The Modern Weird Tale

The Modern Weird Tale

by

S. T. JOSHI

McFarland & Company, Inc., Publishers
Jefferson, North Carolina, and London

Library of Congress Cataloguing-in-Publication Data

Joshi, S.T., 1958–
    The modern weird tale / by S.T. Joshi.
       p.   cm.
    Includes bibliographical references.
    ISBN 0-7864-0986-X (softcover : 50# alkaline paper) ∞
    1. Horror tales, American—History and criticism. 2. American
fiction—20th century—History and criticism. 3. English fiction—
20th century—History and criticism. 4. Horror tales, English—
History and criticism. I. Title.
PS374.H67J67   2001
813'.0873809—dc21   00-54805
                                                              CIP

British Library cataloguing data are available

Manufactured in the United States of America

Front cover: ©2001 Index Stock

McFarland & Company, Inc., Publishers
  Box 611, Jefferson, North Carolina 28640
    www.mcfarlandpub.com

To Stefan R. Dziemianowicz

CONTENTS

PREFACE

This book is an informal follow-up to *The Weird Tale* (1990), in which I discussed six writers of the "Golden Age" of the horror tale (roughly 1880–1940). No reference to that earlier volume is, however, necessary in understanding this one. Probably the most vexing problem I have faced is to decide which authors of post–World War II weird fiction—especially the authors of the horror "boom" of the 1970s and 1980s, many of whom retain a popular following to the present day—should be covered in this study. I do not know if I have evolved any very coherent rationale for the inclusion or exclusion of a given writer; in some cases I will admit frankly that I have written about certain authors simply because I happen to like them. I hope that I have in general covered those weird writers who are either unavoidable on purely literary grounds or because of their promi-nence in the field; the two groups, obviously, are not identical. My dis-cussions generally cover works published prior to 1994.

In the course of my work on this book I have considered (or had sug-gested to me) such authors as Iain Banks, Charles Beaumont, L. P. Davies, Les Daniels, Dennis Etchison, Charles L. Grant, James Herbert, K. W. Jeter, Robert R. McCammon, Richard Matheson, David J. Schow, Rod Ser-ling, Dan Simmons, Steve Rasnic Tem, Thomas Tessier, Chet Williamson, and a number of others. My reasons for excluding these authors are very complex and are not to be taken as judgments on their literary work. I par-ticularly regret that, although I have attempted to probe the relationship between the weird tale and the mystery story in such writers as Robert Bloch and Thomas Harris, I have been unable to explore the very involved interplay between weird and science fiction, especially as represented in the two pioneering writers in this mode, Fritz Leiber and Ray Bradbury. Their work is so voluminous and complex as to be impervious to brief analysis, and it seems to me that my book is already large enough.

My method of citation of works is, in the interests of space, very condensed. I have assigned abbreviations to all important primary works and some secondary works I discuss; these abbreviations can be found in the bibliography at the rear of the volume (an asterisk indicates the edition I have used if it is not the first). In the text, therefore, I cite these works only by abbreviation and page number. My bibliography should not in every instance be considered complete; rather, it lists only those works by and about the author I have consulted for this volume. Save where indicated, however, I have attempted to read all the weird work of the authors I cover.

It is my pleasure to thank the many associates who have assisted me in the writing of this book. I could write an entire essay on the help provided by Stefan R. Dziemianowicz—in the supplying of texts, in suggestions for arrangement, in guidance on individual authors, and in many other less tangible ways—and if this book does nothing more than to encourage him to write his own study, I shall be content. Other individuals such as Lance Arney, Scott D. Briggs, Rusty Burke, Richard Fumosa, Sam Gafford, Jay Gregory, Anna Magee, Steven J. Mariconda, Marc A. Michaud, and Darrell Schweitzer have helped in various ways. I am especially grateful to Ramsey Campbell, T. E. D. Klein, and Thomas Ligotti for reading my chapters on their work and making highly illuminating comments. It is difficult to write about living authors, especially if one is acquainted with them, and I hope that my objectivity has not suffered in these or other instances.

I am aware that some, or much, of this book is deliberately controversial or polemical; but I hope it is evident that I have not come to my views carelessly and that my intent in expressing them is simply the utterance of the truth as I see it (insofar as there can be "truth" in such matters). I may well be wrong, but I would be reluctant to acknowledge that I am malicious. Criticism is not an exact science, and the expression of an informed judgment is my only goal and purpose.

—S. T. J.

INTRODUCTION

During the early part of the twentieth century, weird fiction was not so much a genre as the consequence of a world view, and relatively few authors of what could only retrospectively be called weird fiction were conscious of writing in a specifically weird mode that was to be radically distinguished from "mainstream" writing. H. P. Lovecraft (1890–1937) is in many ways a watershed here: not only was he (because of his early interest in and publication by the American pulp magazines) the first significant writer who understood that his work was "weird," and who for various reasons was repeatedly rebuffed by mainstream publishers, he was perhaps also the last writer whose weird fiction was the systematic embodiment of a world view.

Weird writing has certainly proliferated since Lovecraft's time, and especially since about 1970, but it is not at all clear that much of this mass of writing has any literary significance or much chance of survival. Indeed, there appears to be a consensus among informed critics that the amount of meritorious weird fiction being written today is in exactly inverse proportion to its quantity. One can only ask: what happened?

The query should be interpreted not merely to the causes for the decline in the quality of weird writing just as it is (or was) becoming a spectacularly marketable phenomenon, but to why and how weird fiction became concretized into a definite genre. The answer to this second question may help us to answer the first. By "genre" I mean a certain body of conventionalized scenarios and tropes from which authors can draw and upon which they can, as it were, hang a tale in a formulaic way, since these scenarios and tropes have become so common and readily comprehensible to readers that their mere citation triggers certain stock responses and situates the work in an easily identifiable class. Such tropes, in weird fiction, include the vampire, the ghost, the reanimated corpse, the haunted house, and the like. They were, certainly, already well used by the late Victorian period, and Lovecraft himself felt that many of them were so stale that they ought to be avoided entirely or utilized in some distinctive manner so as to lend them freshness and vigor. His general solution was to transfer the locus of fear from the mundane to what he called the "Great Outside"— the illimitable voids of outer space. As a result, he effected a remarkable union between weird fiction and the emerging mode of science fiction. But few have followed in his footsteps—either because he did what he did so well and so completely, or because it was felt that this sort of "cosmic horror" was best left to Lovecraft's generally mediocre and unimaginative disciples and imitators.

Weird fiction appears now to have become a genre for various historical reasons that I shall examine presently. One of the worst effects of such a development is that certain themes and tropes are used in a very mechanical fashion because they have come to be regarded as staples of a horrific scenario: we are, for example, still inundated, year after year, with vampire novels, only a small proportion of which (e.g., the work of Les Daniels, Anne Rice's *Interview with the Vampire*, Dan Simmons's *Carrion Comfort*) bring any sort of originality to this tired theme. It is as if the evocation of a vampire were felt to be in itself sufficient to raise a shudder. What is more, the vampire is now so common a trope that the more careless writers (and even some of the better ones) feel no need to provide a rationale or justification for the vampire's existence, or to incorporate the entity within any world view.

Moreover, it seems as if the whole approach to weird fiction today is flawed in its very conception. The purpose of most modern weird writing seems to be merely to frighten. This is an inevitable result of the elimination of a philosophical basis for the weird: all that is left (if, indeed, anything is left) is the emotion of horror. If I may utter an apparent paradox: horror fiction is not meant to horrify. This is to say that the *primary* purpose of weird fiction should not be to send a tingle up one's spine; that is merely, as it were, an epiphenomenon of the weird. Winfield Townley Scott said many years ago: "To scare is a slim purpose in poetry."[1] He did not explain this statement, but his meaning can be inferred from his noting that Lovecraft's poetry (unlike his fiction) "touched no depths of human significance." If weird fiction is to be a legitimate literary mode, it must touch depths of human significance in a way that other literary modes do not; and its principal means of doing so is the utilization of the supernatural as a metaphor for various conceptions regarding the universe and human life. Hence the need for a world view that structures and defines the use of the weird in literature. Mere shudder-mongering has no literary value, however artfully accomplished.

All this is why so much modern weird writing is, in the profoundest sense, *lifeless* (I mean no pun): it neither utilizes weird themes and situations in an original way nor embodies a distinctive world view. It is scarcely to be wondered that many have begun to speak direly of the death of weird writing as an art form.[2] This is, no doubt, a little premature, and if the "death of horror" means nothing more than that the legions of second-rate hacks will cease flooding the market with their vapid and slipshod products, then weird fiction may well emerge purged and cleansed and will continue to supply its small modicum of genuine literature to a discriminating readership.

Another perplexing difficulty in dealing with the whole field of weird fiction is that of terminology. Although the term "ghost story" seems to be dying out as a generic designation for the entire field, we now find ourselves facing the ominous and blunt term "horror" as the general designation for the weird. My own term "weird fiction" (which is really Lovecraft's) seems to be gaining some currency among critics, but I do not expect it to be used in those bookstores that have segregated what is believed to be weird fiction into a separate "horror" section. I myself fall into the habit of using the two terms synonymously, but strictly speaking I regard "horror" as a subset of the weird, since fantasy of the Dunsany or Tolkien type is just as much a branch of weird fiction as any other; and "horror" itself must be subdivided into supernatural and nonsupernatural horror.

But there may be a problem with using the term "horror" at all: what other mode of writing is designated by an *emotion*? "Science fiction" is clearly a formal designation, as are "mystery fiction" and "detective fiction." The only other terms that seem even remotely to parallel horror are humor and romance; but the latter has now become so stereotyped that it has in effect become a formal designation, whereas the former is something that can be thought to infiltrate all forms of writing—even weird writing—and is rarely a literary mode in itself.[3] The term "horror" also suggests (falsely, to my mind) that the arousal of fear is somehow the prime concern of weird writing.

I do not know what one is to do about this whole issue. For a time the term "dark fantasy" was used for certain types of weird writing, mostly involving the quiet and purportedly subtle intrusion of the weird into the mundane world, with an emphasis on indirection and suggestion. But I find this term highly paradoxical, since I can think of "fantasy" as meaning only imaginary-world fantasy, and certainly much of Tolkien is about as "dark" as anyone could want. However, this is certainly not what is designated by the term "dark fantasy."

It may be well at this point to discuss in a little more detail the history of modern weird writing. It is my impression that what has frequently been termed the "ghettoization" of weird fiction—especially in America—occurred as a direct result of the pulp magazines. All the standard "genres" we now recognize—mystery, horror, science fiction, western, romance—either grew out of the pulp magazines of the 1920s (even though the pulps as originally conceived at the turn of the century were by no means specialized in terms of content) or received a considerable impetus from them. As a result, weird material in particular disappeared almost entirely from mainstream magazines, since there seemed to develop a notion that such material now had a market of its own.

Lovecraft evidently never even considered submitting his work to magazines such as *Harper's* or *Scribner's* or *Atlantic Monthly*; the loftiest he ever aimed at was the venerable and well-paying pulp *Argosy* (he was rejected). In 1936 he remarked: "After all, a taste for fantasy in large doses is a rather unusual thing. Most readers like it only occasionally—relishing a Machen book now and then, or faintly appreciating the timid and insipid bits (like 'The House of the Laburnums' [by Mollie Panter-Downes] in the Dec. *Harper's*) sparingly scattered through the conventional magazines...."[4] It is interesting to note that, among his several inconclusive dealings with major publishing firms, Lovecraft conducted tentative negotiations in 1930 with Clifton P. Fadiman (then of Simon & Schuster) for a book of his work: Fadiman stated bluntly that he wanted a novel and not a collection of tales.[5] This prejudice against books of short weird fiction persists today, even though it is scarcely to be denied that the weird tale as an art form generally works better in small compass.

The demise of the pulps in the 1940s led to the birth of paperback book publishing; and some of the genres—particularly mystery and science fiction—flourished in this new medium. Weird fiction, for whatever reason, did not. Until recent times, of course, weird fiction was never written in any great quantity; before the establishment of the pulp magazine *Weird Tales*, no periodical was ever devoted exclusively to the weird, and the many competitors to that venerable and long-running journal (1923–54) were all short-lived, so that for most of its history it remained the only genuine market in America for the publication of weird short fiction. After the demise of *Weird Tales* (and, really, even somewhat before), many weird talents felt more attracted to other genres. Robert Bloch, Ray Bradbury, and Fritz Leiber had all published weird work in the pulps, but Bloch then made his reputation in the mystery-suspense field; Bradbury and Leiber in the science fiction field. There simply is no dominant weird writer in America between H. P. Lovecraft and Stephen King. Richard Matheson and Charles Beaumont did good work in the field, but they too spanned several different genres; the unquestionably brilliant Shirley Jackson was always considered simply an odd mainstream writer, and the bulk of her work only borders upon the weird by any conventional standard.

The role of the small or specialty press in this situation is difficult to gauge. Arkham House was established in 1939 by August Derleth and Donald Wandrei initially for the sole purpose of publishing Lovecraft, but it rapidly expanded its scope to issue other weird writers, mainly from the pulps. It certainly seems as if Arkham House and its congeners—Gnome Press, Shasta, and a few others—had some influence in perpetuating the ghettoization of weird fiction: Derleth, after receiving generally hostile or condescending reviews of the first few Arkham House books, ceased altogether to attempt an appeal to the mainstream, and the other small presses made even less of an effort to do so. No one wants to condemn the small presses prior to 1970; they certainly issued meritorious work that might not have seen print in any other venue. I do believe, however, that their self-segregation from general literature and publishing played some role—small but deleterious—in the isolation of the field.

All the above describes the situation in America; in England there was never so much of a distinction between weird and mainstream fiction nor so abrupt a hiatus between oldtime and modern weird writing. The Victorian ghost story, reaching its apotheosis with M. R. James (1862–1936), metamorphosed smoothly into what is really the very different form of the psychological ghost story with such writers as Walter de la Mare, Oliver Onions, L. P. Hartley, John Collier, and Robert Aickman. Aickman and Lovecraft were Ramsey Campbell's two strongest early influences, and as a result Campbell neatly effected a union between the British and the American weird traditions. The imaginary-world fantasy did well in England: the early Dunsany had laid the groundwork, and the field was developed by E. R. Eddison, J. R. R. Tolkien, and Mervyn Peake (and in America by Clark Ashton Smith and, perhaps, A. Merritt, if he is to be classed here). And yet, even here Aickman was virtually a lone voice in the purely supernatural tale in the 1960s until the emergence of Campbell and other writers in the 1970s and 1980s. (The occultist novels of Dennis Wheatley [1897–1977] cannot be said to count as serious literature. They do not, in any event, appear to have influenced later writers.)

It seems to me that the recent boom in horror writing is more a sociological than a literary phenomenon; and yet, I am not sure that anyone has adequately explained *why* horror novels suddenly became bestsellers, why film adaptations of them became blockbusters, and why many average readers who did not previously demonstrate any interest in the weird should suddenly be reading this material. All one can say is that the phenomenon did occur, perhaps as a result of certain writers' conscious tailoring of their work to suit a popular audience not otherwise familiar with the weird. Some believe that the critical event was the publication of Ira Levin's *Rosemary's Baby* (1967), a very mediocre work whose success was augmented by the (much superior) film of the following year; but I see the canonical date as 1971, when William Peter Blatty's *The Exorcist* and Thomas Tryon's *The Other* simultaneously appeared at the top of the bestseller lists.[6] Both were, of course, turned into very successful films, the latter in 1972 and the former in 1973. From this point on there was no looking back. Stephen King published his first book, *Carrie*, in 1974, and has now become the most remarkable publishing phenomenon in literary history. Other writers who have at least some pretensions to literary merit—Peter Straub, Anne Rice, Clive Barker—also regularly make the bestseller lists, as do a number of writers substantially inferior to them on the literary scale (John Saul, Dean R. Koontz, John Farris). There is considerable evidence that this "boom" is coming to an end: even King's more recent works are remaining on the bestseller lists for shorter and shorter periods. It is, of course, a testament to the complete unreliability of bestseller lists as gauges of literary merit that not a single one of Ramsey Campbell's works has ever been a notable commercial success or has ever been made into a film. This applies even more to the work of Robert Aickman and Thomas Ligotti, although T. E. D. Klein's *The Ceremonies* (1984) achieved bestseller status briefly.

There has, of course, been an appalling amount of entirely subliterary material published in the last two decades, as talentless hacks have sought to capitalize on the success of the horror field as a commercial phenomenon. What these writers have failed to note is that even Blatty and Tryon did not sit down to write "horror novels" but were actually trying (and, on the whole, succeeded) to deal with serious human issues through the horror tale (in one instance supernatural horror; in the other psychological horror), and that the commercial success of *The Exorcist* and *The Other* was as much a surprise to their authors as to anyone else. Both these novels are really rather good and deserve to survive as literary documents, not merely as artifacts in the history of publishing. But it is clear that the overwhelming number of hack writers who regurgitate tired old themes have nothing to say and merit the instant oblivion they in any case achieve. The problem with all this, however, is that weird fiction tends to be tainted by these inferior examples and to be judged by them rather than by those relatively obscure or unpopular works that truly raise the weird tale to an art form. This may be more a function of mainstream critics' laziness than anything else: there is no reason why weird fiction should be judged by its worst instances rather than by its best, as all other fields are judged.

One reason why the weird tale has become both commercially successful and, in my view, literarily problematical is what Stefan Dziemiano-wicz has termed the "banalization" of horror.[7] This means the increasing concern of weird writers to depict the minute details of the mundane lives of mundane people, both in an attempt to win the reader's sympathy (most of us are, after all, pretty ordinary) and to lay the groundwork for the intrusion of the weird into a familiar realm. In the end this technique is not so different in *approach* from Lovecraft's brand of realism, although he emphasized topographical over psychological realism. Although this dwelling on issues that are of concern to most normal people—relationships between husband, wife, and children; difficulties on the job; problems of modern urban life—is a very large reason for the popular success of writers like King and Straub, it does not seem to me as if this should be the *primary* focus of weird fiction. This is not what Winfield Townley Scott meant by touching "depths of human significance," especially since most weird writers treat these issues superficially and sentimentally, and without sufficiently integrating them into the weird scenario. Many modern weird writers do not appear to have taken much notice of Lovecraft's words on this matter: "I could not write about 'ordinary people' because I am not in the least interested in them. Without interest there can be no art. Man's relations to man do not captivate my fancy. It is man's relation to the cosmos—to the unknown—which alone arouses in me the spark of creative imagination. The humanocentric pose is impossible to me, for I cannot acquire the primitive myopia which magnifies the earth and ignores the background."[8]

Weird fiction should not be about ordinary people. Even if one does not adopt the "cosmic" attitude of Lovecraft, even if one wishes to depict the insidious incursion of the weird into the ordinary, the emphasis should be on the weird and not the ordinary. It is because so many weird writers emphasize the latter rather than the former that their work seems to me thin and poorly conceived: amidst all the effort spent upon portraying realistic human figures, not enough attention is devoted to what is presumably the raison d'être of the work itself—the weird phenomenon. I do not think this is merely a personal prejudice. If weird fiction is to be a distinct mode of writing, then it should not feel the need to ape so many of the conventions that make mainstream fiction a distinct mode of writing. Even Ramsey Campbell tends to write about wholesome middle-class characters and their charming little children in his novels, and it is this that makes his novels so much less compelling than his short stories, which feature the bizarre not only in terms of the supernatural but in terms of the warped human characters he puts on stage. There is scarcely a single "normal" character in all Thomas Ligotti's work, and this is what gives it much of its effectiveness.

I am not saying that weird fiction should simply deal with odd people; but the overall *scenario* should be odd and strange, with the human figures subordinate to the general weird conception. Stephen King may fancy himself the modern-day Theodore Dreiser, just as Peter Straub imagines that he is our contemporary Henry James, but a plowing through even a single one of their gargantuan tomes full of hackneyed portrayals of boring people and their boring problems that have nothing to do with the weird phenomenon is enough to make one despair for the future of all weird writing. It is only the exceptionally talented writer—a Shirley Jackson or a Robert Aickman—who has the insight to depict human relationships in all their complexity and the skill to incorporate these relationships into the very fabric of the weird situation.

Another matter of great concern to me is the proliferation of the "horror novel" in modern weird writing. Consider the following:

> Critics of supernatural horror fiction have repeatedly observed that the novel is a difficult form for telling a tale of terror. After brooding for years over this matter from the viewpoint of a potential novelist, not to mention the many aborted attempts at actually writing the things, I find this form too difficult for me. The realistic novel makes certain demands that are entirely alien to supernatural literature as I understand its aims and possibilities. The best I could do would be to produce a mystery or suspense narrative with a supernatural plot motive. But such a work bears little resemblance to the masterpieces of the form that it's been my ambition to ape: "The Fall of the House of Usher" [by Poe], "The Willows" [by Algernon Blackwood], "The White People" [by Arthur Machen], "The Colour out of Space" [by Lovecraft], and so on.[9]

This gauntlet has recently been thrown down by Thomas Ligotti, a master of the weird short story. It has its troubling aspects—Ligotti arbitrarily assumes that a weird novel will be "realistic," and in general his argument bears much resemblance to Poe's criticism of the long poem—but it must also be said that many current weird writers have failed to take note of the difficulties of sustaining weirdness over novel length or even to realize that the whole enterprise is highly problematical. The enormous *commercial* success of the contemporary horror novel has been a fatal attraction to writers; even Ramsey Campbell has confessed that he has been forced into writing novels in order to continue being a professional writer. The issues—constantly raised by Lovecraft—of whether there is or ought to be any such thing as a "professional writer," and whether genuine literature can be consistently produced by a such a person, do not, apparently, seem to have occurred to anyone.

Commercial demands for the production of novels (as opposed to collections of short stories), combined with the difficulty of maintaining a "nonrealistic" weird conception over novel length without merely lapsing into conventionalized imaginary-world fantasy, have led to the proliferation of novels whose basic scenarios may have genuine literary potential only in the short story or may not be weird at all in their essence but fundamentally allied to suspense or melodrama. Again I point to Campbell, since this most talented of modern weird writers has himself been only indifferently successful in the novel; many of his works have been spun out to novel length only by increasing the number of characters involved (*Obsession*, *The Hungry Moon*) rather than by the creation of a plot that actually requires a novel for its exposition. There seem to be three solutions to this general difficulty: write a frankly nonrealistic novel; write a novel that is avowedly largely a mystery or suspense tale with supernatural interludes, or perhaps one that does not involve the supernatural at all; or write a novel that is truly structured around a complex supernatural phenomenon. Let us consider each of these in greater detail.

The first has been tried and found quite successful, but it has now become so distinct a form that it is virtually beyond the scope of the purely supernatural horror tale. Dunsany was a pioneer in this regard: *The Blessing of Pan* (1927), *The Curse of the Wise Woman* (1933), *The Story of Mona Sheehy* (1939), and *The Strange Journeys of Colonel Polders* (1950) are all *tours de force* in that, although emphatically set in the "real" world, they are very little concerned with mundane human motivations in the manner of mainstream novels; they are, in some inexplicable way, imaginary-world fantasies without the imaginary world. Subsequent efforts at nonrealistic weird fiction have generally fallen more conventionally into the imaginary-world pattern, and Eddison, Tolkien, Peake, and their followers have certainly produced very brilliant and substantial work in this form, but this is now regarded as a distinct subgenre of its own with little relation to the main body of weird writing. Perhaps only Jonathan Carroll's *The Land of Laughs* (1980) should be cited here—a work that is curiously similar to the novels of Dunsany mentioned above, in that it portrays an imaginary world somehow inserted within the realm of the real. Clive Barker has also attempted something along this line, with relative success in *Weaveworld* (1987), and with spectacular lack of success in *The Great and Secret Show* (1989) and *Imajica* (1991).

It is a fact that the overwhelming majority of weird novels written in the last two decades are subject to Ligotti's complaint that they are merely mystery or suspense tales with or without supernatural interludes. Some of these are nevertheless very successful, even though—especially with

purely nonsupernatural work—it sometimes becomes problematical to classify them within weird fiction at all. There is a lively debate as to whether
the nonsupernatural suspense novels of Thomas Harris are or are not
weird—and there are many other works of this type. A number of unquestionably brilliant novels of this sort have certainly been produced, from
Bloch's *The Scarf* (1947) and *Psycho* (1959), to Campbell's *The Face That Must
Die* (1979), to Iain Banks's *The Wasp Factory* (1984), to Harris's *The Silence
of the Lambs* (1988). But there will always be a question as to whether these
are genuinely weird. It is, however, in those novels that are theoretically
based upon a supernatural premise, but in which that premise that does
not always function in a systematic way, that the "banalization" of horror
is particularly evident. In many of King's or Straub's novels there is not even
a mystery or suspense foundation for the weird but merely long stretches
of irrelevant character portrayal and melodramatic human conflict. This
tendency reaches its nadir in the soap-opera supernaturalism of Charles L.
Grant.

Only rarely are novels actually founded upon a weird situation of novel
length. I do not see any formula for the creation of such a thing, and one
can only point to the successes: Tryon's *The Other* and *Harvest Home* (1973);
Rice's *Interview with the Vampire* (1976); Campbell's *Incarnate* (1983) and
Midnight Sun (1990); Barker's *The Damnation Game* (1985); Klein's *The Ceremonies*; David J. Schow's *The Shaft* (1990); and, of course, the grandfather
(or should one say grandmother) of them all, Shirley Jackson's *The Haunting of Hill House* (1959). It is of note that not a single one of Machen's or
Dunsany's or Blackwood's novels can be called *horror novels* as such. They
may perhaps be weird (although even this is in doubt in the case of such a
tenuous if poignant work as Machen's *The Hill of Dreams*), but they must
be classed more as fantasy than as supernatural horror. There were a few
other fairly successful weird novels prior to Lovecraft (among them William
Hope Hodgson's *The House on the Borderland* [1908] and Leonard Cline's
The Dark Chamber [1927]), but of those written subsequent to Lovecraft,
the above are all I can think of that rank among the authentic masterpieces
of the form. It can be seen that these novels have virtually nothing in common with each other, either in theme or in style or in execution; it is simply that in each instance the author has conceived of a scenario that is
sufficiently complex and sufficiently supernatural in its essence such that a
novel is required for its exposition.

Weird fiction, in spite of the recent appearance of vast amounts of
rubbish, is still a relatively small field, and its best practitioners are all
highly distinctive and individual writers who do not appear to have very
much in common. This is why I find a thematic approach to this field

generally unsatisfying, since it is frequently made only at the expense of ignoring what makes each author's work unique in its employment of a given theme. How, really, can one compare the use of the vampire in the work of Les Daniels and Anne Rice? In the end it seems as if weird authors will simply continue to produce whatever they are moved to produce at the moment, and it is we critics who have the onerous task of tidying up after them and classifying their work in this or that subcategory. But it is also the responsibility of critics to sort the good from the bad, the original from the hackneyed, the substantial from the vacuous, the aesthetically polished from the superficially slick; and in that task we have much work to do.

I. SHIRLEY JACKSON: DOMESTIC HORROR

Shirley Jackson (1916–1965)[1] and Ramsey Campbell are the two lead-ing writers of weird fiction since Lovecraft. In making this assertion I am not merely bypassing other writers who, at least in their own minds, aspire to that title—in particular the best-selling quartet of Stephen King, Peter Straub, Clive Barker, and Anne Rice—but am making the problematical assertion that Jackson is a weird writer at all. In truth, only one of her nov-els is avowedly supernatural—the masterful *Haunting of Hill House* (1959)—while others are weird only slightly or not at all. In addition, only perhaps 15 or 20 of her 100-odd short stories can be said to belong to the weird tale or to the mystery story or to science fiction. Certainly there is nothing supernatural about "The Lottery" (1948), whose impact rests on the very *possibility* of its occurrence. But I wish to place Jackson within the realm of weird fiction not only for the nebulous reason that the whole of her work has a pervasive atmosphere of the odd about it, but, more importantly, because her entire work is unified to such a degree that distinctions about genre and classification become arbitrary and meaningless. Like Arthur Machen, Shirley Jackson developed a view of the world that informed all her writing, whether supernatural or not; but that world view is more akin to the cheerless and nihilistic misanthropy of Bierce than to Machen's har-ried antimaterialism. It is because Shirley Jackson so keenly detected hor-ror in the everyday world, and wrote of it with rapier-sharp prose, that she ranks as a twentieth-century Bierce.

Jackson began her career writing short stories—the first one, "Janice," dating to 1938, when she was attending Syracuse University. In late 1941 she published a sketch, "My Life with R. H. Macy," in the *New Republic*, and from 1943 onward she appeared regularly in the *New Yorker*, *Mademoi-selle*, *Harper's*, *Woman's Home Companion*, *Good Housekeeping*, *Collier's*, *Ladies'*

Home Journal, Woman's Day, and other general fiction or women's magazines. "The Lottery," of course, catapulted her to fame and notoriety, setting off a furor after its appearance in the *New Yorker* for June 26, 1948. Jackson wittily recounts the story's reception in a lecture, "Biography of a Story" (1960; C). Shortly thereafter her first novel, *The Road through the Wall* (1948), appeared. The celebrity of "The Lottery" caused Jackson's publishers to push for a collection of her stories, and it emerged in early 1949 under the same title, *The Lottery*. This heterogeneous volume shows signs of hasty assemblage: the stories are for the most part notable, but their rather disconcerting variety does not produce a unified effect, especially as two of the stories—"My Life with R. H. Macy" and "Charles" (1948)—are plainly, if peculiarly, autobiographical.

This strain of quasi-autobiography became much more pronounced from the late 1940s onward, as Jackson began to write a whole series of stories about her family, most centering around her four children. First published in women's magazines, these stories or sketches were collected in two of her most popular books, *Life among the Savages* (1953) and *Raising Demons* (1957). The former was actually a bestseller for a short time, and it continues to be reprinted.

It is surprising that Jackson never subsequently made an effort to collect her nondomestic short fiction. Not merely did *The Lottery* fail to include all the fiction she had published up to that time (it also included nine stories that, as far as I can tell, were unpublished), but there are some 20 stories written subsequent to *The Lottery* that were not reprinted in the posthumous collection, *Come Along with Me* (1968), edited by her husband Stanley Edgar Hyman. About a dozen of her later family stories also remain uncollected. Some of these are not only among her most famous and most frequently anthologized—including "One Ordinary Day, with Peanuts" (1955), first published in *Fantasy and Science Fiction*—they are among her best.[2]

The course of Jackson's novelistic career (she wrote six novels, not including *Come Along with Me*, left unfinished at her death) reveals both a growing mastery of the novel form and an increasing dosage of the weird, culminating with *The Haunting of Hill House*. *The Road through the Wall* is an entirely mainstream satire on suburban life, but is too episodic to be effective as a whole; it reads like a series of short stories stitched together in no especial order. *Hangsaman* (1951) has more unity and a fine atmosphere of the strange—probably the result of Jackson's employment of stream-of- consciousness, which produces a weirdly hallucinatory effect— but in the end, it is also a nonweird Bildungsroman. *The Bird's Nest* (1954) approaches the weird in its study of a woman with multiple personalities—

a phenomenon explicitly compared by the woman's psychiatrist to demonic possession (B 198–99)—but, aside from being very clumsy in its execution, it involves nothing genuinely supernatural or weird. Indeed, the very analogy of split personality to demonic possession renders the concept wholly natural, since it is now something entirely encompassed by natural science (or, at least, it is so presented by Jackson, whose character is cured in the end by psychoanalysis). *The Sundial* (1958) is wholly unclassifiable: although there are some powerful dream or hallucination sequences, this tale of a twisted family convinced that the rest of the world is soon going to end borders on the weird through the author's bland suggestion that perhaps the family members, far from being insane, may actually be right. It is one of the most pungent satires ever written. *The Haunting of Hill House*, of course, is explicitly supernatural and was so conceived by Jackson, although its true emphasis may lie elsewhere. It is certainly her most polished and integrated novel. *We Have Always Lived in the Castle* (1962) seems to be regarded as a weird tale by many (perhaps because it was initially marketed as such by her publishers, who wished to capitalize on the success of *Hill House*). But if it is weird, it is in a highly peculiar and perhaps backhanded way, for all that it is a gripping work. *Come Along with Me* promised to be supernatural, but I do not know enough about its genesis or purpose to say whether it would actually have turned out to be so.

Jackson's world view does not extend into the realm of metaphysics: it is not possible to deduce from her work any coherent conception of the nature of the universe. She is wholly and avowedly concerned with human relationships, and it is from their complexities that both horror and the supernatural emerge in her work. Both early and late in her career Jackson was affirming that, at least for her, the supernatural is a metaphor for human beings' relations to each other and to society. Consider a remark in 1948:

> I have had for many years a consuming interest in magic and the supernatural. I think this is because I find there so convenient a shorthand statement of the possibilities of human adjustment to what seems to be at best an inhuman world.... [E]verything I write [involves] the sense which I feel, of a human and not very rational order struggling inadequately to keep in check forces of great destruction, which may be the devil and may be intellectual enlightenment [O 125].

It is appropriate, then, that a proper starting-point for the study of Jackson's fiction from a weird perspective may not be her actual weird work but those tales for which she gained an entirely different following: her family chronicles collected in *Life among the Savages* and *Raising Demons*.

DOMESTIC FICTION

The strain of autobiography that is so dominant throughout Jackson's work can be traced to her very earliest writing. Her first professionally published story, "My Life with R. H. Macy" (L), appears to be a lightly fictionalized account of a job she had as a saleswoman at Macy's department store. The stories she wrote about her family date from no earlier than 1948, several years after she began her literary career, but they continued at a fairly constant pace to the end of her life. Jackson admitted to her parents that many of these stories were potboilers: "They are written simply for money ... I won't write love stories and junk about gay young married couples, and they won't take ordinary children stories, and this sort of thing is a compromise between their notions and mine ... and is unusual enough so that I am the only person I know of who is doing it" (O 145). This dismissal of her domestic stories may be somewhat disingenuous: to be sure, they brought in needed income (the $1000 she received for each story came in very handy in supporting four children, as Hyman, a university professor, never made much money of his own from his literary criticism), but the zest, vigor, and wit with which they are written testify to their importance to Jackson.

James Egan, in a thoughtful essay that attempts to reconcile Jackson's domestic fiction and her weird work, sees a twofold division of her work, as "either the expression of an idyllic domestic vision or the inversion of that vision into the fantastic and Gothic."[3] This assessment seems fundamentally correct, but it may require a little more shading. Especially when we examine the chronology of Jackson's short fiction, we will find that the domestic stories themselves undergo a gradual modification, brought on, perhaps, by her marital problems or simply by the fact that her children grew up and no longer exhibited that affinity to "magic" (see O 209) which Jackson thought the very young reveal. The later domestic fiction now and then displays a brooding irony and even misanthropy that bring it surprisingly close in tone to her other work.

Life among the Savages and *Raising Demons* were both stitched together from a number of stories originally published in magazines. Jackson's skill in this process of editing and rewriting the tales into a unified whole cannot be overemphasized, especially in the former work. It is true that both books remain somewhat episodic, but she has weaved the tales together in such a way that they flow naturally one into the other; some of the stories have been so extensively revised as to be nearly unrecognizable from their originals. Although Jackson appears to pay lip service to the conventions of middle-class life in the 1950s, the vibrancy of her writing, the flawlessly exact capturing of her children's idiosyncrasies, and above all her complete lack of sentimentality make these stories pungent and vivid even today.

The overriding question, in regard to these works, is the degree of their veracity; that is, the extent to which they are unvarnished or faithful transcriptions of actual events in Jackson's life and in the life of her family. It is, of course, naive to imagine that any autobiographical writing simply relates events as they occurred; and Jackson's remark that these stories allowed her to see her children "through a flattering veil of fiction" (O 119) may be all we need to infer that her domestic fiction, no less than her other work, is in some sense a creation of the imagination. Egan's reference to this work as "idyllic" is correct insofar as Jackson systematically attempts to present what may in reality have been highly traumatic events as the sources of harmless jests—her son being struck by a car, for instance, in which he suffered a concussion and some broken bones.

The importance of this domestic fiction—as regards her other work, at any rate—rests in its employment of very basic familial or personal scenarios that she would reuse in her weird stories in perverted and twisted ways: things like riding a bus, employing a maid, taking children shopping, going on vacation, putting up guests, and, in general, adhering—or seeming to adhere—to the "proper conduct" expected of her as a middle-class housewife. It is interesting that her function as a writer is almost never mentioned in these nonweird works, or if it is, she pokes fun at it as an anomaly for a wife with four children. "The Third Baby's the Easiest" captures the idea perfectly, as Jackson registers with a desk clerk at the hospital:

> "Age?" she asked. "Sex? Occupation?"
> "Writer," I said.
> "Housewife," she said.
> "Writer," I said.
> "I'll just put down housewife," she said [LS 426].

It is important to note, however, that this body of domestic fiction really does undergo some significant changes over the years; it is in no sense a monolithic block of determined cheer. Some cracks begin to appear as early as "Lucky to Get Away" (1953), in which Jackson emphatically betrays a weariness with the unending round of housework required of her as a mother, especially as her husband contributes nothing to the household chores:

> I got to feeling that I could not bear the sight of the colored cereal bowls for one more morning, could not empty one more ashtray, could not brush one more head or bake one more potato or let out one more

> dog or pick up one more jacket. I snarled at the bright faces regarding
> me at the breakfast table and I was strongly tempted to kick the legs
> out from under the chair on which my older son was teetering back-
> ward [RD 583].

The humor in this passage is, surely, a little sardonic.

Three other pieces show that Jackson's relationship with her husband
might not have been one of unending bliss. One of the many curious things
about these stories is the infrequency with which her husband even appears:
they are all about herself and her children, and when her husband does
make an appearance it is almost always as a clumsy buffoon ("The Life
Romantic," "The Box"). In "Queen of the May," in which Hyman has been
invited to judge a beauty contest, the tone becomes a little more sinister:
the jealousy Jackson felt toward her husband (a known philanderer) is much
in evidence:

> "Daddy is going to see a lot of girls," Sally told Barry. She turned
> to me. "Daddy likes to look at girls, doesn't he?"
> There was a deep, enduring silence, until at last my husband's eye
> fell on Jannie. "And what did you learn in school today?" he asked with
> wild enthusiasm [RD 661–62].

Still odder and still more bitter is "One Last Chance," in which her husband announces somewhat sheepishly that an old flame of his will be dropping by (in fact she cancels her plans and never arrives), tactlessly and
unintentionally suggesting that this woman is much prettier and a better
cook than his wife. I have no idea whether this was an actual incident in
Jackson's life, but it is interesting to note that her vindictiveness here is
directed even at her children:

> I gathered up ten clean sheets and six pillowcases and went first
> into Barry's room, where I removed six Teddy bears ... a green rabbit,
> two hidden lollipops and a wooden train from the bed and stripped
> and made it. Then I took up my armload of linen and went into Sally's
> room, sighed and removed from her bed a stack of coloring books, a
> disintegrated box of crayons, two dolls and an Oz book. I stacked the
> stuff on the floor where she would be sure to fall over it and quickly
> stripped and made the bed.[4]

Most telling is the article "On Being a Faculty Wife," which scathingly lays
bare Jackson's resentment at the ostracism and condescension she suffers
from the academic community of Bennington College, where the young girls
all revere her husband but take scant notice of her. Incredibly, the following

bit of venom was omitted when the piece, which first appeared in *Mademoiselle*, was reprinted in *Raising Demons*:

> ...she [a student] turned to me and asked casually, "How long have you been married?"
>
> "Sixteen years."
>
> "Sixteen *years*? Gosh, he doesn't look that old. Where did you meet him?"
>
> "In college."
>
> "You went to college too? How many years?"
>
> "Four."
>
> "Gosh. How come you just ended up doing housework and stuff? Couldn't you get a job?"
>
> "I have a job. I cook and sew and clean and shop and make beds and drive people places and—"
>
> "No, I meant a *job*. Like ... you know, doing something. Because wouldn't it give you something to talk about at home? Because after all he's a very cultured man, you know."[5]

Note here Jackson's curious response to the query "Couldn't you get a job?" Although by now an author of some stature, she does not reply, "I am a writer," but "I cook and sew and clean..." No doubt the point is to emphasize that housework is indeed a job of some consequence, but, as with nearly all the domestic stories, Jackson suppresses or conceals a major facet of her life—her writing.

Some of the later, uncollected domestic fiction comes off sounding a little tired: Jackson must have realized that her material was running dry, especially as her children were growing up into the less superficially "cute" stage of young adulthood. Indeed, a late piece, "Karen's Complaint" (1959), is quite poignant in depicting Jackson's sense of loneliness and aimlessness as her youngest child begins to go to school and she faces the prospect of an empty house for the first time in nearly two decades. However haphazardly her household appeared to be run, she took evident pride in providing a loving home for her husband and children. It is exactly this sense of togetherness and warmth that is obtrusively lacking in her other fiction. Where the reality of her own family lay, no one but she herself could have answered: perhaps all the carefree and well-adjusted children in her domestic fiction were themselves imaginary—her greatest fantasy.

Domestic into Weird

The transformation of some incidents found in the domestic fiction into something very different and much more disturbing occasionally occurs with scarcely an alteration save that of context. I am reminded of Plautus' remark in the prologue to *Amphitryo*:

> Are you disappointed
> To find it's a *tragedy*? Well, I can easily change it.
> ...I can easily make it a comedy,
> And never alter a line.[6]

The textbook example of this is the story "Charles." Here the transition has occurred in the reverse direction, as the story was first published in a magazine and gathered in *The Lottery* before being reprinted in *Life among the Savages*. In its earlier two contexts the story is subtly menacing and rather grim: her son Laurie (mentioned by name in all three versions), attending kindergarten, tells of a strange boy, Charles, who is by turns extremely unruly or even evil ("'Today Charles hit the teacher.' 'He kicked the teacher's friend.'" [L 71–72]) and excessively well-behaved. Later, when Jackson meets Laurie's teacher, she finds out that there is no Charles in the class. I shall return to the implications of this story later. But here I wish to note what a remarkably different atmosphere this story has when it is buried in the genial confines of *Life among the Savages*: there the whole tale comes off as simply another prank by her cute but headstrong son. In the former instances, though, one has the strong sensation that her son may well have serious problems of adjustment.

Another means for effecting the transition from domestic to weird, or vice versa, is omission. A very peculiar tale, "The House," was reprinted in *Life among the Savages*—but not all of it. The latter portion was excised, no doubt because it is precisely here that the tale veers off into suggestions of the supernatural. At the outset it is difficult to ascertain whether, in its magazine appearance, this story is genuinely autobiographical, since Jackson never refers to her husband or children by name. In any case, the story concerns her family moving into an old, somewhat ramshackle, and faintly sinister house in New England (the precise location is never specified in the original appearance). The narrative of fixing up the house for habitation and moving in is told with mild humor—certainly not with the overt hilarity of pieces like "Look, Ma, We're Moving!" (1952) or "Worldly Goods"—but with an undercurrent of the strange. The house seems almost animate:

There was a door to an attic that preferred to stay latched, and would latch itself no matter who was inside; another door hung by custom slightly ajar, although it would close good-humoredly for a time when some special reason required it. We had five attics, we discovered, built into one another; one of them kept bats, and we shut that one up; another one, light and cheerful in spite of a small window, liked to be a place of traffic and became a place to store things temporarily.

An old clothesline hung across the basement, and after the line I put in the back yard had fallen down for the third time, I resigned myself and hung a new line in the basement, and clothes dried there quickly and freshly.... One bedroom chose the children. It was large and light and showed height marks on one wall, and seemed to mind not at all when crayon marks appeared on the wallpaper and paint got spilled on the floor.[7]

The house controls its inhabitants, not the inhabitants the house. It is on its sufferance that they are there at all. All this may be only mildly disturbing; but then an old lady comes to pay a visit:

"It's a lovely old house," I said.

"Do you think so?" She turned quickly to look at me. "Do you really think it's a lovely old house?"

"We're very happy here."

"I'm glad." She folded her hands and smiled again. "It's always been such a good house," she said. "The old doctor always used to say it was a good house."

"The old doctor?"

"Doctor Ogilvie."

"Doctor Ogilvie?"

"I see they kept the pillars, after all," she said, nodding. "We always thought they gave the house character."

"There was a hornets' nest in one," I said weakly. Doctor Ogilvie had built the house in 1816![8]

The first passage I quoted above was included in *Life among the Savages*, but again context robs it of any undertones of the weird; and that reprint breaks off the tale shortly thereafter. If anything, this story could be a model of Jackson's ability to transform the events of her own life into weird fiction.

Jackson's work returns time and again to certain fundamental domestic themes, sometimes in an autobiographical manner, sometimes in a mainstream manner, and sometimes in a weird manner. It is again worth emphasizing that these distinctions are arbitrary and nebulous; it takes only a small touch to push a story from one of these groups to another, and some stories remain resolutely averse to clear categorization.

Consider, for example, the number of stories by Jackson involving the hiring of a maid. There are at least four such tales, and they all play startling variations of tone and mood upon this one theme. Chronologically the first is "Tootie in Peonage" (1942; C), one of Jackson's earliest stories. It tells of a young woman, Tootie Maple, whom the narrator hires to help with the housework. It is an amusing tale of how Tootie has too many other pressing things to do—painting her toenails, finishing the latest issue of *True Confessions*—to get down to her actual duties. But the real object of satire is the housewife who hired her, who lacks the strength of will either to order Tootie to do her work or to fire her. The next maid story, "Family Magician" (1949), is a rather odd and benign weird tale about a maid, Mallie, who appears to fulfill her household responsibilities through magic. The tale is not of much note save in being Jackson's first avowedly supernatural work. Then comes "Monday Morning," incorporated in *Life among the Savages* and similar in tone to "Tootie in Peonage." In this explicitly autobiographical story we read of the maid Phoebe, who shows up more than an hour late. It is all very amusing:

> "Where's Phoebe?" she [Jannie] said.
> "She didn't come today," Laurie said. "Mommy's *terrible* mad. Mommy's probably going to kill her."
> "Laurie," I said, but they had already started, "Mommy's going to kill Phoebe, Mommy's going to kill Phoebe" [LS 438].

Then we come to the extremely nasty "Strangers in Town" (1959). The tale does not focus upon the maid, named Mallie (as in "Family Magician"), but it is clear that this maid too has supernatural powers: she gathers an acorn, a mushroom, and a scrap of grass and makes a stew out of them.

The simple act of riding a bus or train and traveling to a strange location—usually a big city—has generated a number of Jackson's most powerful stories, whether weird or otherwise. We see an innocuous version of this in chapter four of *Raising Demons*, in which Jackson relates taking her children to New York. Other such tales are much more ominous. "The Tooth" (1949; L) is a queer and meandering story of a young woman who travels to New York to see a dentist. I confess to being at a loss as to what point this story is trying to make, but the atmosphere of shimmering, dreamlike fantasy that was to become a Jackson trademark finds its first genuine embodiment here. "Pillar of Salt" (1948; L) involves a nearly identical scenario, although here a couple from New Hampshire comes to New York for a vacation. The emphasis is, inevitably, on the wife, whose appreciation of the city oscillates between amazement and condescension (looking at a set of miniature milk bottles being sold as toys, she notes archly,

"We get our milk from cows" [L 177]). Gradually the giganticism, pace, and impersonality of the city overwhelm her, and her plight is keenly encapsulated by her complete inability to cross a busy street even when the light is with her:

> The minute the light changes, she told herself firmly; there's no sense. The light changed before she was ready and in the minute before she collected herself traffic turning the corner overwhelmed her and she shrank back against the curb. She looked longingly at the cigar store on the opposite corner, with her apartment house beyond; she wondered, How do people ever manage to get there, and knew that by wondering, by admitting a doubt, she was lost [L 184].

"The Bus" (1965; C) finally takes this topos into the realm of the supernatural. An old woman is dropped off at the wrong stop late at night. Eventually she catches a ride on a truck to some dismal-looking roadhouse. As the atmosphere becomes at once more menacing and more unreal, the old woman imagines herself a child in her room, looks in a closet, and finds her old doll speaking to her: "'Go away, old lady, go away, old lady, go away'" (C 200). At this point the old woman wakes up—it was all a dream and she is still on the bus! Not content with this trite device, Jackson gives it a further predictable twist by having the old woman get off at the same wrong stop as before.

Several other stories speak of the peculiar vulnerability of people on vacation, away from their friends and their familiar environment. "The Summer People" (1949; C) is a mordant tale about an elderly couple who decide to stay on in their summer cottage past Labor Day, something they have never done before. The dour countryfolk of the region appear to resent this decision—"'Nobody ever stayed at the lake past Labor Day before'" (C 73)—and insidiously conspire against them: the couple cannot get kerosene or ice, the mail suddenly stops, the groceries can't be delivered, and so on. This masterful story is worth considering in several other respects, but the gradual isolation of the couple, as one by one the locals turn against them through sheer inaction, is harrowing. There is, of course, nothing supernatural about this tale, but a work like this makes the strongest possible case for the inclusion of the nonsupernatural horror story as a genuine subset of the weird tale.

"The Lovely House" (1952; retitled "A Visit" in C) introduces the supernatural in the subtlest way. A college girl, Margaret, goes with her friend Carla Rhodes to the latter's palatial home, whose location is never specified. Initially it all seems idyllic:

> Carla stopped before the doorway and stood for a minute, looking first
> behind her, at the vast reaching gardens and the green lawn going
> down to the river, and the soft hills beyond, and then at the perfect
> grace of the house, showing so clearly the long-boned structure within,
> the curving staircases and the arched doorways and the tall thin lines
> of steadying beams, all of it resting back against the hills, and up, past
> rows of windows and the flying lines of the roof, on, to the tower... [C
> 98].

The tale develops a powerful atmosphere of weirdness through the deliberately artificial dialogue—it is as if all the characters know they are in a
work of fiction. Carla's brother Paul arrives; Margaret spends much time
with him. She goes up to the tower and has an enigmatic talk with Carla's
grandmother. Throughout the story Mrs. Rhodes is weaving a tapestry of
the house. This is the end of the tale:

> "You will not leave us before my brother comes again?" Carla
> asked Margaret.
> "I have only to put the figures into the foreground," Mrs. Rhodes
> said, hesitating on her way to the drawing room. "I shall have you
> exactly if you sit on the lawn near the river."
> "We shall be models of stillness," said Carla, laughing. "Margaret,
> will you come and sit beside me on the lawn" [C 120]?

What does this mean? What is the significance of Paul's remark that "'without this house I could not exist?'" (C 119). Is this not a pun, meaning that
neither he nor the entire family can live *without* (i.e., outside) the house?
And isn't Margaret now being woven into the fabric of the house by way
of the tapestry? This exquisite and haunting tale—a fantastically transmogrified version of a visit Dylan Thomas paid to Jackson's home in Westport, Connecticut (O 151–52)—exemplifies the "quiet weird tale" at its
pinnacle. And, of course, it embodies a theme that we can already see is a
dominant one in Jackson's work and perhaps also her life: the manner in
which a house can subsume its occupants.

Some of Jackson's strangest stories—which are perhaps only on the
borderland of the weird—seem like satires of middle-class tact and etiquette.
A few of the domestic stories may be of some relevance here, as Jackson
feels (or claims to feel) embarrassment at the unruly antics of her children
in public. In "Shopping Trip" (1953) she tries to control her children as
they act up in a department store. "I was beginning to be aware of a familiar and dreadful feeling: that of being stared at by hordes of people—
salesladies, floorwalkers, mothers, immaculate children, and perhaps truant
officers. 'Come on,' I said nervously, and added just in time, 'my dears'"

(LS 458–59). Some of her nondomestic stories read like exaggerated versions of things of this sort. In "Like Mother Used to Make" (1949; L)—founded, apparently, on a genuine incident experienced by one of her friends (O 102)—a man has invited a woman in a neighboring apartment to a dinner he has taken great pains to make. While they are there together, a male friend of the woman's arrives, thinking it is *her* apartment, and this unwanted intruder makes himself right at home. In fact, so spineless and so afraid of causing (and suffering) embarrassment is the actual owner of the apartment that he simply leaves, pretending that *he* is the guest. A single paragraph etches his character: "David stood up. For a minute he thought he was going to say something that might start, 'Mr. Harris, I'll thank you to....' but what he actually said, finally, with both Marcia and Mr. Harris looking at him, was, 'Guess I better be getting along, Marcia'" (L 34). I suppose Jackson can get away with being a misogynist: Marcia has made no effort to disabuse Mr. Harris of the true state of affairs. A very similar story is "Trial by Combat" (1944; L). A woman, Emily, finds small items missing from her apartment and discovers that an old woman living in the downstairs apartment, Mrs. Allen, is the culprit. But Mrs. Allen is so seemingly "nice" and harmless that Emily cannot confront her on the matter. Jackson again encapsulates an entire life in a paragraph: "Emily found that she was staring at the picture of Mrs. Allen's husband; such a thoughtful-looking man, she was thinking, they must have had such a pleasant life together, and now she has a room like mine, with only two handkerchiefs of her own in the drawer" (L 39).

"The Summer People" might also be worth considering from this perspective, as the elderly couple cannot slough off their exterior of "good behavior" and come to terms with the brutal treatment they are receiving at the hands of the countryfolk. The conclusion finds the two of them cowering in the dark, waiting for the dawn—or for the next piece of viciousness from their once-friendly neighbors.

LANGUAGE, TRUTH, AND HORROR

Many of Jackson's stories turn on the statements uttered by her characters: is what they are saying true? What if, Jackson asks in a number of tales, there is some sort of insane conspiracy to deceive a single individual? Such stories are almost unclassifiable: we cannot know if the supernatural actually comes into play because ambiguity is maintained to the end as to the truth of the matter. Nevertheless, some of her most powerful tales revolve around simple utterances by individual characters, which, when taken together, potentially suggest some horrific and irrational victimization of an individual who is frequently somewhat disturbed to begin with. The standard distinction between what might be called interior and exterior supernaturalism (i.e., that occurring within the confines of an individual's mind and that occurring in the external world) seems to collapse here, or even to fuse together. It is as if Jackson is suggesting that the supernatural falls specifically upon those individuals whose hold on reality is itself shaky.

The celebrated tale "The Daemon Lover" (1949; L) is one of the best of this type. This story inaugurates a curious thread in the works in *The Lottery* (and elsewhere) in which the figure of James Harris, the Daemon Lover, flits in and out of stories, seemingly at random. To my mind, however, not much can be made of this: The name Harris appears in several stories in the collection, and sometimes he is specified as James or Jim Harris. But I do not think that in the end it amounts to much save as a sort of in-joke that has no particular point. Jackson herself admitted to being haunted by a demon lover, from as early as her college years, and she describes it in a sketch as follows (she was in a noncapitalization phase at this point): "but all i remember is that i met him (somewhere where was it in the darkness in the light was it morning were there trees flowers had i been born) and now when I think about him i only remember that he was calling margaret, as in loneliness margaret margaret, and then (did i speak to him did he look at me did we smile had we known each other once) i went away and left him (calling to me after me) calling margaret margaret" (O 49). This is poignant enough, and the several stories she wrote about a demon lover all have this same quality of bittersweet unreality. But the interconnections she attempts to forge by dropping the name Harris in the *Lottery* collection do not add up to a coherent whole.

But "The Daemon Lover" is an exquisite piece. It introduces us to the most easily recognizable character type in all Jackson's work: the lonely, weak-willed, sensitive, overly imaginative, and possibly psychotic young woman who usually ends her pitiable and meaningless existence in madness or suicide. This figure recurs with such obsessive frequency in her stories that one is tempted to see in it Jackson's imaginative view of herself, however much or little it may have coincided with the reality of her personality. In "The Daemon Lover" we encounter such a figure in Margaret, who awakes one morning in her shabby one-room apartment awaiting the arrival of James Harris, to whom she is to be married. We are already a little uneasy, since we learn that she has known Harris only for a month; and our fears seem confirmed when he fails to show up at her apartment at the appointed time. She begins to look for him, reaching the building where he had borrowed the apartment of a Mr. and Mrs. Royster for the last month. Finding the Roysters, who have just returned, she asks about James. Mrs. Royster's reaction is not reassuring: "'O Lord... What'd he do?'" (L 18). At least this appears to confirm Harris's existence, however tenuously. But the Roysters do not really know him—he was a friend of a friend. Margaret begins to ask the neighborhood shopowners whether they have seen a man answering Harris's description. No one has. Finally she so pesters a newsagent that he confesses to have seen him:

> "Now I don't know for sure, mind you, but there might have been someone like your gentleman friend coming by this morning."
> "About ten?"
> "About ten," the newsdealer agreed. "Tall fellow, blue suit. I wouldn't be at all surprised."
> "Which way did he go?" she said eagerly. "Uptown?"
> "Uptown," the newsdealer said, nodding. "He went uptown. That's just exactly it. What can I do for you, sir?" [L 21].

This is the critical point of the story: is the man admitting to having seen Harris only to get rid of the pestiferous Margaret? Why does he agree with such alacrity to having seen him at the time and place she insists he must have seen him? From this point the tale devolves into either a paranoid fantasy or an evil conspiracy, or perhaps both: the florist admits that Harris bought flowers (wouldn't a man going to his wedding buy flowers for his bride?); the shoeshine man admits he shined Harris's shoes (a natural thing for a bridegroom to do), and he directs Margaret to a street (not hers) where he says he saw Harris go; a boy at the corner says he saw Harris go in a building across the street. Margaret goes in and hears voices behind a door. The tale ends inconclusively (as it must) and agonizingly: "She knew there was someone inside the other apartment, because she was sure she could hear low voices and sometimes laughter. She came back many times, every day for the first week. She came on her way to work, in the mornings; in the evenings, on her way to dinner alone, but no matter how often or how firmly she knocked, no one ever came to the door" (L 26). Have all these people lied to her? If so, why? Do they all hate her and wish to torture her emotionally? Or are they simply cheerful sadists? This is the most frightening prospect of the story, more frightening than the prospect that Margaret has imagined much of her relationship with Harris: how can people be so irresponsibly evil?

"The Daemon Lover" has an atmosphere of wistful pathos that somehow works in tandem with the *conte cruel* horror of the tale; another, "The

Renegade" (1948; L), is pure *conte cruel*. A family from the city, the Walpoles, have moved to a seemingly placid country town and appear to be settling in nicely. Then Mrs. Walpole receives a call from a neighbor: the Walpoles' dog has been killing this person's chickens; something must be done. Mrs. Walpole cannot believe it of her gentle pet. Soon the story is all over the town (the phone is on a party line), and everyone has a remedy for stopping a dog from killing chickens. These remedies become more and more hideous: you can chain the dog; you can tie a dead chicken around its neck until it rots, so that the dog hates chickens; you can place it in a pen with some chicks and a mother hen who is sure to scratch the dog's eyes out; or you could put around the dog's neck a collar that has spikes on the inside, and when the dog approaches a chicken you pull on a rope attached to the collar, and (as Mrs. Walpole's own son notes with glee), "The spikes cut her head off" (L 65). Which one is it to be?

In this tale it is a little clearer that the townspeople have conspired to tease Mrs. Walpole mercilessly, although other questions remain unclear. Has the dog actually killed chickens? It is true that the animal comes into the house with blood on its legs—but what does this mean; has it been somehow framed? And why have the townspeople ganged up on Mrs. Walpole? As to this, Mrs. Walpole "wondered briefly if Mr. White had maliciously blamed Lady because they were city folk, and then thought, No, no man around here would bear false witness against a dog" (L 61). What Jackson has done in this story, and in others of this type, is to make us doubt every single utterance made by every character in the tale; at the same time, we are inexorably made to think the worst of all the characters. In this instance, the townspeople are either liars or sadists or both. And the worst part of it is, of course, that her own children are infected with this bloodlust against a dog and happily imagine the many tortures one could inflict upon it to cure it of its reprehensible habit.

The odd story "The Intoxicated" (1949; L) might perhaps be studied in this context. Here a man who finds himself bored at a party wanders into the kitchen, meeting the hostess' daughter Eileen, a girl of 17. She is writing a paper about the future of the world; but she doesn't think the world has much of a future. Rather harrowingly, she chronicles the destruction of civilization—or, at least, this phase of it:

> "Somehow I think of the churches as going first, before even the
> Empire State building. And then all the big apartment houses by the
> river, slipping down slowly into the water with the people inside. And
> the schools, in the middle of Latin class maybe, while we're reading
> Caesar." She brought her eyes to his face, looking at him in numb
> excitement. "Each time we begin a chapter in Caesar, I wonder if this

won't be the one we never finish. Maybe we in our Latin class will be the last people who ever read Caesar" [L 11].

The worst thing about it is that she seems so *certain* of it, and this raises the query: what if she is right? The tale is faintly reminiscent of Margaret St. Clair's famous story, "The Boy Who Predicted Earthquakes," although there the boy is undoubtedly clairvoyant and knows that the world will end. In "The Intoxicated" we are left only with the unnerving thought that the girl is either right (in which case the world will end) or that she is wrong (in which case she is insane) or that she is having a little fun (in which case she is a sadist). None of these is very reassuring. Here again Jackson is simply trying to jolt us out of our conventional ways of thinking, and a tiresome party is the perfect backdrop for such an enterprise.

Jackson's one genuine science fiction (or at least futuristic) story, "Bulletin" (1954),[9] might be studied here, for it not only follows up on the theme of "The Intoxicated" (the future of civilization) but indirectly exemplifies the same issues of language, truth, and horror as the other stories I have been discussing. This very brief tale is surprisingly difficult to interpret. Let us bypass the very crude mechanics of the story: a clumsy editor's note informing us that certain documents have come back in a time machine that was sent into the early twenty-second century, although the scientist who went in the machine did not return.

The first document we find is a fragment of a newspaper dating from May 8, 2123; this indicates little save that the people of that time were given to pompous and empty circumlocution (hardly a unique trait!). A letter from a boy to his parents has the spellings "haveing," "cokies" (for *cookies*), "loveing," and the like, implying either that the boy was illiterate (and perhaps, by extension, the rest of the society?) or that these spellings had by then become standard. The most interesting and problematical document is a high-school or college history exam. Here we find that the twenty-second century has fallen into irremediable confusion about the past, citing such figures as "George Washingham," "Sinclair (Joe) Lewis," and "Sergeant Cuff" (as if he were a real individual). Then there are a series of statements that one is to mark either true or false, and this is where things get complicated. Take this statement: "The aboriginal Americans lived aboveground and drank water." This is obviously true, but carries the suggestion that the people of the twenty-second century do not live above-ground or drink water: in a single sentence an entire mode of future existence is potently suggested. But consider this statement: "The hero Jackie Robinson is chiefly known for his voyage to obtain the golden fleece." The point is not whether this is true or false; the point is: what if the people of the future *think* it to be true? Given their other errors, this is entirely conceivable. Even if the future society knows this to be false, the very manner in which the statement is framed suggests that Jackie Robinson is now regarded as some sort of hero, perhaps in some religious fashion. Other statements carry similarly disturbing implications. But the clincher is at the end. The final document is a card giving someone's weight (presumably the scientist's) and a meaningless machine-generated fortune. But the editor of these documents professes to find this silly thing "of great significance." And it suddenly becomes clear that the time machine was not sent *forward* from our time into the future but *backward* from an infinitely farther future, in which people's grasp of the events of our time and before must be even poorer than people's in the twenty-second century's if they cannot correctly identify an insignificant weight and fortune card.

LONELINESS

Shirley Jackson once wrote that she took to writing out of loneliness:

> when i first used to write stories and hide them away in my desk i used to think that no one had ever been so lonely as i was and i used to write about people all alone. once i started a novel ... but i never finished because i found out about insanity about then and i used to write about lunatics after that. i thought i was insane and i would write about how the only sane people are the ones who are condemned as mad and how the whole world is cruel and foolish and afraid of people who are different [O 40].

It is conceivable that this single utterance encompasses nearly the whole of her fiction, and loneliness may be the single most dominant theme in her work. But note again what a contrast the domestic fiction presents: in that body of work she herself is not lonely because she has her lively and energetic children (I have already noted how infrequently her husband appears in these works). And although she and her family may be isolated from the rest of the community (as in reality they were because of their intellectualism and, it must be admitted, Jackson's snobbishness [O 183–84]), they still participate with gusto in such social rituals as shopping, moving, celebrating Christmas, and participating in sports. If the domestic fiction therefore benignly papers over the true loneliness of Jackson and her family, her other fiction scathingly lays it bare with such force that the tales become genuinely horrific.

Loneliness appears to be manifested in these stories in two parallel ways, as in the domestic fiction: 1) the loneliness of an individual within a wider group (whether that be a family, a community, or the world); and 2) the loneliness of a family within a wider group. In both categories we find some of Jackson's most memorable and terrifying work.

We have already noted individual loneliness in a number of tales—the partygoer in "The Intoxicated," Margaret in "The Daemon Lover," the niece in "The Little House." The opening paragraph of "The Intoxicated" encapsulates the idea perfectly:

> He was just tight enough and just familiar enough with the house to be able to go out into the kitchen alone, apparently to get ice, but actually to sober up a little; he was not quite enough of a friend of the family to pass out on the living-room couch. He left the party behind without reluctance, the group by the piano singing "Stardust," his hostess talking earnestly to a young man with thin clean glasses and a sullen mouth; he walked guardedly through the dining-room, where a little group of four or five people sat on the stiff chairs reasoning something out carefully among themselves ... [L 9].

By implication, the man's loneliness is a product both of his own volition (he does not want to join the singers) and of rebuffs by others (the hostess clearly does not wish to be interrupted in her tête-à-tête with the young man; the people in the dining room are discussing something "among themselves," leaving no room for anyone else). We will find this sort of dichotomy frequently in Jackson. A surprising number of individuals or families will withdraw themselves from society, washing their hands of it entirely. This tendency reaches its apex in *We Have Always Lived in the Castle* (1962). But can we truly be certain that this self-imposed hermitry is solely a result of misanthropy? Might it perhaps not conceal a longing for acceptance that has finally turned to what Lovecraft called the "bitterness of alienage"?[10]

I am not at all certain that "The Lottery" (1948; L) ought to be considered in this precise context, but we may as well do so here as anywhere. Whereas this tale seems generally to convey the notion of a community that willfully isolates an individual within it, Jackson herself appears to have had different ideas. Judy Oppenheimer writes: "She always refused to answer the question put to her by thousands of readers, 'What is "The Lottery" really about?'—but to a good friend she confided very matter-of-factly that it had, of course, been about the Jews" (O 72). Respectful as I generally am to authors' statements about their own work, in this case I must frankly declare Jackson to be mistaken. "The Lottery" cannot be about anti–Semitism because of the fundamental *randomness* of the procedure by which an individual from the community is selected to die. In any case, the community depicted in the story appears racially and culturally homogeneous, and the individual chosen for death—Mrs. Hutchinson—differs in no appreciable way from the other citizens. Indeed, it is exactly this randomness that is the source of horror in the story. Another comment by Jackson seems a little more on target: "I suppose I hoped, by setting a particularly brutal rite in the present and in my own village, to shock the readers with a graphic dramatization of the pointless violence and general inhumanity of their own lives" (O 131). Even this I am not inclined to accept wholly, and in fact Jackson's best commentary on her story may be a stray remark in *Hangsaman*: "Another instance ... of ritual gone to seed" (H 62).

For ritual is at the heart of the story—a meaningless, stupid ritual whose original rationale, whatever it may have been, has now been entirely forgotten. This is made clear by an elderly person's statement that the neighboring town wants to give up the lottery (the implication, obviously, is that the lottery is a widespread if not universal phenomenon):

> Old Man Warner snorted. "Pack of crazy fools," he said. "Listening to the young folks, nothing's good enough for *them*. Next thing you know, they'll be wanting to go back to living in caves, nobody work any more, live *that* way for a while. Used to be a saying about 'Lottery in June, corn be heavy soon.' First thing you know, we'd all be eating stewed chickweed and acorns. There's *always* been a lottery," he added petulantly [L 215].

The lottery has become so inveterate that it has given rise to an axiom. This axiom, "Lottery in June, corn be heavy soon," suggests that the original purpose of the lottery was as a fertility rite, something akin to what Thomas Tryon described at the conclusion of *Harvest Home* (1973). But the need for bountiful crops must have long passed, and yet the lottery continues, much as we might say "Bless you!" when someone sneezes, even though we have entirely forgotten and presumably would no longer even believe in what the expression really means (one must be blessed lest one expel one's soul while sneezing). It is "ritual gone to seed." And it is the young people of the neighboring town who wish to give up the lottery: they are less under the sway of mindless convention than the old people. Indeed, when Old Man Warner remarks at the end, "It's not the way it used to be.... People ain't the way they used to be" (L 218), he means that now some people are actually taking pity on the victim or, at least, are no longer taking pride in having the victim chosen from their own families (the remark previous to his is: "A girl whispered, 'I hope it's not Nancy'" [L 218]).

The artistry of "The Lottery" is indeed remarkable, although there is some justice to some readers' complaints of authorial deceit. One reader wrote to the *New Yorker*, "I resent being tricked into reading perverted stories like 'The Lottery'" (C 231). However naive and conventional this response may be, it underscores the fact that Jackson goes out of her way to conceal the climax by a narrative tone that at the outset is placid, benign, and innocuous almost to excess. Subtle little points throughout the narrative cause unease, however, in particular the matter of why the family that has apparently won the first part of the lottery seems unhappy about being chosen. If they have won a lottery, shouldn't they be pleased? In fact, the person to be killed will be chosen from that family. And it is only one more of Jackson's perversions of domestic bliss that the children of the town take the greatest glee in stoning the victim to death.

I have stated that "The Lottery" is nonsupernatural, and of course the actual events are indeed so. But in a strange way this tale may be *weird* without being supernatural, by merely postulating the existence of the lottery in this town and in at least several others. There are, of course, no lotteries of this sort and never have been. In this sense the story embodies in the most literal way a trait I have described in the weird tale: the refashioning of reality. "The Lottery" is clearly set in the present day and in a world we are all seemingly familiar with; but the mere existence of the lottery, and the clear implication that it has been in practice for decades or centuries, depict Lovecraft's "violation of natural law" in the simple sense of portraying the real world as other than we know it in this one regard.

The central theme of *The Haunting of Hill House* also appears to be individual loneliness, although it could be studied from a number of other perspectives. The focus of this rich, complex, poignant, and atmospheric work—at once the greatest of Jackson's novels and her greatest contribution to weird fiction—is Eleanor Vance, perhaps Jackson's most delicately etched portrait of the weak-willed, love-starved woman. Eleanor has been chosen—along with Luke Sanderson and Theodora (she claims to have no last name)—by Dr. John Montague, an avowed investigator of "supernatural phenomena" (HH 5), to explore Hill House because of her apparent sensitivity to the weird or occult: when younger she had evidently experienced some poltergeist phenomena. Her previous life (she is 32) has been wretched. Up to a few months before coming to Hill House she had to take care of her sick mother, and she now suffers guilt because she thinks she may have contributed to her death by being negligent. She does not get along with her married sister (indeed, it is stated at the outset that she "hated" [HH 7] her) and is forced covertly to take the car they jointly own when the sister refuses to allow her to use it to drive to Hill House.

At the moment I am not interested in many of the supernatural phenomena recounted in the novel. I wish to clarify here not merely Eleanor's loneliness (she admits this herself: "'I am always afraid of being alone'" [HH 113]) but her low estimation of herself:

> Eleanor found herself unexpectedly admiring her own feet. Theodora dreamed over the fire just beyond the tips of her toes, and Eleanor thought with deep satisfaction that her feet were handsome in their red sandals; what a complete and separate thing I am, she thought, going from my red toes to the top of my head, individually an I, possessed of attributes belonging only to me. I have red shoes, she thought—that goes with being Eleanor; I dislike lobster and sleep on my left side and crack my knuckles when I am nervous and save buttons. I am holding a brandy glass which is mine because I am here and I am using it and I will have a place in this room. I have red shoes and tomorrow I will wake up and I will still be here [HH 59].

This is all a little harried: she is seizing upon anything she can find to validate her existence. Has Eleanor only really begun to *live*—to lead a full, emotionally satisfying life—since coming to Hill House? Such is surely the implication of the following:

> Suddenly, without reason, laughter trembled inside Eleanor; she wanted to run to the head of the table and hug the doctor, she wanted to reel, chanting, across the stretches of the lawn, she wanted to sing and to shout and to fling her arms and move in great, emphatic, possessing circles around the rooms of Hill House; I am here, I am here, she thought. She shut her eyes quickly in delight and then said demurely to the doctor, "And what do we do today?" [HH 100–1].

What this passage also suggests is her growing identification with Hill House—she is possessing it or it is possessing her. Early on the doctor says: "'Hill House has a reputation for insistent hospitality; it seemingly dislikes letting its guests get away'" (HH 48–49). Eleanor ominously echoes this idea when she says, "'I don't think we could leave now if we wanted to'" (HH 54).

The Shakespearean tag "Journeys end in lovers meeting" glides through this novel like an elusive ritornello, but what is its true implication? If it is Eleanor's journey that is at an end here (and this is clearly the case, as at the beginning we experience the long trip to Hill House through her eyes), who is her lover? Is it Theodora, with whom she becomes very close—to the point that Theodora must wear Eleanor's clothes when her own are found covered with red paint like blood? Is it Luke, who seems to be dallying with both women? Or is it the house itself? Perhaps it is all three.

Toward the end it becomes clear that Luke, finding Eleanor's behavior increasingly odd, prefers the company of Theodora. Is Eleanor jealous of Theodora? Why else is she suddenly filled with an "uncontrollable loathing" (HH 112) of her?

It is here that some of the supernatural manifestations gain their importance. At one point the guests find some crude writing on the wall: "HELP ELEANOR COME HOME" (HH 103). The wording is significant: it is not "Help Eleanor *go* home" or "*get* home"; the implication is that Eleanor is already home or on the way home (at Hill House), and that some sort of spiritual transition must take place so that she feels *at* home here. Other weird events also seem to single out Eleanor, until finally she appears to begin cracking under the strain. One night she leaves her bedroom to meander through the house. Her absence is noted by the others and they look for her, but she refuses to reveal her whereabouts. "Eleanor clung to the door and laughed until tears came into her eyes; what fools they are, she thought; we trick them so easily" (HH 163). Who is the "we" but she and Hill House? Journeys end in lovers meeting. When the others persuade her to leave, she cries defiantly, "Hill House belongs to *me*" (HH 173), and as she leaves the driveway she turns abruptly and smashes her car into a tree, echoing the fate of the last occupant of Hill House 18 years before, whose "horse bolted and crushed him against the big tree" (HH 49). What life would Eleanor have had if she had left? "'It's the only time anything's ever happened to me'" (HH 171).

At this point it is worth studying the general supernaturalism of the novel. In a lecture written a year prior to the publication of *The Haunting of Hill House*, "Experience and Fiction" (C), Jackson discusses the research and composition of the novel at length. This essay does not seem to be of any genuine help in elucidating the work, although it contains some wry features, as when Jackson notes coming down to her study one morning and finding the words "DEAD DEAD" on a sheet of paper in her own handwriting (C 213), which she takes as a sign that she was destined to write a ghost story. In any case, we learn both from this essay and from the facts of her biography that Jackson had always had an interest in the supernatural, and indeed both she herself and her children made no secret of the fact that she actually believed in the supernatural (O 37, 125). She had an extensive collection of books on witchcraft, and in preparation for her novel she read much about hauntings, including papers by the Society for Psychic Research.

And yet, it must be admitted that the supernatural manifestations in *The Haunting of Hill House* in many cases seem random, unmotivated, and unexplained. What is the significance of the cold spot in the hallway; of the knocking heard intermittently at night on people's doors; of "some animal like a dog" (HH 95) seen by Dr. Montague? It is all very well for the doctor to say that "'psychic phenomena are subject to laws of a very particular sort'" (HH 48), but those laws are never specified, nor are the psychic events actually experienced at Hill House ever plausibly accounted for or harmonized within the overall scheme of the novel. It appears that they are meant merely to enhance the atmosphere of weirdness as a backdrop to the story of Eleanor Vance. It may also have been a mistake for Jackson to introduce Montague's obnoxious and overbearing wife and her pompous and bumbling assistant toward the end; considerable cheap satire is had at their expense, but the atmosphere of the novel is close to being shattered by their obtrusive presence. Nevertheless, *The Haunting of Hill House* remains a masterwork in the field, if only for exhibiting some of the most meticulous character portrayal in weird fiction and for its overwhelming sense of inevitable doom.

A final contribution to the individual loneliness theme is Jackson's last published story, "The Possibility of Evil" (1965). This story of an aristocratic old woman who writes anonymous poison pen letters to other citizens so as to keep her town "clean and sweet" is a trifle obvious, but is redeemed by its unrelenting viciousness. In the end she is detected and someone repays her in kind by destroying her cherished rose garden and writing an anonymous note: "LOOK OUT AT WHAT USED TO BE YOUR ROSES." Jackson's biographer Judy Oppenheimer believes, incredibly, that Jackson identified with the old woman: "Shirley wanted to see herself ... as a proper lady, sure of her place, who sent forth her terrible messages to the world yet remained anonymously secure" (O 272). But surely we are meant to loathe the old woman for her spitefulness and her injustice: "Miss Strangeworth never concerned herself with facts; her letters all dealt with the more negotiable stuff of suspicion." And the irony is a little heavy-handed:

> She had been writing her letters ... for the past year. She never got any answers, of course, because she never signed her name. If she had been asked, she would have said that her name, Adela Strangeworth, a name honored in the town for so many years, did not belong on such trash. The town where she lived had to be kept clean and sweet, but people everywhere were lustful and evil and degraded, and needed to be watched; the world was so large, and there was only one Miss Strangeworth left in it.[11]

The individual loneliness theme has given birth to an interesting offshoot whereby, as I have suggested earlier, some of Jackson's loners flee their confining environment and, sometimes literally, transform themselves into new individuals with new personalities. We have already seen this at work in *The Haunting of Hill House*, where Eleanor Vance's trip to Hill House symbolizes the sloughing off of her old personality—as a weak, colorless, lonely woman—in preparation for the donning of a new one. She can adopt this new personality without fear of contradiction or ridicule, because none of the other guests at Hill House know of her former life; indeed, at Hill House she is, at least at the outset, vibrant, witty, and potentially an object of a man's (and woman's)[12] affections.

Several stories, early and late, also exemplify this trend. I have noted how, in "Like Mother Used to Make," the woman appears as a guest in her neighbor's apartment, then takes on the persona of the legitimate occupant of the place when a second guest arrives. Similarly, "The Villager" (1944; L) is the subtly disturbing story of a woman, Hilda Clarence, who comes to an apartment of someone selling furniture, finds the occupant gone, and wanders in. Another individual (the ubiquitous Mr. Harris) comes in, and Hilda passes herself off—not through any explicit statement, but merely by omitting to state the contrary—as the occupant. The scenario allows her to create a new life for herself: she and her husband (she is in fact unmarried) are going to Paris and must sell the furniture; she herself is a dancer (in fact, the actual occupant of the apartment is a dancer; Hilda had wanted to be one [L 40] but is now a private secretary). Harris leaves without buying any furniture; Hilda leaves shortly thereafter. That is all there is to the story, but in a few pages Jackson portrays vividly a woman's loss of her dreams in the mundane realities of life and the ease with which she can indulge in wish-fulfillment fantasies of what she might have been.

The Bird's Nest might be studied here, even though it is the least successful of Jackson's novels. This work might have been a powerful vehicle for the study of loneliness and the concomitant desire to refashion oneself—for who can be lonelier than a person with multiple personalities?—but the execution is severely flawed. It is about Elizabeth Richmond, who is diagnosed as having four separate personalities: Elizabeth (timid and colorless); Beth (sweet but fragile); Betsy (childishly petulant and potentially violent); and Bess (the most evil of all, a frightening megalomaniac). But the story is marred by structural clumsiness, poor writing, and a feeble conclusion. Jackson makes several mistakes of judgment. Each of the five long chapters is narrated from a different point of view: the first chapter is omniscient; the second and fourth are from the perspective of the psychiatrist brought in to treat Elizabeth; the third (most interestingly) is through Betsy's eyes; and the fifth is from the point of view of Elizabeth's Aunt Morgen. The psychiatrist's narrative tone—flippant, pretentious, cheaply ironic—seriously impedes the progress of the novel, which in any case (as with all Jackson's novels save the last two) tends to meander and digress. In chapter two the reproduction of the psychiatrist's transcript of a discussion with Elizabeth and her various personalities sounds excessively clinical, robbing the scene of the emotive power it might have had if it had been presented more novelistically. And the lame conclusion, in which Elizabeth is magically cured and her personalities integrated, is a woeful anticlimax. Indeed, toward the end the atmosphere changes almost in spite of Jackson's wishes from grim intensity to farce as we watch Elizabeth's four personalities successively assert themselves and take four baths consecutively (B 335–37).

Eventually we are led to understand the origin of the entire personality split: Elizabeth, jealous of her mother's lover (who hates her [B 236]), has caused her mother's death in an altercation and is now suppressing the memory. Jackson may have erred here also on the side of vagueness, as the background is sketched hazily and fragmentarily, so that the connection between Elizabeth's relationship with her mother and her split personality is never adequately clarified.

Jackson's incomplete novel, *Come Along with Me* (1965; C), is the most forthright example of a character leaving the past behind. A middle-aged woman whose husband has died decides to unburden herself of all the impedimenta of her prior existence and start afresh. "So that was how I started out. I'd thought about it for a long time of course—not that I positively expected I was going to have to bury Hughie, but he had a good life— and everything went the way I used to figure it would. I sold the house, I auctioned off the furniture, I put all the paintings and boxes in the barn, I erased my old name and took my initials off everything, and I got on the train and left" (C 12). She takes up a new name, Angela Motorman, almost at random, and, in response to her landlady's query as to her occupation, she remarks: "'I dabble in the supernatural'" (C 18). What this means, apparently, is that from the age of 12 she has heard voices from the dead (C 24–26). The fragment ends after Angela gives a rather inconclusive and unsatisfying séance. I have no idea where this novel was going to go—even what we have seems a little disjointed and unfocused—or whether the supernatural would actually have come into play, but *Come Along with Me* might for once have portrayed a strong, self-controlled figure rather than the birdlike victims so characteristic of Jackson's other work.

The tales that focus on the loneliness or isolation of a family within a community do not differ appreciably in tone from those involving individual loneliness. It might be thought that these tales would be tempered somewhat with hope, in the sense that the family members at least have the comfort of each other's company even if the rest of the world rejects them, whereas the lonely individuals have no one to turn to in their isolation. But in fact these tales can be even grimmer than the others, and several of them represent Jackson's most pungent excursions into satire and misanthropy. This is either because the family unit cannot provide any significant comfort to its members in the face of the overwhelming hostility of the outside world, or because the family itself is torn by tragedy and infighting, so that individuals may feel an added layer of loneliness— both within the family and without.

Consider "The Renegade." The horror of this story lies not merely in the implication that an entire community has, with gleeful vindictiveness, turned against a household because of its supposed chicken-killing dog, but that the family is now being destroyed from within as the children embrace the prospect of killing the dog:

> Mrs. Walpole looked at them, at her two children with their hard hands and their sunburned faces laughing together, their dog with blood still on her legs laughing with them. She went to the kitchen doorway to look outside at the cool green hills, the motion of the apple tree in the soft afternoon breeze.
> "Cut your head right off," Jack was saying [L 65].

"Strangers in Town" (1959) is Jackson's vendetta against the townsfolk who ostracized her when she accused a favorite grade-school teacher of beating her children (see O 213–15). This crude and obvious story is fueled by nothing but hatred, to the point that Jackson's artistry completely forsakes her. Told from the point of view of small-minded neighbors who cannot tolerate a strange family's unconventional ways (they don't seem to do any cooking; they dance the night away), this story is simply void of subtlety:

> "Foreign ways!" I said. "You're heathen, wicked people, with your dancing and your maid, and the sooner you leave this town, the better it's going to be for you. Because I might as well tell you"—and I shook my finger right at her–"that certain people in this town aren't going to put up with your fancy ways much longer, and you would be well advised—very well advised, I say—to pack up your furniture and your curtains and your maid and cat and get out of our town before we put you out."[13]

"'All She Said Was "Yes"'" (1962) is much superior, speaking poignantly of a curious young girl whose parents have been killed in an auto accident. It bears similarities to "The Intoxicated" in that it suggests that the girl is clairvoyant; and like that story, it is told from the point of view of an individual who fails to perceive the girl's powers. This tale is also a little obvious (there is no ambiguity, as in "The Intoxicated," about whether the girl really can see into the future). And a predictable ending does not help matters— the girl tells her neighbor repeatedly not to go on a boat, but the neighbor pays no attention and the story concludes: "we're all going to go on a cruise." But the delicate portrayal of the central figure— an unattractive, tight-lipped, morose girl who knew that her parents would die and is accordingly not shocked but merely saddened and stupefied, and now totally alone in the world—makes this one of Jackson's later triumphs.

The Sundial may be mentioned here, although I wish to study it more extensively elsewhere. This mad and disturbing tale of the large and wealthy Halloran family convinced that the external world will shortly come to an end, with only its house preserved, displays at once their isolation and the internal dissensions that cause them to be a microcosm of the unruly outside world they are purportedly leaving behind. The Hallorans' withdrawal from the world, even before they take up their insane view of imminent global destruction, is entirely self-generated:

> The character of the house is perhaps of interest. It stood upon a small rise in ground, and all the land it surveyed belonged to the Halloran family. The Halloran land was distinguished from the rest of the world by a stone wall, which went completely around the estate, so that all inside the wall was Halloran, all outside was not. The first Mr. Halloran ... was a man who, in the astonishment of finding himself suddenly extremely wealthy, could think of nothing better to do with his money than set up his own world. His belief about the house ... was that it should contain everything. The other world, the one the Hallorans were leaving behind, was to be plundered ruthlessly for objects of beauty to go in and around Mr. Halloran's house; infinite were the delights to be prepared for its inhabitants [S 11].

But this isolation fails to weed out the disharmonies of the world, as we shall see elsewhere. Much of the effectiveness of this book lies in how Jackson totally ignores the outside world, as if it has already ceased to exist. Everything is focused on the house and its occupants; even when some of those occupants have come from that outside world, it is completely forgotten once they enter the house. Background information on the characters is deliberately lacking, as if they had no prior existence before coming there. In the one instance where a character—Maryjane, the daughter-in-law of the domineering Mrs. Halloran—attempts to escape, the scene is depicted in so bizarre a manner that we are uncertain of its reality. And Maryjane, bootlessly trying to flee to the nearby town on foot, finds that she has unwittingly returned to the very house she sought to leave. It is needless to remark that Jackson wisely ends the novel without resolving the issue of whether the world will in fact end.

We Have Always Lived in the Castle is Jackson's grimmest and nastiest portrayal of family isolation. The Blackwood family has been shattered by tragedy: all but three members of the household died by poisoning six years prior to the novel's opening, and one of the survivors, Constance Blackwood, is blamed by the townspeople for the murders even though she was tried and found innocent. She now lives in her spectral house with her younger cousin Mary Katherine (called Merricat) and her uncle Julian, himself crippled from the effects of the poison. Next to the Hallorans in *The Sundial*, this is Jackson's weirdest family. Merricat is the focus of the tale: she alone ventures to the town for groceries and other household needs, enduring the taunts of the townsfolk but in turn hating and despising them. It is clear that we are meant to sympathize wholeheartedly with the Blackwoods and to hate the townspeople as they hate them, and as they are hated in turn by them. But what are we to make of the family's snobbishness?

> Anyone who came to see us, properly invited, came up the main drive which led straight from the gateposts on the highway up to our front door. When I was small I used to lie in my bedroom at the back of the house and imagine the driveway and the path as a crossroad meeting before our front door, and up and down the driveway went the good people, the clean and rich ones dressed in satin and lace, who came rightfully to visit, and back and forth along the path, sneaking and weaving and sidestepping servilely, went the people from the village [W 27–28].

One might be inclined to say that Jackson is introducing a significant ambiguity in suggesting that the Blackwoods and the townspeople are both blameworthy for the ostracism they inflict upon each other, but this does not appear to be the case. We have already seen that Jackson herself looked down upon the townsfolk of Bennington, and her views are identical to Merricat's. She is clearly portraying the attitude here as entirely admirable (it in fact connects with what happens later in the novel), and it is unfortunate that Jackson could not predict the disapproval that later generations would have of this sort of snobbishness. In any case, the rest of the novel compels us to find the townspeople wholly responsible for the events that follow, in particular when they, in a fit of irrational anger, destroy much of the house while putting out a fire that has started inside it. It is at this point that we learn a truth that scarcely any reader could have failed to guess, although Jackson evidently intends it as a stunning surprise: Merricat was the poisoner of her family.

The novel does not end here, however. In what is both a horrific and a heart-rending twist of Jackson's domestic fiction, the two cousins (Julian has now died) continue in their quiet defiance of the townsfolk by trying to resume their lives even when most of their property—furniture, clothes, utensils, food, even much of the house itself—has been devastated. When Constance, successfully locating two teacups with their handles intact, remarks, "We will take our meals like ladies ... using cups with handles" (W 144), we are evidently to regard this as a reaffirmation of the "good breeding" the women have received, a wholly admirable attempt to preserve one's dignity in the face of disaster.

There is, of course, nothing supernatural about We Have Always Lived in the Castle. If anything, it is a mystery story, although the mystery is not very cleverly executed and is by no means the focus of the novel. By any normal criteria it cannot be considered a weird tale, even though it manipulates after a fashion the topos of the haunted house, doing so from the unique perspective of the inhabitants of the house rather than of outsiders seeking to penetrate its mysteries. There is, however, a rather odd way in which perhaps the weird does enter into this novel, and it is this that I now wish to consider.

MISANTHROPY

"Nothing has the power to hurt which doesn't have the power to frighten" (O 42): this single utterance by Shirley Jackson may be all the justification we need to consider some of her darkest and most vicious work, otherwise wholly nonsupernatural, as anomalous contributions to the weird tale. Maurice Lévy remarked of Ambrose Bierce that "One is almost tempted to believe that one day he decided to instill fear into his contemporaries *by hatred*, to gain revenge on them,"[14] and Jackson seems very frequently inspired by the same motivation. Indeed, from this perspective it is possible to consider a very wide array of works—from Juvenal (notably the fifteenth satire, on cannibalism in Egypt) to Swift[15] to Evelyn Waugh's A Handful of Dust (1934)[16]—as quasi-weird, because they are all driven by such demonic misanthropy that they not only hurt but frighten. Perhaps it is this feature that will allow us to sneak in We Have Always Lived in the Castle through the back door of the weird.

It is interesting that *The Sundial* seems to have been singled out by reviewers for its misanthropy. Harvey Swados snorted: "While Miss Jackson is an intelligent and clever writer, there rises from her pages the cold fishy gleam of a calculated and carefully expressed contempt for the human race" (O 218). There are two problems with this assertion: one, the whole of Jackson's work is refreshingly misanthropic; two, the assumption here (as I have noted in connection with Bierce) is that there is something necessarily wrong with misanthropy. I do not know that Jackson anywhere offers an explicit philosophical defense of misanthropy, but perhaps she need not have done so: her work makes it obvious that she had little patience for the stupid, the arrogant, the pompous, the complacently bourgeois, the narrow-minded, and the spiteful—in other words, she hated all those people whom there is every good reason to hate. Since, therefore, I do not acknowledge any prejudice against misanthropy, I can only relish the exquisite nastiness with which Jackson ordinarily displays it. Such a tale as "Strangers in Town" is to be criticized not because it is misanthropic but because in this instance Jackson's blind hatred has resulted in a failure of artistry and subtlety otherwise uniformly evident in the rest of her work.

It may be worth discussing the celebrated "One Ordinary Day, with Peanuts" here. This spectacularly nasty story has, in its quiet way, some stupendous implications. A man leaves home in the morning and seems intent on accomplishing nothing but good: he keeps an eye on a boy while his mother runs an errand; he advises a man looking for an apartment that he has just seen one that is available; he gives a cab driver money and advice for betting on horses. Most remarkably of all, he intentionally stops a young man and a young woman on the street, introduces them to each other, and gives them money to take the day off and have a good time. He is benevolence itself. He comes home, meets his wife, and tells her how his day went. She tells him about hers. "'I had a little nap this afternoon, took it easy most of the day. Went into a department store this morning and accused the woman next to me of shoplifting, and had the store detective pick her up. Sent three dogs to the pound—*you* know, the usual thing.'" They plan the next day:

> "Fine," said Mr. Johnson. "But you do look tired. Want to change over tomorrow?"
> "I *would* like to," she said. "I could do with a change."
> "Right," said Mr. Johnson.[17]

With such ease can people be by turns sadistically mean and superhumanly philanthropic! The one seems as good a way of passing the time as the other. But the true message of the story, beyond the implication that misanthropy and benevolence can be sloughed off and put on like a cloak, is the idea of manipulation: both misanthropy and benevolence involve a fascistic manipulation of human beings as if they were puppets. And perhaps Jackson's real misanthropy is directed here not at the couple but at the spineless and stupid people who allow the couple to do their dirty or good work with such insouciance.

Manipulation of this sort is what Mrs. Orianna Halloran attempts in *The Sundial*. There may perhaps be some justification in singling out this novel for its misanthropy, since here there are no admirable or likeable characters at all, and each of them is portrayed in the most vitriolic manner: Mrs. Halloran, domineering, arrogant, and possibly the murder of her own son so that no one could stand in the way of her control of the household; Mr. Halloran, her husband, broken, feeble-minded, lost in dreams of the past; Aunt Fanny, flighty and confused but startlingly bucking Orianna's authority at unexpected moments; Maryjane, an airhead who only wants control of the house and property for herself; Miss Ogilvie, an utterly ineffectual longtime family retainer; Essex, a sycophant who seeks only to forward his own cause; Augusta Willow, a blowsy matron who wants nothing more than to marry off her two sullen daughters, Julia and Arabella; Gloria, a possibly disturbed young woman with apparently precognitive powers; even little Fancy, Maryjane's young daughter, whose sweet exterior hides a lust for power and control scarcely less intense than that of Mrs. Halloran.

This is the eccentric group Jackson gathers for her pseudoapocalyptic tale. And it can scarcely be doubted that, if nothing else, it represents the most extreme contrast possible with the love, warmth, and unity of her own family as recorded (with perhaps no little exaggeration) in her domestic fiction. The ease with which everyone is convinced—or claims to be convinced—of Aunt Fanny's notion that the world will end (she claims to have heard it from the spirit of her dead father) is certainly meant as a testament to human stupidity. It is conceivable, however, that Mrs. Halloran only goes along with the idea as a means of maintaining control of the household, since she immediately begins laying down orders on preparing for the disaster and makes it abundantly clear that she will be the queen of the new civilization that the family will have to found once all the other people in the world are eliminated.

We Have Always Lived in the Castle is Jackson's most unrestrainedly misanthropic work. Here hatred is everywhere: "The people of the village have always hated us" (W 11); "I wished they were dead" (W 15); "our father said they [the villagers] were trash" (W 17). Let us hear what Merricat feels for the townsfolk:

> I wish you were all dead, I thought, and longed to say it out loud. Constance said, "Never let them see that you care," and "If you pay any attention they'll only get worse," and probably it was true, but I wished they were dead. I would have liked to come into the grocery some morning and see them all, even the Elberts and the children, lying there crying with the pain and dying. I would then help myself to groceries, I thought, stepping over their bodies, taking whatever I fancied from the shelves, and go home, with perhaps a kick for Mrs. Donell while she lay there. I was never sorry when I had thoughts like this; I only wished they would come true. "It's wrong to hate them," Constance said, "it only weakens *you*," but I hated them anyway, and wondered why it had been worth while creating them in the first place [W 15–16].

That last sentence rather reminds me of Lucretius' celebrated comment against the argument from design: *Quidve mali fuerat nobis non esse creatis?* ("What harm would it have been had we never been created?") (*De Rerum Natura* 5.174). In any case, I actually believe we are meant to agree with Merricat's sentiments here, outrageous as they seem: note that when Constance chides her for hating the townsfolk, it is not because such a hatred is abstractly immoral but because "it only weakens you." Constance is recommending a sort of bland indifference as an even purer form of misanthropy than active hatred. The whole novel, in any event, asks us to sympathize with the Blackwoods and not the townsfolk.

The downfall of the Blackwood family is triggered by the arrival of a cousin Charles, who is portrayed with withering scorn as a small-minded, conventional man interested in returning the family to "normality" (as if that is what Constance or Merricat wants) and in making use of the large amount of money that is carelessly hidden in the house. Even after the destruction and burning of the place, Charles returns only because of the money:

> "See?" Charles said, outside, at the foot of our steps. "There's the house, just like I said. It doesn't look as bad as it did, now the vines have grown so. But the roof's been burned away, and the place was gutted inside."
>
> "Are the ladies in there?"
>
> "Sure." Charles laughed, and I remembered his laughter and his big staring white face and from inside the door I wished him dead. "They're in there all right," he said. "And so is a whole damn fortune."
>
> "You *know* that?"
>
> "They've got money in there's never even been counted. They've got it buried all over, and a safe full, and God knows where else they've

hidden it. They never come out, just hide away inside with all that
money" [W 168].

Constance and Merricat don't let him in, and he goes off, never to be heard
from again.

HOUSES

Anyone who has written works with such titles as "The Lovely House,"
"The House," "Louisa, Please Come Home," "The Little House," "Home,"
The Haunting of Hill House, and *We Have Always Lived in the Castle* must find
great inspiration from dwellings. These tales by no means exhaust the cat-
alogue of "house" stories in Jackson's work, and we must add at least *The
Sundial* and, indeed, both volumes of domestic fiction to the list.

Those domestic volumes are again the logical starting point for the
analysis of the house theme in Jackson. It is not simply that the house
functions benignly in these books whereas it is sinister, evil, confining, and
inhibiting in her other work; the relation is again more complex than that.
Recall our discussion of "The House" (1952), the quasi-supernatural tale
whose first section alone was included at the very beginning of *Life among
the Savages*. It is no surprise that the supernatural component of the story
would be excised in its new setting; but the mere context has robbed the
house in the story of its subtly evil character. The narrative of moving into
this imposing but ramshackle house takes on a seriocomic quality, as in
the book Jackson's children play a greater role, dispersing the potentially
chilling atmosphere with their boisterous high spirits. The message is clear:
in the domestic fiction a house is not in itself a cheering and heartwarm-
ing environment, but *becomes* so through the love and closeness of the family occupying it. It is exactly these emotions that are lacking in Jackson's
other work, whether it be in such a nonsupernatural satire as *The Road
through the Wall* or in a quasi-supernatural one as *The Sundial*. In both these
instances the house becomes cold and unwelcoming only because the inhabitants themselves exhibit these same feelings toward each other.

Even in those stories in which the house itself remains relatively pas-
sive, the hostility of its occupants or of the outside community render the
house something akin to a prison. Neither "The Summer People" nor "The
Little House" focuses upon the house as such, but it takes on foreboding
qualities in both. In the former tale, the elderly couple's summer house
becomes a virtual tomb when they decide to extend their stay beyond Labor

Day. In the latter, the spitefulness of elderly neighbors causes a perfectly innocuous house to appear a deathtrap to its new owner, who flees in terror.

And yet, to Jackson's mind—simultaneously conditioned to the domestic pieties of the 1950s and rebelling against them—the house is an unavoidable fixture regardless of what dire qualities it takes on. Even at the beginning of *We Have Always Lived in the Castle* Constance is afraid of leaving the house (W 29), although it has become, for all practical purposes, a grave for her. Her life after the poisoning of her family has been reduced to its walls—with, perhaps, fleeting moments on the grounds—but she regards it at least as a haven against the scorn of the townspeople. And even after much of the house is burned and rendered uninhabitable, Constance and Merricat choose to remain there, calmly and even whimsically reshaping their lives to within an even smaller compass. *We Have Always Lived in the Castle* is Jackson's most searing parody of domesticity: all the things that made the domestic stories so wholesome and touching—love between the family members; the antics of children; the comical excess of furniture, toys, and food; the sense of belonging to a community—have here been perverted. And yet, Constance and Merricat seem strangely content with their impoverished circumstances. And indeed, is it really so bad? They at least have each other.

In *The Sundial* even this comfort is lacking. Each member of this lunatic household clings, like Constance and Merricat, to the belief that the house alone will represent safety and sanctuary even when the rest of the world is destroyed. But among the occupants themselves there is no harmony, only struggles for supremacy, covert affairs, and bungled attempts to escape. Because the outside world so rarely figures in this novel, the house itself becomes the world—it is as if there really is nothing beyond it. Is Jackson saying that the rest of the world functions as the Halloran household does? Is there no harmony or love to be found anywhere?

The Haunting of Hill House is Jackson's most profound and searching treatment of the house theme. Its opening paragraph sets the tone, and I cannot resist quoting it in spite of its celebrity:

> No live organism can continue for long to exist sanely under conditions of absolute reality; even larks and katydids are supposed, by some, to dream: Hill House, not sane, stood by itself against its hills, holding darkness within; it had stood so for eighty years and might stand for eighty more. Within, walls continued upright, bricks met neatly, floors were firm, and doors were sensibly shut; silence lay steadily against the wood and stone of Hill House, and whatever walked there, walked alone [HH 5].

I confess, however, to an uncertainty as to what this is exactly supposed to mean. It is interesting that here insanity is linked to the perception of "absolute reality": I am not so much concerned with quoting T. S. Eliot ("Human kind cannot bear very much reality") as with ascertaining the precise applicability of the remark. Hill House is a place where the superficial masks and deceptions of life are stripped off: it is where Eleanor comes to terms with the wretchedness of her prior life, sees through the sham of Luke's and Theodora's arch lightheartedness, and realizes that she belongs here—because, in fact, she belongs nowhere. A later passage might shed further light on this enigmatic opening:

> This house, which seemed somehow to have formed itself, flying together into its own powerful pattern under the hands of its builders, fitting itself into its own construction of lines and angles, reared its great head back against the sky without concession to humanity. It was a house without kindness, never meant to be lived in, not a fit place for people or for love or for hope. Exorcism cannot alter the countenance of a house; Hill House would stay as it was until it was destroyed [HH 26].

Curiously, the remark that the house "was not a fit place for ... love" is perhaps contradicted by the denouement, for in its twisted way Hill House loves Eleanor—it wants her, it won't let her leave, it perhaps kills her when she tries.

But if whatever walks in Hill House walks alone, are we not to see in this Jackson's ultimate metaphor for loneliness? A house should represent safety, comfort, welcome. But in this house, as Dr. Montague notes, "'the intention is, somehow, to separate us'" (HH 96)—to render each person alone and lonely. If Jackson sees togetherness as the natural and desirable state for human beings, then Hill House, which causes loneliness, is an abomination and even a paradox. If it makes no "concession to humanity," then it has defied the very beings who have created it and inverts the purposes for which it was built.

CONCLUSION

What are we to make of Shirley Jackson? Is she a weird writer even in part? That second question I am still unable to answer in any definitive way, save to note the obvious supernaturalism in a fairly representative core of her work. If *The Haunting of Hill House* is one of the greatest haunted house novels ever written, if "The Lottery" is among the cruelest nonsupernatural horror stories ever written, what do we do with something so nebulous as *The Sundial* or "The Lovely House"? I hope, at any rate, to have suggested the tightly knit unity of Jackson's work, its constant reworking of the interlocking themes of domesticity and loneliness, love and hate, madness and sanity, society and the individual. And I hope we can now see how each of these threads is pursued successively in tales that, from the point of view of genre, might be termed supernatural, nonsupernatural, mainstream, or autobiographical. It is true that Jackson, even in her avowedly supernatural work, presents no coherent metaphysics: her supernatural manifestations fail to suggest any putative reordering of the cosmos. But if she lacks the cosmic perspective of a Lovecraft, a Blackwood, or a Dunsany (or, indeed, of Ramsey Campbell or T. E. D. Klein), if her focus is solely on human characters and human relationships, with even the supernatural phenomena subservient to or symbols for these relationships, then she at least distinguishes herself by the intensity, accuracy, and subtlety of her portrayal of human concerns. As with Bierce, her pitiless and sardonic exposing of human weakness makes her a horrific satirist who does not require the supernatural to arouse fear and horror. Her icy prose, clinical detachment, and utterly refreshing glee at the exhibition of human greed, misery, and evil ought to give her a high rank in general literature. That she chose to devote even a part of her talents to the weird is something for which we all ought to be grateful.

II. THE PERSISTENCE OF SUPERNATURALISM

——— WILLIAM PETER BLATTY: ———
THE CATHOLIC WEIRD TALE

The career of William Peter Blatty (b. 1928) is most peculiar. His first book, *Which Way to Mecca, Jack?* (1960), is a humorous account of his years spent with the United States Information Agency in Lebanon. There followed several comic novels—*John Goldfarb, Please Come Home!* (1963), *I, Billy Shakespeare!* (1965), and *Twinkle, Twinkle, "Killer" Kane!* (1966)—which achieved little or no critical or commercial success. Then, in 1971, Blatty published *The Exorcist*, and not only his literary career but the fortunes of the entire field of weird fiction were changed forever. Coming out in the same year as Thomas Tryon's *The Other*, Blatty's novel helped to usher in the tremendous popularity of the supernatural novel over the next two decades. It is no surprise that Stephen King once came up to Blatty and said, "You know, in a way, you're my father" (FF 39). But if Blatty's role in the propagation of horror fiction is clear, it was not so clear how his subsequent career was to progress.

As if overwhelmed by the success of *The Exorcist*, Blatty has failed to produce a work that measures up to that novel either as a popular success or even as the modest critical success it was. His next book, *I'll Tell Them I Remember You* (1973), is an account of his Arabian-born mother, and toward the end Blatty—a committed Roman Catholic—manages to convince himself that her spirit has somehow survived the death of her body. *The Ninth Configuration* (1978) is a rewriting of *Twinkle, Twinkle, "Killer" Kane*, and it is not clear that the original has been improved. *Legion* (1983),

50

the long-awaited sequel to *The Exorcist*, is disappointing for more than one reason, and Blatty has yet to issue the new novel that he has evidently been working on for years. Douglas E. Winter has described it as "a suspense thriller with a theological theme" (FF 46), and Blatty himself has labeled it "much bigger in scope and size than either [*The Exorcist* or *Legion*]" (FF 46–47).

I am under a severe handicap in discussing William Peter Blatty, for as an atheist I find his brand of tortured Catholicism nearly incomprehensible. It is difficult for me to be impartial in dealing with a theology or philosophy that I find so entirely misguided. Although theological discussion does not seem to figure seriously in his work prior to "*Killer*" *Kane*, it is prevalent to the point of obtrusiveness in everything he has written since. Blatty is not merely a writer who happens to be Catholic; he is, like Arthur Machen, ardently striving to convert his readers to Catholicism and rid them of the godless secularism that he feels is undermining modern society. His novels are platforms from which he openly debates (through characters who are transparent vehicles for the views he is advocating or disputing) the existence of God, the soul, and the afterlife, and the nature of good and evil. Blatty is, however, neither a sufficiently competent philosopher to discuss these matters with any depth or persuasiveness, nor a sufficiently adept storyteller to integrate these discussions adequately into the fabric of his works.

I do not wish to be accused either of a lack of sympathy for Blatty's opinions or of inconsistency in my general notion of weird fiction as a vehicle for the conveying of a world view. In the first place, it is true that I do not share Blatty's religious or philosophical outlook, but it is also true that it takes very little effort to find the most elementary errors of philosophical reasoning and a grievous ignorance of the facts of science in Blatty's disquisitions, as it does in the case of the mystic Algernon Blackwood. In the second place, my objection to Blatty—as with Machen in some of his fiction—is not that he is trying to convey a world view but that he is doing so ineptly or inappropriately. Blatty's set pieces, in which characters simply stop the flow of action and dispute theological issues, seriously mar the unity and coherence of his novels. It is as if he does not trust his readers to understand his message merely from the logic of the story, but feels the need to insert these clumsy signposts of what his novels are really all about. There is also the clear intent to convert: Blatty is not merely expressing a Catholic world view, but wants his readers to adopt it also or, rather, writes in such a fashion that only spiritually confused Catholics like himself can truly empathize with his work. Lovecraft's and Dunsany's work is, I believe, motivated by an equally strong atheistic world view, but I never get the impression of being preached at by them as I do with Blatty. Indeed, it is only because *The Exorcist* has relatively less of this sort of moralizing that it is at least a partial success.

In a sensitive essay on him, Scott D. Briggs has identified four of Blatty's works as weird: *Twinkle, Twinkle, "Killer" Kane!*; *The Exorcist*; *The Ninth Configuration*; and *Legion*.[1] But although *"Killer" Kane* and *The Ninth Configuration* have a certain bizarrerie to them (Briggs refers to them, and to Blatty's work as a whole, as psychological horror), they are not supernatural at all and, to my mind, are not genuinely weird, and I shall study them here only tangentially. Both deal with a madhouse where some highly distinguished soldiers and astronauts have been confined for observation. A supposed psychiatrist, "Killer" Kane (Hudson L. Kane in the first novel; Vincent Kane in the second), is brought in to ascertain whether they are actually afflicted with madness or are only feigning it. But this is merely the vehicle for a series of discussions between Kane and his principal adversary, the astronaut Manfred Cutshaw, on the nature of God. In a prefatory note to *The Ninth Configuration* Blatty states that he wrote *"Killer" Kane* "when I was young and worked very hastily and from need"; but there is much reason for preferring the zany surrealism of the earlier work (it is fundamentally a comic novel, rather like *One Flew Over the Cuckoo's Nest*) than its dour revision. In both novels, however, Blatty raises questions that would provide the intellectual backbone of his weird work, in particular the pointed query: "How can there be evil coexistent with a good God?" (T 67). This single utterance could serve as the hallmark for Blatty's entire work. It of course never occurs to him to define what "evil" actually is or to believe that it may be entirely a result of the conflicts inherent in human society.

"Killer" Kane is so full of preposterous theological arguments that a single example will suffice to destroy forever any standing Blatty might be thought to have as a moral or religious philosopher. Consider Kane's case for the existence of an afterlife:

> "...every man who has ever lived has been born with desire for perfect happiness. But unless there is an afterlife, fulfillment of this desire is a patent impossibility. Perfect happiness, in order to be perfect, must carry with it the assurance that the happiness won't cease; that it will not be snatched away. But no one has ever had such assurance; the mere fact of death serves to contradict it. Yet why should Nature implant—universally—desire for something that isn't attainable? I can think of no more than two answers: either Nature is consistently mad and perverse, or after this life there's another; a life where this universal desire for perfect happiness can be fulfilled. But nowhere else in creation does Nature exhibit this kind of perversity; not when it comes to a basic drive. An eye is always for seeing and an ear is always for

hearing. And any universal craving—that is, a craving without exception—has to be capable of fulfillment. It can't be fulfilled *here*; so it's fulfilled, I think, somewhere else, some*time* else" [T 137].

This really does seem to be Blatty's own view, since he repeats it (in the mouth of Lieutenant Kinderman) in *Legion* (L 196–97). We are therefore robbed of the faint hope that this is merely meant as an example of Kane's utter fatuity. It is difficult to enumerate all the philosophical mistakes in this passage. In the first place, the desire for perfect happiness (whatever that is) is not universal but only exists, apparently, in those who have been mentally crippled by millennia of religious wishful thinking. Secondly, Blatty has illegitimately personified Nature (note the sophistical use of the capital N), regarding it as a sort of conscious entity rather than merely the sum total of all existence. Thirdly, it is false to equate this desire for perfect happiness with such a "basic drive" as sight or hearing: the desire has so obviously been socially conditioned that it cannot be considered on the same metaphysical or epistemological level as basic instincts. In *"Killer" Kane*, as in other works, Blatty resembles Plato in not allowing his philosophical opponents (here Cutshaw) sufficient intelligence to refute such obviously false or improbable opinions. Perhaps Blatty could not do so himself.

But *"Killer" Kane* is more interesting for its being, although entirely nonsupernatural, a manifest anticipation of themes, characters, and scenarios found in *The Exorcist*. Kane himself—a self-confessed "confused" Catholic (T 66)—is clearly the model for Father Damien Karras, the angst-ridden priest who confronts the demon in *The Exorcist*. Indeed, at one point Kane has a dream in which Cutshaw pleads with him to perform an exorcism on another inmate (T 135). Later there is an extended discussion of black magic, exorcism, and the like; a book on exorcism is referred to by Kane as "'Better than horror films on The Late Show'" (T 154). Finally, at the very end of the novel another priest reports one of Kane's apophthegms: "'He said that evil doesn't spring out of madness—that it's the other way around'" (T 183).

I believe this final remark is the foundation for *The Exorcist*. Let us consider one of the epigraphs Blatty has affixed to this novel, from Dr. Tom Dooley: "There's no other explanation for some of the things the Communists did. Like the priest who had eight nails driven into his skull.... And there were the seven little boys and their teacher. One soldier whipped out his bayonet and sliced off the teacher's tongue. The other took chopsticks and drove them into the ears of the seven little boys. How do you treat cases like that?" The only "explanation" for evils like this, Blatty is suggesting, is the influence of Satan or some other transcendent evil. *The*

Exorcist is loosely based upon an actual case of exorcism performed in 1949. Blatty investigated it thoroughly and also read voluminously on the literature pertaining to exorcism. He became convinced that the exorcism was a highly significant event theologically. "...I thought, 'Oh, my God. At last, proof of transcendence, or at least of the reality of spiritual forces.' I mean, intelligent, discarnate entities—demons, devils, whatever. It seemed a validation of what we were being taught as Catholics, and certainly a validation of our hopes for immortality. Because if there were evil spirits, why not good? Why not a soul? Why not life everlasting?" (FF 41). I hardly know how to react to this. Firstly, Blatty has assumed, merely from the testimony of the priest involved in the case (hardly an impartial witness!), that the exorcism actually revealed the existence of transcendent forces. Secondly, he has then inferred, illogically, that the existence of evil forces necessitates the existence of good ones (an entirely false corollary, especially as several religions and philosophies have consistently postulated only the existence of transcendent evil, with no corresponding good); thirdly, he leaps from the existence of transcendent evil to the existence of a soul and afterlife by a series of logical somersaults that escapes me utterly. But let it pass. The end result is that Blatty wishes to see *The Exorcist* as a work that indirectly affirms the existence of good by the portrayal of the existence of evil. Everything in the novel is tailored to lead to this conclusion. It is, as a result, somewhat problematical to call it a weird tale at all, for all the weird phenomena are merely props to convey this religious message and are not intended to be of interest in themselves.

This is perhaps why the actual nature of the supernatural entity in the novel—the demon Pazuzu (E 7)—is so nebulously defined: it does not matter who or what he is, for his sole function is merely to exist and thereby to confirm the existence of a transcendent evil that makes the existence of transcendent good theoretically possible. This is also why it takes rather a long time for the confrontation between the demon and the exorcist to occur: much of the novel must necessarily be spent in exhausting the natural explanations for the odd behavior of the little girl Regan MacNeil, so that in the end only the supernatural explanation (demonic possession) remains.

Initially, once Regan begins exhibiting uncharacteristic traits, she is taken to a psychiatrist, that modern replacement for a priest. Some drugs are prescribed, but they have little effect, and her behavior becomes more and more bizarre. One especially harrowing incident occurs at a party, when Regan walks into the room and states bluntly to an astronaut, "'You're going to die up there'" (E 73). I wonder if we can relate this to *"Killer" Kane*. When Cutshaw finally gives his true reasons for not wanting to go to the moon, he states that it is a result of his fear of dying alone—"'especially if there's no God; that makes it even more horribly lonely'" (T 172). In any event, even when a seemingly supernatural event occurs—the bed on which Regan is lying begins to shake violently (E 79)—it too is explained away naturalistically, if somewhat implausibly. There then ensues a series of tests to trace some known medical cause for Regan's symptoms. The novel drags a bit at this point, but it is all vital to Blatty's purpose in showing that no rationale known to science can account for all the strange phenomena of the case.

Even when the matter of demonic possession and exorcism is first raised, it is done so in a quasi-psychological way. A doctor tells Regan's mother: "'We call it somnambuliform possession. Quite frankly, we don't know much about it except that it starts with some conflict or guilt that eventually leads to the patient's delusion that his body's been invaded by an alien intelligence; a spirit, if you will. In times gone by, when belief in the devil was fairly strong, the possessing entity was usually a demon'" (E 166). Note Blatty's circumspection: in order to convince the modern (and presumably atheistic, or at the very least skeptical and nonorthodox) reader of the reality of the demon and the need for exorcism, he must begin by postulating a psychological account of demonic possession and, later, even a psychological motive for the use of the rite of exorcism.

> "...[there is a] stylized ritual now out of date in which rabbis and priests tried to drive out the spirit. It's only the Catholics who haven't dis-carded it yet, but they keep it pretty much in the closet as sort of an embarrassment, I think. But to someone who thinks that he's really possessed, I would say that the ritual's rather impressive. It used to work, in fact, although not for the reason they thought, of course; it was purely the force of suggestion" [E 169].

Here is the rationalist account of the entire matter. Regan only believes (if subconsciously) that she is possessed; therefore, since all other remedies (medical and psychological) have failed, an exorcism might work—but only as a result of "autosuggestion" (E 169). Exorcism is, after all, a bit primitive nowadays—even Karras tells Regan's mother, when she asks about it, that "'it just doesn't happen anymore'" (E 199). But in the end we are led to believe that this rationalistic explanation simply cannot account for the facts of the case. Ergo, there must really have been demonic possession and the rite of exorcism must really have worked! There is a God (there must be, if there is a demon), and Catholicism is the one true religion.

In this entire scenario Regan's mother, the successful actress Chris MacNeil, plays an integral role—not as a character in her own right but as a vehicle for convincing the unbelieving reader. She is an atheist (E 43) who has serious doubts as to the afterlife (E 22): if *she* can come to believe that only a genuine act of exorcism can cure her daughter, then how can even the most irreligious of us think otherwise? It is she who pleads with Karras to perform the rite; it is she who overcomes his grave reservations.

The conclusion of the tale appears ambiguous (it is more so in the film version) but a careful reading of the text will both explicate it and reveal the optimism with which Blatty wishes us to leave his work. It is vital for Blatty to portray both Karras's spiritual doubts about God ("*Ah, my God, let me see You! Let me know! Come in dreams!*" [E 49]) and the sense of aimlessness he feels. The death of his mother—perhaps the most powerful and moving segment of the entire novel—fills him with grief and remorse, and he feels adrift in a world that seems to lack the guidance of any spiritual entity. He gains some small comfort when he, himself a psychiatrist, briefly brightens the life of a lonely young priest, but later he wonders what he has actually accomplished: "The psychiatrist grew weary; found himself drifting into private sorrow. He glanced at a plaque that someone had given him the previous Christmas. MY BROTHER HURTS. I SHARE HIS PAIN. I MEET GOD IN HIM, it read. A failed encounter. He blamed himself. He had mapped the streets of his brother's torment, yet never had walked them; or so he believed. He thought that the pain which he felt was his own" (E 88–89). But the exorcism allows him genuinely to share someone else's pain and so to meet God, even if it also means his death. Enraged by the demon's having caused the death of an old priest, Father Merrin, whom Karras had brought in to aid in his exorcism, he turns upon the demon in fury and cries: "'Come on! Come on, loser! Try *me!* Leave the girl and take me! Take *me!*'" (E 328). The demon enters his body, and Karras promptly leaps out of the bedroom window and down to his death on the stairs below. Father Joseph Dyer, Karras's friend, comes to him just as he is dying: "He pulled back his head and saw the eyes filled with peace; and with something else: something mysteriously like joy at the end of heart's longing. The eyes were still staring. But at nothing in this world. Nothing here" (E 331).

The death of "Killer" Kane appears to be the model for Karras's self-destruction. In *Twinkle, Twinkle, "Killer" Kane!*, however, that death (by suicide) is singularly ambiguous. Is it that Kane, having cured Cutshaw of his "madness" (actually, his spiritual loneliness), now senses no further purpose to his existence? Is suicide his way of seeking redemption for all the enemy soldiers he has killed in battle? The conclusion of *The Ninth Configuration* is no less puzzling. Kane and Cutshaw have been subjected to vicious brutalization and humiliation by a gang of motorcycle punks, but Kane revives and kills four of them with his bare hands. (I am not sure how Christian this is, since, as Kinderman notes in *Legion*, "When I read, 'Love your enemy,' I tingle, I go crazy, and inside of my chest I can feel something floating, something that feels like it was there the whole time" [L 98].) Later Kane is found with a fatal knife wound in his stomach: was this self-inflicted or did he receive the injury from one of the punks? An officer first remarks, "'He's killed himself,'" then quickly amends the statement: "'He gave up his life'" (N 128). The distinction intended here is, apparently, that Kane has performed some kind of necessary self-sacrifice. His death—and, one imagines, the spiritual tranquility he has achieved through it—is the model for Karras's.

The death of Damien Karras, poignant as it is, only briefly distracts us from an issue that has troubled us all along: why has this demon, an apparently supernatural being, possessed this little girl in Georgetown? What could such an act possibly accomplish? Surely the demon is capable of greater things than merely causing a little girl a certain amount of discomfort. Blatty addresses the issue at one point in the novel when Merrin says to Karras:

> "Yet I think the demon's target is not the possessed; it is us ... the observers ... every person in this house. And I think—I think the point is to make us despair; to reject our own humanity, Damien: to see ourselves as ultimately bestial; as ultimately vile and putrescent; without dignity; ugly; unworthy. And there lies the heart of it, perhaps: in unworthiness. For I think belief in God is not a matter of reason at all; I think it finally is a matter of love; of accepting the possibility that God could love *us*" [E 311].

This is all rather dismaying. Is a loving God required to make us feel other than "bestial"? Does the absence of God rob us of dignity? In any case, this appears to be the rationale Blatty provides for the entire novel. In the death of Karras we are to see redemption, not despair: his death was the only way to banish or suppress the horror, and it is also a symbol for the renewed belief in God he has attained and the fulfilling of his mission of sharing another's pain and making it his own.

Twelve years passed before Blatty published *Legion*, a loose sequel to *The Exorcist*. And it has become clear that his hostility to the modern-day lack of spirituality increasingly troubles him, to the point that he must hector his readers with long, tiresome, and aesthetically disastrous theological diatribes. Already in *The Exorcist* we hear Lieutenant Kinderman tell his wife, "'Mary, the entire world—the *entire world*—is having a massive nervous breakdown'" (E 133); and when Kinderman in the early parts of *Legion* thinks to himself that "the materialist universe was the greatest superstition of his age" (L 13), we can already see the direction this novel is going to take. More than any other of his works, *Legion* is hamstrung by vacuous and pompous philosophizing that simply halts the flow of action and bears little relation to the actual outcome of events. Perhaps Blatty was irritated that (as we shall shortly see) the moral message of *The Exorcist* was so universally overlooked; in *Legion* he is determined that no reader will make that mistake. The result is a potentially dynamic and suspenseful story that flounders in a morass of theological speculation before the writer actually gets down to the business of telling it.

William F. Kinderman has now suddenly taken on the role of Kane and Karras, even though he showed little interest in religion in his fleeting appearances in *The Exorcist*. But Blatty must have his mouthpiece for the expression of his writhing reflections on God. Other characters in *Legion* are still less important in their own right than in other of Blatty's works. In one especially ludicrous digression a neurologist, Vincent Amfortas, writes a letter to Father Dyer telling of his experiments in trying to tape record voices from beyond the grave. He claims success in the effort, and we are evidently to conclude that the question of life after death is now solved once and for all. (I am rather more saddened and disturbed that Blatty himself has made such experiments [FF 48–49]).

When the novel finally pays attention to its purported subject—the apparent revival of the so-called "Gemini murders," even though the murderer was presumably killed 20 years ago—it becomes highly compelling. Kinderman eventually finds the link between the gruesome crimes: all the victims were somehow related to the exorcism of 1971. The demon in Karras's body did not die with him. And, in sardonic irony, he actually revives the priest's corpse and causes it to escape from its coffin just prior to burial. Although it is now confined in a psychiatric ward, he compels it to continue committing his murders by possessing the minds of other inmates and having them do the killing. *Legion* would be, without its theological baggage, a powerful supernatural detective story. As it is, the core of the plot (which, Blatty's worries to the contrary notwithstanding, would have been sufficient to convey his theological message to intelligent readers) is simply not given adequate attention or related as adeptly as it could have been. The film version of this novel, titled *The Exorcist III*, was written and directed by Blatty, and it is far superior to the novel. As an experienced scenarist, he knows much about the pacing of films, and in this one he has removed much of the theology of the book and focused his attention on the actual storyline. As a result, a tense but surprisingly restrained horror film has been produced. Even the confrontations between Kinderman and the demon in the psychiatric ward gain power through crisp dialogue and dramatic lighting effects. And the ending of the film is far more potently cataclysmic than the novel's. I wish Blatty would import some of the good sense he brings to filmmaking into his novels.

Blatty concludes *Legion* with the following words of wisdom from Kinderman:

> "The physicists now are all certain," he said, "that all the known processes in nature were once part of a single, unified force." Kinderman paused and then spoke more quietly. "I believe that this force was a person who long ago tore himself into pieces because of his longing to shape his own being. That was the Fall," he said, "the 'Big Bang': the beginning of time and the material universe when the one became many—legion. And that is why God cannot interfere: evolution is this person growing back into himself" [L 269].

Incredibly, Blatty remarks of this farrago of bad science, incomprehensible theology, and naive optimism that "I had finally had the answer—a really satisfactory answer to the problem of evil. That is to say, if you grant its assumptions, there is not a loophole or a flaw to be found in it" (FF 47). Well, I suppose if one grants the assumption that the earth is flat, then there is no flaw in believing that one may fall off the edge of the earth.

The singular—and, for Blatty, bitter—irony in all this is that in his work, especially *The Exorcist* (both the book and the film), there is such a compound of gruesome horror, sex, violence, and sacrilege that it becomes very easy to bypass his preaching and relish his work for the pleasant shudders it provides. This is, indeed, exactly what has happened with *The Exorcist*. And Blatty is right to complain that the film only augmented this effect: "Let's face it—the message was adroitly snipped out of the film. It wasn't there" (FF 43). In spite of the oceans of blood and gore that have been spilled in books and movies in the last two decades, there are portions of *The Exorcist* that retain their power to shock:

> Chris plunged down the hall and burst into the bedroom, gasped, stood rooted in paralyzing shock as the rappings boomed massively, shivering through walls; as Karl lay unconscious on the floor near the bureau; as Regan, her legs propped up and spread wide on a bed that was violently bouncing and shaking, clutched the bone-white crucifix in raw-knuckled hands, the bone-white crucifix poised at her vagina, the bone-white crucifix she stared at with terror, eyes bulging in a face that was bloodied from the nose, the nasogastric tubing ripped out.

"Oh, please! Oh, no, *please!*" she was shrieking as her hands brought the crucifix closer; as she seemed to be straining to push it away.

"You'll do as I *tell* you, filth! You'll *do* it!"

The threatening bellow, the words, came from *Regan,* her voice coarse and guttural, bristling with venom, while in an instaneous flash her expression and features were hideously transmuted into those of the feral, demonic personality that had appeared in the course of hypnosis. And now faces and voices, as Chris watched stunned, interchanged with rapidity:

"*No!*"

"You'll do it!"

"*Please!*"

"You *will,* you bitch, or I'll kill you!"

"*Please!*"

"Yes, you're going to let Jesus *fuck* you, *fuck* you, f—"

Regan now, eyes wide and staring, flinching from the rush of some hideous finality, mouth agape shrieking at the dread of some ending. Then abruptly the demonic face once more possessed her, now filled her, the room choking suddenly with a stench in the nostrils, with an icy cold that seeped from the walls as the rappings ended and Regan's piercing cry of terror turned to a guttural, yelping laugh of malevolent spite and rage triumphant while she thrust down the crucifix into her vagina and began to masturbate ferociously, roaring in that deep, coarse, deafening voice, "Now you're *mine,* now you're *mine,* you stinking cow! You bitch! Let Jesus *fuck* you, *fuck* you!" [E 189–90].

It would be difficult to find passages more arresting than this even in the so-called splatterpunk writers, whose sensibilities are, of course, very different from Blatty's. But Blatty must nevertheless acknowledge, however grudgingly, that he is indeed the "father" of Stephen King and modern weird writers generally. *The Exorcist* was one of the first best-selling novels to use explicit profanity in this fashion, and I distinctly recall being stunned by it when I read the novel as a youth; the film, of course, has already achieved the status of an icon in popular culture. All this is, as we can see, profoundly contrary to Blatty's moral purpose, but he must still bear some of the credit—or blame—for it. If his gruesome passages had not been written so vividly and so accessibly, with a deliberate effort to offend his readers' (and his own) religious sensibilities, then his novel would not have achieved its bestseller status.

I can imagine two general objections to my treatment of William Peter Blatty. First, it might be thought that it is the very essence of supernatural fiction to postulate the existence of transcendent forces, so that Blatty should not be criticized for basing his work on the existence of God and the Devil. Second, it is to be wondered whether it is right for a critic to take an author to task for the world view that informs his work rather than merely assessing the success or failure of that work as an aesthetic entity independent of its philosophical or religious orientation.

The first objection is easier to deal with than the second. The postulation of supernatural forces in weird fiction is, generally, done on an *aesthetic*, not *metaphysical*, plane: Lovecraft does not believe in the literal reality of Cthulhu; Dunsany does not believe in the actual existence of Pegana. In both cases, these imaginary entities or realms serve as symbols: in the first instance, a symbol for an infinite, unknowable cosmos in which human beings count as nothing; in the second instance, a symbol for the imagination that cannot find beauty in the prosiness of the contemporary world. Blatty, however, really believes in the existence of God and the Devil, and he wishes us to believe in them also; it is this significant divergence of attitude that makes it problematical to classify his work as within the realm of the weird at all, since its motivations are antipodal to those of most writing in this field. In this sense, Blatty is more similar to certain eccentric or occultist writers—Charles Fort, Ignatius Donnelly, Erich von Däniken—than he is to Lovecraft, Blackwood, or Dunsany. Donnelly really wants us to believe in his Atlantis; Dunsany knows, and knows that we know, that his Pegana is only figurative.

As for the second objection, Blatty is again an unusual case. I know of few writers, especially in this realm, who are so desperate to convert their readers to religious orthodoxy. Blatty may like to imagine himself a modern-day Dostoevsky, wrestling torturously with problems of faith and belief, but his theological reflections lack both the intellectual substance and the aesthetic integration that is found in the best work of this kind. In any case, the whole idea of not taking a stand on a writer's philosophical position strikes me as critically pusillanimous, especially when Blatty so insistently pushes his theology in our faces. I cannot see how it is possible for anyone to contemplate Blatty's work in a purely aesthetic way; indeed, Blatty would be the first to urge us against such a practice. Accordingly, I offer no apologies for criticizing not merely the manner but the content of Blatty's work: there is, surely, a real problem in founding one's entire work upon a religion that is very likely to be false. Blatty does not, like Dante or Milton or even the later Evelyn Waugh, have enough other literary virtues to survive the destruction of the religious underpinnings of his work: the sole function of his writing is to reconcile us to Catholicism, and if he fails in that task, his writing as a whole fails. As it is, William Peter Blatty occupies his humble niche in the realm of supernatural horror because a sufficient number of readers, religious and nonreligious alike, are willing to ignore his windy theologizing and appreciate his work for its occasional moments of terror and grue.

STEPHEN KING: THE KING'S NEW CLOTHES

Stephen King (b. 1947) is the most remarkable publishing phenomenon in modern literature. To say this, however, is not in any sense to say that he is the most remarkable *literary* phenomenon in modern literature or even in the narrow confines of weird fiction. King is remarkable principally in the quantity of books he has sold over the past 25 years. And before I consider his work on its actual literary merits (which is my chief interest here), it may be worth giving brief attention to the possible sources of his tremendous popular success. Three factors seem paramount.

First is the popularity of the film adaptations of King's work. It should be recalled that King's first novel, *Carrie* (1974), was not a bestseller until the movie version appeared the following year. And subsequent films—which in terms of their actual merits as films range from the moderately successful (*The Dead Zone, Stand by Me, Misery*) to the spectacularly wretched (*Children of the Corn, It*)—have in many cases done little save serve as publicity for the author.

The second is King's relentless prolificity, a factor that has perhaps not been given much attention. Unlike former titans of the bestseller lists such as Harold Robbins and Irving Wallace (remember them?), who wrote for only about two decades before lapsing into a merciful silence, King has been writing since the late 1960s—he began his career by publishing short stories either in genre magazines (*Startling Mystery Stories*) or in men's magazines (*Cavalier, Penthouse*), and these were eventually collected in *Night Shift* (1978) and *Skeleton Crew* (1985)—and he has issued at least one book a year since 1974 with no signs of surcease.

The third factor in his success is the aggressive marketing of his work by his publishers. King benefited by the tendency in commercial publishing—clearly evidenced from the early 1980s to the present day—of spending a majority of the advertising budget on the vigorous promotion of a small number of preordained "bestsellers" at the expense of the now nearly vanished midlist. King, in effect, became less an author than a brand name and was marketed as such. The result was inevitable. It is certainly not the case that those works of his which (even in the view of King's supporters) are lower on the literary scale than others sold more poorly than those which are higher.

As for the overriding question of why readers lapped up horror fiction at this exact time, I have stated earlier that I am not prepared to make any conjectures. Certainly, the *type* of horror fiction King wrote has much to do with his commercial success. He chose horror fiction, to be sure, because in youth he absorbed a great deal of it in literature, films, television, and comic books, but his particular approach to the field is not at all that of an innovator—he has, as far as I can tell, come up with not a single original weird conception or original treatment of a preexisting weird conception—but that of a writer who has purportedly "humanized" the weird tale by enmeshing it in the everyday lives of ordinary people. As King himself has remarked in an interview, "my idea of what a horror story should be [is that] the monster shouldn't be in a graveyard in decadent old Europe, but in the house down the street" (UM 94). King maintains, correctly enough, that this notion was evolving in the generation just prior to his, with such writers as Ray Bradbury, Shirley Jackson, and Richard Matheson. All these writers (and many others one could name) handle the human element with vastly greater literary skill than King. What we find in King's own works is an array of supposedly "real" human characters encountering conventionalized weird scenarios, augmented by the dropping in of a great many surface objects of our contemporary material civilization (frequently in the form of brand names) to engender immediate, if superficial, reader recognition.

King's writing, considered abstractly, is a mixture of cheap sentiment, naive moral polarizations between valiant heroes and wooden villains, hackneyed, implausible, and ill-explained supernatural phenomena, a plain, bland, easy-to-read style with just the right number of scatological and sexual profanities to titillate his middle-class audience, and a subscribing to the conventional morality of common people. Whether King actually subscribes to this morality or whether he has merely adopted it in a calculated attempt to appeal to a wide and indiscriminate audience, only he can answer. I am willing to give him the benefit of the doubt on the matter and assume his sincerity, if the pathetic earnestness of his disquisitions on the subject is any gauge of his real beliefs.

By the early 1980s King, now a perennial bestseller, became uncomfortable with his typecasting as a supernatural horror writer. He first attempted to break out of the mold with a disastrous nonsupernatural horror novel, *Cujo* (1981), then with a collection of four mainstream novellas,

Different Seasons (1982). This latter work was received with a certain amused tolerance by the general literary community, but most reviewers urged him to stick with horror, and for the next decade he did so in spite of one further nonsupernatural novel, *Misery* (1987). Some of his most recent works— *It* (1986), *The Tommyknockers* (1987), *The Dark Half* (1989), *Four Past Midnight* (1990)—have met with almost uniform condemnation from critics, largely on account of their staggering prolixity, although that has not stopped them from mechanically achieving bestseller status. Strangely enough, in the last few years he has not merely returned to nonsupernaturalism (*Gerald's Game* [1992], *Dolores Claiborne* [1993]), but has apparently striven to shake free of the commonplace expectations of his audience, writing works whose challenging morality have made them relatively unpopular to his supporters precisely because they are in such stark contrast to the saccharine sentimentality of his earlier output.

An interesting aspect of King's work is a group of five novels written under the pseudonym Richard Bachman. These novels, published between 1977 and 1985, are actually among his more literally successful works, even though only one of them—*Thinner* (1985)—is genuinely weird (it is also by far the poorest of the lot), while two others—*The Long Walk* (1981) and *The Running Man* (1982)—can be classified as science fiction. The other two, *Rage* (1977) and *Roadwork* (1981), are entirely mainstream. King makes a simple but revealing statement about why he wrote under a pseudonym: "I think I did it ... to do something as someone other than Stephen King" (BB vii). The Bachman books—written with verve, flair, and a bracing toughness of conception, setting, and mood—are the best evidence possible that King could have been an able writer had he not felt the need to cater to an undiscriminating public. Here he could write under the persona of someone other than the megabucks publishing superstar who was expected to dish up the same tired supernaturalism and sweet, lovable, and unadventurous characters year in and year out.

BUNGLED SUPERNATURALISM

One wonders how King's early short stories could have developed any sort of following, for they are on the whole facile, mechanical, and implausible. "Jerusalem's Lot" (NS) is a longwinded and half-baked imitation of Lovecraft. "The Mangler" (1972; NS) is, if one can imagine it, about a haunted ironer in an industrial laundry. "Gray Matter" (1973) tells of a disease caused by bacteria in beer that turns individuals into "'a great big gray lump'" (NS 116); the influence of Lovecraft's "The Colour out of Space" and Machen's "Novel of the White Powder" is very obvious, and King's tale reads like an unwitting parody of these masterworks. "Battleground" (1972; NS) is about toy soldiers coming to life; this is, of course, a very old idea, but the treatment here is at least somewhat amusing. "Sometimes They Come Back" (1974; NS) may be of value only in reflecting King's own teaching experiences, for the premise—a schoolteacher who summons a demon to despatch some punks who have come back from the dead—makes one desperately but bootlessly wish the story were intended as a parody. "Children of the Corn" (1977; NS)—not to be judged by the truly awful film adaptation of it—is not a bad tale about the perversion of religion in a remote Nebraska town, but it is too close in texture and conception to Tryon's *Harvest Home* (1973) to be considered meritorious in its own right.

These early stories already exhibit the utter commonplaceness of King's supernatural scenarios. Most have been much better utilized by his predecessors and contemporaries, and all he has done is to thrust them into a modern, middle-class setting in order to trigger reader identification and to milk as much cheap emotion out of them as he can. Later stories are subject to the same defects. "Gramma" (1984; SC) would have been an able tale of a boy left alone with his aged, bedridden, and rather terrifying grandmother if King had not clumsily dragged in some Lovecraftian elements at the end. "The Raft" (1982; SC) is the foolish story of college youths stranded on a raft in a pond with some inky monster menacing them; inevitably, no plausible account of this monster's existence or purpose is provided. "The Monkey" (1980; SC) asks us to believe that people or animals die when a toy monkey claps the cymbals in its hands, although why this should be so is anyone's guess. King's novels continue this trend, containing supernatural notions that are so poorly thought out that they collapse under the weight of their own improbability.

'Salem's Lot (1975) could serve as a prototype for what is wrong with King's work. It is trite, conventional, sentimental, and poorly written. This novel is a radical expansion of a short story, "One for the Road" (NS), which is just as conventional in its treatment of the vampire theme and also entirely preposterous in its failure to account plausibly for an *entire town* of vampires (how do they subsist? how do they escape detection by the outside world?). Ben Mears comes to the Maine hamlet of Jerusalem's Lot, where he had grew up as a boy, in order to write a book about a strange old house called the Marsten place, in which a man murdered his wife and then committed suicide. Two mysterious individuals, Richard Straker and Kurt Barlow, move into the establishment, and shortly thereafter deaths occur with remarkable frequency. It becomes rapidly obvious that these deaths are the product of vampires, and Straker and Barlow are the clear

suspects. What else can Mears do but gather together a stalwart band of citizens and extirpate the monsters? Moreover, although people are dying like flies all over town, Mears manages to have a sloppily sentimental love affair with the fetching Susan Norton; regrettably, it is curtailed when she herself becomes a vampire. After an action-packed series of violent deaths, the principal vampires are finally dispatched, and the novel ends with Ben's vow to rid the rest of the town of vampires as well.

King has done absolutely nothing to enliven the worn-out vampire theme. Indeed, he has confessed that the novel is nothing more than a sort of updating of *Dracula* (DM 37–39; DS 519). King actually seems to relish reproducing the vampire myth as unoriginally as he can ("'I suspect [Barlow's] origins may have been Romanian or Magyar or Hungarian'" [SL 320]). It is particularly amusing how King, although having launched a vicious attack on the Catholic church ("It was the steady, dead, onrushing engine of the church, bearing down all petty sins on its endless shuttle to heaven" [SL 149]) and having Barlow assert that he is far older than Christianity (SL 354), nevertheless makes his principal heroes soberly go through confession prior to their final encounter with the villain. Also typical is a needlessly lengthy dwelling on the funeral of Danny Glick (SL 127–30), a young boy who has succumbed to vampirism: King wrings as much heartrending sentiment as he can out of this meaningless episode, even though Glick is only one of dozens who have fallen victim to the vampires.

A number of King's other novels have serious problems of conception, especially in regard to the central supernatural phenomenon. Consider *Christine* (1983). There seem to be two antecedents of this novel (about a car that somehow comes to life) among King's short stories. An early tale, "Trucks" (1973; NS), is a ridiculous account of trucks that turn against human beings. Rather better is "Uncle Otto's Truck" (1983; SC): this tale of a truck avenging the murder of its owner is effective because of the relative gradualness with which the supernatural manifestation is introduced. In *Christine* the notion is handled with extreme ineptitude. The problem facing King is to endow an object whose origin, manufacture, and functioning are so thoroughly understood with some sort of supernatural mystery—he can never quite turn the trick. Dennis Quilter, a high school senior whose friend Arnie Cunningham has fallen under the influence of the car, Christine, which he has bought from a mysterious old man named Roland LeBay, ponders the matter: "This was a car, not a she but an it, not really Christine at all but only a 1958 Plymouth Fury that had rolled off an assembly line in Detroit along with about four hundred thousand others" (Ch 156). This incontrovertible truth makes the car's supernaturalism implausible at the very outset.[2]

It is then suggested that the car has somehow stored up the hate that fueled the personality of LeBay, a man embittered at the world since youth. LeBay's brother remarks: "'I do believe that emotions and events have a certain ... lingering resonance. It may be that emotions can even communicate themselves in certain circumstances, if the circumstances are peculiar enough'" (Ch 106). This idea, as we shall later see, had already been used in *The Shining* (1977), but it is just as paradoxical here as there: if the car has somehow absorbed LeBay's hate and become animate, why have not other cars behaved like Christine? Is LeBay the only car-owner who has been angry at the world? The much later suggestion that LeBay was a changeling (Ch 432) is so preposterous and poorly developed that it sounds like some sort of joke.

Then there are the actual supernatural manifestations. Christine is purchased by Arnie, and LeBay dies shortly thereafter. At this point it appears that either Arnie or the car itself or both become possessed by the spirit of LeBay; but which is it to be? Not only that, LeBay is somehow bodily resurrected in a manner that is never explained. On top of this, all Christine's *victims* are magically resurrected as decaying corpses after the car has dispatched them. In effect, there is *too much supernaturalism* in this novel, all of which seems designed merely to jolt the reader from time to time rather than to harmonize into a coherent whole. Dennis thinks the matter over toward the end: "What was it? Some sort of *afreet*? An ordinary car that had somehow become the dangerous, sinking dwelling-place of a demon? A weird manifestation of LeBay's lingering personality, a hellish haunted house that rolled on Goodyear rubber? I didn't know" (Ch 414–15). Neither, apparently, does King.

Pet Sematary (1983) is also full of paradoxes and implausibilities. We are asked to believe that there is a region near the rural town of Ludlow, Maine, that the Indians have deemed a "magic place" (PS 117). This region has the power to reanimate dead animals and human beings when they are buried there. This itself is pretty remarkable, and we must simply accept King's word on the matter, since he provides absolutely no justification or account of how such a piece of land could have gained this miraculous property. There are, in addition, some other, lesser implausibilities (a man who dies in an accident comes back from the dead to utter a prophetic warning; the protagonist's daughter suddenly begins to have precognitive dreams, even though she never possessed this trait before). But the true failing of the novel is an utterly maudlin and dripping sentimentality. This problem dogs nearly all King's work, but here it is worse than usual. King wants us to be intimately concerned with the fate of a nice, wholesome, middle-class family—husband, wife, young daughter, and infant son—as they move into this region and encounter the weird topography. But who aside from other nice, wholesome, middle-class people could possibly care about what happens to them? Consider the wife's reaction when her son dies in a car accident:

> "I moved the couch while you were in Bangor ... I thought running the vacuum around would take my mind off ... off things ... and I found four of his little Matchbox cars under there ... as if they were waiting for him to come back and ... you know, play with them..." Her voice, already wavering, now broke. Tears spilled down her cheeks. "And that's when I took the second Valium because I started crying again, the way I'm crying now ... oh what a fucking soap opera all of this is ... hold me, Lou, will you hold me?" [PS 262].

Can one imagine Robert Aickman writing something like this? If King's self-proclaimed virtue lies in bringing horror down to ordinary people, then things like this are the best possible argument for believing that horror has no business with ordinary people.

Then there is *Thinner* (1985), one of the poorest excuses for a novel in the history of weird fiction. This, the last and worst of the Richard Bachman books, is the fatuous tale of a man, Bill Halleck, who kills an aged Gypsy woman in a car accident and is cursed by her father so that he inexorably loses weight day by day. This novel is severely flawed in its very conception: since the supernaturalism of Halleck's weight loss is made transparently obvious at the outset, the sole dramatic interest in the novel rests in watching what Halleck will do about the situation. Will he plead with the dead Gypsy's father? Will he kill him? But we cannot possibly be interested in Halleck's fate, as he is an utterly unsympathetic character who is clearly guilty of killing the Gypsy by negligence. King compounds the problem by asking us to sympathize with Halleck when he hires a small-time hood to terrorize the Gypsy until he finally lifts the curse. There is some attempt at social commentary—the Gypsies as outcasts from the rarefied upper-class atmosphere of suburban Connecticut—but the treatment is so crude as to seem a caricature. King evidently wrote this novel as the secret of his Bachman pseudonym was coming out, so that he felt no need to adopt the bold persona of Bachman, lapsing instead into his usual middle-class sentimentality.

Another of King's recent ventures into supernaturalism, *Needful Things* (1991), received very hostile reviews, even from his supporters; but it is in some ways superior to many of his recent works. The premise of this novel is childishly simple: a strange individual, Leland Gaunt, opens a shop called

Needful Things, in which he sells rare commodities to the townspeople of Castle Rock, Maine, and asks in return only that they play increasingly nasty tricks on one another. But the execution of the story, although inevitably prolix, is deft. What is perhaps most striking about Needful Things is its refreshingly bleak view of humanity—the notion that greed for possessions is so inexorable that it will cause human beings to violate the most fundamental moral norms in society and in interpersonal behavior. As one character ruminates: "Everyone loves something for nothing ... even if it costs everything" (NF 628). After an endless series of works in which King has paid lip service to conventional bourgeois pieties, this dark vision is a tonic. And, in contrast to The Shining, the novel's supernaturalism augments rather than confounds this message: although Gaunt is clearly a supernatural being, his prime function is only to set up a scenario whereby one individual will wish to do harm to another. It is abundantly obvious that most of the increasingly vicious actions on the part of the townspeople are, after Gaunt's initial urging, performed freely, willingly, and even with sadistic glee. What King (in this novel, at any rate) sees as the basic motivating factors of small-town life, and perhaps of American life generally, are greed, stupidity, revenge, and arrogance.

There is no question that supernaturalism does indeed come into play in this work, although in many cases it seems as if Gaunt achieves his purposes merely through a kind of hypnosis. In the first place, Gaunt, even before getting to know the townspeople, is familiar with each person's most secret desire: a young boy desperately wants a Sandy Koufax baseball card; a woman yearns for some token of Elvis Presley; a man wants a fishing pole like the one his father had. Gaunt appears to have all these items in his shop, but it is gradually revealed that he has managed to cast some sort of hypnotic spell over individuals so that they think they have become the owners of these cherished objects when in fact they have not. Also, Gaunt has uncanny mind-reading capabilities, and he performs other actions that clearly signal him to be superhuman.

What, then, is Gaunt? Is he the Devil? Almost nothing is told about him until the very end: we hear only that his career began in the Middle Ages (NF 547). Finally it is revealed that Gaunt is only a demon, albeit a powerful one (NF 681). Even so, King has awkwardly painted himself into a corner: his desire for a happy ending of sorts—in spite of the fact that the bulk of the town of Castle Rock has gone up in flames and many of its citizens have perished—results in absurdity and disappointment. Sheriff Alan Pangborn has finally grasped the fact that Gaunt is the fount of all the troubles in his town, and in the end he confronts him. But how is a mere human to deal with a demon? In some inexplicable and ludicrous fashion, Pangborn momentarily develops supernatural powers of his own and dispatches Gaunt with remarkable ease. It is, aside from verbosity, the one significant drawback in an otherwise respectable novel.

One gains the impression that King wishes this novel to be a sardonic commentary on the pettiness and hypocrisy of small-town life, as he folksily writes at the beginning: "call it Peyton Place or Grover's Corners or Castle Rock, it's just folks eatin pie and drinkin coffee and talkin about each other behind their hands" (NF 6–7). The novel was criticized for its "unsympathetic" treatment of its multifarious characters—no one aside from Pangborn, his girlfriend Polly Chalmers, and a few other minor characters are portrayed in any sort of favorable light. But what these criticisms overlook is that the novel is primarily a satire: we are meant to feel scorn and contempt for these people, and King seems to take a charming pleasure in killing them off one after the other. The only drawback in all this is that so many characters are presented that their deaths after a time lose emotional potency.

I am not entirely sure why King has felt the need to destroy the town where so many of his novels and tales have been set. The dust jacket proclaims *Needful Things* as "The Last Castle Rock Story," although oddly enough this designation appears nowhere in the book itself. Perhaps it is his way of calling an end to a very heterogeneous and thematically unrelated cycle of works. In any event, I enjoyed *Needful Things* for precisely the reason that many of King's enthusiasts did not: because it, like several of the Bachman books, outlines an unwonted but challenging *moral* brutality in addition to, and working in tandem with, the abundant physical brutality. As Gaunt smugly declares: "'I know all about that peculiar thing people call "pride of possession." I have made it the cornerstone of my career'" (NF 431).

Nevertheless, King's supernaturalism in general fails to convince. There are, aside from the hackneyed and paradox-riddled plots he has devised in many of his works, two fundamental reasons for this: his much vaunted mundane realism and his lifeless, working man's prose. This is a fatal combination. King spends so much time portraying his bland, middle-class characters going about their bland, middle-class activities (and does so with a prose style as flat and atmosphereless as any I have encountered in and out of weird fiction) that the intrusion of the supernatural comes to seem utterly preposterous and extraneous. When, in "The Mist" (1980; SC), tentacles suddenly appear at the loading entrance of a supermarket, the spectacle is more comical than frightening. This may be a general difficulty of the "mundane realists" of weird fiction as a whole—so different from such topographical and psychological realists as Lovecraft and Shirley Jackson—but it is a difficulty that King exemplifies most notably, and catastrophically.

THE POWERS OF THE MIND

Many of King's novels focus on the anomalous powers of the human mind. *Carrie* (to be studied more extensively elsewhere) deals with this theme, but the handling is unsatisfactory. The central phenomenon of telekinesis is here presented in a science-fictional manner, but difficulties result from this procedure. We are asked to believe that telekinesis is some sort of genetic trait: a fictional document extensively cited by King in the novel, a book on the case entitled *The Shadow Exploded*, speaks of a "TK gene" that is "more or less assumed in the scientific community" (C 224). There is a double mistake here: first, this wholly improbable pseudoscientific "explanation" causes the supernatural component of the novel to be assumed as a given rather than something to be accounted for plausibly; second, there must be thousands of Carries in the world if this supposed capability were genetic, and one wonders why we have not heard of them. Predictably enough, King suggests at the very end that another individual has the same telekinetic ability as Carrie, so I suppose we are to imagine another holocaust, like the one that concludes the book, occurring sometime in the future.

In *The Shining* (1977) the focus is on a young boy, Danny Torrance, who seems to be gifted with second sight. Once again, however, King has failed to think through this conception satisfactorily. Danny appears to be able both to read people's minds and to see (dimly) into the future; but there are paradoxes in King's presentation of both these attributes. Danny comes to the Overlook Hotel with his parents, Jack and Wendy Torrance, who will be tending the place while it is vacant during the winter season. He encounters an elderly woman who is leaving the hotel and whose bags are being stowed away by a handsome bellboy. Danny reads her thoughts: "*(i'd like to get into his pants)*" (S 70). But he misunderstands this: "Why would she want to get that man's pants? Was she cold, even with that long fur coat on?" (S 70). But what Danny is doing here is not, apparently, reading the woman's thoughts but—oddly—reading the woman's *verbalization* of her thoughts. This is an extremely peculiar method of mind reading, especially since at a later point he *is* able to read a doctor's thoughts imagistically: "he tried to catch Edmonds's thoughts or at least the color of his mood. And suddenly he got an oddly comforting image in his head" (S 139). Therefore, the appropriate vision he should have received in regard to the woman is some picture of the woman going to bed with the man (and Danny already knows something about sex [see S 83]). But King is forced into this bizarre expedient because a critical plot element rests upon it: one of Danny's persistent images is the word "REDRUM," which is finally explained (as if anyone could have failed to guess it) as "MURDER" seen in a mirror. As for Danny's precognitive abilities, Dick Hallorann, an elderly man who has befriended Danny and who has a limited capacity for precognition himself, tells him: *"Those things don't always come true"* (S 86). Why not? How can they be genuinely precognitive—rather than merely good guesses—if they don't? King again needs this escape valve in order that his characters can perform certain actions that prevent the worst of these precognitive visions from occurring.

The central supernatural scenario of *The Shining* is also poorly conceived. Why do various weird phenomena (an elevator that moves of its own accord; the ghost of an old woman that appears in the bathtub where she died; a bar whose patrons seem to materialize at random moments) afflict Jack Torrance and his family so relentlessly? The hotel certainly has a shady past, full of corruption and Mafia-style murders, but what does this have to do with Torrance, who seems especially victimized by the ghostly manifestations? These questions are not adequately answered. At one point Jack says that the ghosts may be *"like the residues of the feelings of the people who have stayed here. Good things and bad things. In that sense, I suppose that every big hotel has got its ghosts"* (S 264. But then why are other hotels not plagued with ghosts as this one is? We have already seen that this same motivation is used, with equal implausibility, in *Christine*. Still later it is said that "little by little a force had accrued" (S 420) in the hotel—but how, and for what purpose?

Perhaps Danny's precognitive power (called "shining") is involved in some way. He reports Hallorann telling him that "'this was a bad place for people who shine'" (S 248); Wendy wonders whether "in some unknown fashion it was Danny's shine that was powering" (S 371) the hotel. "Unknown" is certainly right, for this idea is never developed or clarified. Then there is Jack's increasing sense of identification with the hotel: "He felt that he and it were *simpático*" (S 251). The ghost of Grady, the bartender, says to Jack in a hallucination or vision: "'*You're* the caretaker, sir.... You've *always* been the caretaker'" (S 349). Is Jack some sort of reincarnation of a previous employee of the hotel? And what of the "huge dark shape" (S 437) seen floating out of the hotel as it is burning to the ground? All these variegated supernatural accounts never solidify into a whole, and in the end we are left completely at sea as to the exact cause of the incidents at the Overlook Hotel.

Even the portrayal of Jack's growing alienation from his family is bungled. His pseudopossession by the spirit of the hotel is presumably meant to serve as a symbol for his increasingly bad treatment of his wife and child, but several passages in the novel explicitly repudiate such an interpretation. Wendy asks Danny, "'Is Jack ... is he going to hurt us?'" to which Danny answers, "'They'll try to make him'" (S 324)—"they" being, one imagines, the sum total of the weird phenomena in the hotel. Jack is therefore absolved of any moral guilt in the matter, since he is now under the control of outside forces. A later passage confirms this view: "There was nothing of the real Jack in that howling, maundering, petulant voice" (S 410). Hence, *The Shining* cannot even serve as an effective metaphor for the breakup of a familial unit. *Roadwork* (1981), written under the Richard Bachman pseudonym, is a much more telling and unsentimentalized account of troubled family life.

The same supernatural phenomenon that caused a minor difficulty in *The Shining*—Danny Torrance's second sight—is a much greater problem in *The Dead Zone* (1979), since it is the very foundation of the plot. In this novel John Smith has had a slight precognitive ability ever since a boyhood accident in which he injured his head: he has "hunches" (DZ 4) of what the future will bring. This ability is augmented tremendously by a serious car accident in which he nearly dies. He spends four and a half years in a coma, and when he emerges from it he finds that mere contact with a human being enables him to visualize that person's past history, present circumstances, and future. In some cases, however, these visions are either vague or entirely lacking. A doctor attempts to account for this by the notion of a "dead zone":

> "A part of John Smith's brain has been damaged beyond repair—a very small part, but all parts of the brain may be vital. He calls this his 'dead zone,' and there, apparently, a number of trace memories were stored. All of these wiped-out memories seem to be part of a 'set'—that of street, road, and highway designations. A subset of a larger overall set, that of where is it. This is a small but total aphasia which seems to include both language and visualization skills" [DZ 145].

The crux of the novel is Smith's contact with Greg Stillson, a brash and dangerous right-wing politician. When Smith shakes Stillson's hand at a rally, he sees visions of Stillson becoming president and, more vaguely, causing an atomic holocaust through his rash and violent actions. Smith feels that the only way to prevent this from happening is to kill Stillson. Although he fails in his attempt, he manages to discredit Stillson so that his presidential ambitions are permanently destroyed.

There is, however, a fatal paradox in this entire conception. All Smith's previous precognitive visions have in fact come true regardless of his own actions in the matter—unfailingly so. Indeed, in a notebook Smith himself confesses: "I *have* to do something about Stillson. I *have* to.... There is absolutely no question in my mind. He is going to become president and he is going to start a war—or cause one through simple mismanagement of the office, which amounts to the same thing" (DZ 328). It is true that one of the impressions Smith receives when touching Stillson is vague (he sees blue and yellow stripes around him) but this is ultimately explained as the stripes of a child's coat, as Stillson holds the child up in front of him to prevent Smith from shooting him. But the mere vagueness of an impression has never previously prevented it from coming true in some fashion or other.

King is trying to have his cake and eat it, too. The whole dramatic tension of the novel rests upon Smith's heroic attempts to foil Stillson, but in order to have this tension King has fallen into a Catch–22 situation. If the vision that Smith sees is of the future, how can that future be altered by anyone's actions? If it *can* be altered, how could Smith have seen the vision to begin with? What is the future, after all, but the sum total of all actions by every entity in the universe from the present onwards? Smith's own actions would presumably be part of the sum total leading to the event he has visualized. King tries to get around this difficulty by a previous episode, but this is equally paradoxical. Smith, touching Chuck Chatsworth, a youth whom he has been tutoring, has a vision of a fire at the restaurant where Chuck's class is to celebrate its graduation that evening. He frantically and successfully persuades Chuck not to go, and sure enough there is a fire at the restaurant, in which many of Chuck's schoolmates are killed. But here again, if Chuck were among those who would perish in the fire, then this event is fated to happen and Smith could do nothing about it (or, rather, any actions Smith took would still lead to that result). If Chuck were— through whoever's actions—*not* among those who would perish, then Smith, by touching him, *could never have had a vision of the fire to begin with.* He would have had to touch some *other* person who *was* going to perish.

My whole point is that King has not thought through this entire supernatural phenomenon so that it avoids insuperable paradoxes. There has never been any indication, prior to the restaurant fire incident, that Smith's or anyone else's actions could have any effect in altering the future, and even that incident is fraught with conceptual difficulties. The "vagueness" of the vision, especially as it relates to Stillson, is not a sufficient escape valve for King, for here the vision has been completely *negated*, not merely altered in some insignificant way.

When *Firestarter* (1980) appeared, it was widely thought to be a rip-off of the central idea in *Carrie*: here, instead of a girl endowed with telekinesis, we have a little girl who has what King calls "pyrokinesis" (a singularly unfortunate coinage),[3] or the ability to start fires with her mind. She gained this power by being the offspring of two individuals, Andy McGee and Vicky Tomlinson, who were given some strange drug in a test administered by the Shop, a very secret branch of the Department of Defense devoted to research on the use of mental powers in warfare. Andy and Vicky themselves gain certain mildly anomalous mental faculties (Vicky seems to have dim precognitive abilities, while Andy is able to influence people's thoughts and behavior with his mind) but it is their child, Charlie, who has the greatest power. This idea is, I confess, a little hard to swallow, and King has to rely on the unknown powers of the mind to suggest that a mixture of relatively harmless mental faculties in two adults could produce such a radically new faculty in a child. This faculty, indeed, makes one individual think of Charlie "as a crack—a chink, if you like—in the very smelter of creation" (F 306). It is stated on a number of occasions that the child, when she grows up, might be able to crack the entire planet in two.

But, to be honest, the weird phenomenon in *Firestarter* is not conveyed with any sort of plausibility; we must simply accept it when we see Charlie start fires, large and small, at every turn. The novel is, in fact, largely a suspense story involving a laborious chase of Andy and Charlie by the Shop (who have already murdered Vicky) and, when they are finally captured, an equally laborious attempt by the government to harness Charlie's powers. As is so often the case, King's verbosity destroys whatever suspense this novel may have had. And, ironically, his anomalously inadequate depiction of Vicky—who is seen only in a series of flashbacks—causes her death to lack any emotive impact. There are, besides, King's usual platitudinous attacks on science ("Andy had no great faith in Modern Science, which had given the world the H–bomb, napalm, and the laser rifle" [F 30]) and the government ("The Shop, like the FBI and CIA, had a long history of killing the money" [F 214]). The story culminates a big shoot-'em-up scene in which Charlie torches everything in sight while agents try to gun her down. In an unintentionally hilarious afterword King tries to justify his "pyrokinesis" by appealing to that old charlatan Charles Fort and then gives an owlish lecture on what his novel is all about. "If I mean to suggest anything, it is only that the world, although well-lighted with fluorescent and incandescent bulbs and neon, is still full of odd dark corners and unsettling nooks and crannies" (F 402–3).

ADOLESCENCE

If King has any virtue as a writer, it is his really remarkable sense of identification with adolescence, particularly with teenage boys. Some of his more successful works—*Rage* (1977), *Christine* (1983), "Apt Pupil" and "The Body" in *Different Seasons* (1982), to be studied elsewhere—deal with this critical stage of human development. His portrayal of boys (and men) is much more perceptive than his portrayal of girls (and women), the latter tending to be depicted either sentimentally or with bizarre hostility. But when King is writing about high-school-age boys, he appears to be on familiar turf.

Carrie is King's first lengthy treatment of adolescent life; it is, however, a failure in every way. This is the story of Carrie White, a high-school girl endowed with the power of telekinesis. She is the daughter of Margaret White, a fanatical fundamentalist Christian with a ferocious loathing of sex that causes her to be psychotically overprotective of Carrie lest she succumb to the lure of men. Carrie is the ugly duckling of her high school: she has no friends; she is taunted at every turn; and, in an incident that opens the book, she is jeered at by her classmates when she experiences her first menstrual period in the school locker room and is unaware of what is happening. One student, furious at Carrie because she has been banned from the school prom for her part in the locker room incident, plans revenge by planting a booby trap for Carrie at the prom. But the plan backfires, as Carrie unleashes her telekinetic powers and causes mass destruction to the entire town. She finally dies herself.

This could have been an interesting work that probed many different issues—the effect of religious fundamentalism upon people's lives; the social difficulties of high-school life; telekinesis as a metaphor for repressed anger and anxiety—if King had had the ability to handle any of these elements well. But, at this point in his career, he did not. The portrait of Margaret White is so broad and ludicrous a caricature that she becomes preposterous and unbelievable. The high school setting is also poorly developed, and none of the characters are anything but hackneyed stereotypes. Structurally, the novel is very clumsy in narration because of King's unwise attempt at a documentary style. All sorts of books and articles and court testimony produced after the events are quoted in an attempt to create verisimilitude, but they are entirely unconvincing in their pompous banality and produce a fragmented narration that fails to bring the characters alive.

Curiously, one of King's best works overall—and certainly his most telling and perceptive account of adolescence—is *Rage* (1977), the first published Richard Bachman novel. This is in no sense a weird tale, but a gripping and psychologically acute narrative of a boy, Charlie Decker, who runs amok, kills several teachers, and holds his high school class hostage for several hours with a shotgun before finally giving up to the police.[4] This simple incident becomes a forum for the students to voice their personal and social hostilities and resentments, and especially a means for Decker himself to provide a bitter account of his past life, in particular his relationship with his parents and other schoolmates. The entire novel (mercifully short by King's standards) is told crisply, and the potentially explosive situation creates a grim tension that is scarcely relieved even at the end. King's ability at character portrayal has rarely been finer.

> Susan Brooks was one of those girls who never say anything unless called upon, the ones that teachers always have to ask to speak up, please. A very studious, very serious girl. A rather pretty but not terribly bright girl—the kind who isn't allowed to give up and take the general or the commercial courses, because she had a terribly bright older brother or older sister, and teachers expect comparable things from her. In fine, one of those girls who are holding the dirty end of the stick with as much good grace and manners as they can muster. Usually they marry truck drivers and move to the West Coast, where they have kitchen nooks with Formica counters—and they write letters to the Folks Back East as seldom as they can get away with. They make quiet, successful lives for themselves and grow prettier as the shadow of the bright older brother or sister falls away from them [BB 39].

Why can't King summon up the energy to write like this all the time? This single passage points to the most noteworthy feature of this novel—its morally challenging tone and, in contrast to the work written under his own name, its utter disregard for conventional middle-class pieties. If he had written more works of this kind, then there might be some small justification for giving him some standing as a social commentator. Surely, in spite of the raucous pleas of his supporters, he could never gain such standing on his work overall.

    Christine (1983) is one of King's abler treatments of adolescence—or, I should say, part of it is. The first third of the novel is narrated in the first person by Dennis Quilter, a senior in high school and the best friend of Arnie Cunningham, whose love affair with a 1958 Plymouth Fury leads to his downfall. This section is full of pungent and tellingly accurate reflections on high school life—sports, teenage love, problems with parents—and, moreover, is for once narrated wholly without the sugary sentiment and moral commonplaceness so uniform in King's work. Perhaps King felt that, under the persona of another character, he could shrug off his usual tired conventionality. But in the second part of the novel King's own voice takes over in a third-person narrative, bogging down in needless detail and windy verbosity. By this time the bizarrerie of an animate automobile has already been well established, but King cannot resist stringing out every incident to interminable length. When Quilter resumes his narrative in the final third of the novel, the damage has already been done and the novel never recovers. Still, the first third of *Christine* may embody some of King's most vibrant writing outside of his Bachman books.

It (1986), another novel largely about adolescence, cannot be regarded as even a modest success; indeed, it may be one of the most spectacular fiascos in modern literature. King, in the first place, should be ashamed of stealing the title from a magnificent novelette by Theodore Sturgeon, just as he has ripped off many particulars of the weird scenario from Ray Bradbury.[5] This grotesquely bloated novel (1150 pages long) is so crippled by inessential and superficial character description that the actual horrific scenario has no chance to develop. We encounter seven children, six boys and one girl, in the Maine town of Derry in 1958. Aside from having to escape frequent pummelings from the school bully, Henry Bowers, they each find themselves facing some loathsome entity they can only label "It." After about 700 pages pass, we finally learn that this entity is a manitou or shapeshifter (I 674), which has the unique capacity of presenting itself in the form most terrifying to its observer. Years pass. The children grow up to become entirely undistinguished adults (one of whom, Bill Denbrough, is another in a long line of Stephen King stand-ins, being a best-selling horror writer). It transpires that It reawakens in Derry every 27 years or so to murder children or, indeed, anyone who has the misfortune to cross its path. The children had taken a vow to return to Derry if It ever showed its face again. So sure enough they come marching back from all across the country to battle the evil thing and, naturally, conquer it. This entire scenario allows King to go on at appalling length about both the youthful and the adult lives of his utterly unremarkable characters. In the actual manifestation of the manitou, however, he faces the same difficulty that Peter Straub encountered in *Ghost Story* (1979), from which the central weird phenomenon was surely derived: the manitou is a virtually eternal entity (see I 763), so how is one to dispatch it? But in some utterly inexplicable fashion our courageous band manages to do so. This novel indicates, more than any other of King's works, how fond he has grown of his own voice: it must be comforting to have the colossal arrogance to fancy that readers will be willing to put up with more than a thousand pages of windy maundering about characters as mundane as these. King himself has, through one of his characters, delivered an apt verdict on the novel: "But if this is a story, it's not one of those classic screams by Lovecraft or Bradbury or Poe" (I 146). For once he has understated the issue.

APOCALYPSE

Stephen King is worried about things to come. He sees all sorts of dreadful things occurring in the rather near future, from nuclear holocaust to thought-control, and his novels and tales return obsessively to these scenarios. In many cases the government is to blame for these horrors in the offing, and this idea also fills King with concern to the point of paranoia.

Some of King's short stories anticipate his novels in the treatment of these themes. "Night Surf" (1974; NS) might be thought of as a kind of synopsis of *The Stand*, telling of a flu that has ravaged mankind, leaving a handful of youths to lead an aimless, violent existence. This bitter and poignant tale, technically a science fiction story, is narrated effectively in a series of impressionistic vignettes. "The Mist" (1980; SC) is virtually a short novel, but not nearly as effective as "Night Surf." A strange cloud of mist comes over a small New England town. It is apparently produced by some nuclear power plant, and for some utterly mysterious reason it affects only insects, making them become huge and threatening. This grotesquely implausible scenario (no doubt derived from some comic book King read in his youth) is further weakened by his focusing not on the weird phenomenon, which is left wholly unaccounted for, but on the emotions of the individuals affected by it. King directs his attention to a group of people caught in a supermarket and their efforts to come to terms with the mist and the giant bugs and tentacles that menace them. But his characterization is, as always, crude and melodramatic. Rod Serling wrote a far more compelling tale on a roughly analogous premise (and in much shorter compass) in his gripping tale "The Shelter."

The Stand is the first of King's apocalyptic novels. It was first published in 1978. In 1990, at the height of his marketability, the cuts made in the first version—amounting to some 400 pages—were restored and a "complete and uncut version" was published. King, in his 1990 preface to the novel, remarked with a sobriety that borders upon deadpan humor: "After all, many critics ... regarded it bloated and overlong to begin with" (St x). I have had neither the energy nor the inclination to make a collation between the two versions, so I shall have to accept King's word that the uncut edition "is not a brand-new, entirely different version... You will not discover old characters behaving in new ways, nor will the course of the tale branch off at some point from the old narrative" (St ix); random references to George Bush and AIDS suggest that a token amount of updating has been done. What we have, then, is a staggering, 1154-page novel in which every incident is elaborated at endless length, characters' past and present actions related in mind-numbing detail, and the pace of the action so lumbering that one wonders where the novel is going at all. King simply does not have the intensity of vision to carry a work of even a quarter of this size. He himself has again unintentionally written the epitaph to this novel when a character remarks: "'It was a quest with no object in view at the end of it'" (St 417).

A "superflu" has killed off nearly the entire population not merely of the United States but of the world. It was caused by an "accident" (St 110) when the U.S. government was experimenting with germ warfare. Random individuals prove immune to the disease, and *The Stand* narrates their efforts to reconstruct civilization after the decimation of the rest of the human race.

There are a number of oddities here. Let us consider the political implications. King's characters all seem fired with the notion that the foundations of American government must be restored. They gather together in Nebraska (no doubt because it is the center of the country) and immediately reratify the U.S. constitution and the Bill of Rights—this in spite of the fact that it is the government's actions that caused the destruction of the world in the first place. At one point there is a debate as to what to do about certain individuals who have sabotaged the group. There is a lot of talk about summary execution, but then one character intercedes: "'We was Americans once!' Whitney cried at last. 'This ain't how Americans act. I wasn't so much, I'll tell you that, nothin but a cook, but I know this ain't how Americans act, listening to some murderin freak in cowboy boots—'" (St 1081). King's reading of American history must be very selective, since vigilante justice has thrived during the length and breadth of this country's existence. His supporters like to speak of the "epic" dimensions of *The Stand*, yet in reality it is curiously parochial in outlook: recall that *the entire world* has been killed off, but there is no hint of what is going on outside the borders of the United States. It is in this regard that the work suffers most when compared to such a superb apocalyptic work as M. P. Shiel's *The Purple Cloud* (1901), which in a fifth of the length manages to convey spectacularly and poignantly the desolation of the entire planet. Even Pat Frank's *Alas, Babylon* (1959) is a more interesting treatment of the same basic theme.

And what would a King book be without a cardboard villain? Randall Flagg, a superhuman figure who has organized a competing band of people near Las Vegas and seeks to exterminate the good folks in Nebraska, is described as "'the purest evil left in the world'" (St 514). Well, that settles that: all you can do is kill him and his band. But the final conflict between good and evil takes enormously long to develop, and the climax, when it finally arrives, proves to be grotesquely absurd. We have no vast pitched battle between the Nebraskans and the Nevadans; instead, four individuals are sent as scouts to Las Vegas, and, by what appears to be a freak accident, an atomic explosion destroys Flagg's camp. This would itself be bad enough (I have rarely read of a nuclear warhead detonated with less fanfare and less psychological preparation than this one), but King then compounds the blunder by suggesting with apparent seriousness that it was not the atom bomb but *the hand of God* (yes, really!) that caused Flagg's destruction (St 1084). Where was God when the superflu and its effects were ravaging the world? On top of which, King concludes the novel by showing Flagg somehow reemerging, with a threat to cause further havoc. An even more horrifying threat to my mind is the prospect of a sequel to this novel sometime in the future. (This pulling of Flagg out of a hat at the end is one of the dubious additions to the uncut version of *The Stand*. In the original version he remained mercifully dead.)

Two Richard Bachman novels also deal with a future gone wrong, *The Long Walk* (1979) and *The Running Man* (1982). Of these, the former is much less substantial, but it still has several points of interest. *The Long Walk* is set in the very near future (1989) and speaks of a time when the national pastime has become a grueling, hundred-mile walk that teenage boys are forced to undertake without stopping and under strict rules lest they be summarily executed. In the end the last of the hundred contestants who remains alive claims the prize, apparently a vast sum of money (BB 169). This scenario certainly allows King to get in a number of telling jabs at the increasing dominance of violent sports and of the media in our society. But he seems more concerned (as in *Rage*) with the fluctuating emotions of the young competitors under the pressure of this dire situation. Although many of the individual characters are rendered crisply, the novel is a little too diffuse and unfocussed to be truly successful.

Of *The Running Man*, however, no praise can be too high. It is far and away King's best work; on no account should one judge it from the entertaining but insubstantial film adaptation. Here again we are dealing, a little implausibly, with a relatively near future, the early twenty-first century, a time when the gap between rich and poor has become so extreme that the lower classes are forced to live in vast, filthy slums under the constant threat of disease and violence. The government and television have united and formed an evil conspiracy to preserve the power of the wealthy few. They have set up a hugely popular game show in which an individual is shown on television, thrust into the world, and must survive undetected for a month to claim an enormous sum of money, while everyone in the country attempts to track him down and claim an equally grandiose prize for his capture or death. It is difficult in a summary to convey the clipped tension of this novel. Ben Richards, needing money to prevent his daughter from succumbing to disease, is haunted by the prospect of sudden death from every side and from every individual he meets, learning along the way that the government is intentionally withholding protection from the deadly air pollution of the cities in order to kill off its own citizens. But it is Richards' isolation that is the most frightening aspect of this entire scenario. "Richards hung up his jacket, slipped off his shoes, and lay down on the bed. He realized how miserable and unknown and vulnerable he was in the world. The universe seemed to shriek and clatter and roar around him like a huge and indifferent jalopy rushing down a hill and toward the lip of a bottomless chasm. His lips began to tremble, and then he cried a little" (BB 581). And the final confrontation between Richards and the government agents who ultimately track him down may be the single most intense and hypnotic episode in all King's work. *The Running Man* is, strictly speaking, a science-fiction novel, but it certainly has enough horrific overtones to be classified well within the weird tale.

KING AS MAINSTREAM WRITER

I have already noted that two of the Richard Bachman novels, *Rage* and *Roadwork*, are purely mainstream without any suggestion of the weird. They are among King's abler works. *Roadwork* (1981) is the disturbing story of a man who, faced with the demolition of both his house and his business by the extension of a highway, runs quietly amok and seeks to sabotage the highway rather than relocate. It is a tense and gripping tale, but I am not certain that the protagonist's psychological motivations have been satisfactorily clarified: is he homesick; has his placid middle-class life become intolerable to him; is some imp of the perverse guiding his actions? One never knows.

Several short stories are also purely mainstream. "The Woman in the Room," the final and best tale in *Night Shift*, is a lightly fictionalized account of the death of King's mother from cancer, and is full of a terseness and stinging wit that King can only dream of now that he has babbled himself out in harmless verbosity. "The Last Rung of the Ladder" (NS) is a touching story of a boy's increasing loss of emotional contact with his sister as he grows to manhood. It is conceivable that King could have had moderate success as a mainstream writer, but he chose to make his career in the horror field. And yet, he has been uncomfortable with the simple label of "horror writer" and has repeatedly tried to flex his muscles in the realm of mainstream fiction. *Different Seasons* (1982), a collection of four long tales, is his most ambitious attempt in this regard.

The first and last of these tales can be dismissed immediately. "Rita Hayworth and Shawshank Redemption" is a long-winded story about a man, falsely convicted of murder, who spends 27 years digging a tunnel out of his cell and escapes to live the remainder of his life in peace, contentment, and wealth in Mexico. He supplies the handy moral to the story in a letter to an inmate friend: "Remember that hope is a good thing, Red, maybe the best of things, and no good thing ever dies" (DS 100). I fear that King's treatment of this idea is not sufficiently compelling to justify a tale as long as Lovecraft's *At the Mountains of Madness*. "The Breathing Method" is the mawkish story of an unmarried woman in the 1930s who gets pregnant, decides to have the baby (King's characters don't like abortion), but dies tragically in a car accident on the way to the hospital. This tale is dedicated to Peter Straub, and it is a clear homage to Straub's *Ghost Story* in that it involves a club of men who meet to tell odd and disturbing stories. (A roughly contemporaneous story, "The Man Who Would Not Shake Hands" [1982; SC], reuses the club setting, although it is a weird tale of a supernatural curse.)

King's greatest claims to respectability in *Different Seasons* are two long, nearly novel-length stories, "Apt Pupil" and "The Body," both of which have been filmed (the latter as *Stand by Me*). Both are quite noteworthy— they contain some of his best writing and most poignant scenarios—but both are severely flawed. "Apt Pupil" tells of a teenage boy, Todd Bowden, who develops a fascination for Nazi concentration camps and then discovers that the commandant of one such camp, Patin, has escaped detection and is living in his own southern California town under an assumed name. Rather than expose the Nazi, Kurt Dussander, Todd forces him to speak repeatedly of his experiences at the camp. A bizarre symbiotic relationship develops between the boy and the now aged Nazi. To his parents and to the townspeople in general it appears that Todd has merely befriended an old man out of kindness and sympathy, but in fact Todd's fascination for the horrors of the camp has made him as much a monster as Dussander.

All this is handled quite well, if a little verbosely. But King errs in the area of psychological motivation at one critical juncture. Todd, developing a love-hate relationship with Dussander, wishes to sever his ties to him, by murder if necessary. He cannot kill him, however, because the latter has told him (falsely) that he has placed a letter telling of their relationship in a safety deposit box, to be opened if Dussander were to die. This letter, speaking of Todd's bland acceptance of Dussander's Nazi past, may destroy Todd's future. In rage and frustration, Todd takes to killing derelicts all over town. Curiously, Dussander does the same, luring them into his house, dispatching them, and burying them in his cellar. Why does Dussander do this? What psychological purpose is served by this procedure? King compounds this anomaly by an implausible use of coincidence. A Jewish man who had been at Patin happens to wind up in the same hospital room as Dussander, who is recovering from a heart attack—this in spite of the fact that the town is described as "'a quiet little suburb'" (DS 282). The Jew eventually recognizes Dussander and exposes him, leading to Todd's downfall as well. These failings mar an otherwise powerful and grim tale, one that might nevertheless stand as one of King's relative triumphs.

The problems with "The Body"—which otherwise contains some of King's freshest and most vibrant writing and imagery—relate not to psychological motivation but to overall conception. This could have been an utterly delightful novelette about four 12-year-old boys who undergo a rite of passage from boyhood to incipient manhood when they find the body of a boy who has died mysteriously in their town. But King spoils his delicate and empathic portrayal of adolescence by becoming pretentious and inserting into the narrative two wholly fatuous stories written later by one of the boys, Gordon Lachance. King does this because his true but misguided purpose in this story is to depict the Evolution of a Writer. Indeed, since it becomes obvious that Lachance is one more stand-in for King ("I've since written seven books about people who can do such exotic things as read minds and precognit [sic] the future" [DS 370]), what "The Body" is really about is the Evolution of Stephen King the Writer. King lets us know the real import of the story in a passage highlighted with self-important italics: "*The only reason anyone writes stories is so they can understand the past and get ready for some future mortality; that's why all the verbs in stories have -ed endings ... even the ones that sell millions of paperbacks. The only two useful artforms are religion and stories*" (DS 411). You tell 'em, Steve.

If *Different Seasons* is only a middling success, then some more recent nonsupernatural or mainstream works by King reveal a surprising competence that may yet redeem him. He has by no means abandoned supernaturalism, but his last several works clearly point to a change of focus or emphasis away from comic-book scenarios and toward more serious issues dealing with individuals' relations with themselves, with others, and with society.

AUTHORSHIP

It should by now be obvious that King has become obsessed with his own role as author and the advantages and drawbacks of being a best-selling genre writer. As early as Ben Mears in *'Salem's Lot*, he has populated his novels and tales with transparently autobiographical figures. Both Bill Denbrough in *It* and Roberta Anderson in *The Tommyknockers* write popular bestsellers (horror novels and westerns, respectively), and both betray a violent resentment against the mainstream community that refuses to take them seriously. "The Body" is, as we have seen, one long meditation on King's own literary development. *Misery* (1987) and *The Dark Half* (1989) complete this pattern; in both novels King, and King alone, is the subject.

Misery must, I suppose, be accorded one of King's modest triumphs, if only because of its brevity. This is a wholly nonsupernatural *conte cruel* about Paul Sheldon, a best-selling writer of romance novels featuring Misery Chastain as their heroine, whose car slides off the road in a remote area of Colorado and who is rescued by Annie Wilkes, a crazed ex-nurse who is Sheldon's "number-one fan" (M 6). Wilkes keeps Sheldon prisoner, and—when she learns that Sheldon has killed Misery off in his last novel— forces him to write another novel bringing her back to life. *Misery* is wholly focused upon Sheldon's attempts to escape from Wilkes's clutches.

Considered abstractly as a novel, *Misery* isn't bad, although it is not as good as King thinks it is. He seems to fancy that he has presented a powerful psychological portrait of an insane serial killer (for Wilkes has murdered dozens of people both before and during her career as a nurse), but the extreme hostility of the portrayal robs it of subtlety and acuteness: she is, in the end, just another in King's long line of utterly evil villains. There is no attempt to probe her mental state from within, as there is in Ramsey Campbell's *The Face That Must Die* (1979) or John Fowles's *The Collector* (1963), a clear model for King's work and one to which he alludes (M 151). *Misery* is really nothing more than an adventure story in which we are expected to sympathize entirely with Sheldon and to loathe and despise Wilkes and wish for her death.

The novel is much more interesting in what it tells us about Stephen King. From this perspective, it comes across as a hostile snarl against his own legions of readers and against critics who treat him condescendingly, as well as a sort of pitiable wish-fulfillment fantasy in which King fancies himself an unrecognized literary master. Sheldon, we are told, "wrote novels of two kinds, good ones and best-sellers" (M 6); unfortunately, no one reads the good novels and even critics fail to accord them more than marginal notice (See M 41). The new novel Sheldon has written—not a Misery novel—is one that he thinks has a chance of winning the National Book Award! (M 14). Wilkes forces him to burn it because it contains too many obscenities.

As for Sheldon's hack work, Sheldon/King cannot bring himself to condemn it entirely. Writing the Misery novels may have been "whoredom" (M 66), but they at least have the power to keep the reader turning those pages, more so than his "real" work (M 224). Of the novel Wilkes forces him to write, Sheldon thinks, "The story was hot, but the characters as stereotyped and predictable as ever" (M 137); but, by gum, it "was still a goddam good yarn" (M 237). In a last-ditch attempt to escape Wilkes, Sheldon pretends to burn the completed manuscript of the new Misery novel, but he has in fact hidden the actual manuscript away and burns mere blank sheets. He cannot bring himself to destroy his hack work, even if it may cost him his life.

All this is rather sad. Wilkes's compelling Sheldon to write a Misery novel is a transparent metaphor for King's readers clamoring for a new horror blockbuster every year. King feels fenced in, feels like a whore, feels unable to devote his energies to his "real" work (which the critics don't like anyway). He comes extremely close to biting the hand that feeds him: does he imagine that all his readers are Annie Wilkeses? At one point Sheldon thinks disdainfully, "She was the embodiment of that Victorian archetype, Constant Reader" (M 57)—but this is exactly the term that King would use ingratiatingly in the 1990 preface to The Stand! (St xii). The afterword to Different Seasons, with its weirdly defensive tone and manifest hostility toward his lukewarm critics, is also worth reading in conjunction with Misery. What is finally amusing is that King is really condemning his own work by attacking Wilkes's inept fondness for Sheldon's: how can his work be any good if it is adored by the likes of her?

If, in my analysis of Misery, I have failed to appreciate the distinction between author (King) and persona (Sheldon), it is because there does not seem to be any. Sheldon's Misery novel bears uncanny resemblances to King's work, with its melodramatic one-sentence paragraphs, frequent italicized passages recording the thoughts of his narrators, ponderous repetition of significant phrases, and other crude devices of popular bestsellerdom found throughout King's own novels. King may whine about being typecast as a genre writer, but he is whining all the way to the bank. And on the basis of his actual mainstream work, there does not seem to be much of a case for his being a "real" writer.

The Dark Half (1989), while definitely supernatural, is a sort of inversion of both Misery and of King's own life, but it is as self-obsessed as its predecessor. Here we are to imagine that George Stark, the pseudonym of

Thad Beaumont, has somehow come to life after Beaumont has ceremonially "buried" him by vowing to write no more best-selling crime novels under the Stark name and to resume mainstream writing under his own name. An author's note at the beginning records King's debt to the "late" Richard Bachman, and one can see the novel as a neat reversal of the facts of King's own life: it was the genre novels under King's own name that were the bestsellers, while the more mainstream work of Bachman was relatively unsuccessful. Indeed, at the outset *The Dark Half* is a lightly fictionalized account of how King was finally compelled to acknowledge the Bachman pseudonym.

And yet, as a novel, *The Dark Half* is not entirely unsuccessful. The central supernatural premise—a pseudonym coming to life—is, of course, entirely preposterous and never adequately explained. King tries various methods—a fleeting reference to Poe's "William Wilson" (DH 124); a suggestion that Beaumont, as a boy, had a peculiar operation in which an "eye, ... part of a nostril, three fingernails, and two teeth" (DH 9) were removed from his brain, these being the remains of the twin whom Beaumont had consumed or absorbed in the womb, but none of them work and the whole idea sticks in one's craw like a piece of meat. And yet, if one simply grants the premise, the working out of the novel is rather entertaining. Stark viciously kills everyone involved with the revelation of the pseudonym. Then he tries to compel Beaumont to revive him by writing a new Stark novel, for he is "losing cohesion" (DH 266) and literally falling apart because Beaumont is not using the pseudonym. Only toward the end does *The Dark Half* become anything other than a ridiculous but amusing adventure story, as King finally states openly the psychological relationship between Beaumont and Stark:

> Hadn't there always been a part of him [Beaumont] in love with
> George Stark's simple, violent nature? Hadn't part of him always
> admired George, a man who didn't stumble over things or bump into
> things, a man who never looked weak or silly, a man who would never
> have to fear the demons locked away in the liquor cabinet? A man with
> no wife or children to consider, with no loves to bind him or slow him
> down? A man who had never waded through a shitty student essay or
> agonized over a Budget Committee meeting? A man who had a sharp,
> straight answer to all of life's more difficult questions? [DH 328].

The conclusion, in which King borrows the idea of birds as psychopomps from Lovecraft's "The Dunwich Horror," is surprisingly powerful. *The Dark Half* may be considered King's answer to the growing number and popularity of serial killer novels. It is as if he wished to show how this nonsupernatural form could be melded into the supernatural horror novel. If he had only worked out the supernatural premise of *The Dark Half* more convincingly, he would have produced a very able and unique amalgam.

NONSUPERNATURALISM

Nonsupernatural horror has been an element of King's work from the beginning of his career. A number of short stories in *Night Shift* and *Skeleton Crew* are really nothing more than *contes cruels*, many of them undistinguished and too reliant on trick endings. "The Ledge" (1976; NS) is the suspenseful tale of a wealthy man who dares another man to walk all the way around the narrow ledge of his penthouse apartment. Less successful are "I Know What You Need" (1976; NS), a maudlin story about a love triangle that leads to murder; "Strawberry Spring" (1975; NS), about some gruesome murders at a small college; and "The Man Who Loved Flowers" (1977; NS), a crude and superficial portrayal of a man who becomes a mass murderer from an inability to accept the death of his lover. Of King's later nonsupernatural tales, "Nona" (1978; SC) is a windy account of a homicidal maniac and "Survivor Type" (1982; SC) is a rather nasty story in which a man, trapped on a desert island with no food, eats parts of his own body to remain alive. Four of King's novels are nonsupernatural: *Cujo* (1981), *Misery* (1987), *Gerald's Game* (1992), and *Dolores Claiborne* (1993). *Misery* has already been examined, and it is time to give consideration to the other three. The last two are among his most provocative and successful works.

Cujo is, however, close to the nadir of King's output. It was greeted with much ridicule by the horror community because it was believed, correctly, to signal the complete exhaustion of King's imagination, coming so soon after *Firestarter*, his self-plagiarism of *Carrie*. *Cujo* is about a huge Saint Bernard who gets bitten by a bat, develops rabies, and rampages through the community of Castle Rock, Maine. This does not sound like a very prepossessing premise for a novel, and it isn't. *Cujo* is wholly nonsupernatural (although with some attempted shenanigans that I shall examine presently) and is in fact a long-drawn-out soap opera about various people in the town whose paths the dog crosses: Joe Camber, owner of the dog, a beer-swilling mechanic who mistreats his wife Charity; Gary Pervier, his lush of a friend; and Vic Trenton, an advertising executive whose wife Donna and son Tod have the misfortune to be terrorized by the dog in their car in a remote part of town. King has, however, not sufficiently vivified these white-trash characters to make any reader care about their fate.

The problem with this novel is that the horrific element—a rabid dog running amok—has absolutely no broader meaning or symbolism. King tries to fill this void by dwelling at interminable length, and in his usual stereotypical and sentimental fashion, on the personal problems of his characters—problems that have nothing to do with the central situation. Vic's advertising agency is in serious trouble; Vic's wife is cheating on him; Joe Camber doesn't want to let his wife and son visit his wife's sister; Gary Pervier is embittered because one of his testicles was blown off during World War II. King, I imagine, fancies all this to be the stuff of life, but what of it? What connection does any of it have to the dog?

As if realizing his poverty of conception in *Cujo*, King tries to infuse a quasi-supernatural element into it, but the result is ineptitude and confusion. Tod is terrified of a monster that may lurk in his bedroom closet. His parents dismiss the idea, but King frequently suggests that there may be some linkage between it and Cujo. At the end of the novel, however, this thread is simply dropped, as if King had forgotten about it. Similarly, Vic dreams that his wife and child are being attacked by some monstrous entity, but again it is never clarified whether he is, as a result, somehow clairvoyant. Finally, Donna, trapped in her car, tries to think of the situation rationally: "She did not believe in monsters from closets; she believed in things she could see and touch. There was nothing supernatural about the slobbering wreck of a Saint Bernard sitting in the shade of a barn; he was merely a sick animal that had been bitten by a rabid fox or skunk or something" (Cu 203). Shortly thereafter, however, she reverses herself: "In that instant she knew—she did not feel or just think—she *knew* that the dog was something more than just a dog" (Cu 207). But this is mere trickery, for in fact the dog is simply a dog. The plight in which Donna finds herself is somewhat analogous to those in the Bachman novels, which all focus upon the conflicting emotions of an individual in a critical and life-threatening situation. But Donna's reflections are all hackneyed and stereotyped, and cannot match the intensity of Charlie Decker's in *Rage* or Ben Richards' in *The Running Man*.

Of *Gerald's Game* and *Dolores Claiborne*, the latter is virtually a mainstream work, with scarcely any horror element in it at all. Both are surprisingly creditable performances. *Gerald's Game* was, like *Needful Things*, not well received even among King's own supporters, and yet it is far superior to much of the rest of his output. One reviewer, sympathetic to King, called it "something of a Bachman book,"[6] and the tone of the remark suggests disapproval or even a sort of disdain. The designation is exactly on target, however, for like the best of the Bachman books this novel chooses as its focal point a single, highly anomalous, and tension-filled moment and, by a series of flashbacks, seeks to explain how things have come to such a pass.

It is possible that *Gerald's Game* was disliked because of its very stark premise: a woman whose husband was fond of sex games finds herself handcuffed to a bed in a remote cabin in Maine after her husband has died of a heart attack. The entire novel is concerned with her attempts to escape and her harried reflections on how she has arrived—both literally and figuratively—at this state. Jessie Burlingame spends two-thirds of the novel wearing nothing but bikini briefs and handcuffed to the bed. Her husband—whom she kicked because she was tired of the "game," inducing his heart attack—lies on the floor and later becomes food for a starving stray dog. In spite of this outrageous premise, the novel is not at all gratuitous in its violence or cheaply titillating in its sexual scenario. King's writing here is crisp, deft, and suspenseful. A ten-page set piece in which Jessie attempts to reach for a glass of water, finally succeeding after she has given up the cause as hopeless, is as vivid a passage as any in his entire work.

But there is much more to *Gerald's Game* than merely witnessing a woman escape from an appalling and life-threatening situation (she finally does escape by cutting her wrists and using the blood as a lubricant to wriggle out of the handcuffs). Since Jessie has caused her husband's death by kicking him after he refused to release her from the handcuffs, she understandably feels a certain amount of guilt ("I never meant to kill him" [GG 30]), even wondering whether she deserves her fate. Some have criticized King's (and Jessie's) failure to give any account of her 17-year marriage to Gerald, but this silence is deliberate, for it is clear that the marriage was emotionally empty and unfulfilling on both sides. And Jessie finally comes to realize that her husband's need to play increasingly harsher bondage games with her (they had progressed from scarves to ropes to handcuffs) merely to perform sexually is much more a reflection on his inadequacies than hers.

As Jessie struggles to escape, she ponders on the course of her life. Some harrowing incident involving her father occurred to her as a ten-year-old child during a total eclipse of the sun in the summer of 1963, and she racks her brain to recall it. Finally the incident is revealed in a long flashback: her father molested her by masturbating while holding her on his lap. This entire lengthy tableau is told with the utmost delicacy and emotive power, and it inevitably leads Jessie to wonder: "How many of the choices she had made since that day had been directly or indirectly influenced by what had happened during the final minute or so she had spent on her Daddy's lap...? And was her current situation a result of what had happened during the eclipse?" (GG 179). There are no clear-cut answers to these questions, but King has supplied enough background for readers to come to their own conclusions.

The novel unfortunately suffers a letdown at the end. During and after her escape, Jessie thinks she sees some shadowy figure (Death?) staring at her from a dark corner of the room. The reader is naturally inclined to think this a mere delusion, but King dwells on the episode in such a way as to suggest the actual—and grotesquely implausible—incursion of the supernatural. This would be bad enough, but then we are asked to believe that this figure was a real individual, a man who committed a series of horrible sex murders. The entire latter third of the novel deals with this matter, and concludes with Jessie writing an interminable letter to an old roommate telling of her pursuit of the facts of the case. This long digression seriously disfigures the unity of the novel, taking interest away from Jessie's plight and forcing the reader to dwell at needless length upon the hideous practices of the crazed serial killer. In spite of this blunder, *Gerald's Game* ranks close to the pinnacle of King's achievement. And it may be a welcome sign that he is no longer slavishly paying lip service to reader expectations and is beginning to write about tough, emotionally sensitive issues uncompromisingly and unsentimentally.

Dolores Claiborne exhibits these same features somewhat less strikingly. This is a very curious novel, at least formally. Written without chapter divisions, it is a 300-page monologue by an ill-educated 63-year-old cleaning woman, Dolores Claiborne St. George, who is giving her statement to the police in an attempt to clear herself from accusations that she murdered a wealthy woman, Vera Donovan, for whom she worked for decades, and who has conveniently left her millions of dollars in her will. In the process she confesses to the decades-old murder of her husband, Joe St. George, but presents a convincing case that she did not murder Vera.

The novel is not, however, primarily a murder mystery, but rather a character study. Dolores admits at the outset that "I'm just an old woman with a foul temper and a fouler mouth, but that's what happens, more often than not, when you've had a foul life" (DC 5), and her account certainly verifies this utterance. She married a slothful, beer-guzzling wretch; she has worked herself to exhaustion taking care of the ageing and increasingly disoriented Vera; and, to top it off, she killed her husband (during the same eclipse of 1963 that was the focal point of *Gerald's Game*) because he started sexually molesting his daughter Selena. *Dolores Claiborne* is a convincing picture of lower-class life—full of ignorance, coarseness, and filth—which is perfectly captured by Dolores's own ignorant, coarse, and filthy monologue. But King extends sympathy both to her and the upper-class Vera, who, as we learn at the end, also killed her husband many years ago, thereby establishing a bond that overcomes class distinctions. I could have done without the coy and meaningless references to *Gerald's Game* (during the eclipse Dolores has visions of a little girl who is clearly no other than ten-year-old Jessie) and an implausible happy ending whereby Dolores is reconciled to her daughter and son. Otherwise, though, *Dolores Claiborne* is another strong performance, and it is certainly not the sort of novel one would have expected a writer like King to have produced.

It is, of course, more than the eclipse that unites *Gerald's Game* and *Dolores Claiborne*: it is the sensitive portrayal of women who, in their very different ways, have been victimized by men but who struggle to establish their identities as strong, competent individuals capable of triumphing over the most daunting obstacles. King is perhaps reacting to frequent criticisms of his women characters, who are either saintly or unimitigatedly evil. And, aside from a few conventional diatribes of the "all men are beasts" variety, he has succeeded in depicting well-rounded, courageous women who are no longer defined by the men around them—their fathers, their husbands, their sons.

For me, however, the prime virtue of *Gerald's Game* and *Dolores Claiborne* is in their possibly revealing a new Stephen King. Is it conceivable that King, now assured of bestseller status, is belatedly achieving an independence of vision? Is he abandoning horror entirely and tackling difficult personal and social issues without catering to the sentimental expectations of his audience? Has perennial bestsellerdom paradoxically inculcated a sort of "art for art's sake" attitude in him, and is this (rather than the undeniable mediocrity of his more recent horror work) the true cause of his somewhat decreasing sales? It is too early to answer these questions, but one would like to think that there is still hope for an author who has been long on popularity but short on literary substance.

CONCLUSION

I have focused in this chapter on relatively basic, even mundane aspects of King's work—in particular, the plausibility of his supernatural conceptions—because there does not seem to me much else to study. King himself has admitted that he has nothing to offer as a prose stylist ("the literary equivalent of a Big Mac and a large fries from McDonald's" [DS 524]), and this makes one doubly perplexed one as to his precise motivations for generating such staggering excursions into logorrhea as in *The Stand, It,* and *Four Past Midnight.* His resolutely pedestrian style, full of colloquialisms, profanities, and a superficial attempt to imitate the thoughts and speech of average Joes, becomes unutterably wearying after prolonged exposure: how many burgers and fries, after all, can one eat? This is why such works as *The Talisman* (1984), written in collaboration with Peter Straub, and *The*

Eyes of the Dragon (1987) are such colossal failures: in trying to capture the atmosphere of a fairy tale, these novels are so handicapped by King's abrasively modern style that they become totally unconvincing. They sound like a Tolkien story narrated by a sportscaster.

Recently, as if perceiving the absurdity of vaunting King purely on the basis of his supernatural conceptions, some of his supporters have attempted to make a case for some kind of social significance in his work. Tony Magistrale appears to be the leading flag-waver of this campaign,[7] the idea being that King has all sorts of insights into the lives of ordinary Americans. I cannot see much in this argument. Can one really believe that King's comic book plots, TV movie dialogue, and soap opera sentimentality have any value as social commentary? Consider this bit of wisdom from "Apt Pupil": "More and more it seemed to Ed that there was a vicious downside of American life, a greased skid of opportunism, cut corners, easy drugs, easy sex, a morality that grew cloudier each year" (DS 267). One would have to have been comatose for the last three decades to come up with an observation less illuminating than this.

It is also of interest that King's unswervingly middle-class vision has nothing good to say about either the lower or the upper class. Nearly all of King's lower-class characters—Watson, the furnace tender in *The Shining*, Gary Pervier in *Cujo*, Roland LeBay in *Christine*, Joe St. George of *Dolores Claiborne*, to name only a few—are portrayed with a scornful satire bordering upon caricature. They are ignorant, uncouth, racist, and irrationally violent. Randall Flagg, the cosmic villain in *The Stand*, is an apotheosis of lower-class savagery, as are Henry Bowers, whom the entity in *It* possesses to do its dirty work, and George Stark, the vicious murderer in *The Dark Half*.

As for the upper class, consider this description of Regina Cunningham in *Christine*: "Regina ... was forty-five and handsome in a rather cold, semi-aristocratic way—that is, she managed to look aristocratic even when she was wearing bluejeans, which was most of the time" (Ch 18). This is doubly interesting in that Regina is not an actual aristocrat but merely a college professor: King is as suspicious of the intellectual aristocracy as he is of the actual aristocracy (many of his sympathetic characters are indeed teachers, but almost always at the high-school level). A number of King's villains are also of the upper class or ape upper-class mannerisms: Richard Straker in *'Salem's Lot* inspires immediate suspicion and hostility by the hauteur and courtliness of his speech and actions among the down-home farmers of the town. *Thinner* purports to be a scathing satire on the hoity-toity airs of upper-middle-class yuppies in Connecticut, but the treatment is too coarse and obvious to be effective.

What becomes tiresome in King's work is not merely the mechanical replication of a standardized nuclear family in novel after novel (husband, wife, cute children) but the clear implication that this bourgeois lifestyle is self-evidently the optimum state for human beings. In many of his works the weird phenomena appear to have as their primary goal the destruction of this wholesome familial unit, and this is what King sees (and what he expects his readers to see) as genuinely horrifying, not the spectacular defiance of natural law embodied by the mere existence of the supernatural. It is not enough to say that King ignores the powerful metaphysical implications of his weird conceptions; it is that he uses the supernatural as a makeshift prop for dwelling upon the conventionalized emotions of his uninspiring characters. It is no wonder that King has put so little thought into the logic of his supernatural scenarios: they are not in fact the focus of his work at all. Strange as it may sound, King is not primarily a supernaturalist but a sort of male Harlequin romance writer.

It may be well to say a word about the proliferation of Stephen King "criticism" in recent years. King's purported scholars appear to divide generally into three groups: first, the mere sycophants who hope to gain fame and fortune by riding on King's coattails; second, those who, through an ignorance either of weird fiction or of mainstream fiction, vastly inflate King's status and are unaware of the degree to which his weird conceptions are stale, flawed, and unimaginative and his work as a whole is flat, superficial, sentimental, and uninsightful; and third, those so dazzled by King's fame and reputation that they fancy there must be something to the fellow (the hoary and fallacious argument "Millions of readers can't be wrong!") or are simply afraid to speak out against him. It would be invidious to name names; but when one scholar blithely compares King to Hawthorne and Faulkner and another ranks him with Dostoevsky without the faintest realization of the outrage to critical standards they are effecting, they have surely destroyed whatever credibility they may have had as analysts. These critics have fallen into a trap many of their academic counterparts have stumbled into: the failure or inability to cast *evaluative judgments*. The thinking is that because King writes about the *same subjects* as Hawthorne, Faulkner, and Dostoevsky, he has some significant relationship to them. No attempt is made to ascertain whether King's treatment of these subjects is anything but trite, jejune, and undistinctive. One might as well say that Judith Krantz and Tolstoy are significantly related because they both write about love and death. It is, indeed, a fact that King has more in common with Krantz, Danielle Steel, Sidney Sheldon, and other purveyors to popular sentiment than he does with Poe, Lovecraft, and Blackwood, let alone Hawthorne and Faulkner.

My general verdict on King is that his weird conceptions are unoriginal and poorly conceived, his style plebeian and verbose, his morality conventional and unadventurous, and his characterization hackneyed and sentimental. Only a few of his books—*Different Seasons*, *Christine*, *Misery*, and *Needful Things*—are even partial successes; his two Bachman novels, *Rage* and *The Running Man*, along with *Gerald's Game* and *Dolores Claiborne*, may actually be his greatest achievements, in spite or because of their relative unpopularity. Juxtaposed to these are some of the most stupendous failures in modern weird fiction—*Carrie*, *'Salem's Lot*, *Cujo*, *Thinner*, *It*, *The Tommyknockers*, *The Stand*, *Four Past Midnight*—failures that would have caused any other writer to have been laughed out of the field.

King's domination of the bestseller lists over the last two decades has been an unmitigated disaster for the weird tale. By being the chief exemplar of the "banalization" of horror, he has caused an inferior strain of weird fiction (commonplace, flabby, sentimental work full of "human interest" but entirely lacking in originality of conception) to gain popular esteem. As a result, genuinely artistic and dynamic work—the work of Robert Aickman, Ramsey Campbell, T. E. D. Klein, and Thomas Ligotti—has been relegated to comparative obscurity, while a whole phalanx of King imitators and wannabes have attempted to churn out their own bulging blockbusters of middle-class folks dauntlessly fighting to save their wholesome families and their suburban lifestyle from evil monsters from the other side of the tracks.

But perhaps the tide is finally turning. King is no longer regarded by the horror community with that mixture of envy and awe which he receives in his earlier years, and several of his recent failures have met with uniform derision both from the horror field and from mainstream reviewers. No doubt King will continue to appear regularly on the best-seller lists for some time to come. But one can confidently look to the day when he—like Marie Corelli, Robert W. Chambers, and other bestselling authors of a prior day—is relegated to his proper position as an insignificant footnote in literary history.

— T. E. D. KLEIN: URBAN HORROR —

THEORY AND PRACTICE

The lamentably small body of weird fiction by T. E. D. Klein (b. 1947) is among the most distinguished in the field of the weird. Klein's corpus comprises less than a score of short stories and novelettes and one long novel, *The Ceremonies* (1984), aside from stray reviews, essays, and poetry. Four long tales were gathered in *Dark Gods* (1985), which ranks with Campbell's *Demons by Daylight* as one of the premier weird collections since the heyday of Lovecraft and Blackwood. Klein has been working for years on a second novel, but it does not appear close to completion. He also edited *Twilight Zone* magazine from its inception in 1981 to 1985, and in that period it was the flagship journal of the field.

Klein is a master of horrific technique: he knows just what hints, suggestions, and allusions can allow the intelligent reader to sense the intrusion of the supernatural. In his best work he so modulates the pace of a tale that it grows cumulatively to a spectacular climax, but never with the least violence of diction and with scarcely any visible horror at all. But perhaps his greatest feat is a seamless blending of the mundane realism so prevalent in weird writing today (Dziemianowicz's "banalization" of horror) with the cosmic horror of Machen, Blackwood, and Lovecraft. His eye for the telling detail can humanize his characters and render them immediately recognizable. He can do in a paragraph or sentence what Stephen King cannot do in any number of his plodding pages. Of the central character of "Children of the Kingdom" (1980) it is said that "there still hung about him a certain air of comedy, as if it was his doom to provide the material for other people's anecdotes" (DG 5). But while paying meticulous attention to details of character and setting, he does not fail to paint a broader mood picture that suggests the grim and pitiable lot of human beings in a universe ruled by gods or forces that may be either cruelly indifferent or actually hostile to human life. *Dark Gods* is a highly appropriate title for Klein's best book, for his view of the world is dark, bitter, and pessimistic—almost in spite of himself.

What is strange about Klein is that in some of his nonfictional work he has uttered opinions suggesting that he is, or wants to be, an optimist who yearns for happy endings both in life and in literature. But his innate good sense as a writer and thinker prevails in his actual fiction, so that it doggedly fails to succumb to any Pollyanna-like resolutions. Klein has, indeed, acknowledged that he had no religious upbringing (FF 126). With Lovecraft, he maintains that "religions, all of them, the occult included, strike me as nonsense—pernicious nonsense, as often as not,"[8] and he goes on to claim that his view of the world is "pretty bleak": "I see it, really, as a crusher of dreams—a place where most living things experience a lot more pain and fear than pleasure, and where most hopes and ambitions are ultimately disappointed" (FF 133). But on the other side, in speaking of his editorial preferences for *Twilight Zone* magazine, he states the following:

"I preferred tales of a milder, more sentimental sort to the mailbags full of *contes cruels*, and remain to this day a sucker for happy endings" (RG 27). And elsewhere: "I'm a real sucker for sentimental stuff, stories that leave me with a lump in my throat" (FF 131). It is as if Klein knows the world is a pretty awful place, but finds literature appealing precisely when it papers the awfulness over with homespun sentimentality.

Why, then, does Klein write horror stories? Surely they tend—at least in the work of Lovecraft, Ramsey Campbell, and other writers whom Klein himself acknowledges as his models—to paint the universe as a cold, hostile, and perhaps evil place. But Klein the theorist apparently does not see it that way, although Klein the fiction writer does. Klein has written two significant essays on the aesthetics of weird fiction: the first a series of articles for *Twilight Zone* published under the collective title "Dr. Van Helsing's Handy Guide to Ghost Stories" (1981); the second a booklet charmingly titled *Raising Goosebumps for Fun and Profit* (1988), originally written for *Writer's Digest*. The latter derives much of its theoretical apparatus from the former, and the two taken together form a virtual *Poetics* of weird fiction—its purpose, appeal, and philosophical foundations. I am not at the moment concerned with assessing the merits of these elegant and sensitively written disquisitions, although they are considerable; I wish rather to emphasize how Klein's notions on the function of weird literature stand in antipodal contrast to his actual practice as a weird writer. We have already noted Klein's predilections for happy endings in literature. Now consider the following: "... the 'intended action' that Elizabeth Bowen spoke of as surviving death is, traditionally in ghost stories, an act of revenge, the fulfillment of some furious dying curse. And in delineating its consequences, the ghost story is capable of providing still another pleasure—the pleasure of returning to a moral order" (RG 9). And again: "There's another sort of comfort the horror tale provides. Its vision of a world menaced by dark supernatural forces has, within it, a happier corollary, one that may offer a further clue to the genre's appeal. The existence of a supernatural evil presupposes the existence—or at least the possibility—of an equal force for good" (RG 8).

The first is nothing more than a restating of the "happy ending" idea, but this time the notion is rendered explicitly philosophical and there is the suggestion that a representative proportion of weird literature conforms to a "moral order" wherein evil is defeated by good.[9] Unfortunately, Klein's fiction is almost never of this sort. The second passage, with its naive and erroneous metaphysics (there is no reason to imagine a balancing force of good in the world if there is a force of evil, and several religions and philosophies have conceived of only the latter), seems to me mere wishful thinking. We have already seen it in the thought of the Catholic William Peter Blatty, where the idea is propounded just as ridiculously as here. In any case, Klein, throughout the Van Helsing articles, is keen on employing I. A. Richards' distinction between intellectual and emotional belief in order to get around the awkward problem of unbelievers writing and reading about entities (ghosts, spirits, and the like) in which they manifestly do not believe: it is emotional belief that allows us to entertain the quasi-reality of these entities for the duration of the story, as we do when watching a play. But now Klein unwittingly applies intellectual belief to the ideas of the existence of life after death and of the triumph of good versus evil—ideas that can, on his own principles, only elicit emotional belief. Surely Klein cannot imagine that Lovecraft, thoroughgoing materialist that he was, is somehow ascribing actual belief in the various undead creatures with which he populates his tales.

Klein concludes that the real appeal of the weird tale is "vicarious fear":

> What we're dealing with, after all, are not real horrors; they are, in effect, defanged, to be enjoyed in a spirit of play. And the emotion they inspire is not fear, but a kind of toothless substitute—vicarious fear, if you will. It's what Dr. Johnson called "terror without danger ... a voluntary agitation of the mind, that is permitted no longer than it pleases," and what Virginia Woolf was alluding to when she remarked upon "the strange human craving for the pleasure of feeling afraid," noting that "it is pleasant to be afraid when we are conscious that we are in no kind of danger" [RG 5].

This is, as Klein's citations of Samuel Johnson and Virginia Woolf attest, an old and popular idea—we can always shut the book if we are too frightened!—but Klein doesn't seem to realize that it only applies to the innocuous "Christmas supplement" ghost story that was never meant to probe very deeply into the nature of the universe or the nature of human life. Of course we are in no physical "danger" when we read a weird tale. But are its effects so easily dispelled after we have finished it? And would any serious writer wish his work to be so "defanged" that it would have no effect upon us after we put the book aside? Do we not retain in our minds the notion of mankind's insignificance after we finish reading a tale by Lovecraft (or by Klein)?

All this signifies Klein's evidently sincere desire to make weird fiction a light-hearted amusement, although his own fiction is emphatically nothing of the sort. He has actually admitted that "If I had my druthers, I suppose I'd be writing light, humorous fiction with perhaps a touch of weirdness here and there."[10] Once again we see a sort of schizophrenic writer or, at the very least, a writer torn between what he wants in life and literature and what he is somehow compelled to do once he actually sits down to write a tale. Klein likes happy endings in literature, but where are they in his own work? Only a single story ends with the complete eradication of the horror, and this tale, "Hagendorn's House" (1987), is unconvincing precisely because the protagonist's triumph over the evil entity menacing him seems forced and contrived. Jeremy Freirs, the central figure in *The Ceremonies*, manages to subdue the horror at the end and get the girl in true sentimental romance fashion, but even he wonders whether the creature is permanently dispensed with. *The Ceremonies* is an elaboration of Klein's early tale, "The Events at Poroth Farm" (1972). In that tale Jeremy makes the remarkable assertion that "I remain, despite all that's happened, an optimist" (EP 3) (as Klein himself appears to be, or wishes he were) in spite of the fact that he is clearly being pursued by the supernatural entity that dogged him at Poroth Farm. Jeremy himself, like Klein, is a student of weird literature, and one of his comments is very revealing:

> Read some Shirley Jackson stories over breakfast, but got so turned off at her view of humanity that I switched to old Aleister Crowley, who at least keeps a sunny disposition. For her, people in the country are callous and vicious, those in the city are callous and vicious, husbands are (of course) callous and vicious, and children are merely sadistic. The only ones with feelings are her put-upon middle-aged heroines, with whom she obviously identifies. I guess if she didn't write so well the stories wouldn't sting so [EP 23].

Who is speaking here, Jeremy or Klein? Perhaps both. What Klein appears not to realize is the degree to which his own fiction mirrors the dark, dismal world of Shirley Jackson.

Klein's notions of a "moral order" supposedly affirmed by weird literature may be of some relevance in the analysis of one of his most powerful tales, "Nadelman's God" (1985). This is the only one of Klein's stories in which the religious or philosophical orientation of the protagonist is sketched in detail. As a young man Nadelman, raised in conventional belief in a benevolent God, finds that the reality of the world does not tally with such a rosy view: too many innocent people appear to have suffered harm and injustice. Nadelman then attempts to find a sort of logic to it all:

> By the time he'd reached high school, he'd discovered that, with a little intellectual effort, he could justify damned near anything—and it certainly helped stave off despair. Innocent people, it turned out, were

in no real danger; it was only the guilty who died. Did cigarette smok-
ers cough their lives away? They'd clearly brought it on themselves. Did
some alcoholic poet drink himself to death? It served him right. When
a planeload of nuns went down over the Andes, he told himself that
this was what happened to people who tried to jam their religion down
other people's throats. Pious do-gooders! [DG 197].

But this sort of sophomoric rationalization fails to stand up to scrutiny: it
is simply impossible to blame certain obviously guiltless persons for the mis-
fortunes they suffered. Nadelman revises his theology:

> He himself had reached a somewhat more reasonable conclusion:
> rather than worshiping God as a divine and highly arbitrary execu-
> tioner, it made more sense to see the position as vacant. There was no
> one in control up there. The office was empty. Nobody home.
>   Or maybe ... there was simply another god in charge, deranged
> and malign, delighting in cruelty and mischief [DG 198].

This seems to be simply cheap (and scarcely original) cynicism, but in any
event this world view serves as the basis for a long poem Nadelman writes
in college and publishes in the school literary magazine. To his surprise,
the poem is set to music years later by a heavy metal rock band, and so
comes to the attention of a half-deranged individual, Arlen Huntoon, who
sets about creating a "servant" to worship Nadelman's god, a servant "in
this new god's image" (DG 189). At this point Nadelman seems to be concerned only with a lunatic. But, through the subtlest of implications, it is
suggested that Huntoon's servant, made—as Nadelman's poem dictated—
of garbage (the symbolism of which scarcely requires elucidation), has actually come to life. Does this mean that Nadelman was right in thinking that
there is a malign god ruling the universe? Harried (so he believes) by the
garbage creature, he thinks back to a childhood vision he had of seeing a
vast, leering face in the sky. "Just as the sky darkened, beneath the glare of
eyes as big as galaxies, he had felt his foot slide, then sink into a hollow in
the sand. And the sand had opened beneath him, then pressed in upon
him, clutched him, tried to draw him in. As if the earth were yearning to
crush him, smother him, blot out the very memory of him. As if the planet,
all nature, all creation, the very fabric of reality, were inimical to breeds
such as his" (DG 247).
     I shall return to this tale elsewhere. Here I can point out what a bleak,
nihilistic picture of the cosmos Klein has painted in this masterful tale. If
there is any "moral order," it is "inimical to breeds such as his." Nadelman,
walking along the seashore, sees some lonely old men staring at the vacant

sea—"he wished he could conjure up a ship for them to watch, or even a small fishing boat" (DG 244)—but he can only conjure up an evil god and a servitor of garbage. And Nadelman the atheist can find little comfort at the end as he crawls into a synagogue and waits cowering for the dawn, hoping that his pursuer will be gone but knowing all too well that optimism of this sort is pathetically futile.

New York and Environs

As a lifelong New Yorker (aside from four years spent at Brown University and one year teaching high school in Maine) and a self-confessed "quintessential urban man" (FF 129), Klein has understandably been drawn to New York City as the source of both horror and fascination. Nearly every one of his tales is defined by its relation to New York: some are actually set there ("Children of the Kingdom," "Nadelman's God," "Black Man with a Horn" in part), others are set in locales physically close to but topographically and psychologically far from the metropolis ("The Events at Poroth Farm," "Petey," *The Ceremonies*).[11] It is as if New York City were a touchstone both for his life and for his work. Just as Klein himself seeks to escape the grinding strain of city life with brief jaunts to the country (he owns a cottage in a rural region well north of the city) but finds himself inexorably drawn back to the throbbing vitality of the urban milieu, so his fiction portrays New York as the locus of all horror; but the placid countryside presents only a spurious safety and proves to be as infested with the monstrous as the city.

"Children of the Kingdom" (1980) is a tale of cosmic horror that plays upon and inverts the racial tensions that have recently torn the city apart. The first-person narrator reflects the standard white New Yorker's fear of people of color ("Except for my reflection, I saw not one white face" [DG 3]) and a distaste for the decline of a neighborhood. But the true center of the story is the narrator's grandfather, Herman Lauterbach, who, although feisty and full of life, has reached the stage where he must be put in a nursing home. One is found for him in the Upper West Side, and this drab and dispiriting building serves as the setting for a tale that transmogrifies the daily horror of life in the city. The locus of horror in this tale is the basement (specifically the laundry room) of the nursing home. Klein sets the stage brilliantly by subtly altering his description of the home from the wry to the sinister when this critical location is reached:

> Our tour ended with the laundry room in the basement. It was hot
> and uncomfortable and throbbed with the echoes of heavy machinery,

> like the engine room of a freighter; you could almost feel the weight of
> the building pressing down on you. The air seemed thick, as if clogged
> with soapsuds, and moisture dripped from a network of flaking steam
> pipes suspended from the ceiling. Against one side stood four coin-
> operated dryers, staring balefully at four squat Maytag washers ranged
> along the opposite wall [DG 11].

The weird is introduced with Klein's characteristic deftness. Lauterbach collects a motley band of friends from the neighborhood, including
an aged black woman, Coralette, and a Costa Rican priest whom he nick-
names Father Pistachio. Coralette tells the strange tale of a black woman
who finds an intruder in her bedroom "just a lookin' down at her and
doin' somethin' evil to hisself" (DG 25). But this intruder turns out to be
a "*white* boy" (DG 25). Later we hear of another black girl who is found
dead in her room, an apparent suicide. Coralette finishes her tale laconi-
cally. "'I guess that boy of hers done left her all alone.' Coralette shook her
head sorrowfully. 'Seems a shame when you think of it, leavin' her like that,
'specially 'cause I recollect how proud she been. Say he was the first white
boyfrien' she ever had'" (DG 43).

It is at this point that Father Pistachio tells the bizarre tale of his
researches into an ancient and hideous race of beings who preyed upon
the Indians of central America until, as the legend goes, God first cursed
them by making their women sterile and then—when the creatures resorted
to mating with human women—by causing the males' penises to fall off.
Pistachio affirms that this loathsome race died long ago—but did it? And
what relevance does this wild tale have to the increasingly strange occurrences in modern New York? The connection is made when the narrator,
surveying a room of the nursing home in which an old woman was attacked
by some man, sees a strange mark on the door—"the outline of a crude,
five-pointed holly leaf scratched lightly in the wood" (DG 53). He thinks
of some pictures Pistachio had shown him:

> They say the night remembers what the day forgets. Pulling out
> the crudely bound orange book, I opened it to one of the drawings.
> There it was, that shape again, in the outline of the flipperlike
> gauntlets which Pistachio claimed his *usurpadores* had worn.
>   I got up and made myself some tea, then returned to the living
> room. Karen was still at her Wednesday evening class, and would not
> be back till nearly ten. For a long time I sat very still, with the book
> open on my lap, listening to the comforting rattle of the air condi-
> tioner as it shielded me against the night. One memory kept intruding:
> how, as a child, I liked to take a pencil and trace around the edges of
> my hand. This shape, I knew, is one that every child learns to draw.

I wondered what it would look like if the child's hands were webbed [DG 54].

This is one of the absolute high points in modern weird fiction, and prototypical of what may, perhaps not entirely accurately, be termed "quiet horror." Note that there is no explicit horror here, merely hideous suggestion. Note also that the horror is entirely mental and comes to the narrator in the relative security of his own apartment. As with Lovecraft, it is not what the horrors *do* that is so awful, but the mere fact that they *exist*: they suddenly render our rulership of the earth very tenuous. And yet, even this moment may be excelled by the gripping conclusion where the narrator, during the 1977 blackout, must descend the pitch-black stairs of the nursing home to the basement, where he encounters the monsters. "The door exploded in my face. I went down beneath a mob of twisting bodies pouring through the doorway, tumbling out upon me like a wave. I was kicked, tripped over, stepped on; I struggled to rise, and felt, in the darkness, the touch of naked limbs, smooth, rubbery flesh, hands that scuttled over me like starfish. In seconds the mob had swept past me and was gone; I heard them padding lightly up the hall, heading toward the stairs" (DG 59–60).

But a plot outline cannot begin to convey the atmospheric richness of this tale, with its crisp character portrayal, cumulative suspense, and most of all the "hints and portents" (as Steven J. Mariconda has termed it[12]) that typify Klein's horrific technique. Once again, however, I cannot resist drawing attention to a glaring contradiction between Klein's theory and his practice. In *Raising Goosebumps* he writes: "The world, with its troubles, is indeed too much with us, and the horrors it lays before us each day are all too real, ranging from the petty to the monstrous to the nearly unthinkable. Horror fiction offers us a means of keeping these realities at bay" (RG 1–2). The idea is, apparently, that imaginary horrors can somehow make us forget about the real horrors of life. But surely the reverse is the case in "Children of the Kingdom," which makes the horrors of city life *more real* than they were before. I am not merely referring to Klein's searing portrayal of the breakdown of the social fabric of the city in the blackout; rather, his loathsome white monsters who prowl maggotlike in the bowels of Manhattan are clear metaphors for the horrors of robbery, rape, murder, and other terrors that have made city life a sort of ongoing pitched battle in many of the metropolises of the world. There is no comfort in the existence of an added horror on top of (or, rather, beneath) the daily horrors of the city. And is there a political message here as well? Do the monsters who live underground, like the homeless people who actually live in the tunnels beneath Grand Central Station, symbolize the

underclass that threatens to topple a city that has deprived them of the
sustenance they require for a normal life?

"Petey" (1979) is another enormously skillful tale in which social satire
and horror again go hand in hand. Here we are taken out of the city into
the seemingly idyllic wilds of Connecticut, where a man has bought a large
estate for what he admits was a virtual steal. "'I have to keep reminding
myself how near we are to the city'" (DG 84), one character notes, compactly conveying both how near (literally) and how far (figuratively) this rural
domain is to New York, which now seems a haven of civilization in contrast to the dark woods of the Connecticut interior. The entire story is
nothing but a series of vignettes about a housewarming party held by the
new owners for their city friends; and what seems on the surface to be relatively innocuous satire directed at the various foibles of the guests is in
fact a vehicle for conveying with consummate subtlety hints of the menace
lurking nearby. These hints accumulate slowly: the place "stank like a sewer"
(DG 92) (from what?) when the owner, George Kurtz, first moved in; Kurtz
got the house so cheaply because the previous owner went mad (DG 84)
(how?); the house has a nursery, but the previous owner had no children
(DG 109–10); the man "'may have had a dog *or something* [my italics] to keep
him company'" (DG 93); the metal legs of the bed in the master bedroom
looked "chewed" (DG 93) (by what?); similarly, a department store man-
nequin that the previous owner had looks "pretty chewed up" (DG 94).
All this makes us now think twice about some earlier incidents, as when
one of the guests drove up in the dark and nearly hit some creature like a
bear (DG 81–82), or when someone gets lost on the road, comes upon a
little cabin near the house, and hears "something lumbering in the bushes"
(DG 83). I shall study the nature of this entity in a later section; here it
will suffice to point out that this seemingly rambling tale of a chaotic and
rather boring party of protoyuppies in fact contains not a single wasted
word. As in "Children of the Kingdom" and all Klein's best work, deft
character portrayal and an abundance of dialogue do not compromise the
gradual build-up of the horrific atmosphere (as they so often do in the
work of Stephen King and other lesser writers) but rather augment it. The
tale has perhaps a single flaw, and that is in the critical issue of *why* the
entity—raised by the original owner—chooses to attack the new occupants.
We learn that Kurtz gained the property in part through illegal collusion
with a government official (DG 107). But, in a series of interludes in which
we meet the original owner, now confined to a madhouse, we are led to
believe that he is concerned that his monstrous pet is merely hungry (DG
110, 118),[13] and there is no suggestion that this man is trying to gain revenge
on Kurtz for being ousted from his own house. So is Kurtz morally guilty

and therefore deserving of being set upon by a hideous creature, or isn't he? This question is never satisfactorily resolved, so that the broader rationale for the events of the tale remains perpetually clouded.

I wish to study *The Ceremonies* here, because I believe that in Klein's miraculous transformation of a 40-page novelette into a 500-page novel the work has undergone a considerable change of focus. This is not to say that either work is superior to the other: that question is now unanswerable, for the two have become entirely different entities, having nothing in common but the skeleton of the plot. "The Events at Poroth Farm" involved merely some strange goings-on in an obscure New Jersey community, and was primarily a masterful exercise in subtle suggestion and atmosphere. The novel has, as it were, *cosmicized* the idea to suggest a threat to the world at large, something only implicit in the novelette. The novel takes a considerable time gathering steam, but once it does it becomes hypnotic and compelling as few other weird novels of recent years. Once again we must admit that, while bulky, *The Ceremonies* contains very few extraneous words.

The entire novel rests upon the idea of manipulation. The Old One is an entity from the depths of space who, after thousands of years, possesses the body of a boy, Absolom Troet, in the late nineteenth century. He grows up and becomes a harmless-seeming old man, Mr. Rosebottom, who stage-manages the entire scenario: he has arranged for Jeremy Freirs to see the Poroths' advertisement for a summer guest; he has arranged for Carol Conklin to get a job at a library where she will meet Freirs; and he has even contrived it so that the Poroths take in a stray cat, Bwada, who serves a critical function in the fulfilling of the Ceremonies that the Old One must enact to bring about the destruction of the world. Jeremy mirrors Rosebottom in a bungling way by trying to manipulate Carol into sleeping with him. He fails in this attempt both through his own ineptness and through Rosebottom's timely interventions: he must keep Carol pure (she is a virgin) until the culmination of the Ceremonies.

Although Rosebottom's manipulation of the naive Carol (under the guise of using her as a research assistant in his study of ancient rituals) is one of the most chilling aspects of the novel, I think we could have done without the routine portrayals of the Old One's hatred of humanity:

> Once he had something in common with the figures crowding
> past him on the sidewalk; once, more than a century ago, he was one
> of them, part of the loathsome race that swarms over this planet. Now
> only the semblance remains, the organs, bones, and flesh. He has been
> washed clean of humanity; he feels no trace of kinship for these odious
> doomed beings, only a cold and unremitting hatred. As he passes down
> the avenue they part before him like stalks of corn [C 40].

This is textbook misanthropy, and it assumes that we will find these sentiments dreadful and reprehensible—as if human beings, by their mere existence, are worthy of benevolence. Half-hearted writing like this makes us long for the genuine misanthropy of Bierce or Shirley Jackson. Two other flaws that do not appreciably affect the novel's general excellence can be pointed out here: the curious introduction of Sarr Poroth's mother as a force of good, even though in the end she has little to do with the suppression of the horror; and the remarkably quick recovery, both physical and psychological, that Carol makes at the end after being loathsomely raped by an extraterrestrial. These things must be acknowledged and forgiven, for *The Ceremonies* remains in spite of them one of the landmarks of modern weird fiction.

The city-country dichotomy is played up much more in this work than in "The Events at Poroth Farm." It is not only that the novel (narrated in the omniscient third person rather than, as in the novelette, the first-person voice of Jeremy) continually shuttles between Freirs in New Jersey and Carol in New York; it is that the seemingly placid countryside becomes increasingly sinister and subject to incursions of the supernatural, and the city paradoxically becomes a haven of safety in spite of its well-known hazards. It is no surprise that Jeremy says at the outset in wonderment, "'Boy ... I feel as if New York's a thousand miles away'" (C 31). But it is noteworthy that much later we find he "was surprised how much he'd begun to miss the *Times*" (C 374), especially since exactly the opposite sentiment was expressed in the novelette ("'...it's strange how, after a week or two, you no longer miss it'" [EP 21]). Jeremy even seeks to leave Poroth Farm well before the summer is over; various events conspire to keep him there, however, which is just as well, or else he could not have played the hero and triumphed over the Old One just before (or, it is harrowingly suggested, just after) the Ceremonies are completed.

One of the most engaging aspects of *The Ceremonies* is its adaptation of certain basic themes from Arthur Machen's "The White People." Klein himself has admitted that the novel was an "attempt to update Arthur Machen" (FF 134); but in reality it is not so much an updating as an elaboration—a sort of partial clarification of the hints that Machen left perhaps too vague. It should be noted at this point that Klein is one of the most well-read figures in the field. As opposed to the off-the-cuff and frequently erroneous remarks that made Stephen King's *Danse Macabre* an embarrassment, Klein has written a comprehensive if discursive honors thesis on Lord Dunsany's influence on Lovecraft, a landmark appreciation of Ramsey Campbell, two sensitive introductions to books by Lovecraft, and reviews that are unfailingly acute. He has accordingly taken the basic framework of "The White People"—the initiation of an innocent young girl into the witch cult—and made it his own, a reconstructive task scarcely less impressive than the expansion of his original novelette (which bore far fewer Machenian parallels) into a novel. Rosebottom takes the place of the evil nurse who instructs Machen's little girl into loathsome but strangely alluring acts of sacrilege and perverted sex. Like the nurse who teaches the girl "the old language,"[14] Rosebottom claims to be initiating Carol into the "study of Agon di-Gatuan, the so-called 'Old Language'" (C 76). When, in "The White People," the girl remarks, "Besides these, I have the dances" (M 125), we suddenly understand Rosebottom's patient but insistent tutoring of Carol in archaic and vaguely hideous dances that have a bearing on the ceremonies to come—what Machen's little girl merely cites, with tantalising vagueness, as "the White Ceremonies, and the Green Ceremonies, and the Scarlet Ceremonies" (M 125). After reading Klein we know what these ceremonies really are. When Machen's little girl says, "The Scarlet Ceremonies are the best, but there is only one place where they can be performed properly" (M 125), it becomes clear why the Old One must make such elaborate contrivances to have his Scarlet Ceremony take place in the exact spot where he came to earth millennia ago. *The Ceremonies* is a textbook for creative and imaginative pastiche. The result is a vital and independent work that nonetheless draws strength and texture from previous work in the field.

WORDS AND THINGS

A curious subtheme, working entirely independently of the city-country idea, is evident from the beginning to the end of Klein's work. Put very simply, it could be termed the relation of words and things, of language and reality. To what degree does language govern reality? Is it conceivable that words can, in some direct way, affect the course of events? Considered in the abstract, these questions must clearly be answered in the affirmative, and they seem to involve nothing especially remarkable. But Klein poses the question in such a way that we may no longer think of words as harmless little spots on a page. The most clear-cut instance of the interrelation between words and things occurs in a recent story, "Ladder" (1990).

This deceptively simple tale has potentially stupefying implications. We are here introduced to a Scotsman reflecting upon his tragedy-scarred life. The lesson he has learnt is seemingly a grim one: "you live, you struggle, you learn and grow and suffer, and you realize, after nearly seventy years of searching, that your life has been nothing but a metaphor" (L 188).

What does this mean? The Scotsman has concluded that God works by a "ladder," the game in which one word can be changed into another by the successive substitution of a single letter (*dog* can become *cat* by progressing from *dog* to *cog* to *cot* to *cat*). His own life has progressed with the ladder of *birth* to *firth* to *forth* to *forts* to *ports* to *posts* to *costs* to *coats* to *boats* to *beats* to *heats* to *heath*. Along the way various awful things happen to ensure that this ladder is maintained (e.g., a crate of coats falls seemingly at random upon the man's friend). And only at this point do we realize that each segment of the story begins with the word that governs that stage of the man's life.

There are, I suppose, two interpretations of this story: either the man is mad or the world actually operates by the "ladder" device. I believe that the implication of the story, if not explicitly the latter, is at least meant to make us wonder harriedly: *What if God's ladder is a reality?* What if the fabric of the universe really is governed by words? This carries an added implication: *Nothing happens by accident*; what looks haphazard or serendipitous is in fact the secret workings of the "ladder" that rules and shapes all our lives. This story might be dismissed as a trick (it might, in fact, be called a kind of prose acrostic), but the "trick" is a singularly compelling and haunting one. It is only one of several Klein stories that ruminate on the power of words in human life.

Consider "Petey." If "Ladder" is based on a trick, this novelette is based upon a pun—and in two languages. When the mad owner of the house cries, "Petey!" it is thought that he is calling out to his son (DG 108); but the man has no son. He is crying not "Petey" but "P.D.," or "*Petit Diable*," or "Little Devil"—in other words, the lumbering bearlike entity that makes so dramatic an entrance at the end of the tale. Klein's concealment of this denouement is almost of the nature of a puzzle. We are first introduced to the term "Little Devil" (DG 111), then to a strange jar labeled "P.D. #14" (DG 113), and finally to the term "Petit Diable" (DG 121). But all this is buried under such a wealth of seemingly irrelevant description of the house party that one might be excused for not catching on to it until the end. I do not know that "Petey" has such staggering implications as "Ladder," at least in regard to the words-and-things issue, but it demonstrates how language can first mask and then reveal the horrors that lurk in the dark corners of life.

"Black Man with a Horn" (1980) may be considered in this context, for it too plays upon the possibility of words actually creating horror. This consciously Lovecraftian tale, written for Ramsey Campbell's *New Tales of the Cthulhu Mythos*, centers around a man clearly based upon Frank Belknap Long, an aged member of the "Lovecraft Circle" now remembered almost solely for his association with Lovecraft and not for his own voluminous but sadly mediocre fiction. The opening of the story is itself a play upon literary convention: "There is something inherently comforting about the first-person past tense. It conjures up visions of some deskbound narrator puffing contemplatively upon a pipe amid the safety of his study, lost in tranquil recollection, seasoned but essentially unscathed by whatever experience he's about to relate. It's a tense that says, 'I am here to tell the tale. I lived through it'" (DG 131). In this case, the first-person past tense is far from reassuring because this single individual's "safety" is the least of his own concerns. He may have "lived through it," but he is aware that it is not his own fate but the world's that is at stake. The narrator comes across a harrowing instance of words blending insidiously into reality when, in a museum, he sees a display of ancient Malayan figures to which the catalogue applies the term "Tcho-tcho." The narrator knows of the term only through Lovecraft's reference to "the wholly abominable Tcho-Tchos," and had always fancied that Lovecraft had invented the term in a spirit of fun. Now he finds that the entities to which the term refers are, in some sense, real. "I'd been put in the uncomfortable position of living out another man's horror stories" (DG 151). This piquant expression is not meant entirely literally (the idea, of course, is that what one once thought to be fiction may have a reality of a sort) but it again suggests that insidious mingling of words and things which we have seen elsewhere. And I cannot resist quoting a later passage describing the entity introduced in this tale, where a Malay boy is interviewed by a filmmaker:

> INT: This Malay youth has sketched a picture of a demon he calls Shoo Goron. (To Boy) I wonder if you can tell me something about the instrument he's blowing out of it. It looks like the Jewish *shofar*, or ram's horn. (Again to Boy) That's all right. No need to be frightened.
> BOY: He not blow out. Blow in.
> INT: I see—he draws air in through the horn, is that right?
> BOY: No horn. Is no horn. (Weeps) Is *him* [DG 162–63].

This too is one of the most shuddersome moments in modern weird fiction—rarely have two words packed such a concentrated dose of loathsome implication.

"Nadelman's God" more explicitly foreshadows the theme of "Ladder." It is bad enough that the crazed Huntoon has created the servitor in accordance with the instructions embedded in Nadelman's poem, which was, of course, written in a spirit of iconoclastic satire. What is worse is that "Huntoon had all but suggested not only that the god was a reality, but that Nadelman himself was responsible for its existence" (DG 241). This is because Huntoon refers to the god as The Hungerer, a term not found in the published version of Nadelman's poem but only in his original draft, which Huntoon could not possibly have seen. It is this occurrence that really transforms the tale from one of mere paranoia (Nadelman pursued by a lunatic) to one of supernatural horror. Nadelman reflects:

> Was it possible?—that, in some latter-day Naming of Names, he had given the god life in the very act of naming it, and given its flesh substance with every new line of his poem?
> How weird that would be: the notion that the universe might in fact be listening to him, waiting upon his decisions, his carefully chosen words, responding to his commands. How had that line from the poem gone? "'I'll create Me a Creator,' He would say"—a god made to order?
> But what a dreadful responsibility to contemplate! For it meant that he might in some way be the original cause of the very things that had always appalled and horrified him, all the work of the dark god he'd invented: the fathers stabbed, the mothers raped, the children left to starve [DG 241–42].

To this little need be added. If an undistinguished and insignificant person like Nadelman can create an evil god out of words, then our life on this planet may be one long series of miseries. Here again, as in "Ladder," nothing happens at random: all the evil in the world is the product of an idiot god created by the cheap cynicism of a sophomore.

It is now time to return to "The Events at Poroth Farm." The premise of the novelette is the arrival of Jeremy at Poroth Farm for the summer so that he can bone up on a class on supernatural fiction that he will be teaching in the fall semester. Jeremy spends much of his time reading the classics of weird fiction (more here than in the novel), and indeed he admits that he is "bookish" (EP 27). It is possible, therefore, to interpret the tale (as I have done in an earlier article[15]) as centering around the disjunction between words and things, literature and reality: Jeremy is so wrapped up in books and, more generally, accustomed to reacting to "real" events in a self-consciously literary way, that he is doubly shattered when actual horror breaks loose upon him. For Jeremy, horrors ought to be confined to the printed page, and he is woefully inadequate in dealing with them when they occur to him in reality.

Jeremy both plays upon and flouts literary convention—or, at any rate, the conventions of the standard horror novel or film. In clearing his rented room (a converted chicken coop) of the many bugs, especially spiders, that infest it, he likens himself to the victim of a trite horror film who suffers the revenge of the spiders (EP 7). And yet, he remarks at the outset, "Rural townspeople are not so reticent as the writers would have us believe" (EP 4), indicating a sophisticated awareness of how misleading certain literary stereotypes can be. Later, when he hears something strange outside his room, he declares: "I had no intention of going out there with my flash-light in search of the intruder—that's for guys in stories. I'm much too chicken" (EP 20). But he can still long for the "happy ending" (EP 19) that he notes with satisfaction in Wilhelm Meinhold's *The Amber Witch*: why can't life turn out that way? I have already noted how Jeremy sees himself as an "optimist" even after all the horrible events of the tale, and with the prospect of worse to come. He presents himself to us, then, as a strange combination of naiveté and sophistication: naive about life, but sophisti-cated about literature.

Is this his failing? Is it that he cannot comprehend how real life can turn into a horror tale? Certain passages toward the end suggest this. Jeremy has written a diary throughout his stay at Poroth Farm, and he is now pre-senting it to us, although in an artfully edited form. (This itself, as he well knows, is an old literary convention, and it creates exactly the sort of nar-rative within narrative that he ridicules in Charles Robert Maturin's *Mel-moth the Wanderer* [EP 10], although his interior narrative is much more integrated into the overall tale than Maturin's.) But toward the end, when the real horror finally emerges and he flees the farm, he notes tellingly: "Here my journal ends. Until today, almost a week later, I have not cared to set down any of the events that followed" (EP 35). In other words, he finds that his literary reactions are simply inadequate to encompass what he has actually experienced. In a sense Jeremy's diary has been a *shield* against the horrors that increasingly impinge upon him: by setting them down on paper he has partially exorcised them. But the concluding hor-ror is so overwhelming that this method of rationalization is denied him; the written word is insufficient to negate it. Later he remarks: "Lord, this heat is sweltering. My shirt is sticking to my skin, and droplets of sweat are rolling down my face dripping onto this page, making the ink run. My hand is tired from writing..." (EP 40). The symbolism here is very telling: the ink runs because what Jeremy has experienced is literally "ineffable"— it cannot be told. He is tired of writing because the vicarious emotions inspired by literature are pathetically inadequate in the face of real horror. By referring so constantly to literature and writing, and by implying how secondary and inadequate they are, Klein augments the sense of the *real-ity* of what Jeremy has experienced.

This interpretation—the inadequacy of language to express reality—

can, I believe, be derived quite plausibly from "The Events at Poroth Farm." But I now wish to present an entirely different interpretation, one that may link the story more closely to such tales as "Nadelman's God" and "Ladder" with their notions of the power of words to create a reality out of whole cloth. Is it conceivable that all the works of horror literature Jeremy reads while at Poroth Farm in some way affect or even shape the events that occur there? Whereas in "Nadelman's God" the mere act of writing seems to have engendered a horrific god, does the act of reading actually cause the events at Poroth Farm?

Such a formulation may perhaps be too strong, but it is possible to see in Jeremy's readings a sort of symbolic echo—or, in some cases, anticipation—of the increasingly disturbing manifestations that take place around him. His readings generally progress in a chronological sequence, from the Gothic novels of the late eighteenth century to selected works of the middle twentieth century. His reaction to the Gothic novels—*The Mysteries of Udolpho, Melmoth the Wanderer, The Castle of Otranto, The Monk*—are what one might expect of a sophisticated twentieth-century reader: they are too long, the events they depict are implausible, they are structurally flawed. Taken together, these comments may well be a metafictional hint of what Klein himself does *not* want to do: his tale will be compact; it will be grimly realistic by capturing the minutiae not only of setting and mood but also of character; and the incorporation of the diary will result not in structural confusion but in a smooth-flowing narrative. A further comment by Jeremy on *Udolpho* may have some bearing on the psychology of the tale. In remarking on its length, He tries to compensate by putting himself into the frame of mind of an eighteenth-century reader with "plenty of time on his hands." The result: "It works, too—I do have plenty of time out here, and already I can feel myself beginning to unwind. What New York does to people..." (EP 8). This proves to be a short-lived attempt by Jeremy to adjust his city mentality to the pace of country life. It is interesting that when he later tries to read *Walden* as a break from his diet of literary horror, he finds himself unable to do so—on account of his watery eyes, he claims (EP 20), but also, perhaps, because he is increasingly coming to believe that the country is not the haven of repose he initially fancied.

Two interruptions in the chronological sequence of Jeremy's Gothic readings are of great importance. He first reads Machen's "The White People." A clearer tip of the hat to the literary influence that governs this tale would be harder to find, the influence primarily being in the device of the diary and in the notion of dark secrets concealed in the untamed wilderness. (As we have noted, *The Ceremonies* owes much more to the Machen story than does "The Events at Poroth Farm.") Shortly thereafter he reads

Algernon Blackwood's "Ancient Sorceries," which he describes as a "witch/cat story" (EP 11). The significance of this detail is also obvious, as the cat Bwada plays a central role in the unfolding of the horrific scenario.

Jeremy then reads *Dracula*, which, like "Ancient Sorceries," at least suggests the theme of psychic possession, the dominant motif in "The Events at Poroth Farm." Later comes LeFanu, and Jeremy's comment is of interest: "Read some LeFanu. 'Green Tea,' about the phantom monkey with eyes that glow, and 'The Familiar,' about the little staring man who drives the hero mad. Not the smartest choices right now, the way I feel, because for all the time that fat grey cat purrs over the Poroths, it just stares at me" (EP 18). These stories do not simply disturb Jeremy's equilibrium, both tales, in addition, are a sort of commentary on what has happened (we are dealing here not with a phantom monkey but, virtually, a phantom cat—one that is possessed by the baleful entity of the tale) or what will happen (one of the entity's failings, as Sarr notes toward the end, is that "Sometimes we forget to blink" [EP 38], so that it just stares and stares).

It is at this point that Jeremy reads Shirley Jackson, with her bleak and misanthropic world view. Is he simply too naive to acknowledge the truth of what Jackson writes, or is it that her tales of unhappy husbands and wives point chillingly to the impending dissolution of the Poroths' marriage in horror and death? Worse, Jeremy then reads Ruthven Todd's *Lost Traveller*, which he describes as "Merely the narrative of a dream turned to nightmare, and illogical as hell" (EP 27). But has not Jeremy's dream of a summer full of pleasantly shuddersome reading in the tranquil countryside turned into a nightmare? And the events he has experienced over the last several days are certainly illogical as hell—at least to him, who cannot see the overall pattern of possession as the entity leaps from one being to another, perhaps ad infinitum.

It is, perhaps, not possible to juxtapose all Jeremy's readings with the events at Poroth Farm, but a representative number of them seem to be clear reflections or foreshadowings of what is going on around him. Words are again intimately interconnected with things. I do not think that the two interpretations I have put forth for this tale are mutually exclusive; they could well work in tandem. Indeed, I wish to draw attention to one passage in particular which could be said to harmonize with both interpretations. As the horror is reaching a climax, Jeremy remarks plaintively: "What if some horror stories aren't really fiction? If Machen sometimes told the truth? If there *are* White People, malevolent little faces peering out of the moonlight? Whispers in the grass? Poisonous things in the woods? Perfect hate and evil in the world?" (EP 31). On one level, this passage could be taken as another instance of Jeremy's naiveté about life, but, conversely, it could be a summation of what has actually transpired in the tale. In other words, Jeremy is right. It should be noted that the final sentence has been altered in the latest version of the story: the word "perfect" has been added (just as the word "unsuspected" was added when this passage appeared in *The Ceremonies* [C 439]). This addition may be of significance: whereas the query as to whether there is "hate and evil in the world" might lead one to dismiss Jeremy as hopelessly naive (of course there is hate and evil in the world), the revised sentence points to a supernatural or transcendent hatred and evil that no amount of sophistication could anticipate. Just as, I believe, Klein wishes us to think that the battered Scotsman of "Ladder" is correct in his theology, so here we are to take Jeremy absolutely at his word: he is uttering nothing but the harrowing truth.

"The Events at Poroth Farm" ranks with the best of Klein's novelettes and has in no way been superseded by *The Ceremonies*, impressive as that novel is. If the tale is a sort of hundred-yard dash, the novel is a marathon: the former must be consumed in a sitting; the latter lived with for days to absorb its cumulative effect. The cosmic scope of the novel is only tangentially evident in the novelette, but the latter is nevertheless a masterwork of indirection and subtlety, fit to take its place with "Nadelman's God," "Children of the Kingdom," and "Petey" at the very pinnacle of Klein's shorter work.

In close to 25 years of writing Klein has only two books and a handful of scattered tales to his credit, and yet his achievement towers gigantically over that of his more prolific contemporaries. There is, indeed, a virtue to such compactness—let us recall that Lovecraft's collected fiction, also the work of two decades, fits comfortably into only three substantial volumes. But Klein's many readers are left in a perpetual state of frustration over the paucity of his output. He blithely promised us his second novel by 1986 (FF 135), but there is now no telling when or if this is likely to appear. Even his short fiction is not abundant. Several early tales—"Magic Carpet," "Renaissance Man," "Camera Shy"—have already found the oblivion they deserve, and he has written very few stories since *Dark Gods*.

We have already noted Klein's greatest accomplishment in weird fiction: his melding of the cosmic horror of Lovecraft and Blackwood with the psychological realism of the modern weird movement. In this he is rivaled perhaps only by Ramsey Campbell. But where in Campbell this melding is achieved through an enhanced emphasis on a disturbed psyche, Klein effects the union more harmoniously, so that there is an exquisite balance between external and internal horror—the horror of a hostile cosmos and the horror of a possibly deranged mentality. In wielding a prose style of great suppleness but also of quiet strength, in being a master technician of the weird short story, in delineating character and setting with both humor and piquancy, in painting mood and atmosphere with seemingly effortless ease, Klein so far outdistances his colleagues in weird fiction that he ought to achieve significant recognition in general literature. One simply wishes that his pen flowed a little more freely.

CLIVE BARKER: SEX, DEATH, AND FANTASY

When Clive Barker's *Books of Blood* were published by Sphere Books in London in 1984–85, the world took notice. Hitherto known only as a dramatist whose plays had been performed but not published, Barker (b. 1952) accomplished a feat almost unheard of in publishing by having not one but six paperback volumes of his short stories issued by a major firm. At a time when even established authors in the field had difficulty in publishing collections of short fiction, Barker's achievement was more than unusual. Barker has now issued a novel, *The Damnation Game* (1985), a novella, "The Hellbound Heart" (1986), and three more novels, *Weaveworld* (1987), *The Great and Secret Show* (1989), and *Imajica* (1991), along with a short novel, *Cabal* (1988), a young adult novel, *The Thief of Always* (1992), and random other short stories. *The Great and Secret Show*, subtitled "The First Book of The Art," was the first in a projected series of four or five novels. Barker has also attempted to write and direct films, with middling success, and has allowed his work to be adapted into comic books (or "graphic novels," as they are pretentiously called), although he himself has had little to do with their conception or execution.

Early in his career Barker was lauded by Stephen King with the now famous tag, "I have seen the future of horror ... and it is named Clive Barker." In consequence, not only has Barker received generally more favorable reviews in the mainstream press, but higher expectations have been generated for his work than for popular bestseller material such as King's. And it is reasonable to demand greater literary substance from Barker, especially as he himself is not shy about claiming such substance for himself. But whether he belongs in the class of Blackwood, Dunsany, and Lovecraft (or of Shirley Jackson and Ramsey Campbell) is far from clear.

The keynote of Barker's early work is a frenetic mix of gruesome physical horror, rather conventional supernaturalism, and explicit sex. It would be untrue to say that Barker is aiming purely at shock value in all this, but it is also untrue to believe that he has the literary skill to raise this subject matter very much above the level of sensationalism. Barker is a writer of considerable imagination but extraordinarily slipshod style, conception, and execution. Like many writers, he has already written (or published) too much. It would not be an exaggeration to say that, of his voluminous work, perhaps only five or six stories from the *Books of Blood* and *The Damnation Game* are all that are worth reading.

What I find most interesting about Barker is his place in the history of weird fiction. He is in many ways a herald of the complete and possibly irremediable decadence of the field. He is the prototypical example of the tendency I have noted in my introduction: the failure to give a plausible *account* of supernatural phenomena. Everything in Barker is directed toward the level of pure sensation.

Let us consider "Sex, Death and Starshine." Here we are asked to believe that ghosts of old actors are presiding over the final performance of a Shakespeare play at an old theatre about to be demolished. But Barker provides no rationale (not even one acceptable on supernatural grounds) for how the bodies of those old actors, and the living actors whom they kill, simply come back to life for this final curtain call. Consider the resurrection of Tallulah, an aged employee who has been at the theatre since its heyday 50 years before. She is killed by Lichfield, the leader of the band of deceased actors, but this is of no consequence: "She'd cool easily in the chill of the room, and be up and about again by the time the audience arrived" (BB1, 156). This single sentence encapsulates what might be called the *fossilization* of weird fiction: its transformation from an outgrowth of a philosophical position to a conventionalized genre in which certain events have become standardized because they have been used so often. Barker has no doubt encountered so many instances of the resurrection of the dead (in stories, novels, movies, and comic books) that he no longer feels the need to explain it—it simply provides an excuse for a certain type of frisson that is to be experienced as such without any thought of its plausibility or its philosophical or aesthetic purpose. In this case, we are evidently to be entertained at the prospect of witnessing a dead actress giving a still living director a blow job (he is amazed that she does not breathe during the process). It never seems to occur to Barker to wonder, if these particular corpses can be reanimated so effortlessly, why all corpses do not behave this way.

This identical problem mars another, later work, *Cabal*, and in such a way as to suggest that the absence of a rationale for the supernatural is not merely a technical failing on Barker's part but something that he feels is simply not necessary in a tale of this sort. *Cabal* rests upon the presupposition that there exists a place called Midian where only "monsters" (i.e., those who have apparently committed heinous crimes) are welcome. In fact, these monsters are simply the resurrected dead. How did this happen? A desperate man who thinks he has committed a series of murders seeks out Midian. Although he discovers that it is not on any map (C 32), he and other characters end up finding it relatively easily in the north of Canada. He is eventually gunned down by a pursuing posse of police but calmly walks out of the morgue for further adventures. Only toward the end of the novel do we get a faint rationale for how this could have occurred: he was previously bitten by one of the undead and was therefore "infected" (C 154). But this only pushes the question back one step further: how did the undead become "infected"? Is there something about criminals that causes them to come back from the dead? It is all entirely unaccounted for, and this short novel simply collapses from its own absurdity.

Other stories in the *Books of Blood* also suffer from serious conceptual difficulties. "The Midnight Meat Train" is riddled with implausibilities of plot. Although Barker now spends much of his time in New York, it is painfully obvious that he had not been there at the time he wrote this story, since its account of horrors on the subway is full of transparent mistakes (there is no "Avenue of the Americas" line; one cannot hear conversation from one subway car to the next). These implausibilities, however, could have been acceptable if Barker had restricted the story to one of suspense in which a man going home late at night on the subway is attempting to escape a serial killer in the next car. But the story rapidly becomes preposterous when we are asked, with apparent seriousness, to believe that the serial killer is really feeding the bodies he kills to the "City fathers" (BB1, 47) who live in the bowels of the subway. Here again we are presented with the ludicrous proposition that these City fathers must eat human flesh to remain alive (BB1, 46)—why should this be the case?

The height of absurdity is reached when, at what is presumably meant to be the grand horrific climax, we encounter "the original American" (BB1, 48) who rules this band of cannibals. "It was a giant. Without head or limb. Without a feature that was analogous to human, without an organ that made sense, or senses. If it was like anything, it was like a shoal of fish. A thousand snouts all moving in unison, budding, blossoming and withering rhythmically. It was iridescent, like mother of pearl, but it was sometimes deeper than any color Kaufman knew, or could put a name to" (BB1, 49). But Barker has failed to think out this conception adequately. What significance, political or otherwise, is intended here? Evidently the only

object of this "original American" is to inspire physical disgust at its repulsive appearance. Barker is saying nothing of importance about the horror
and decadence of the city, or of their causes.

Even some of Barker's better tales have flaws in conception, especially
on the key issue of where and how the supernatural enters into the matter. "Son of Celluloid" is a powerful tale of a criminal who dies behind the
screen of an old movie theatre and in some fashion causes the revival of
the famous actors and actresses who enlivened that screen, but again the
critical issue of how this is actually accomplished is not carefully worked
out. Here is Barker's account:

> The space however, like the air itself, had lived a life of its own in
> that fifty years. Like a reservoir, it had received the electric stares of
> thousands of eyes, of tens of thousands of eyes. Half a century of
> movie goers had lived vicariously through the screen of the Movie
> Palace, pressing their sympathies and their passions on to the flickering
> illusion, the energy of their emotions gathering strength like a
> neglected cognac in that hidden passage of air. Sooner or later, it must
> discharge itself. All it lacked was a catalyst.
> Until Barberio's cancer [BB3, 8].

Cancer, I suppose, is one of the great horrors of our time, but that it makes
the resurrection of Marilyn Monroe possible might strain anyone's credulity.
The imagery and atmosphere of the story are highly effective, but, like so
much of Barker, the tale is crippled by its ludicrous premise.

"Rawhead Rex" is the moderately entertaining story of a huge, nine-
foot-tall creature who crawls out from under a rock in a field and rampages
through the countryside; but the only account we get of the entity is from
a human who has fallen under its influence: "'There were things that owned
this land. Before Christ. Before civilization. Most of them didn't survive
the destruction of their natural habitat: too primitive I suppose. But strong.
Not like us; not human. Something else altogether'" (BB3, 57). Barker evidently feels that this half-baked anthropology is sufficient. It is clear that
the true aim of the story is simply to inspire disgust at the creature on
account of its penchant for munching on innocent children:

> It was half past eleven at night. Rawhead Rex lay under the moon
> in one of the harvested fields to the southwest of the Nicholson Farm.
> The stubble was darkening now, and there was a tantalizing smell of
> rotting vegetable matter off the earth. Beside him lay his dinner, Ian
> Ronald Milton, face up on the field, his midriff torn open. Occasion-
> ally the beast would lean up on one elbow and paddle its fingers in the
> cooling soup of the boy child's body, fishing for a delicacy.

> Here, under the full moon, bathing in silver, stretching his limbs and eating the flesh of human kind, he felt irresistible. His fingers drew a kidney off the plate beside him and he swallowed it whole. Sweet [BB3, 80].

One winces at this—not at what is being described but at Barker's fatuity in believing that such ham-fisted sadism can genuinely affect an adult reader.

It is already evident that much of Barker's work contains an element of political or social criticism, but it is equally evident that much of this is superficial in the extreme. "In the Hills, the Cities" contains, as Ramsey Campbell states in his introduction to the *Books of Blood* (BB1, xii), one of the more original monsters in horror fiction: a huge figure made up of thousands of human beings who practice for years to perfect the motions suitable for their respective places in the entity's anatomy. But the whole conception becomes trivialized by being used as a facile satire on the collectivist state: we are behind the Iron Curtain, where the "illusion of petty individuality was swept away in an irresistible tide of collective feeling" (BB1, 197). As if this passage, and others like it, were not enough, Barker feels the need to editorialize bluntly in order to convey his message to even the least astute reader: "Locked in their positions, strapped, roped and harnessed to each other in a living system that allowed for no single voice to be louder than any other, nor any back to labor less than its neighbor's, they let an insane consensus replace the tranquil voice of reason. They were convulsed into one mind, one thought, one ambition. They became, in the space of a few moments, the single-minded giant whose image they had so brilliantly recreated" (BB1, 196–97).

"Babel's Children" is an exercise in cheap political satire. It is a tale of a young woman traveling on an island off the coast of Greece and stumbling upon a group of aged individuals who are actually governing the world because elected heads of state are too stupid to do so. "'We run the *world*. It wasn't meant to be that way, but as I said, systems decay. As time went by the potentates—knowing they had us to make critical decisions for them—concerned themselves more and more with the pleasures of high office and less and less with *thinking*. Within five years we were no longer advisors, but surrogate overlords, juggling nations'" (BB5, 89). After a time these people no longer rule the world by reason but merely by playing games of chance to determine the resolution of events. And when all but one of them die in an escape attempt, the woman is forced to take over their position. All this is presented in a somewhat lighthearted manner, but it cannot conceal the poverty of genuine and penetrating political insight that a story like this must offer.

"The Forbidden" is the one story in Barker's work that seems to promise a somewhat more interesting and subtle social commentary. Here a middle-class woman working on a thesis on graffiti enters a ghetto seeking source material. Instead, she encounters vague rumors of a horrible murder that took place there recently. She has trouble verifying the account, and her friends scoff at her and think she has been taken in by a hoax or fabrication. But as the woman becomes more and more acclimated to her ghetto surroundings, she comes to find her friends effete and smart-alecky. She has undergone a slow cultural transformation. "Nor was it simply the presence of so many people that reassured her; she was, she conceded to herself, happy to be back here in Spector Street. The quadrangles, with their stunted saplings and their grey grass, were more real to her than the carpeted corridors she was used to walking; the anonymous faces on the balconies and streets meant more than her colleagues at the University. In a word, she felt *home*" (BB5, 29). She meets the Candyman, a figure who embodies the rumors that come out of the ghetto. Eventually she succumbs, in a scene that poignantly combines horror, pathos, and bitter cynicism:

> Perhaps they would remember her, as he had said they might, finding her cracked skull in tomorrow's ashes. Perhaps she might become, in time, a story with which to frighten children. She had lied, saying she preferred death to such questionable fame; she did not. As to her seducer, he laughed as the conflagration sniffed them out. There was no permanence for him in this night's death. His deeds were on a hundred walls and ten thousand lips, and should he be doubted again his congregation could summon him with sweetness. He had reason to laugh [BB5, 37].

The story continually wavers between mundane fear (fear of rape or murder) and metaphysical fear. It is one of Barker's few early successes.

From a slightly different perspective, sociopolitical considerations enter indirectly through the dismal, grim, and generally lower-class settings and characters of the majority of his tales. Is Barker saying that horror only affects such areas and such figures? This presupposition is very strong. As he writes in *The Damnation Game*:

> Hell is reimagined by each generation. Its terrain is surveyed for absurdities and remade in a fresher mold; its terrors are scrutinized and, if necessary, reinvented to suit the current climate of atrocity; its architecture is redesigned to appall the eye of the modern damned. In an earlier age Pandemonium—the first city of Hell—stood on a lava

mountain while lightning tore the clouds above it and beacons burned on its walls to summon the fallen angels. Now, such spectacle belongs to Hollywood. Hell stands transposed. No lightning, no pits of fire.

In a wasteland a few hundred yards from a highway overpass it finds a new incarnation: shabby, degenerate, forsaken. But here, where fumes thicken the atmosphere, minor terrors take on a new brutality. Heaven, by night, would have all the configurations of Hell [DG 327].

Accordingly, Barker's settings include prisons ("Pig Blood Blues," "In the Flesh," "The Body Politic" in part), seedy hotels ("Revelations"), and the ghetto ("The Forbidden"). Among his characters are sadists ("Dread"), ignorant and uncouth townspeople ("The Skins of the Fathers"), criminals ("Son of Celluloid"), pornographers ("Confession of a (Pornographer's) Shroud"), prostitutes both female ("Jacqueline Ess: Her Will and Testament") and male ("Human Remains"), young thugs ("The Inhuman Condition"), oily fundamentalist preachers ("Revelations"), and the like.

But it would be too comforting to imagine that horror never strays beyond the prison or the ghetto, and some of Barker's most powerful tales are those in which middle-class characters are drawn inexorably into what Bruce Springsteen has called the "darkness on the edge of town." We have already seen this mingling of class in "The Forbidden." "Confession of a (Pornographer's) Shroud" also effects this union, involving an accountant who unwittingly works for a group of pornographers and loses his wife, children, and ultimately his life as a result. This is, however, not the end but the beginning of the story: in some unexplained fashion the accountant's spirit remains alive (Barker's offhand comment that "There was still a will to revenge in him" [BB3, 99] is wholly useless as a plausible rationale) and actually animates his shroud into a human form. The influence of M. R. James's "'Oh, Whistle, and I'll Come to You, My Lad'" is very obvious, and Barker makes no secret of it: his remark that "He'd seen what freak creases could do, making faces appear in a crumpled pillow" (BB3, 104), precisely echoes James's climactic statement whereby the invisible entity in his story reveals a "face of crumpled linen."[16] Nevertheless, the story, although merely a tale of revenge, is effectively grim. We will see later, in *The Damnation Game*, that even the wealthiest of us are not immune from the intrusion of horror emerging from the depths of history and of the underclass.

As it is, one of the most interesting features of Barker's work is a powerful mix of sex and death in such a way that the one leads to the other, and vice versa. In Barker there is an intimate connection between sex, violence, and death. As he wrote with some pungency in *The Damnation Game*: "It wasn't difficult to smudge sexuality into violence, turn sighs into screams, thrusts into convulsions. The grammar was the same; only the punctuation differed" (DG 153). It is interesting that one of the most wholesome sexual passages in all his work occurs toward the opening of "In the Hills, the Cities," in which we are given a lengthy, explicit, and powerful vignette of homosexual love between two male companions. The heterosexuals in Barker's tales rarely act with such honesty and purity.

"The Age of Desire" is perhaps Barker's most powerful story. Here a man is given a drug that so stimulates his sexual desire that everything becomes seductive:

> Aroused beyond control, he turned to the wall he had been leaning against. The sun had fallen upon it, and it was warm: the bricks smelt ambrosial. He laid kisses on their gritty faces, his hands exploring every nook and cranny. Murmuring sweet nothings, he unzipped himself, found and accommodating niche, and filled it. His mind was running with liquid pictures: mingled anatomies, female and male in one undistinguishable congress. Above him, even the clouds had caught fire; enthralled by their burning heads he felt the moment rise in his gristle. Breath was short now. But the ecstasy?; surely that would go on forever [BB4, 132].

The sociological message here is clear—a commentary on the complete sexualization of our minds and our age. As one character remarks, "'All our so-called higher concerns become secondary to the pursuit [of sex]. For a short time sex makes us obsessive; we can perform, or at least we *think* we can perform, what with hindsight may seem extraordinary feats'" (BB5, 136). Later it is said of the drugged patient: "His back ached, his balls ached: but what was his body now?; just a plinth for that singular monument, his prick. Head was *nothing*; mind was *nothing*" (BB5, 140–41). It is clear what we have become: "The world had seen so many Ages. The Age of Enlightenment; of Reformation; of Reason. Now, at last, the Age of Desire. And after this, an end to Ages; an end, perhaps, to everything. For the fires that were being stoked now were fiercer than the innocent world suspected. They were terrible fires, fires without end, which would illuminate the world in one last, fierce light" (BB5, 136).

Other stories on this theme are rather less successful. Two are feminist in their suggestion that men are useless encumbrances in the entire process of birth, life, and death. In "The Skins of the Fathers" we encounter bizarre monsters who have impregnated a woman in a small desert community. The intimation is that these creatures have created all earth life: "The creatures who were his fathers were also men's fathers; and the marriage of semen in Lucy's body was the same mix that made the first males. Women had always existed: they had lived, a species to themselves, with the demons. But they had wanted playmates: and together they had made men" (BB2, 147). But this transparent reversal of the myth of Eve's creation from Adam is presented too bluntly to be effective, and the story rapidly devolves into an exercise in bloodletting. Somewhat better is "The Madonna," in which a loathsome monster called the Madonna, the "Virgin Mother" (BB5, 66), is shown to give birth without the need of men. A male character who has had intercourse with her wakes up one day to find that he has become a woman. But what is the true point of the story? It is never made clear. "Jacqueline Ess: Her Will and Testament" (BB2) may be mentioned in this connection, as it deals with a woman who, purely through the power of her will, is capable of physically destroying human beings, usually men. If anything, the story hints at the superior strength of women, but beyond this it seems to lack direction and focus.

"Dread" is less obviously sexual, but, as Barker's most effective non-supernatural story, it carries a clear message about men's habitual abuse of women. A philosophy professor decides to carry out an experiment on a bright young female student whom he perhaps considers too challenging to his intellectual supremacy: he subjects her to hideous torture whereby she, a vegetarian, is locked in a room with a gradually rotting piece of meat as her only means of sustenance. She eventually succumbs and eats the rancid flesh. Powerful as this *conte cruel* is, it is ultimately no more than a tale of vengeance, as a man on whom the professor attempts a similar torture comes back to kill him. The story aims at profundity by means of pseudophilosophical discussions on the nature of fear, but these in the end don't amount to much.

"The Hellbound Heart" also attempts a union of sex and death, but the result is clumsy and superficial. Frank, a jaded and unruly wastrel, stumbles upon a curious box ("How had he first heard about Lemarchand's box? He couldn't remember. In a bar maybe, or a gutter, from the lips of a fellow derelict" [NV 218]). This box summons up mysterious creatures called Cenobites who promise him unheard-of pleasures. But Frank, in his limited way, conceives of these pleasures purely sexually. He pays for his misconception, suffering a nameless fate that nearly obliterates his body. He survives, after a fashion, only because he spilled his semen in the room he was occupying: "Dead sperm was a meager keepsake of his essential self, but enough" (NV 220). When Julia, married to Frank's brother Rory but secretly in love with Frank, moves into the house Frank occupied, she eventually detects his presence. She finds that he requires copious amounts of blood to reanimate himself, and promptly poses as a prostitute to lure unwitting johns into her house so that she can kill them and feed their blood to Frank, who gradually dons bone, flesh, and skin once more. All this is an entertaining mix of sex and death (rather more effective in the film version directed by Barker, *Hellraiser*, with its fine special effects), but ultimately no broader conclusions are drawn. Is sex our destroyer or our salvation? What significance does Julia's pseudoprostitution have? Once again the tale lapses into a story of adventure and revenge, as the Cenobites exact punishment upon Frank for trying to escape their clutches.

A serious deficiency in Barker's work is a very naive good versus evil morality that renders many of his characters one-dimensional. He makes many pretensions toward mainstream writing by elaborate character portrayal, and this occurs even in his *Books of Blood*: most of these tales are not so much short stories as novellas, which might, at least in theory, allow for such characterization. But both his heroes and villains are flat and wooden. He has a penchant for depicting vengeful small-town policemen ("The Skins of the Fathers," *Cabal*), amoral criminals ("Cleve knew in his heart he was a leopard born and bred. Crime was easy, work was not"— "In the Flesh" [BB5, 104]), and diseased psychopaths ("The Life of Death"). And those evil Europeans who have come to disturb the peace-loving natives in the Amazon in "How Spoilers Breed" are marked for destruction from the beginning. Les Daniels has rightly referred to this sort of scenario not as tragedy but as melodrama:[17] this is not what adults want to read. In other cases, Barker's attempts at fleshing out his characters in a short story or novelette seriously disfigure the unity of the work: the meandering interludes depicting the sorry state of Jerry Coloqhoun's love life in "The Madonna" are entirely irrelevant to the central plot of the story.

Miraculously, however, all this changes in *The Damnation Game*. In some fashion or other, Barker has here produced a sparklingly flawless weird novel that redeems all the absurdities of his earlier *Books of Blood* and all the verbosity of his later novels. What is more, it fulfills the conditions of an actual weird *novel*, or at least avoids Thomas Ligotti's criticism of the average weird novel as merely a mystery or suspense tale with horrific or supernatural interludes. *The Damnation Game* has indeed been conceived as a weird novel, and the supernatural manifestations are of such a sort as to require novel length for their proper realization.

The first thing that strikes us about this work is the pervasiveness of the game motif. We have already seen indications of its fascination for Barker in "The Inhuman Condition" (the knots whose resolution releases the horror), and we shall see it later in "The Hellbound Heart" with its mysterious box that must be decoded to unleash the Cenobites. Here, however, it structures the entire novel. Joseph Whitehead, a petty thief and gambler preying upon the ruins of postwar Warsaw, hears of a mysterious figure, Mamoulian, who has never lost at cards. Moreover, those who play against him and lose often meet hideous deaths. Whitehead, his curiosity piqued (and also perhaps offended by this challenge to his own prowess at games of chance), seeks out Mamoulian (or is perhaps led to him), challenges him to a game of cards, and wins (or is perhaps allowed to win). Years pass, and Whitehead returns to England. It transpires that, as a result of his victory over Mamoulian, he has gained spectacular wealth, power, and prestige. But now he increasingly senses that Mamoulian is after him in order to exact some sort of revenge, the purpose of which Whitehead cannot clearly ascertain.

The crucial point in the novel is the exact nature of the "game" that Whitehead "won" from Mamoulian. Marty Strauss—who, although merely an ex-convict hired by Whitehead to be his bodyguard, becomes the focal character of the novel—is made aware of the means by which Whitehead accumulated his fortune:

> Life was a random business. Whitehead had learned that lesson years ago, at the hands of a master, and he had never forgotten it. Whether you were rewarded for your good works or skinned alive, it was all down to chance. No use to cleave to some system of numbers or divinities; they all crumbled in the end. Fortune belonged to the man who was willing to risk everything on a single throw.
>
> He'd done that. Not once, but many times at the beginning of his career, when he was laying the foundations of his empire. And thanks to that extraordinary sixth sense he possessed, the ability to preempt the roll of the dice, the risks had almost always paid off.... When it came to knowing the *moment*, for sensing the collision of time and opportunity that made a good decision into a great one, a commonplace takeover into a coup, nobody was Old Man Whitehead's superior... [DG 48].

This is not mere rhetorical praise for a business genius; it is all meant literally, as Strauss begins to sense. "Suppose Whitehead *could* put his finger on the wheel anytime he wanted to, so that even the petty chance of a fox running to the right or left was available to him? Could he know the future before it happened—was that why the chips tingled, and fingers too?—or was he *shaping* it?" (DG 141). The game Whitehead "won" from Mamoulian was the control of chance. As Mamoulian once told Whitehead, "'All life is chance.... The trick is learning how to use it'" (DG 230).

But how did Mamoulian himself gain this quality? He is merely a human being, albeit with superhuman powers. He scoffs at Whitehead's query toward the end as to whether he is the Devil: "'You know I'm not.... Every man is his own Mephistopheles'" (DG 348). We finally learn of Mamoulian's past through Whitehead's daughter Carys, a "sensitive" who can probe people's minds. She ultimately summons up the courage to enter Mamoulian's mind and finds that, as a sergeant in the army, he was nearly executed before a firing squad when "'Chance stepped in on your behalf'" (DG 309), as a monk who rescues him remarks. This monk teaches Mamoulian all he knows: how to resurrect the dead, how to "'take life from other people, and have it for yourself'" (DG 309), and how to control chance. Mamoulian kills the monk, so that this knowledge is his alone, but later he realizes that the monk really *wanted* to die once he had passed on his information (the influence of *Melmoth the Wanderer* is very obvious here). And what does Mamoulian himself want if not the same thing? "'Don't you see how terrible it is to live when everything around you perishes? And the more the years pass the more the thought of death freezes your bowels, because the longer you avoid it the worse you imagine it must be? And you start to long—oh, *how* you long—for someone to take pity on you, someone to embrace you and share your terrors. And, at the end, someone to go into the dark with you'" (DG 311). Whitehead is that person whom Mamoulian wants to accompany him in death, but Whitehead has cheated him.

> "He squandered all my teachings, all my knowledge, threw it away for greed's sake, for power's sake, for the life of the body. *Appetite!* All gone for appetite. All my precious love, wasted!" Marty could hear, in his litany, the voice of the puritan—a monk's voice, perhaps?—the rage of a creature who wanted the world purer than it was and lived in torment because it saw only filth and flesh sweating to make more flesh, more filth. What hope of sanity in such a place? Except to find a soul to share the torment, a lover to hate the world with. Whitehead had been such a partner. And now Mamoulian was being true to his lover's soul: wanting, at the end, to go into death with the only other creature he had ever trusted. "We'll go to nothing..." he breathed, and the breath was a promise. "All of us, go to nothing. Down! Down!" [DG 312].

The portrait of Mamoulian is extraordinarily complex, inspiring at once horror, pathos, and awe. For the one and only time in his writing Barker has abandoned his good versus evil dichotomy to present a rich and intricate conflict of wills. There is no flaw in *The Damnation Game*: its structure is perfect, its characters substantial and fully developed, its style pure and clean (he must have had a good copy editor), and its denouement powerful and satisfying. Although it is part horror story, part historical novel, part mainstream novel, and part detective story, the supernatural premise structures the entire work.

With *Weaveworld*, *The Great and Secret Show*, and *Imajica* Barker is attempting to do something very different. Perhaps irked by the charge that he writes only about gruesome physical horror, Barker in these novels seeks a union between imaginary-world fantasy and supernatural horror. The union is reasonably successful in *Weaveworld*; much less so in *The Great and Secret Show* and *Imajica*. What is still more curious is that the fundamental theme of the first two works is really very much the same, and one wonders why Barker needs two very hefty novels (and the prospect of at least three more sequels to *The Great and Secret Show*) to expound a theme that is not intrinsically interesting—or, at any rate, one that Barker does not treat in a very interesting manner.

This theme is the power of art and the imagination: this is all that both these novels are about. In *Weaveworld* we encounter an elaborately woven carpet endowed with magical powers: it contains an entire realm of entity within its substance. It quickly becomes clear that the Weaveworld is nothing but a symbol for art. "Every inch of the carpet was worked with motifs. Even the border brimmed with designs, each subtly different from its neighbor. The effect was not overbusy; every detail was clear to Cal's feasting eyes. In one place a dozen motifs congregated as if banded together; in another, they stood apart like rival siblings. Some kept their station along the border; others spilled into the main field, as if eager to join the teeming throng there" (W 32). And the Weaveworld itself, full of wondrous landscapes and bizarre but enchanting creatures, is also a transparent symbol for the power of the imagination to transform the ordinary into the magical. As is stated toward the end, "Magic might be bestowed upon the physical, but it didn't *reside* there. It resided in the word, which was the mind spoken" (W 428).

Once this symbolism is established, however, nothing in particular is done with it. Instead, we lapse again into a good versus evil paradigm where some cardboard villains—the oily salesman Shadwell, the evil policeman Inspector Hobart—attempt to gain control of the carpet either for personal gain or in order to rule the Weaveworld. Two young people, Cal and Suzanna, with assistance from various cute denizens of the Weaveworld, come to the carpet's rescue and save it from desecration. Indeed, the last two-thirds of the novel are nothing more than an adventure story relating the battle for the possession of the carpet. All symbolism pertaining to the Weaveworld and its appurtenances is ignored.

The remark in *Weaveworld* that the basic "story" of the weave is "'about being born, and being afraid of dying, and how love saves us'" (W 348), however platitudinous it may be, seems to be the fundamental message of *The Great and Secret Show*, subtitled "The First Book of The Art." Here we are involved with a mysterious "dream-sea" called Quiddity, which appears to us at three critical junctures of our lives: "'It's a dream of what it means to be born, and fall in love, and die. A dream that explains what *being* is for'" (GSS 211). The whole of this interminable and tiresome novel involves the attempts by various good or evil persons to gain control of Quiddity, which again is nothing more than a symbol for our imaginations.

> He no longer cared what words were most appropriate for this reality [Quiddity]: whether it was another dimension or a state of mind was not relevant. They were probably one and the same anyhow. What did matter was the *holiness* of this place. He didn't doubt for a moment that all that he'd gleaned about Quiddity and the Ephemeris was true. This was the place in which all his species knew of glory got their glimpses. A constant place; a place of comfort, where the body was forgotten (except for trespassers like himself) and the dreaming soul knew flight, and mystery [GSS 566].

And when we put together statements like this with other remarks such as "'The real mystery—the only mystery—is inside our heads'" (GSS 211) and with the assertion that one of the villains wants to "'own the dreamlife of the world'" (GSS 344), there is little doubt as to the nature of Quiddity. But the brutal truth is that Barker has not made this conception interesting enough to sustain a novel of such enormous length, much less the three or four projected sequels he has in mind. If he really carries through his threat of writing four books the size of this one on a theme he presents with such a poverty of interest and complexity, then he may have made the greatest mistake of his career.

Perhaps affected by the poor response to *The Great and Secret Show*, Barker has temporarily (and one hopes permanently) abandoned the continuation of "The Art" and written another imaginary-world fantasy. *Imajica*, however, is as beset with conceptual difficulties as its predecessor. And its gargantuan length (it is by far the longest of his novels) painfully emphasizes its diffuseness and lack of focus and makes one wonder whether, in discarding supernatural horror for pure fantasy, he has not made a disastrous aesthetic decision.

It would be tedious and unprofitable to examine the plot of this shambling behemoth of a novel. Suffice it to say that we are dealing with one John Furie Zacharias, a womanizer and painter of forgeries who proves to

be the hand-picked "Reconciler" of the Five Dominions. The Fifth Dominion is the Earth, and the other four exist in some wholly undefined relation to it. Opposing him is an ancient society called the Tabula Rasa, which
wishes to maintain the barriers between this Dominion and the others,
but is wiped out with surprising ease by the Autarch Sartori, the ruler of
the Second Dominion who comes to Earth to establish his dictatorship
here.

Barker's supporters (like those of Stephen King) are fond of referring
to the "epic" imaginative sweep of this novel, as if mere bulk is sufficient
to give a work an "epic" quality. The fact is, Barker's imagination (or sense
of logic) fails at key points: in defining the relationship between the Dominions; in distinguishing one Dominion from another; in depicting a plausible means of traveling between Dominions (one character, evidently
speaking for Barker, announces, "'I don't fully understand the mechanisms
that carry us over.... I'm not sure anybody does completely'" [I 333–34]);
and, most significantly, in specifying what a "Reconciliation" of the Dominions will actually mean. This last failure is critical: with readers kept utterly
in the dark about the nature, purpose, and effect of Zacharias's quest, the
novel cannot even gain any sense of dramatic tension as to whether the
reconciliation will or should come about.

There is some suggestion of a conflict between reason (now preemi-
nent in the Fifth Dominion) and magic. In referring to the attempt by one
minor character, Chant, to cross Dominions, the narrator remarks, "...the
power to do so, which was usually—and contemptuously—referred to as
magic, had been waning in the Fifth since Chant had first arrived. He'd
seen the walls of reason built against it, brick by brick" (I 24). But beyond
such fleeting mentions, very little is made of this. One wonders, in any
event, what purpose will be served by the Reconciliation, since—aside from
sundry odd-looking animals and quasi-human beings—the other Dominions seem just as mundane as our own. "A sizeable part of him wanted to
exit this Dominion once and for all. Take himself off to Yzordderex and
set up business with Peccable; marry Hoi-Polloi despite her crossed eyes;
have a litter of kids and retire to the Hills of the Conscious Cloud, in the
Third, and raise parrots" (I 74). This passage also reveals Barker's uncanny
knack of creating the most ungainly imaginary names I have lately run
across in fantasy fiction.

Along the way various other themes and motifs are thrown out, but
in such a haphazard and confused way that they fail (if I may say so) to be
reconciled into a unified whole. There are innumerable archly pretentious
descriptions of sex (between man and woman, man and man, woman and
woman, and man and some third gender from one of the Dominions) with

the suggestion that sex has some transcendent power or function associated with the Reconciliation, but one never knows what it is. There is a half-baked parody of feminism in the notion that the goddesses of the other Dominions are imprisoned or killed by the "God of Gods" (I 294), Hapexamendios; there are suggestions that the spirits of all the dead people in the world will somehow return once the Reconciliation takes place. And on and on and on. Once again Barker has bitten off more than he can chew: he does not have either the philosophic vision or the narrative skill to unify these diverse threads, and the novel peters out ridiculously at the end. One can only hope that he does not intend a sequel to this ambling leviathan.

A curious aspect of Barker's supernatural work is that the horror revolves wholly around the physical harm that may come to human beings. There is no sign of Lovecraft's "cosmic" vision, whereby human events are seen against the vast backdrop of the uncaring universe, nor even much of an indication that harm to the physical body may not be the apex of horror. No doubt Barker, by consciously tailoring his work to "mainstream" criteria regarding the importance of human relationships, imagines that this limiting of perspective might render his work more acceptable to the general literary community, but the end result is simply a narrowness of vision and conception. Even his most "cosmic" monster—the huge entities in "In the Hills, the Cities"—is made up of human beings. And even this impressive spectacle suffers from a bathetic anticlimax as Barker remarks at a key point in the narrative, "Was there ever a sight in Europe the equal of it?" (BB1, 207). "Rawhead Rex," although not human, is simply a giant somewhat larger and stronger than a human being; even in *The Damnation Game* all the characters are simply human or (as with Anthony Breer, a loathsome individual resurrected from the dead by Mamoulian) perversions of the human. In Barker's later work it is certainly suggested that the mind controls the body and that therefore the horrors of the mind surpass those of the body. But, firstly, we are still dealing with a human perspective and, secondly, there is still vastly more harm done to the characters' bodies than to their minds or spirits or imaginations.

And yet, Barker reveals himself (in the many interviews he has given and in the critical essays and introductions he has written) to be a surprisingly articulate and stimulating spokesman for weird fiction in general and for his brand of weird fiction (explicit, physically extreme horror) in particular. Even here, however, I have some problems. He speaks repeatedly of the need for weird fiction to be grounded in "metaphysics." We live, Barker feels (surely correctly), in a world where the "banal" reigns supreme—in television, in newspapers, in most of our daily lives. Accordingly, weird fiction must be "confrontational" and "subversive," waking us up from our listlessness and lethargy (SE 202–3). I believe he is on firm ground here, but I am not convinced that his own fiction actually embodies these principles. (This is what used to be called the gap between intention and achievement, before intention was banished from critical theory.) Barker criticizes Stephen King for his all too frequent good-versus-evil scenarios wherein the monster is portrayed as a "pure other" that must be extirpated for the good of the world (SE 74–75), but we have already seen that Barker has himself fallen into a very similar pattern in some of his own work, notably *Weaveworld* and *The Great and Secret Show*. Perhaps Barker expressed his views most clearly and succinctly in a 1988 interview:

> I'm not just writing to horrify, I'm writing to disturb, excite and subvert. Those functions are best served by the clearest possible views of the imagined scenes. I never cut to shadows—never cut away the moment of maximum revelation. What is revealed can be a moment of transcendence or disgust or self-comprehension or all three. It can be erotic, it can be funny, it can be foul. Those ambiguities and paradoxes are best arrived at if you show all there is to see [SE 77].

This sounds good in theory, but in practice I fear that repeated doses of mere physical horror do not excite terror or disgust as much as...boredom. Barker says in a cocksure fashion that "What you can't do to most of the images in my books is ignore them" (SE 202). Well, yes you can, since after a while they all start sounding the same. The only solution for someone in Barker's position is either to increase the dosage (as in *The Damnation Game* and his films) or to opt for a different mode of writing altogether (as in *Weaveworld* and its successors). In a sense I can understand and even sympathize with Barker's impatience with the subtlety, indirection, and suggestiveness of much traditional weird fiction, which can on occasion lead to excessive obscurity (Robert Aickman) or tameness (some of M. R. James and most of his disciples). But Barker's own frenetic pyrotechnics have drawbacks of their own. I defy anyone to read his "The Midnight Meat Train" and then T. E. D. Klein's "Children of the Kingdom," and not come away with a vastly greater impression of the horrors that may dwell on the underside of New York City from Klein's tale than from Barker's. Klein cannot possibly be accused of pulling any punches—his denouement is as horrifying as anything I have read in modern literature. It is simply that his tale is written with an elegance, meticulousness, and atmospheric tensity that Barker can only dream of. Indeed, Barker at times disingenuously makes a virtue of his carelessness in conception and style, as if such a thing is somehow inextricable from in the message he is trying to convey:

>I'm an inclusionist.... Whatever is going through my head at a given time goes into the mix.... I don't think of myself as a slick artist. I think I'm kind of clunky in lots of ways. I don't actually mind the clunkiness. It's part of what I am.... I think everything I've done is rough-hewn. If it were not rough-hewn, I'd actually be simplifying it, I'd often be taking out paradoxes, I'd often be taking out contradictions, I'd often be taking out a kind of richness. Which would be highly regrettable.[18]

Barker may not be "slick," but this is just about the slickest defense of clumsy, ill-conceived writing I can think of.

What, in the end, is the verdict on Clive Barker? The honest truth is that, with the sole exceptions of *The Damnation Game* and a handful of stories, the entirety of his work is marred by poor conception and construction, slipshod writing, excessive violence that serves no aesthetic purpose, and, in general, simply a lack of depth and substance. His later novels make vast pretensions to profundity but fail utterly to deliver on the promise. If *Weaveworld* effects a fairly convincing union of horror and fantasy, then he has seriously erred in embarking on what appears to be an interminable multinovel series with *The Great and Secret Show*, which exhibits a complete lack of focus, direction, or purpose. If Barker truly is, as Stephen King claimed, the "future" of horror, then the field is in deep trouble.

III. Ramsey Campbell:
The Fiction of Paranoia

Although British writer Ramsey Campbell (b. 1946) does not have even a fraction of the popular following of Stephen King, Clive Barker, Anne Rice, or Peter Straub, there seems to be general agreement among critics in the field that he is the leading weird fictionist of our time. But like Lord Dunsany and Algernon Blackwood, Campbell has more often been praised than studied, and little critical work of substance has been devoted to him. We are now, however, at a stage where important study of him can begin. Not only does he now have an impressive and voluminous body of writing, but he has recently made available a bibliography of his own work, arranged chronologically by date of writing, so that it is possible to trace his literary evolution with much precision. (Throughout this essay, accordingly, all dates appearing in square brackets refer to years of composition.)

His bibliography shows that Campbell is not merely one of the most prolific of modern weird writers, but perhaps the most precocious. His first volume, the piquantly titled *The Inhabitant of the Lake and Less Welcome Tenants* (1964), was issued by Arkham House when Campbell was 18, but some of the stories in that collection actually date to as early as his fourteenth year. (He has even been so generous as to make available a juvenile volume, *Ghostly Tales*, that he wrote when he was about 11. In the introduction to *The Height of the Scream* he reprinted a poem published when he was five and a story written at the age of seven and a half [HS xiii–xx].) It is true that the tales in his first published volume are, on the whole, rather lurid and bombastic imitations of Lovecraft's "Cthulhu Mythos," but they are written with such vitality and enthusiasm as to be on the whole superior to the mechanical imitations of such purportedly mature authors as Brian Lumley and even August Derleth. It was nine years before Campbell published his next volume, *Demons by Daylight* (1973), a towering landmark in the history of weird fiction. What has not been known until now is that some versions of those stories (leagues beyond his early imitative work) date to his seventeenth year, and several final drafts were completed by the time he was 21. His development from competent apprentice to assured master was remarkably rapid.

If we date the commencement of Campbell's mature writing to 1965, then it would be a full decade before he would complete his first novel, *The Doll Who Ate His Mother* [1975]. In the 1990 introduction to *Demons by Daylight* he speaks of conceiving a science-fiction novel around 1973, although it was never begun. In the introduction to *The Height of the Scream* he notes: "I never did have the staying power to finish writing a novel. But that won't be true of the one I'm writing now, however" (HS xx). He had written nearly 150 short stories before writing *The Doll Who Ate His Mother*; from 1976 to 1992, however, he wrote 11 novels (excluding three novelizations of films written rapidly in 1976 and published under the house name "Carl Dreadstone") but fewer than 100 short stories. This shift from short story writing to novel writing has been a mixed benefit. To be sure, the novels have given Campbell greater visibility in the literary arena, and several are notable successes (*The Face That Must Die, Incarnate, Midnight Sun*), but one cannot help feeling that his distinctively hallucinatory and elliptical style, like Robert Aickman's and Thomas Ligotti's (the one a mentor of his, the other a disciple), is best suited to the short story. Only two or three of Campbell's novels rank with the absolute masterpieces of the form, but easily a score of his short tales can take their place with the best weird writing of all time, and several dozen others are tales we would be much the poorer without.

Campbell has passed through several stages in his short story writing, and these stages are exhibited with fair accuracy in his five principal short story collections. *The Inhabitant of the Lake* (1964) gathers many of his stories written between 1960 and 1963; *Demons by Daylight* (1973) prints stories written from 1966 to 1969 (although some were drafted as early as 1963); *The Height of the Scream* (1976) collects stories written from 1967 to 1974 (with the exception of "The Cellars" [1965]); *Dark Companions* (1982) contains one story ("Napier Court") written in 1967 but otherwise collects stories written between 1974 and 1978; and *Waking Nightmares* (1991) collects stories written from 1980 to 1988 (one was written in 1974 and another in 1976). Other of Campbell's collections—*Cold Print* (1985), *Black Wine* (1986), *Night Visions 3* (1986), *Scared Stiff* (1986)—contain stories written over a wide interval, while the chief virtue of the recent *Strange Things and Stranger Places* (1993) is that it makes available to American readers his scintillating novella *Needing Ghosts. Dark Feasts* (1987) is a fine retrospective of some of his best work over the entirety of his career, from 1960 to 1986, but is superseded by its revised edition, the magnificent *Alone with the Horrors* (1991), an omnibus that may rank as the finest single volume of weird fiction since Lovecraft's *The Outsider and Others* (1939). Quite a number of Campbell's stories, however, remain uncollected.

Campbell's progression as a short fictionist is suggestive. Leaving behind the Lovecraftian imitations of *The Inhabitant of the Lake*, he adopted a hallucinatory, dreamlike, and almost surrealist style (derived jointly from Robert Aickman and Vladimir Nabokov) in *Demons by Daylight*. In his 1990 introduction to that collection he wryly notes Donald Wandrei's belief that "one underlying theme of the book was drug use."[1] By 1968 Campbell had already mined this vein nearly to its limit, and he seemed for the next several years to be searching for a new or different style to express his vision. *The Height of the Scream* strikes me as in some ways more experimental than its predecessor, or at any rate more tentative and heterogeneous. The very diversity of tone of the tales in this collection makes it less unified than *Demons by Daylight*, and many of the stories seem uninspired, overly obscure, and even a little self-indulgent. Perhaps he was simply writing too much. He wrote 17 stories in 1973 and 27 in 1974: more than he has written in any other year.

But *Dark Companions* shows that he found a new voice as a short story writer. The dream imagery of the *Demons by Daylight* period is not abandoned but harnessed: the stories are set more firmly in the mundane world, but Campbell's focus on individual psychology allows dreamlike effects to enter precisely at the moment when the horror is beginning to manifest itself. His fascination with the complexities of human relationships, typical of *Demons by Daylight*, has given way to an intense concern with loneliness, both physical and psychological. Recall that it was in this period that he wrote his masterwork of solitary paranoia, *The Face That Must Die*.

With the stories of the *Waking Nightmares* period we see Campbell at the very height of his short story technique. He is now no longer content to work in a single style or mood, but varies them as the theme or subject warrants. Perhaps this is a result of his relative sparseness of output in the short story: in the ten-year period of 1981–90 he wrote only 28 short stories; in the years 1981, 1982, and 1989 he wrote none at all.[2] Accordingly, we have stories of all types here, from dreamlike prose poems ("Just Waiting" [DF]) to an updating of the conventional English ghost story ("Watch the Birdie" [WN]) to fiercely paranoid first-person accounts ("Next Time You'll Know Me" [WN]) to grimly realistic tales of supernatural horror

("Old Clothes" [WN]). A curious development is a very faint optimism in some of these tales (perhaps derived from his novels, many of which have provisionally "happy" endings): whereas previous Campbell protagonists meet their loathsome fates with dreary resignation, we find that "In the Trees" (NV) the narrator escapes bodily harm, even though his spirit is shattered; in "Old Clothes" the narrator manages to transfer the horror (embodied in a raincoat) to someone else; and in "Apples" (DF) children actually suppress a horror in the end. I do not know that much is to be made of this: Campbell's world remains, on the whole, as profoundly dispiriting as ever.

I am less certain of the overall course or development of Campbell's novels, as they do not appear to have very many thematic connections either with his short work or with each other. There is, on the whole, a regrettable tendency to describe at great length and detail the lives of commonplace middle-class characters, with a special concentration on personal relationships and family life. The weird scenarios frequently grow out of or are directed toward these relationships. He seems to forgo the distinctively warped view of the world he or his characters adopt in the short stories, replacing it instead with a conventional outlook that suggests that these ordinary people and their concerns are somehow significant in themselves. I myself find his novels compelling only when they are told from some twisted perspective (*The Face That Must Die, The Count of Eleven*) or when they suggest that human beings are symbols for vaster phenomena (*Incarnate, Midnight Sun*). There are many writers who can write about cheerful bourgeois characters and their wholesome, well-adjusted children, but only Campbell can write the fiction of paranoia. This is why the novelette *Needing Ghosts* may be his finest work.

BEFORE AND AFTER LOVECRAFT

Campbell's *Ghostly Tales* [1957/58] is a delight. Consisting of 16 stories (some very short, others quite long) the volume reveals a rather surprising diversity of tone and style, and Campbell need feel no embarrassment at the exhibition of his 11-year-old juvenilia: certainly Lovecraft's story "The Mysterious Ship" (1902), written at the age of 12, is far worse. Lovecraft, in fact, is not the focus of this collection. It opens with a weird poem rather in the manner of Thomas Lovell Beddoes, and at one point M. R. James is cited by name (GT 37). The one explicitly Lovecraftian reference is amusing: coming upon the term "shoggoth," a character looks it up in the dictionary (!), where it is defined: *"evil spirit or demon in the shape of a tree with mouths scattered over its trunk"* (GT 9). Lovecraft would, no doubt, have been startled to read this definition, since his shoggoth is a 15-foot protoplasmic amoeba. But Campbell has mentioned to me that the definition is derived from Robert Bloch's "Notebook Found in a Deserted House." Nevertheless, by 1960–61, when the first of the tales to be included in *The Inhabitant of the Lake* were written, Campbell had grasped, and even begun very tentatively to go beyond, the Lovecraftian influence.

"The Tomb-Herd" and "The Tower from Yuggoth" [both 1960–61] testify to Campbell's desire, as he writes in the 1990 introduction to *Demons by Daylight*, "to sound as much like H. P. Lovecraft as I could." The former is set in Lovecraft's Kingsport; the latter in Arkham. Moreover, both seem to take place in Lovecraft's own era rather than in Campbell's: although the date of "The Tomb-Herd" is not specified, "The Tower from Yuggoth" is clearly set in 1929, and its hero is given the transparently Lovecraftian name of Edward Wingate Armitage. In terms of style, the opening of "The Tomb-Herd" says it all: "There are myriad unspeakable terrors in the cosmos in which our universe is but an atom; and the two gates of agony, life and death, gape to pour forth infinities of abominations. And the other gates which spew forth their broods are, thank God, little known to us" (TH 3). It is just as well that neither of these stories was actually included in *The Inhabitant of the Lake*. The first of Campbell's stories that *was* included is "The Horror from the Bridge," and it is in this story that Campbell introduces his British analogue for Lovecraft's mythical New England topography. In the course of his early stories Campbell (at the suggestion of August Derleth [CP 4]) invented such towns as Severnford, Temphill, Brichester, Camside, Goatswood, and Clotton, all evidently set in the Severn valley and all conforming approximately to Lovecraft's Arkham, Dunwich, Kingsport, and Innsmouth. But even "The Horror from the Bridge" is still set in 1931, as if he were satisfied in merely transplanting the Lovecraftian scenario to another location.

Mechanically imitative as most of these early stories may be, some of them already betray signs that Campbell was seeking to move beyond the Lovecraftian influence. "The Church in High Street" [1960–61] and "The Render of the Veils" [1962] contain considerably more dialogue than was Lovecraft's wont. The former tale, a revision of "The Tomb-Herd," is now set in Temphill. Other tales reveal a clever adaptation of Lovecraftian themes. "The Insects from Shaggai" utilizes the notion of insects penetrating a man's brain, which, as Campbell admits (CP 5–6), was taken from a late entry in Lovecraft's commonplace book, as were the plots of a number of other early Campbell stories. "The Inhabitant of the Lake" resembles

Lovecraft's "The Whisperer in Darkness" in its use of the documentary style—in this instance, correspondence between the two protagonists—to achieve narrative distancing and verisimilitude. And, of course, Campbell cannot resist concocting his own Lovecraftian god (Glaaki, first cited in "The Room in the Castle") and mythical book (*The Revelations of Glaaki*, first cited in "The Render of the Veils"). All these devices would be used to much greater effect in some of the *Demons by Daylight* stories.

Even before the publication of *The Inhabitant of the Lake*, however, Campbell was seeking to shed the Lovecraftian cloak he had donned. In 1963 he produced the first draft of "The Interloper," one of the more memorable tales in *Demons by Daylight*. "Before the Storm" [1965] is an exceptionally bizarre dream-fantasy, although it is still rooted in Lovecraft's Mythos. But if we are to look for any single story of Campbell's that marks his declaration of independence from Lovecraft, it is "The Cellars" [1965]. Not only is this Campbell's first tale to be set in his native Liverpool, it is in other ways typical of his later work—in its focus on human relationships, its evocation of the squalor of urban decay, its oblique narration, and its nebulous, indirect, and nearly incomprehensible horrific climax.

Campbell has spoken frequently of Lovecraft's influence upon his work, most extensively in the introduction to *Cold Print* (1985), a collection of his Lovecraftian tales; but other remarks are also illuminating. In the 1990 introduction to *Demons by Daylight* he remarks that in that collection he was striving to be as *unlike* Lovecraft as possible: "Having imitated Lovecraft, I rejected him with all the obstreperousness of a fanzine contributor determined to make a name for himself at the expense of his betters." His most insightful comment may be in the introduction to *The Height of the Scream*: "Lovecraft had rooted his horrors in recognizable settings; I wanted to root mine in recognizable human behavior, an altogether more universal thing" (HS xi). This may not be entirely fair to Lovecraft; there is far more realism in Lovecraft than mere settings, and the absence of vivid characters or relationships in his work is a direct result of his portrayal of humanity's inconsequence in an infinite and uncaring cosmos. But it adequately conveys not merely Campbell's own difference from Lovecraft but the overall tendency of all post–Lovecraftian weird fiction, a tendency that Campbell has exemplified more distinctively and powerfully than any of his contemporaries. This tendency may be very crudely defined as the shift from the cosmic to the human. When Campbell remarks that Lovecraft's "minimal characterization and plot work because they are right for him" (HS x–xi), he is suggesting that it is not characters but phenomena that form the true heart of Lovecraft's fiction, whereas for Campbell (as for most other modern weird writers) the human characters become not merely the object of the reader's sympathy but the sole or prime focus of the horrific scenario. At its worst this tendency leads to Dziemianowicz's "banalization" of horror: the creation of an obvious and sentimental realism based upon the mundane activities of ordinary middle-class people (Stephen King, Charles L. Grant), or else an emphasis on crudely physical horror centering around the harm that can be done to the human body (Clive Barker). In Campbell, however, the focus on the human takes the form of an extremely intense concentration on individual consciousness, to the degree that much of his work approaches stream of consciousness while still retaining a sort of clinical detachment. As a result, his vision is distinctly lacking in Lovecraftian cosmicism, and even later tales in which he attempts to arouse a sense of cosmic fear ("The Tugging," "The Voice of the Beach") seem half-hearted and unconvincing. Indeed, some of Campbell's most genuinely cosmic tales tend to be entirely un–Lovecraftian, such as the nightmarish "Playing the Game" (WN).

Two magnificent tales in which Campbell reveals himself to have fully assimilated the Lovecraftian influence while at the same time speaking in his own voice are "Cold Print" [1966–67] and "The Franklyn Paragraphs" [1967]. The former vividly etches the milieu of Brichester, with its dismal slums and its inhabitants stunted and imaginationless from poverty and urban decay. Campbell's later admission that Brichester had by now become merely a metaphor for Liverpool ("My invented town of Brichester, originally intended as the Severn Valley equivalent of Lovecraft's Arkham, was Liverpool by now in all but name" [FD xxi]) only confirms what we suspected all along. His great innovation in this story was to revivify the stale concept of the mythical book of occult lore (which, even toward the end of Lovecraft's own career, had become more and more of a game or in-joke) by linking it to the world of violent pornography. His seedy narrator, entering a bookstore on the edge of town, is not some scholarly antiquarian seeking forbidden knowledge: he has come to find books analogous to those he has purchased elsewhere—*Miss Whippe, Old-Style Governess* and *Prefects and Fags* (CP 199); but the *Revelations* prove more than he bargained for. It is exactly in such a place that the horror originally inspired by Lovecraft's *Necronomicon* can be re-created in the present day.

"The Franklyn Paragraphs" is Campbell's most audacious attempt to mimic—and perhaps also to parody—Lovecraft's documentary style. Campbell himself appears as a character in the story, acting as narrator and engaging in a correspondence with the eccentric writer Errol Undercliffe.[3] At one point Undercliffe criticizes one of Campbell's own stories, "The Stocking" (elsewhere in *Demons by Daylight*), dismissing it as "elaborately pointless"

(DD 33): it is as if Undercliffe is a sort of maturer version of Campbell himself, one who can examine Campbell's work with the objectivity that greater years and greater experience as a writer bring. The story is written as if it were a critical article, with Lovecraft's own Mythos the subject of the commentary. Undercliffe discovers a strange volume by one Roland Franklyn, *We Pass from View*; Campbell (the narrator) claims that it "displays marked affinities with the Cthulhu Mythos in certain passages, [but] such Lovecraft scholars as Derleth, Lin Carter, Timothy d'Arch Smith and J. Vernon Shea can supply no information on the book" (DD 31). Later Campbell reproduces the British National Bibliography entry for the book (his years spent working in a library were not spent in vain) and also the scornful *Times Literary Supplement* review of it.

But "The Franklyn Paragraphs" is more than a succession of playful in-jokes; it is one of the most insidiously horrific tales of Campbell's early period. Its power stems both from the subtlety and the indirection of its execution. As frequently in Lovecraft, narrative distance is taken almost to an extreme: at one point Campbell the narrator quotes a letter from Undercliffe who quotes a passage of Franklyn's book. In fact, there is an additional level of narrative distance here, since Campbell the author must be separated from the persona he has adopted as narrator of the story. Moreover, the story, as frequently in his later work, probes the relationship between writing and reality. What happens if an actual horror descends upon the writer of supernatural fiction? Should he not be prepared for it, given his predisposition to the weird? Undercliffe concludes that the opposite is the case: "Even the supernatural-story writer who believes what he writes (and I'm not saying I don't) isn't prepared for an actual confrontation. Quite the reverse, for every time he fabricates the supernatural in a story (unless based on experience) he clinches his skepticism; he knows such things can't be, because he wrote them. Thus for him a confrontation would be doubly upsetting" (DD 42). And when Franklyn's widow tells Undercliffe what would happen if he were to experience the supernatural ("'God! You'd never write about it, you'd never write about anything again'" [DD 42]), we see the reason for the fragmentary and halting nature of Undercliffe's last letter.

This richly textured story—with its complex network of narrative voices, its attempt to maintain a harried sobriety in the face of unthinkable horror, and its gradual build-up to a spectacularly powerful climax—is the summation of Campbell's Lovecraftian work. Undercliffe's final message—"No longer could I trust the surface of the world" (DD 44)—is exactly the burden of Lovecraft's work, but is here expressed with a vividness that is Campbell's own. In the contributors' notes to his anthology *New*

Tales of the Cthulhu Mythos (1980) Campbell notes that "One of his ambitions is to write a single successful Lovecraftian story" (NT 255). If this is so, then he can rest at ease, for in "Cold Print" and "The Franklyn Paragraphs" he has twice accomplished the feat.

Although he has returned sporadically to the Lovecraftian mode in subsequent stories, it is well that Campbell so quickly decided to speak in his own voice, however adept and powerful some of his Lovecraftian imitations are. His manifesto in this direction was *Demons by Daylight*. I am not alone in remembering the shock I experienced when coming innocently upon that volume, for who could have predicted that its 27-year-old author would develop so quickly from the pastichist he had been?

DREAM AND REALITY

What makes many of the *Demons by Daylight* stories so successful is the dreamlike—or nightmarish—atmosphere they evoke through an almost Proustian focusing upon the shifting thoughts and emotions of the protagonists. This quasi–stream of consciousness helps to blur the distinction between dream, hallucination, memory, and reality in such a way that the supernatural phenomena—which might otherwise appear highly implausible or ludicrous if narrated with the objective realism of a Lovecraft—seem both strangely natural and chillingly intense. "The End of a Summer's Day" is prototypical. In this story a couple, Maria and Tony, enter a cave as part of a tour group. Tony gets lost in the cave, but no one believes Maria when she pleads that he is still inside when all the others have emerged. This simple scenario raises a host of unanswerable queries: is there a conspiracy against Maria to deprive her of her lover; did Tony ever exist at all outside of her imagination; and who is the blind man whom all the others in the tour group insist is her companion?

"Concussion" is, to my mind, the finest tale in *Demons by Daylight*, and it again displays Campbell's ability to mingle pathos and horror seamlessly. The premise of the story seems grotesquely unlikely—an old man finds that a young woman he meets on a bus is the same woman he once loved as a youth, as in some strange fashion she has gone back in time to reenact the same scenario 50 years ago. But the heart-rending poignancy of the tale rests not only in Campbell's insight into the emotions of young lovers but in the highly disturbing way in which he flits back and forth between the present and the past, to the point that we scarcely know which is which. (A much later story, "Just Waiting" [1983; WN], employs this same device.)

It would be futile to attempt to analyze the other stories in *Demons by Daylight*: they are as elusive as a dream or a memory, and yet they haunt us as only dreams or memories can. "The Guy," "Potential," "The Sentinels"— all are masterpieces of atmosphere and indirection. They still rank as some of Campbell's finest tales. The greatness of *Demons by Daylight* stems both from the intrinsic excellence of its contents—there is not a single weak story here, and several are among the best in Campbell's work in particular and in modern weird fiction in general—and from its historical importance. In this volume—with its uncompromising realism of character and setting, its evocatively dreamlike prose style, its sexual frankness, its extremely oblique narration—Campbell has almost single-handedly ushered in the dominant mode of modern weird fiction. The influence of Robert Aickman, whose own work embodies many of these same characteristics, is evident in the volume, but Aickman's work has not had nearly the impact of Campbell's. Although most of the tales in *Demons by Daylight* were completed by 1968, only four years after the publication of *The Inhabitant of the Lake*, they have completely abandoned the pulpish and derivative tone of that volume. Campbell himself was aware of breaking new ground with these stories, as he writes in the 1990 preface to the collection: "Accurately or otherwise, I tended to feel that nobody else was writing horror fiction quite like this, and perhaps that meant everyone else was right and I was wrong." Fortunately for weird fiction, Campbell received encouragement from colleagues and editors and persisted in his revolutionary work. At times *Demons by Daylight* seems to have been written by an entirely different author from that of *The Inhabitant of the Lake*; at other times it seems to have been written in a different century.

Incarnate (1983), one of Campbell's richest novels, might be worth studying in this context. As with his later short stories, this work probes the tenuous distinction between dream and reality but in an opposite fashion from the tales in *Demons by Daylight*. Instead of blurring the real world by dream imagery, *Incarnate* presents dreams that have all the clarity of waking life. As with all Campbell's work, this effect is created by an intense focus upon individual consciousness; but here we are dealing not with one or two but five or six highly distinct personalities. One of the many triumphs of the novel is the skill with which their lives, thoughts, and experiences are skillfully integrated into a complex fabric.

The novel opens with an experiment in which several very disparate individuals are gathered together because they all appear to have had dreams of the future: many have woken up to find their dreams embodied in the morning paper. But in fact the scope of the work is larger, treating broadly of the insidious incursion of dream phenomena into what we call the waking world. The general focus of the novel is Molly Wolfe, an assistant producer for a television station who has had disturbingly prescient dreams all her life. In a penetrating essay on the novel, Michael A. Morrison has noted that one of the most jarring moments in all Campbell's fiction occurs when Molly discovers that the humiliation she has suffered at the hands of the police, while investigating the possible murder of a black man by some police officers, was all a dream: Campbell never breaks the realistic narrative flow to signal where the waking world has ended and the dream has begun. But is this experience "only" a dream? When she sees a police officer whom she has never met before but whom she saw in the dream, she reflects: "She'd dreamed of him before she'd met him in what most people would call reality, and that proved the dream" (I 261). The suggestion is that dream is really another form of perception; or, as one of Campbell's characters says much later in a celebrated remark, "'Dreaming isn't a state of mind ... it's a state of being'" (I 425).

Startling as the scene with Molly and the police is, an even more striking tableau is a long episode in which another character, a gawky young man named Danny Swain, encounters the leader of the original experiment, Dr. Guilda Kent, years later. The reader, having read of Molly's evident confusion of dream and reality (or, rather, of their confusion between themselves), is prepared to accept that this entire scenario—involving Danny's frequent visits to Dr. Kent's office in a seedy area of Soho—is also a dream. And so, evidently, it turns out to be. Danny appears to lure Dr. Kent into the movie theatre in which he works and then sets it afire, apparently killing her. But is it then only his imagination that causes Dr. Kent to come to his home later? How can this be only an apparition, since Danny's parents see the figure themselves? (I 404–5). And what of the fact that the real Dr. Kent has all along been interred in a madhouse? With this entire scenario Campbell has shown how utterly chimerical is the supposed distinction not only between dream and reality but also between internal and external horror—i.e., horror that is a product of a deluded mind and horror that is postulated to exist in the external world.

It is at this point that some of the epigraphs with which Campbell prefaces the novel come into play, in particular one from a letter by Lovecraft: "Surely the strange excrescences of the human fancy are as real—in the sense of real phenomena—as the commonplace passions, thoughts, and instincts of everyday life." Lovecraft, as a mechanistic materialist, was far from wishing to abolish the distinction between dream and reality, as another letter testifies: "I confess to an over-powering desire to know whether I am asleep or awake—whether the environment and laws which affect me are external and permanent, or the transitory products of my own brain."[4] What Campbell is doing in *Incarnate* is interpreting Lovecraft's phrase "real phenomena" in a very literal manner, suggesting that dreams have some sort of ill-defined but "real" existence and that they can somehow obtrude upon the "real" world in some hideous fashion.

Toward the end of the novel Campbell generalizes the notion, stating through his characters that dreams have become stronger by being repressed. The real Guilda Kent states bitterly:

> "We've allowed them to grow stronger by trying to explain them away, don't you understand? Don't you know yet what dreams are?"
> ..."Don't answer that," she said. "The trouble is, we thought we knew. Science thinks it can distinguish between reality and dreaming. People who can't are locked up in places like this. You can't lock dreams up. All that does is make them stronger" [I 424].

Dream, in essence, "'wants to feed on what we call reality ... so it can take its place'" (I 427). The conclusion of the novel tells the mesmerizing story of characters drifting through a dream-world of their own invention in a desperate effort to send dreams back to their own domain.

Incarnate remains Campbell's most ambitious work of fiction, and by and large he has succeeded in writing a compelling and vividly realized novel in which the human characters are at once distinct individuals in their own right and symbols for the broader thematic purpose he is seeking to achieve. If I still hesitate to rank *Incarnate* among the very best works of its kind, it is because of a certain slackness of style that affects all Campbell's novels, as well as some apparently unresolved issues. Most notable among these is Sage, a mysterious figure who appears to be manipulating events so that the dreams can overrun the waking world. Sage is one of Campbell's most piquant villains, but it is never clarified what his real purpose is in fostering the conquest of dream over reality: what, exactly, will he gain by such a procedure? It is also not very clear to me why some of the precognitive dreamers join Sage in his quest and others do not: has he gained control of them somehow? Some other minor loose ends, perhaps inevitable in a novel that places so many characters on the stage, could also be enumerated. Nevertheless, *Incarnate*, in spite of its great length, is perhaps the most readable and one of the most unified of Campbell's novels, being guided by a single theme—dream versus reality—that is on the surface extremely simple but in actuality highly complex and baffling. Only *The Face That Must Die* and some of his short stories can match the intensity of *Incarnate*'s concluding portion.

ART AND REALITY

From the problematical relationship between dream and reality it is a short step to the equally troubling relationship between art (usually writing) and the real world. We have already seen this theme emerge in "The Franklyn Paragraphs": the genuinely supernatural obliterates writing, renders one speechless (a theme to be found also in T. E. D. Klein's "The Events at Poroth Farm"). But the tale is still more complex than this, and one of its most potent moments is when Errol Undercliffe, reading Franklyn's *We Pass from View*, sees words appearing of their own accord on the page: "FEEL THEM COMING SLOWLY BURROWING WANT ME TO SUFFER CANT MOVE GET ME OUT SAVE ME SOMEWHERE IN BRICHESTER HELP ME" (DD 37). We can think of this as a vast refinement of the Lovecraftian narrator's penchant for scribbling until the bitter end, but in reality it symbolizes the writer's heroic effort to maintain his art in the face of the most overwhelming obstacles.

"Beyond Words" [1985; NV] presents a much more pessimistic account of the artist's plight in the modern world. A struggling but sincere writer of weird tales develops a horrible ringing or tinnitus in his ears, which builds day by day until he can no longer hear or write: what can this be but a symbol for the impossibility of maintaining one's aesthetic integrity in the face of rampant commercialism (a publisher wishes him to write a fantasy trilogy and be the next Tolkien) and the grinding realities of urban life? The story ends with the monotonous repetition of "must go on, must go on" (NV 94)—but to what end will the writer go on? He has already lost everything that means anything to him, and he is nothing but an automaton whose life will be a mechanical series of endlessly repeated gestures void of art or meaning.

It is possible that we should study here the several Campbell stories involving films and their nebulous relationship to the real world. This is, indeed, the subject of one of his earliest stories, "The Childish Fear" [1963], about the horrors to be found in a movie theatre. Other tales continue to address this theme, some to my mind very successfully—such as "After the Queen" [1969; BW]—and others not so successfully—such as "Horror House of Blood" [1973; HS]. But the tale that sums up this entire theme is "Boiled Alive" [1986], a magnificently chilling and nightmarish story about the ubiquity of television, films, and computers in our age, and of the degree to which they can simulate a reality so unnervingly real and complete in itself that the actual world begins to take on the aspect of a fiction.

> The idea of living in a film wasn't entirely unappealing. If it had been a better film he might even have been flattered. Being able to repeat favourite moments and speed up the boring parts was certainly tempting, not to mention the ability to say of bad times "it's only a film" or to have a hidden voice explain things when he looked at them. But how much control would he have? About as much as one generally has of one's life, he thought, then felt as if the voice that knew its lines could put him right if he could just work out how to respond [DF 337].

Anyone who has remarked of some event in real life, "It's just like a movie," or anyone who has been exposed to the "virtual reality" propagated by certain computer programs, will find much in this story that is both harrowing and prophetic.

Campbell's most exhaustive—but not, perhaps, his most interesting or satisfying—treatment of the relationship of film and reality occurs in his novel, *Ancient Images* [1987–88]. This work purports to deal with a film made in England in 1938 featuring Boris Karloff and Bela Lugosi, almost all copies of which appear to have been lost or suppressed. It is suggested at the outset that there is something supernatural about the film itself: many of those who worked on it died or suffered strange accidents, and those few who have seen it found it almost impossible to watch (this rather reminds one of Lovecraft's commonplace book entry about a "Book or MS. too horrible to read"[5]). But in fact the film turns out not to be the focus of the supernatural element of the novel at all, even though much of the story is spent in the protagonists' desultory search for a print of the movie by tracking down all those who were involved with it. It transpires that the true reason for the tragedies surrounding the making of the film is an obscure curse upon the region in which the film was made, a curse that requires the sacrifice of human beings every 50 years lest nameless horrors emerge and overrun the world. All this is rather hard to swallow, and as a result not much is ever made of the connection between film and the real world. *Ancient Images* is, in the end, only a moderately entertaining supernatural adventure story, with the protagonists constantly sensing the presence of loathsome creatures all around them: a doglike entity that is heard scratching behind doors; an incredibly thin figure lurking just out of sight; hideous rotted scarecrows that come to life. As with an earlier novel, *The Nameless*, the rich thematic and philosophical issues raised by the scenario fail to be developed in depth or detail.

A curious theme can be found throughout the length and breadth of Campbell's work—what might be called the relationship between dolls and human beings. This theme can be related to the art/reality trope because of the suggestion of a possible connection between human beings and some representation or duplicate of them. We find this motif appearing as early as the strange tale "Cyril" [1968], in which an older woman seeks to seduce a shy young man she has met. He has given her a doll, whom she names Cyril, but he himself seems regrettably immune to her charms, even though she has convinced him that it is too late for him to go home and that he will have to spend the night with her. In her fury she tears the doll to bits. "But Flora only dragged her head down and wished, cursed, prayed that the screams from the next room would stop" (HS 153).

"Dolls" [1974; SS] is somewhat similarly conceived, although on the whole it seems to be an oblique treatment of the voodoo legend. John Norton appears to have the power to cause injury or death with the dolls that he creates, but then suffers a similar fate from a lifesize doll he has fashioned to act as the "devil" for his witch coven. A slightly different working out of the idea is found in "Playing the Game," which deals with an individual who manipulates a gameboard of snakes and ladders that has a disturbing correlation with the real world. Perhaps, Campbell is saying, we are all dolls or puppets made to dance along the course of our lives by some unseen hand.

An ingenious variation of the doll/man theme occurs in "The Gap" [1977], in which a writer, Lionel Tate, puts together a jigsaw puzzle that happens to have himself in the picture. Why does the puzzle also have another figure (that of a rival author, Don Skelton, whose book, *The Black Road*, Tate sees everywhere) who appears to be stealthily creeping up on him? And why is the piece containing Tate's face apparently missing from the puzzle? With these typically Campbellian elements a superbly atmospheric tale develops. At one point Tate, seemingly pursued by some nameless figure, finally flings away the copy of *The Black Road* that he has been idly carrying: "It caught at his feet in the dark until he trampled on it; he heard its spine break. Good riddance."[6] It would be comforting to think that his actual pursuer could be disposed of so easily.

It may be possible to extend this doll/man metaphor even further to cover instances where any sort of reproduction of a person's form or personality has the power to overtake and destroy its original. Consider "Broadcast" [1969; BW], wherein a man's essence appears to be drained by a microphone, or "The Next Sideshow" [1977], in which a mirror maze first presents distorted images of a man who wanders casually within it, then physically distorts him. This latter tale, however, appears to involve the notion of psychic or inner distortion under the surface of outward normality.

I do not know if "In the Trees" [1983; NV, WN] fits exactly into this paradigm, but it is such a magnificent story that I cannot forbear discussing it. This is one of the few Campbell tales to be set in a rural milieu—specifically, a forest into which a jaded bookdealer wanders, where he continually mistakes various pieces of wood for telephones, human beings, and other objects. I am not sure what symbolism is meant by this rather hideous omnipresence of wood, but the cumulative atmosphere and suspense of the story is well-nigh unexcelled in the whole of Campbell's work.

Horrors of the City

Campbell is the poet of urban squalor and decay. More so than T. E. D. Klein's New York or Clive Barker's London, the Brichester or Liverpool of Campbell's mature stories evokes not merely the noise, grime, and dangers of the city, but also the inhabitants—both lower- and middle-class—who find themselves crushed within its omnipresent coils. Only Campbell could instill horror in the commonest objects of our daily existence: plastic bags ("In the Bag" [DC]), garbage ("Litter" [HS]), a raincoat ("Old Clothes" [WN]). "Lilith's" [1975] presents a prototypical account of Campbell's world:

> He rode home that way every weekday evening. The district
> depressed him; its sameness did—the same colorless tower-blocks every-
> where on the slope above the river, the same slow procession of
> derelict terraces as the bus ground uphill, the same hostilities scrawled
> on walls, attacking the nearby travellers' camp. The January rain on the
> glass of the bus made the view worse, more the same: the houses were
> smudged brown blotches, the boards in their windows were bedraggled
> slashes of dark crayon; huge pale unsteady lumps of tower-blocks floated
> past. Palin sat swathed in layers of tobacco-smoke, coughing; the driver
> had driven him upstairs when he'd tried to stand, bloody little Hitler.
> The bus throbbed throatily to a stop [SS 49].

This single paragraph shows that his technique in depicting the urban milieu is not realism at all but impressionism. The most telling evocations of the city in his work occur not through simple description but through the metaphor-laden visions of his jaundiced narrators.

In later work, such as "Beyond Words" [1985], Campbell finds that more recent urban developments have not enhanced either the physical or psychological environment of the city:

> Liverpool's dying of slogans, Ward thinks. Several thousand city
> council workers are marching through the littered streets under placards

and banners and neon signs, Top Man, Burger King, Wimpy Hamburgers, Cascade Amusements. Songs that sound like a primer of bad English blare from shops under failing neon that turns words into gibberish. The chants of the marchers and the chattering of signs lodge in Ward's skull, crushing fragments of the story he's trying to complete. He dodges between stalls that have sprung up in Church Street, hawking cheap clothes and toys and towels imprinted like miraculous shrouds with a pop star's face... [NV 81].

How different this is from Stephen King's mechanical and uninspired brand-name-dropping! It becomes evident from such passages that Campbell's eye for the urban landscape is as keen as his eye for the finest gradations of human character. This is why some of his most powerful work depicts individuals who are as tired and rundown as their cheerless environment. It is not the urban landscape itself, but its effect upon those who dwell in it, that makes Campbell's work so dispiriting. It is scarcely to be wondered that his dominant theme is paranoia, for what else could emerge from a realm that crushes people and their dreams under the grind of metal and filth and crime?

"The Depths" [1978] provides the philosophical justification or rationale for Campbell's emphasis on the horrors of the city. It contains one of the most ingenious premises in modern weird fiction: an author finds that if he does not frantically write down his horrible nightmares of violence and sadistic crime, they come true in actuality.

> Before he'd begun to suffer from his writer's block, there had been occasions when a story had surged up from his unconscious and demanded to be written. Those stories had been products of his own mind, yet he couldn't shake them off except by writing—but now he was suffering nightmares on behalf of the world.
>
> No wonder they were so terrible, nor that they were growing worse. If material repressed into the unconscious was bound to erupt in some less manageable form, how much more powerful that must be when the unconscious was collective! Precisely because people were unable to come to terms with the crimes, repudiated them as utterly inhuman or simply unimaginable, the horrors would reappear in a worse form and possess whoever they pleased [DC 79].

This is, of course, a scarcely veiled metaphor for the indifference to society's ills that typifies urban life, especially middle-class life. Just as the repression of dreams causes them, in *Incarnate*, to emerge in a still more bizarre and dangerous form, the repression of our sense of responsibility for urban violence causes it to erupt in a still more explosive manner.

Many of Campbell's stories seem to be what I would call *supernaturalizations* of the horrors of the city; in other words, they are metaphors for the very real and chilling dangers of urban life. "The Scar" tells of what might happen in a dark alley in a bad part of town; "Down There" (DC) hints of what might lurk in the basement of an office building; "After the Queen" (BW) warns us not to linger in movie theatres too long; "The Man in the Underpass" is a magnificent tale of the dangers of a pedestrian underpass, that distinctively British topographical landmark which has exercised a great fascination for Campbell; and perhaps the early "The Cellars" is an exemplification of a mother's warning to her daughter not to go to strange places alone with a man. I wonder, however, whether some of Campbell's less successful stories are *nothing but* transmogrifications of urban paranoia: is, for example, the predictable "Reply Guaranteed" [1967; HS] anything more than a tale of women's fear of rape? Analogously, "Smoke Kiss" [1973; HS] seems to be little more than an allegory on the evils of cigarette smoking, and it draws much of its imagery from the earlier "Ash" [1969; HS].

"Mackintosh Willy" [1977; DC] is perhaps Campbell's masterpiece of this type; it may well be the single most frightening story he has ever written. This triumph of suggestiveness tells, through a boy's eyes, the relatively simple story of a derelict who dies, haunts the bicycle shelter he used to occupy in life, and then pursues a boy who mutilated his corpse by putting bottle caps over his eyes. No reason is given for the resurrection of the derelict's body, but the subtlety of the story's prose and the richness of its atmosphere cause such an omission to fall to the background, in contrast to such of Clive Barker's failures as "Sex, Death and Starshine" or *Cabal*, whose prosaic narration makes the lack of a convincing explanation for the supernatural phenomena obtrusively evident. Consider the hideous description of Mackintosh Willy drowning the boy in a pond: "When I tried to raise him, I discovered that he was pinned down. I had to grope blindly over him in the chill water, feeling how still he was. Something like a swollen cloth bag, very large, lay over his face. I couldn't bear to touch it again, for its contents felt soft and fat" (DC 15). That "swollen cloth bag" is reminiscent of a famous climax in one of M. R. James's stories, in which a supernatural entity is described as resembling "some rounded light-coloured objects ... which might be bags."[7] Indeed, the subtlety of the supernatural manifestation in "Mackintosh Willy" is very Jamesian, but with a power and poignancy drawn from a decaying urban milieu that James could not have imagined.

Paranoia

Paranoia is, for Campbell, the inevitable outcome of the ceaseless and grinding squalor and decadence of the urban milieu. The palpably real horrors of the inner city—crime, violence, poverty—compel its inhabitants to adopt an eternal vigilance that can easily metamorphose into irrational suspicion and vigilante justice. The emblematic work by Campbell in this mode is *The Face That Must Die* [1976–77].

This novel (virtually the sole instance of purely nonsupernatural horror in Campbell's early work) may still rank as his finest for its compactness, intensity, and relentless portrayal of a paranoid personality. I do not propose to study his enlightening, and disturbing, introduction to the 1983 edition of the novel. Suffice it to say that Campbell's upbringing, which has some similarities to that of Robert Aickman as recorded in *The Attempted Rescue*, gave him first-hand experience of paranoia.

What allows *The Face That Must Die* to be a genuine work of horror fiction—in contrast to the work, say, of Thomas Harris, which falls just outside the realm of the weird—is the almost unbearably intense and unrelenting way in which we are forced to inhabit the mind of a paranoid schizophrenic. We participate in his actions, we see (and, after a fashion, understand) the twisted logic of his reasoning, and we ultimately learn why he fears and suspects every person and even every object he encounters.

Our initial meeting with the semi-invalid Horridge prepares us for his gradual descent into mania. Entering a shop, he overhears a conversation by the owners and immediately thinks to himself: "Was she referring to him?" (FD 10). When he goes to a park and hears children shouting, he reflects: "People spoiled his peace" (FD 12). At this point we might think him merely a somewhat crotchety recluse, but more unpleasant traits emerge: a violent antipathy to homosexuals, fear and hatred of women ("she wore trousers, which were unnatural" [FD 13]), racism against blacks and foreigners. It is not long before Horridge enunciates the archetypal paranoid complaint: "Was the whole world mad?" (FD 45).

Gradually we learn the origins of Horridge's state: as a boy he had been accused by some girls of being gay; his father, also afflicted with severe misogyny, warns him against masturbating and going out with girls; and his father had himself caused the leg injury that forces him to walk with a humiliating limp. Slowly a still more horrifying fact dawns upon us: but for certain accidents of upbringing, Horridge could have been a relatively normal person—or, conversely, but for those same accidents we ourselves could have become a Horridge. The fact that many of his views are not entirely unusual among certain classes and certain segments of British and

American society makes us wonder how many more Horridges are dwelling quietly in our midst, ready to explode.

For it is not, of course, Horridge's simple paranoia but the actions he takes as a result of it that create the horror of this novel. Seeing a police sketch of a murderer in the paper, he fancies that an individual (a gay man) living in a nearby apartment is in fact the killer. He tries to notify the police, but they do not appear to believe him. As a result, he feels he has no recourse but to kill the man himself, and he does so.

Interweaved with Horridge's hideous pursuit of an innocent man are the lives of other occupants of the apartment building, in particular Peter and Cathy Gardner, a young couple who seem destined to become Horridge's next victims. Cathy is (aside from Roy Craig, the gay man whom Horridge kills) the only individual in the novel who is portrayed sympathetically. And yet, even she experiences paranoia on occasion, first when meeting Peter's mother ("Was it an accident of words, or was she criticizing Cathy?" [FD 108]), then when Horridge compels her to drive him to Wales ("Could he read her mind?" [FD 197]). It is as if Horridge's own paranoia were a sort of contagion that infects everyone around him.

The gradual deterioration of Horridge is masterfully handled. Just prior to killing Craig, he concludes, with shuddersomely unconscious irony, that he "had to remind himself that he was dealing with a madman" (FD 92). After hearing that someone else has confessed to the original murders, Horridge thinks his radio is mocking him (FD 114); and again later: "He shut off the radio, which was trying to distress him" (FD 159). The concluding twist of the novel is a fittingly cheerless end to a work whose unremittingly bleak vision is singular even amid Campbell's own dark oeuvre.

The Count of Eleven (1991) will inevitably be compared to *The Face That Must Die*, but this most unclassifiable of Campbell's novels defies neat categorization or comparison: who but Campbell could have written a *comic* serial killer novel? It is this anomalous mixture of paranoia, gruesomeness, and pure hilarity (and, perhaps, the fact that Campbell does not offer a facile moral condemnation of a murderer) that caused the novel to receive very mixed reviews upon its appearance. But it must be regarded as one of his great triumphs if only for its scintillating wordplay, unexcelled in all his work.

In this novel we are presented with the bumbling but undeniably likeable Jack Orchard, who becomes obsessed with numbers and begins killing people in order to preserve the logic he fancies is inherent in his number mysticism. But it would be erroneous to assume that Campbell fails to condemn Orchard for his increasingly aberrant actions. Campbell's purpose in displaying Orchard as an "ordinary" man (husband, father, struggling shop owner) is not to point the tired moral platitude that any of us could become murderers, but rather to depict the insidious way in which "normality" slowly devolves into psychosis. The characterization of Orchard is much more finely modulated than that of Horridge. The latter, when we first see him, is *already* a psychotic; on the other hand, Orchard immediately wins our sympathy for the sheer ill luck that seems to dog his every attempt to provide for himself and his family, so that it becomes impossible to determine at what precise point his increasingly harried but seemingly well-intentioned actions cross the line successively from rationality to eccentricity to dangerous insanity.

It is, however, the mingling of slapstick humor with hideous violence that gives *The Count of Eleven* its utterly distinctive tone. A scene at the beginning, in which an old man blunders about in Orchard's video store and causes a fire that burns the place down, could not have been surpassed by Wodehouse. A later scene, where Orchard, now a murderer, kills a man by blasting him with a blowtorch and hurling him into a river, presents the surface atmosphere of a Three Stooges episode but gradually devolves into one of the most loathsome murders in all weird or crime fiction:

> [Jack] trained the jet of flames on the largest target within reach, the top of Foster's head. In a very few seconds the man's hair hissed and withered, and he was both bald and piebald. During these seconds he emitted an almost inarticulate crescendo of sound—"Mmmur"—and Jack had the dismaying impression that he was crying out for his mother. His hands were convulsively slapping the water and keeping him afloat, so that he was unable to move out of range of the flame. His scalp was peeling by the time shock or helplessness or a yearning for the cool water caused him to sink [CE 199].

And yet (as with Patricia Highsmith's series of novels about the clumsy but engaging murderer Tom Ripley) we cannot help liking Orchard even after he commits the first several of his murders, especially as in some cases he resorts not to murder but to mere arson, making sure that no "innocent" individuals are killed or even injured. This sort of consideration could not have been imagined by a Horridge. A recent commentator, Joel Lane, also sees an interesting political dimension to the novel. "The problems faced by the Orchard family are synonymous with Thatcherite economic culture: the slick, cold mechanisms of banks, employers, insurance agents, estate agents. Life becomes a lottery, a numbers game in which survival depends on 'chancing.' Jack Orchard takes this value distortion literally, reducing people to numbers and placing absolute trust in luck."[8] Truly, *The Count of Eleven* has turned the hackneyed serial killer novel on its head: we may all be murderers, but we are also all victims, and it is becoming increasingly difficult to tell the difference between the two.

Next to Horridge and Jack Orchard, Danny Swain, the pockmarked youth who gradually becomes the focus of evil in *Incarnate*, is Campbell's most powerfully realized paranoid personality, especially as he is sketched in this magnificent character portrait:

> He couldn't say he hated Mr. Pettigrew for treating him like a dog, not when Mr. Pettigrew might be a friend of hers. He couldn't say that he wanted a job he had got for himself instead of the job Mr. Pettigrew had given him as a favor to his father because it was clear nobody else would employ him, just because he wasn't very good at speaking. He wanted to be somebody, that was all, somebody more than the schoolboy who had never been able to speak up when the teacher had said, "Got a bone in your throat, Danny?"; more than the teenager who'd locked himself in the toilet to hide from the girls who said, "Got a bone in your trousers, Danny?"; the girls kicking the toilet door and telling him what they were going to show him, until he hadn't dared go out when the afternoon bell rang because the girls would be waiting for him in the classroom. He couldn't say any of this, he mustn't get confused, mustn't let his enemies confuse him. His trousers were hurting his crotch, his stomach felt squeezed and he was afraid he was going to fart ... [I 87].

In this compact and bitter passage we can see Danny's entire young life encapsulated, as well as the origin of his hatred of women and of people in authority. Once again Campbell has taken care to supply the psychological background of his characters so that their paranoia seems an entirely natural product of their stunted upbringing. And Danny, although ignorant, clumsy, and full of repressed rage, earns our sympathy far more than Horridge does.

Campbell's short stories feature some of his most notable paranoid characters. In "The Little Voice" [1976; DC] horror is evoked by the simple repetition of the meaningless syllables *la, la, la*. A schoolteacher, Edith Locketty, hears the sounds repeatedly from the house next door, which appears to have been inhabited only by an old blind man who has just died. But surely, Edith thinks, the voice must be of some poor child who has been left alone in the house. She herself is a prototypical paranoiac, close to the edge of insanity. "She read her book to her class, and watched their faces dull. Ranks of uniformed waxworks stared at her, drooping a little. Did they think they were too old for the story, or that she was out of date? She saw the old man trembling. Noise from next door floundered about her room, like a clumsy intruder. If she didn't act she would lose control of herself. 'Talk quietly until I come back,' she said" (DC 107). But what of that *la, la, la?* Is it real or is it simply a product of Edith's imagination? Is it, indeed, the child that she aborted years before? This brooding and atmospheric story ranks as one of Campbell's finest in its careful etching of a disturbed personality who at once repels us and in some strange fashion excites our horrified pity.

The paranoid character stalks through the length and breadth of Campbell's work—from "Cold Print" [1966–67] to "A Street Was Chosen" [1990]—and may well be, in addition to and working in conjunction with his portrayal of decayed cityscapes, his most distinctive and easily recognizable contribution to weird fiction. Hawthorne, Machen, and Lovecraft found the sinister in the untenanted wilderness, but Campbell is the archetypal weird fictionist of the metropolis. Jobs that lead nowhere and accomplish nothing; sex, drugs, and crime as the only escapes from crushing poverty or aimless ignorance; caution and vigilance devolving into irrational suspicion and freakish violence: this is Campbell's city, and it is something that those of the urban milieu can recognize very plainly. And yet, Campbell's erstwhile mentor H. P. Lovecraft prophesied just such a development in his warning about the dangers of mechanization:

> Granted that the machine-victim has leisure. What is he going to do with it? What memories and experiences has he to form a background to give significance to anything he can do? What can he see or do that will mean anything to him? ... We shall hear of all sorts of futile reforms and reformers—standardised culture-outlines, synthetic sports and spectacles, professional play-leaders and study-guides, and kindred examples of machine-made uplift and brotherly spirit. And it will amount to just about as much as most reforms do! Meanwhile the tension of boredom and unsatisfied imagination will increase—breaking out with increasing frequency in crimes of morbid perversity and explosive violence.[9]

SEX AND DEATH

Scared Stiff: Tales of Sex and Death (1986) is one of Campbell's finest collections. Most of its seven tales were originally written for anthologies compiled by Michel Parry (including two anthologies of sex-horror stories edited under the piquant pseudonym "Linda Lovecraft"), and they are among his most affecting stories. But the mingling of sex and horror commences at a very early stage in Campbell's career. In the introduction to *The Height of the Scream* he remarks wryly of the unconscious sexual symbolism to be found in "The Inhabitant of the Lake" (HS x), while as early a tale as "The Moon-Lens" [1963] already hints tentatively at a union of sex and the weird. Other early tales treat intensely of human relationships at the same time that they treat of the supernatural. "The Cellars" [1965] is once again a landmark in this regard, since the premise of the story is the attempt of a dubious character named Vic to seduce a coworker, Julie, by luring her into some deserted catacombs in Liverpool.

An entire section in *Demons by Daylight* is titled "Relationships," and we find here some of Campbell's earliest and best tales of love and death. We have already made note of the exquisitely poignant "Concussion," where the bizarre decades-spanning love affair is the very core of the supernaturalism of the tale. And we must make note of the elusive "The Second Staircase," which initiates a theme to which Campbell returns again and again. Let us consider the opening paragraph. "DELTAFILMS INTERVIEW MEET EUSTON 9.00— But never having met Mike Parry, Carol bobbed above the crowd and thrust through trajectories as the clock edged on to 9.15, finding Mike finally beneath the clock, hopefully holding aloft as identification a copy of *Castle of Frankenstein*. Mike smiled recognition, then his mouth dropped as the minute hand turned downward" (DD 96). What sounds like another of Campbell's many tales of a female protagonist turns out to be nothing of the sort, for Carol is actually a male—but a male whose androgynous name symbolizes his doubt of his own virility. As a result, he has become a misogynist ("Women—he hated them, their soft helpless bodies, passively resisting, unattainable" [DD 104]); but, in some dreamlike way that only Campbell could have devised, Carol finds himself turned into a woman.

This fluidity between the male and female bodies is an idea that fascinates Campbell, for it recurs in "The Seductress" [1975]: "When Betty lay trembling, unable to look, the face stooped for her to see. It was Alastair's mother, smiling triumphantly. She passed a hand over her face. As though that reversed each aspect of it she was James again; his long face replaced her square one, her small plump nose was all at once slim and straight. She passed her hand upward and was herself, as if she'd changed a mask. The mask smiled" (SS 92). It also recurs, in a somewhat different way, in "Stages" (SS), where, perhaps as a result of drug taking, a man's personality and body merge insidiously with those of his lover.

"Lilith's" [1975] may perhaps be the best story in *Scared Stiff*, for a number of reasons—its gritty evocation of Campbell's derelict world of slums and tenements, its utilization of the doll/man theme in a particularly vivid and provocative way (here with the use of a sex doll, which has some nebulous relation to the seductive owner of the store where a man bought it), and in its portrayal of utterly cheerless passion, as the man dreams of making love to the doll after having fished it out of the garbage:

> He was making love to a girl. Her eyes sparkled; she panted, she smiled widely, laughing—he made her feel alive as she never had before. As soon as he was free he'd gone to her. He'd dressed and run to find her. He was laughing too, as they worked together toward orgasm. He'd found her and carried her easily to bed. Her left arm lay carelessly above her head, carelessly twisted, impossibly twisted. He'd found her and dragged her out the rest of the way, as cats struggled from between her limbs.
>
> When he awoke screaming he was lying face down on the bed, in her [SS 67].

Other tales are nearly as striking, although less explicitly sexual. "The Previous Tenant" [1969; BW] treats poignantly of a painter who becomes increasingly fascinated with the spirit of a young woman who committed suicide in the flat he now occupies. But as the tale unfolds it develops into a story of jealousy (the painter's wife "accidentally" destroys the few remaining tokens of the woman's existence in the apartment) and of the irreconcilability of artistic and domestic existence. "The Other Woman" [1974; SS] also involves a painter, this one a commercial cover artist, who becomes fascinated with the picture of a woman he himself has painted for some trashy bestseller, and whom he renders with one blue eye and one brown eye. He imagines violently raping the woman, and finds that he can no longer perform sexually with his wife unless he keeps the image of the woman, and the violence he wishes to inflict upon her, in his mind. This tale is conceivably nonsupernatural until the very last line, when we read of the painter's wife: "Then her legs closed over his, and he stared down to see her eyes gazing at him: one blue eye, one brown" (SS 47). The subtlety and rich texture of this story make this conclusion both startling and inevitable. The overriding metaphor of the tale, of course, is the male instinct for rape, a desire for sexual control that can cross over insidiously into ugly violence. "You would throw her down on the floor. You'd lie on top of her so that she couldn't kick, you'd pin her flailing forearms down with your elbows. You'd lean your weight on your thumbs at her throat. Her throat would struggle wildly as a trapped bird. Her eyes would widen, trying to spring free of the vise: one blue eye, one brown" (SS 26).

Aberrant sex is rarely presented in Campbell's novels (here again his concern for the sensibilities of his middle-class readers becomes evident), but it cannot be said that the depiction of sex, love, and marriage in his longer work is any more comforting than in his short stories. One of the principal goals or functions of a supernatural manifestation in Campbell is to insinuate itself into human relationships and corrupt them from within by bringing to the surface all the dissatisfactions and resentments—between husband and wife, parent and child, or entire generations of a family—that lurk beneath a superficially placid and loving household. All this again points to the unusually noncosmic range of Campbell's supernatural phenomena, which almost always operate upon individuals rather than upon the world or the universe at large.

The sexual frankness that Campbell introduced to weird fiction in *Demons by Daylight* has had wide ramifications for the field, not all of them good: many writers have neither the skill nor the restraint to produce anything but cheap titillation out of the mingling of sex and horror. In many of Campbell's own tales, indeed, sex is nothing but tawdry and emotionless, a mating of animals in a garbage-strewn alley. But such a depiction harmonizes drearily well with the desolate urban panorama, where the sighs of love and passion devolve into the grunts and grinding of meaningless sex.

CHILDHOOD

In the introduction to *Waking Nightmares* Campbell remarks that "parenthood seems to keep sending me back to the theme of the vulnerability of children" (WN 2), and children figure as protagonists—both as the victims and as the perpetrators of evil—from the beginning to the end of his work. Perhaps Campbell's sensitivity to the world of childhood comes from the very early initiation of his own writing career. In adhering faithfully to the old adage of "write what you know," he has drawn extensively in early and late writings upon his own experiences as a youth.

Campbell can treat every aspect of the life of children with uncanny psychological insight: games ("Little Man" [1978; ST], "Apples," "The Old School" [1988; WN]); the traumas of attending school ("The Interloper" [1968; DD]); relationships with parents ("The Chimney" [1975; DF]); the slow emergence from childhood into the adult world ("Being an Angel" [1988; WN]). Of course, some of these themes are also treated from an adult perspective: recall the sour schoolteachers in "The Little Voice" and "The Other Side" (WN), and the game motif prevalent in "Playing the Game" and many other stories. But the themes gain a particular poignancy when focusing upon children. And yet, Campbell's children are frequently not the beatific innocents of Victorian wishful thinking but the tough, hard, street-wise youths of the inner city. It is no wonder that, in "Apples," they manage to gang together and overcome the supernatural horror (in the form of an old man) that threatens them. Even these children, however, have not yet been bludgeoned into the jaundiced cynicism that affects so many of Campbell's adults.

One of the first serious treatments of children in Campbell's fiction occurs in the chilling tale "The Man in the Underpass" [1973], among the earliest of his tales to be narrated from the point of view of a child. As in Machen's "The White People," the prototypical instance of this approach, the effectiveness of this tale rests in the naiveté of the narrative voice: the children playing in a pedestrian underpass fail to understand the hoary antiquity and menace of the Aztec rites that animate the crudely drawn figure of a man in the underpass.

> "Oh, it's only that stupid thing on the wall," June said. "No it isn't," Tonia said. "There's a real man down there if you look." "Well, I don't want to see him," June said. "What's so special about him?" I said. "He's a god," Tonia said. "He's not. He's just a man playing with his thing," June said. "He probably wouldn't want you to see him anyway," Tonia said. "I'm going down. You go home." "We'll come with you to make sure you're all right," I said, but really I was excited without knowing why [DF 93].

"Eye of Childhood" [1978; WN] presents a converse scenario, telling moodily (and a little confusingly) of a seemingly normal child who practices witchcraft.

Then there is the highly disturbing story "The Chimney," a bizarre tale of a lonely, frightened child and his parents. Campbell has referred to it as "disguised autobiography—disguised from me at the time of writing, that is" (DF x). This account of a boy terrified of seeing his father (or something else) come down the chimney as Father Christmas can only make us think of some passages in the introduction to *The Face That Must Die*, where Campbell tells of how his estranged parents occupied separate floors of their house, so that he had almost no contact with his father: "For most of my childhood ... my father was heard but not seen.... I used to hear his footsteps on the stairs as I lay in bed, terrified that he would come into my room.... Worst of all was Christmas, when my mother would send me to knock on his bedroom door and invite him down, as a mark of seasonal goodwill, for Christmas dinner. I would go upstairs in a panic, but there was never any response" (FD xvi–xvii).

And now "The Chimney":

> ...I heard the slithering in the chimney.
>
> Something large was coming down. A fall of soot: I could hear the scattering pats of soot in the grate, thrown down by the harsh halting wind. But the wind was emerging from the fireplace, into the room. It was above me, panting through its obstructed throat.
>
> I lay staring up at the mask of my sheets. I trembled from holding myself immobile. My held breath filled me painfully as lumps of rock. I had only to lie there until whatever was above me went away. It couldn't touch me [DF 148].

It should be remarked that the tale's power in no way depends upon our knowledge of Campbell's biography: "The Chimney" is a masterwork of brooding horror that requires no commentary, biographical or otherwise, to elucidate it. But a knowledge of Campbell's unusual upbringing lends a poignancy to the tale that somehow augments its horrific effect.

Nearly all of Campbell's novels feature children, mostly as innocent victims meant to attract the reader's sympathy, but occasionally as foci or instigators of supernatural evil. Susan, the daughter of Helen Verney in *Incarnate*, is perhaps Campbell's most delicately etched child character, and her apparent destruction, as the mysterious young girl Eve (a facet of Sage) usurps her body, lends an aura of bitterness and tragedy to the novel. (I am, in fact, not entirely clear what happens to Susan, as Campbell never mentions her once her personality has apparently been ousted from her body by Eve.) Other child characters—such as the stereotypical and excessively well-adjusted Francesca and Russell in *Obsession*—are less well realized.

The Influence [1986–87] seems to reenact the Susan/Eve scenario of *Incarnate* by featuring a battle between child-as-victim and child-as-villain. The plot of this novel is not at all new. An elderly woman, Queenie, is so fiercely determined to perpetuate her existence by sheer willpower that she usurps the body of a little girl, Vicky, on the way to overtaking the personality of her grandniece, Rowan. Nor is the execution very subtle (the moment the girl Vicky mentions her name, we think of Queenie—i.e., Queen Victoria). And yet, the confrontation of childlike naiveté and preternaturally aged sophistication is ably handled. The novel contains one of the most spectacular dream sequences in all Campbell's work, a long, moody chapter in which Rowan, fleeing from the home of her aunt (who has been violently murdered by Queenie/Vicky), undertakes a laborious and seemingly endless trek back to her own home—first by train, then, when she senses Vicky pursuing her, mile after mile on foot—only to discover when she gets there, days or perhaps months later, that Queenie has evicted her spirit from her body and occupied it instead. This novel too suffers somewhat from sentimentality, and some of the quarrels between Rowan's parents are embarrassingly reminiscent of soap-opera bickering, but its conclusion is poignant and satisfying.

RECENT WORK

Aside from *The Count of Eleven*, Campbell's most recent major works include two novels, *Midnight Sun* (1990) and *The Long Lost* (1993), and a novelette, *Needing Ghosts* (1990). These three seem, in their very different ways, to be grand summations of everything Campbell is and stands for. All the themes that dominate his writing—dream and reality, art and reality, urban life, paranoia, childhood—come to a head here and in many ways receive their most potent and concentrated expression. What is more, they indicate that Campbell, already a writer of 30 years' standing, may perhaps not even now have reached the pinnacle of his career. Brilliant and revolutionary as some of his work already is, there may be even better yet to come.

Needing Ghosts [1989–90] is virtually the only one of Campbell's works (with the possible exception of a science fiction tale, *Medusa*) that can be classified as a novelette—that unique form which seems especially suited for weird writing, if the best of Lovecraft, Aickman, and Klein is any indication. And it may well be his single greatest acheivement. Everything that defines Campbell's work is here, from the cheerless urban milieu and paranoia to the spiritual loneliness of the modern city-dweller. And the whole tale (told in a nightmarish, third person *present* tense that recalls the best of the *Demons by Daylight* stories) is a long rumination on the interrelationship of words and life. Steven J. Mariconda, in a sensitive review of the work, has identified the plot of the story as involving "a horror writer who has gone mad, murdered his family, and then turned the knife on himself. The events of the story, told from the perspective of [the writer] *after* his death, are a surreal series of episodes that lead to his realization of the murders. The entire narrative, Campbell hints at the end, is—somehow—simply a *dream* of the dead author."[10] Persuasive as Mariconda's arguments are, I think a different interpretation of events could be made.

The protagonist, Simon Mottershead, wakes up one day unaware of who he is and what he is supposed to be doing. Gradually, as he ventures forth into an utterly hallucinatory world, certain facts dawn upon him: he is an author, having written at least one book, *Cadenza*; he is to deliver a lecture at a library; he has (or had) a wife and children. At the outset it appears as if he is simply another in Campbell's long line of paranoiacs, perhaps similar to Horridge in *The Face That Must Die*. But as events unfold, Mottershead desperately attempts to maintain a hold on what he believes to be reality and sanity in a world that appears to have gone completely mad. He stumbles into a bookstore and finds a copy of his own book; its first line, "He knows this dark" (NG 27), is the first line of *Needing Ghosts* itself. What does this mean? Already the problematical distinction between art and reality is being broken down, as it does further when Mottershead, blundering into the library (which is bizarrely juxtaposed to a shopping mall) for his lecture, tells his audience how it feels to be a writer.

> "Every day I'd be wakened by a story aching to be told. Writing's a compulsion. By the time you're any good at it you no longer have the choice of giving it up. It won't leave you alone even when you're with people, even when you're desperate to sleep.... When it comes to life ... it's like seeing everything with new eyes. It's like dreaming while you're awake. It's as if your mind's a spider which is trying to catch reality and spin it into patterns" [NG 34].

"When it comes to life"—what can this refer to but Mottershead's own writing? Another fragment of the truth (if it is that) comes toward the end, as Mottershead wends his way to what appears to be his own former home and finds a videocassette containing an interview he evidently once gave. A commentator remarks:

> "In one of his stories a man who's obsessed with the impossibility of knowing if he has died in his sleep convinces himself that he has, and is dreaming. Another concerns a man who believes he is being followed by a schizophrenic whose hallucinations are affecting his own perceptions, but the hallucinations prove to be the reality he has tried to avoid seeing. The reader is left suspecting that the schizophrenic is really a projection of the man himself" [NG 73].

This is a remarkably accurate description of what has transpired throughout the story, as Mottershead harriedly attempts to escape pursuit from a bald-headed man who dogs him for no apparent reason. When Mottershead finds his family killed (a knife has impaled a book to their necks) he wonders: "Did he once write about doing away with his family, or wasn't he able to write it?" (NG 77). It is my belief that what has really happened to Mottershead is that, alive or dead, he has *fallen into his own fictional universe*. The reality of his stories has subsumed the reality of his life.

And yet, perhaps in the end it is not possible to decide what exactly has happened in *Needing Ghosts*. Is Mottershead alive or dead? Is he caught in a dream? Is the world around him a dream or a hallucination? I believe that a number of entirely contradictory interpretations could be made of this tale, each with just as much validity as the next. All we are left with in the end is pure nightmare.

Midnight Sun is of an entirely different sort. It is the pinnacle of Campbell's realistic novels of character, written in a fluid, supple, richly textured prose superior to that of any of his previous novel-length works, even *Incarnate*. It tells the story of Ben Sterling, who as a boy was fascinated with a book written by his great-grandfather, the explorer Edward Sterling, entitled *Of the Midnight Sun*. This curious book of fairy tales haunts Sterling's imagination even after his aunt (who looks after him after his entire family has been killed in a car accident) takes the book away from him in fear of its being a bad influence. Growing into adulthood, Sterling marries and becomes a writer of children's books himself. At this point the novel suffers a perhaps inevitable letdown, as Campbell, forsaking the intense psychological portrait of Ben as a boy, lapses into conventionality by depicting his usual novelistic scenario of husband-wife-and-happy-children, although in a somewhat less sentimental manner than in other works. But this depiction is necessary to the thematic development of *Midnight Sun*, whose focus is Ben's search for what haunted him about Edward Sterling's book as a boy.

Throughout the novel Ben senses that he is on the brink of some stupendous revelation, which is somehow connected with the dense forest behind his ancestral home ("It seemed to him that the silent luminous dance was constantly about to form a pattern in the air—that if he could only distinguish the pattern, unimaginable revelations might follow" [MS 103]; "he felt as though an inspiration or a vision larger than he could imagine was hovering just out of reach" [MS 136]). Finally the revelation comes. Edward Sterling was found dead of exposure in the icy forest, and Ben realizes that

> Edward Sterling's death had been only the beginning. The forest concealed what his death had liberated—what had accompanied him beyond the restraint of the midnight sun.
>
> Perhaps it had been waiting for as long as there was ice there, waiting for someone it could ride beyond the light. Perhaps that hadn't been Edward Sterling who had come back, but only a shell of him compelled to walk and talk. It must have been the source of the strength which had driven him north again in search of somewhere it could hide, but his body had failed before it reached anywhere secret enough. The forest had hidden it while its power grew during the long nights, and now it was awakening [MS 210–11].

Now Ben feels as if he must take up the task of ushering in this ice-entity back into the world. It is one of Campbell's great triumphs that this nebulous creature, as well as Ben's apparent yielding to it, is never described as anything but awesome and cosmic: fear has no place in this scenario. Campbell himself, in the acknowledgments of the novel, places it in the category of "visionary horror fiction," and indeed much of the novel is reminiscent of Algernon Blackwood's portrayal of the throbbing vitality of nature, a portrayal as devoid of horror (in the sense of fear for the harm that might be caused to human beings) as Campbell's. And yet, at the end Ben has a change of heart and seeks to combat the entity and thrust it back into the dark again. Mariconda's comment that this reversal is "inadequately motivated" is itself charitably inadequate: Ben's actions seem to me entirely unmotivated. It is true that Ben's self-immolation in the depths of the forest bring to mind the impromptu fairy tale he was told as a boy—of the people who live "at the edge of the coldest place in the world" (MS 34) and whose responsibility it is to tend to the fires that will keep the ice from overrunning the world—but the thrust of Campbell's entire narrative has been leading up to the conclusion that the release of the ice-entity is in no way a horrific but simply an awesome event. "The world and the stars had been less than a dream, nothing more than a momentary lapse in its consciousness, and the metamorphosis which was reaching for the world was infinitesimal by its standards, simply a stirring in its sleep, a transient dream of the awful perfection which would overtake infinity when the presence beyond the darkness was fully awake" (MS 323). And yet, Ben, by choosing his family over the entity ("The only light he wanted to see now, too late, was the light in Ellen's and the children's eyes" [MS 319]), is also choosing the safe and bourgeois comforts of family life over the awesome and supremely impersonal force of nature, even though Campbell has been suggesting all along that the former is, in cosmic terms, utterly insignificant in relation to the latter. Despite this severely flawed ending, Midnight Sun must still rank as one of Campbell's finest novels for its exquisitely modulated prose, its perfect unity of construction, and the genuinely cosmic and visionary imagery evoked throughout the entire work.

Overt supernaturalism is reduced almost to the vanishing point in The Long Lost, which could easily pass for a poignant mainstream tale of domestic life. This novel shows how keenly Campbell has learned to depict—again in prose of exquisite fluidity that unites the subdued vitality of Midnight Sun with the intermittent comedy of The Count of Eleven—the manifold ironies and absurdities of everyday existence. He displays an uncanny knack for showing how ordinary people can fall haplessly into the most grotesque situations, and his deft strokes of character portrayal put to shame the plodding verbosity of Stephen King and instead bring John Fowles or Evelyn Waugh to mind.

The Long Lost is based on the theme of the sin-eater—a stranger who, according to ancient Celtic legend, must come to the home where a wake is being held and eat the food (usually a small cake) symbolizing the sins of the deceased. The stranger is then given money and hounded away lest he spread the sins he has absorbed. In fact, the sin-eater motif is not immediately evident in this tale of modern England, although anyone who has read Fiona Macleod's superb story, "The Sin-Eater" (1895)—or its skillful adaptation on Rod Serling's "Night Gallery"—will develop an awareness of it from the obscure hints Campbell supplies. In this case, the sin-eater is an old woman, Gwendolen, who is found lying in a catatonic state in a cottage on a small island off the coast of Wales by David and Joelle Owain, who are vacationing there; Gwendolen claims that her last name is Owain, so that David takes her for a long-lost relative. Bringing her back to Chester, the Owains invite her to a barbecue with some of their friends, at which time she distributes certain odd-tasting cakes she has made.

While it is a shame to spoil the suspense of this novel by revealing its denouement, one must do so in order to study it. Gwendolen is a sin-eater, and has been for years, decades, and perhaps centuries: David only realizes toward the end that the old photograph showing his grandfather as a small boy also showed Gwendolen *as an old woman*. And yet, Gwendolen is far from being an "evil" figure. Indeed, her portrayal as ineffably sad person who seems to bear very heavily the ills of a long life ("'I doubt you'll meet anyone who believes in sin more than I do'" [LL 71]) is a masterstroke of characterization. In effect, Gwendolen distributes the cakes—the sins she has accumulated from her anomalous occupation—lest she herself die with them. David asks her at the end: "'Did being frightened keep you alive somehow, Gwen? ... What could make you so scared?'" (LL 367–68).

The effect of the eating of the cakes by the guests at the barbecue is nothing more than an emphasis of the "sins" or flaws of character each of them possesses. David himself, although otherwise a loving husband, begins to develop an unhealthy sexual attraction to Angela, the 14-year-old daughter of a friend. Angela herself seems to be trying to seduce David with her young, healthy body. Herb Crantry, whose wife has left him for another man, kills himself and the man in a fit of jealousy. Doug Singleton, a lawyer, adopts a coldly legalistic attitude toward even his friends. And so on. In one of the most harrowing tableaux in all Campbell's work, Richard Vale, owner of an unsuccessful computer store, falls into despair over his economic troubles and seeks to kill himself, his wife, and his two teenage children. The long chapter in which this scene is narrated—beginning with the family's wholesome day at the seaside but with the reader's slowly dawning realization that Richard both loves his family and believes that killing them is the only solution to his problems—is one long *conte cruel* unrivaled by anything even in *The Face That Must Die*.

Perhaps the only drawback to the novel is the lack of explanation as to why the effects of the cakes abate toward the end. Somehow—and especially during and after the funeral of Richard Vale's family—the Owains and their friends develop some sense of community that allows them to put aside their conflicts. Whatever the case, the characters of all the protagonists in the novel are etched with exquisite felicity, and although the novel almost entirely lacks the "visionary" scope of *Midnight Sun*, the sin-eater theme causes *The Long Lost* to achieve a cumulative sense of weirdness that is not compromised by the seeming mundanity (and, toward the beginning, the occasional buffoonery) of the surface events. Campbell's growing interest in the complexities of language, exhibited in *The Count of Eleven*, is also on display here, as we come to realize that every single utterance by Gwendolen is a double entendre that refers covertly to her baleful and perhaps unwillingly adopted mythic occupation.

Midnight Sun and *The Long Lost* may indicate that Campbell is finally comfortable working in the novel form. He has conceived plots of sufficient spaciousness that a novel is required for their exposition, and a novel that does not involve the mere multiplication of human characters to carry the theme forward, as was the case even with *Incarnate*. But if we have the right to expect more novels of this sort from Campbell, how much more may we hope that he will write a few more works like *Needing Ghosts*. A volume gathering three or four tales of the calibre of *Needing Ghosts* would constitute the greatest weird collection in the history of literature.

STYLE AND TECHNIQUE

It is singularly difficult to specify, in short compass and without extensive quotation, the precise methods Campbell uses to create his horrific effects. Certainly much of the power of his work derives purely from his prose style, one of the most fluid, dense, and evocative in all modern literature. Campbell can vivify anything. His eye for the details and resonances of even the most mundane objects, and his ability to express them crisply and almost prose-poetically, give to his work at once a clarity and a dreamlike nebulousness that is difficult to describe but easy to sense. Consider his description of so prosaic a thing as an airplane's safety card: "Red arrows poked at cartoon passengers, who leaned forward in attitudes of despair, clutching their heads. Passengers slid down a yellow chute and hurried away; in their haste they'd left their mouths on the plane. A woman helped a child don a life jacket. Panic had frozen the child's face into a bland mask, identical in three pictures. However the woman turned her head, its outline remained exactly the shape of a strawberry" (P 100). And such a description not merely enlivens what might otherwise be a tiresome description of a routine flight, but also helps to create that air of brooding ominousness that makes Campbell's work so powerfully hypnotic.

It is largely as a result of his distinctive style and imagery that Campbell is able to resurrect some of the hoariest and most hackneyed themes in weird fiction and give them new life. An early story, "Napier Court" [1967], is one of the finest haunted house stories in recent years, telling mesmerically of a house whose previous inhabitant, a suicide, expressed the desire to "fade into the house" (DC 21). In the end a young woman meets the same fate.

> The house was empty. Alma was surrounded by a vacuum into which something must rush. She stood up shaking and fell into the vacuum; her sight was torn away. She tried to move; there was no longer any muscle to respond. She felt nothing, but utter horror closed her in. Somewhere she sensed her body, moving happily on her bedroom carpet, picking up her ruined flute, breathing a hideous note into it. She tried to scream. Impossible.
>
> Only in dreams can houses scream for help [DC 32].

In other stories Campbell has given refreshing treatments to the themes of the werewolf ("Night Beat"), the mummy ("Wrapped Up" [ST]), the zombie ("Jack in the Box" [WN]) and the vampire ("Drawing In" [DC]). "The Proxy" [1977; DC] ingeniously melds two old themes by presenting the ghost of a house.

But it would be unjust to Campbell merely to suggest—as Gary William Crawford has done in a mediocre booklet on Campbell—that he has *only* revitalized standard weird scenarios. If the grim realism of his urban settings, his hallucinatory style, his ability to mingle sex and horror, and the insidiously subtle manner of his weird manifestations are not sufficient indications of his fundamental originality, then several of his stories are founded upon strikingly novel premises. Consider "The Pattern" [1975]. This story—dealing with a man who comes to a seemingly placid rural town only to find increasingly disturbing hints of strangeness all around him— gives the impression of being somewhat long-winded, but its magnificent conclusion both redeems and justifies its length. An inhabitant of the town tells the man and his wife what a spiritualist conjectured when he investigated a loathsome murder that had occurred some years before. "'Oh, he had an explanation, he was full of them. He tried to tell the police and me that the real tragedy hadn't happened yet. He wanted us to believe he could see it in the future. Of course he couldn't say what or when. Do you know what he tried to make out? That there was something so awful in the future it was echoing back somehow, a sort of ghost in reverse'" (DC 148). Can this somehow account for the screams the man keeps hearing around his house? What else can he conclude when he finds his wife horribly butchered? "As all the trees quivered like columns of water he heard movement behind him. Though he had no will to live, it took him a long time to turn. He knew the pattern had reached its completion, and he was afraid. He had to close his eyes before he could turn, for he could still hear the scream he was about to utter" (DC 150). I am inclined to connect this with such a story as "Playing the Game": perhaps Campbell senses that we are mere pawns in the control of a force or a "pattern" vastly larger than us.

"Hearing Is Believing" (DF) is an interesting attempt to evoke horror purely from sounds—in this instance a demonic stereo that continues to produce noises even when it is not plugged in. This tale may have had a dim antecedent in the early tale "The Plain of Sound" [1962; TH], in which the entities inhabiting a desolate region are actually *living sounds*. Campbell is a great appreciator of classical music and has written many record reviews for Liverpool newspapers; it is, accordingly, not surprising that music plays a key role in many of his tales. In "Cat and Mouse" music helps to sustain the atmosphere of weirdness: "I thought *Curlew River* might help me define my thoughts. But I didn't get as far as the second side, with its angelic resolution. Peter Pears' eerie vocal glissandi in the part of the madwoman chilled me like the howls of a sad cat; the church which the stereo re-created seemed longer and more hollow, like a tunnel gaping invisibly before me in the air" (ST 26). In "Hearing Is Believing," however, sound itself becomes a source of horror. "Though the stereo wasn't plugged in, the sounds filled the speakers: a gust of wind splattered rain across sagging wallpaper, waterlogged plaster collapsed, a prolonged juicy noise" (DF 282). From a slightly different perspective, note should perhaps be made of the early story, "Among the pictures are these:" [1973; CP], a sort of prose poem describing some drawings Campbell had himself made in 1961.

If Campbell can vary the tone of his work at will, he can also utilize a number of ingenious narrative devices when his themes call for them. One of the most frequent of these is second-person singular narration in the present tense. He is, of course, not the originator of this device—the pioneering, and perhaps still the finest, example of it is Thomas Burke's

"Johnson Looked Back," in *Night-Pieces* (1935)—but it is, once again, a particularly vivid means for Campbell to isolate an individual's thought processes as they are occurring. A number of tales in *The Height of the Scream* and *Dark Companions* employ it, but none more effectively than "Heading Home." This tale—in which the severed head of a scientist manages to emerge from a basement where it has been dumped and reunites with its body—falls just short of being a trick story (as "Conversion" [DC] does not). The "you" of the tale seems to refer to the entire person when in fact it refers only to the head, but this very fact underscores the philosophical point that the head—or, rather, the brain within it—*is* the person because that is where all thought and consciousness lie. The metaphor by which this conception is expressed is the scientist's discovery of a formula that allows the brain to function independently of the body.

> You recall the day you perfected the solution. As soon as you'd quaffed it you felt your brain achieve a piercing alertness, become precisely and continually aware of the messages of each nerve and preside over them, making minute adjustments at the first hint of danger. You knew this was what you'd worked for, but you couldn't prove it to yourself until the day you felt the stirrings of cancer. Then your brain seemed to condense into a keen strand of energy that stretched down and seared the cancer out. That was proof. You were immortal [DC 48].

Another device favored by Campbell is what I would call *double narration*. This technique involves the successive narration of the same event through the eyes of different characters. It is yet another testimonial to Campbell's intense interest in individual consciousness. Indeed, one might almost say that he is curiously reluctant to abandon this perspective: it is strange how infrequently he uses omniscient narration as opposed to narration centered upon a given individual's thought processes. Although double narration is employed in several of his novels, its most striking usage occurs in *The Face That Must Die*. Its power here stems from the juxtaposition of a "normal" and a "paranoid" view of the same event. The murder of Roy Craig is dealt with in this manner: in Chapter 11 we follow Craig's thoughts and actions up to the time of his sudden death on his own doorstep; Chapter 12 then compels us to relive the event through the eyes of Horridge. It is exactly because we know what is coming that the technique gains its gruesome effectiveness. Chapters 22–24 of the novel form an interlocking network of double narrations; they also present an anomalous reversal of roles, as Cathy, spotting Horridge but thinking him a private detective, wishes to speak to him, while Horridge, thinking that

Cathy is helping the police, flees her in the fog. Each chapter replays a certain portion of the events of the previous chapter, then carries the narrative forward a little further so that the next chapter can again replay these events and carry them on still further.

Campbell's general lack of humor in his tales has been noted (and, evidently, rather foolishly regretted—as if his intense vision required a dollop of comic relief now and again!), but one wonders whether some of his later stories do not in fact parody his own manner. There was a period in the later 1970s when his tales were becoming almost formulaic—one could predict that at the end some hapless individual would finally come face to face with the supernatural force that had been lurking just beyond his vision. Perhaps his virtual surcease of short-story writing in the early 1980s gave him a fresh perspective from which to regard his own work, for his later tales have, as I have remarked, become more varied in style and tone. But parody is very evident in such a tale as "Seeing the World" [1983; DF], in which a seemingly conventional middle-class couple invite their neighbors to watch the slides of their trip to Europe, during which they visited some catacombs and returned as undead corpses. There may be parody even in Campbell's early story "The Whining" [1973], although here the joke is directed at the hackneyed conventions of the moribund "ghost story" tradition. A man kills a pestiferous dog but finds that it haunts him continually. How to get rid of the thing? He remarks petulantly, "'You realize it's impossible to exorcise an animal? They don't understand English, never mind Latin'" (HS 30). *Needing Ghosts* is full of twisted humor, although the laughter it provokes may be the hysterical laughter of the insane at the sane.

PHILOSOPHY

Ramsey Campbell has discussed his own work on many occasions. He has, indeed, rather a fondness for talking about himself, although—in contrast to a number of other writers one can name—he always does so with a refreshing candor and lack of self-congratulation. Almost every one of his short story collections bears an introduction. A number of later editions of his novels (several of which have been revised after first publication) contain introductions or afterwords, the most riveting and disturbing being that for the 1983 edition of *The Face That Must Die*. And he has given several illuminating interviews. He makes no secret of the fact that much of his work is autobiographical. But why, exactly, does he write horror fiction at all? He purports to discuss this issue in two of his introductions,

but to my mind neither of these provides a satisfactory answer. In the introduction to *The Height of the Scream* he conducts a sort of self-interview.

> Why do I write horror fiction?
> Because there's nothing I enjoy more than writing.
> But why *horror* fiction?
> Because it's what I do best. And it seems to me one ought to
> spend as much time as possible doing what one does best [HS ix].

This is not very helpful, and he never returns to this particular issue. In
the introduction to *Dark Companions* he appears to take up the matter
again, but his answer there is no more conclusive. "My most vivid memories of my early childhood are of being frightened ..." (DC xi). What, in
the end, does Campbell hope to *achieve* by writing horror fiction? I am not
sure that I know.

It is, accordingly, difficult to trace a coherent philosophy in Campbell's
work: the supernatural phenomena in his stories are not—or are not consistently—metaphors for his metaphysical or ethical concerns. The weird
is most frequently used by him as a vehicle for the examination of a wide
array of psychological states and the probing of an individual's relationship either with others or with his or her environment.

If Campbell is not seeking to convey a unified vision in his work, as
Lovecraft, Blackwood, and Machen did, he is also not concerned with using
fiction as a means of achieving easy moral solutions to difficult problems.
Indeed, it is exactly when Campbell is at his most didactic that he is least
successful. "The Words That Count," for example, as he has himself admitted,[11] is an attempt (rather ill-conceived, to my mind) to combat religious
fundamentalism. He seems to have a peculiar fondness for this tale, including it not only in *The Height of the Scream* and *Dark Feasts* but submitting
it as his contribution to Dennis Etchison's *Masters of Darkness*. Campbell
returns again and again to the theme of religious zealotry, sometimes quite
effectively—as in "Another World" [1987; WN], a nonsupernatural tale of
paranoia bred by religious fanaticism—and sometimes rather less so, as in
the rather nasty and predictable "It Helps If You Sing" [1987; WN]. Then
there is the curious early tale "Made in Goatswood" [1968]. Here some heathenish stone figures built by Terry Aldrich, an unbeliever, for his lover
Kim, a conventional Catholic, serve to underscore their religious differences. But then Terry saves Kim when the figures come to life and threaten
her, and he appears to reconvert to Catholicism in order to preserve their
relationship: "Silently he made the sign of the cross. Then he walked toward
the house" (DD 153). It is disturbing how readily Terry gives up his
principles simply for an emotional attachment.

Religious fundamentalism is the focus of *The Hungry Moon* [1984–85]. Campbell evidently based the central character, Godwin Mann—an American evangelist whose followers overrun a small English town which in ancient times was a druid settlement—on Billy Graham. And certainly the portrayal of the odiously hypocritical and self-important Mann, and his gradual infection of the entire town with his dogmatic fundamentalism, is vivid and pungent, if in a sort of irritating way. But Campbell suggests that Mann may have bitten off more than he can chew when he causes the townsfolk to give up a nominally pagan ceremony whereby a deep cave is decorated every year as a sort of peace offering to the presiding deity or force residing within it. The townsfolk have all imagined that this is merely a harmless tradition, with no more real significance than the hanging of mistletoe at Christmas, but strange forces are released thereby.

At this point the novel begins to gather steam and becomes quite compelling; and one of the most cosmic tableaux in all Campbell's work occurs in a fascinating vision experienced by one of the characters, in which a loathsome and titanic creature flees the dying moon at the dawn of history and approaches the steaming earth. "Meteors still rained down, but caught fire in the atmosphere. Huge continents were splitting, drifting apart as storms picked at the world. Mountains reared up, seas flooded into gaps that were beginning to outline continents she could almost recognize. There might soon be life as she knew it—and then she realized what she had known instinctively. Life on earth was what the watcher on the moon was waiting hungrily for" (HM 214). This entity infects various characters so that they glow with a sickly white phosphorescence (just as the moon does) and become loathsome spiderlike creatures whose only goal is to destroy human beings as a prelude to the entity's regaining its sway over the earth.

The symbolism of the novel is very carefully worked out. In effect, *The Hungry Moon* could (as with Dunsany's *The Blessing of Pan*) be read as the triumph of paganism over Christianity. Campbell slyly alludes to a number of classical myths as the novel develops: the three dogs who tear apart the town's police chief can hardly fail to make us recall three-headed Cerberus; the feast of human flesh that the moon-entity possessing Mann's body serves up to the townsfolk recalls the many such banquets in Graeco-Roman myth; and when an already blind man gouges out his eyes as he feels himself near the horror, we immediately think of the blinding of Oedipus when the truth of his actions dawns upon him. In the central portion of the novel an eerie darkness, reminiscent of Hodgson's *The Night Land*, covers the town like a pall; but it may well be a metaphor for the mental darkness of fundamentalism. The blinding of several of the most fervently religious inhabitants, when the (secular) heroes of the novel banish the darkness and restore the sun, can only suggest the blindness to truth and enlightenment that affects so many religious extremists.

And yet, in the end I am not sure that the withering satire directed against these fundamentalists does not obscure the general moral message of the novel. The fanatics are portrayed as so loathsome that one almost wants them to be possessed and destroyed by the moon-entity, even though that entity is also a threat to the planet at large. And Campbell appears to take great relish in disposing of his fundamentalists in some particularly grisly fashion, as with the sanctimonious police chief:

> They were dogs—mad dogs, to judge by the sounds of snarling and cloth tearing. The flashlight beam swung toward them, and Nick saw them bring the policeman down, one slavering red mouth burying its teeth in his thigh, another ripping at his fist as he tried to defend himself. The man screamed once, and then there was only an agonized gurgling. The next swing of the flashlight showed the third dog on top of him, paws on his chest, worrying his throat like a rat. He must have been as good as dead when his free leg kicked out, his boot smashing the flashlight against the wall. Then there was darkness in the main room, and the sounds of panting and snarling and teeth ripping flesh [HM 196].

Aside from his novels, in which it might be said that he becomes overly attached to his own sympathetic characters, Campbell rarely indulges in naive struggles of good and evil or supernatural revenge in which a crime is fittingly punished by a force from beyond the grave. This is taking the easy way out, and Campbell realizes that much weird fiction that rests on such premises is now hopelessly dated in an age that has seen injustice triumph with impunity on too many occasions.

Accordingly, Campbell's world is dark, brooding, and pessimistic, but not cynical or misanthropic. Even his portrayals of paranoid personalities are free of cheap scorn or contempt, and the care with which he probes the psychological state of these psychotics bespeaks a consuming interest in it and a desire to understand its sources and ramifications. But the bleakness of his vision has frequently stirred comment. T. E. D. Klein—that pessimist who wants to be an optimist—wrote in his landmark essay, "Ramsey Campbell: An Appreciation" (1974): "Yet horror per se can be, in the end, somewhat limiting; and now that he has mastered it, one might hope for an occasional ray of light to alleviate the gloom.... An occasional vision of something behind a glass of stout and a secretary's knickers might add a needed dimension to the world Campbell has created."[12] All this is a little silly, bringing to mind many myopic critics' complaints of Bierce's pessimism. Campbell is perfectly entitled to his unmitigatedly glum outlook: this is clearly how he sees the world, and he is under no obligation to present rosy pictures to satisfy Klein's naive optimism. I have already remarked that the half-hearted and unconvincing "happy endings" to many of Campbell's novels weaken them considerably. It is not merely that these sudden reversals of fortune seem unmotivated and contrived, it is that they appear to confound Campbell's general vision of the world, in which we are helpless pawns in the face of devastating horrors that can overwhelm us at any moment and for any reason, or for no reason at all. If Campbell is doing more than simply transmogrifying the dangers of urban life—and I believe he is—then he must remain true to his world view, cheerless as it may be.

Ramsey Campbell is the only writer in the entire range of weird fiction, with the exception of Lord Dunsany, to combine an almost prodigal bountifulness of output with remarkably high and consistent level of quality. Even if some of Campbell's short tales do not entirely succeed, and even if some of the novels tend to fall flat, every one of his works is written with meticulous care: he is an author, like Machen, Dunsany, Lovecraft, Shirley Jackson, T. E. D. Klein, Robert Aickman, and Thomas Ligotti, whose every work can be read purely for the pleasure of reading it. And yet, as of this writing Campbell is only in his mid-fifties—although he has been writing seriously for more than 35 years, it is possible that he is only at the midpoint of his literary career. The prospect of hundreds more short stories and a dozen or so more novels from Campbell's pen in the next two or three decades—works that will continue to probe new directions in the field as they continue to give further shape and coherence to his own *oeuvre*—is one of the few reasons for maintaining an interest in modern weird fiction.

IV. THE ALTERNATIVES
TO SUPERNATURALISM

KILLING WOMEN WITH ROBERT BLOCH, THOMAS HARRIS, AND BRET EASTON ELLIS

ROBERT BLOCH: HARD-BOILED HORROR

Robert Bloch (1917–1994) is a particularly apt writer illustrate both the distinctions between and the uniting of the suspense story and the weird tale, for it seems undeniable that he has written works of both types as well as works that fuse the two. I have no intention of studying the whole of Bloch's prodigally vast output—which comprises some two dozen novels, hundreds of short stories collected and uncollected, articles, introductions, screenplays, teleplays, and miscellany,[1] and which runs the gamut from pure mystery to supernatural horror to science fiction—nor is such a thing necessary. To be honest, Bloch is by no stretch of the imagination a great writer but merely a competent craftsman whose most distinctive work combines mystery and horror in a seamless fashion. And because his writing is on the whole transparently clear and generally void of subtlety and complexity (I do not necessarily intend this as a criticism), it can be studied for its purely formal qualities in ways that other, denser works cannot be.

Bloch's entire writing career has been a dance on both sides of the supernatural fence. In his teens he wrote entertainingly lurid supernatural tales (many of them in the Lovecraftian vein[2]) for *Weird Tales*. But as early as the late 1930s he was approaching the realm of nonsupernatural horror.

175

"The Cloak" (1939; OW) concerns a cloak, once owned by a vampire, which appears to endow the wearer with vampiric inclinations. This seems rather conventionally supernatural, but Bloch handles it in such a fashion as to imply initially that the vampiric tendencies are being brought on only through psychological suggestion, and it requires the very last line of the story to push the tale into the supernatural. Another, rather similar story is "The Man Who Collected Poe" (1951), in which a man claims that he has rifled Poe's grave, removed the contents therefrom, and actually resurrected the body of Poe and compelled him to write new tales. When a colleague is shown some clearly recent work that appears to be in Poe's handwriting, he feels that his friend has become so obsessed with Poe that he has taken to writing like him. Only at the end do we learn that Poe has in fact been resurrected.

In some of his tales Bloch suggests that certain natural events, usually murder, are so horrible that they must be accounted for supernaturally. "Yours Truly, Jack the Ripper" (1943) is of this sort. A fanatical Jack the Ripper scholar maintains that a series of murders committed around the world over a period of 50 years proves that the Ripper must still be alive, even though he would now be in his eighties or more. The idea is that the grisliness of these murders bears the stamp of some especially deranged fiend, as the Ripper must have been. We have seen that William Peter Blatty has presented this idea from a religious perspective, suggesting that the heinousness of certain crimes necessitates belief in Satan. Bloch broaches the idea in a secular fashion, but this celebrated tale nonetheless suffers from implausibility and triteness. I am not giving away much by revealing that the first-person narrator in the end turns out to be the preternaturally aged Ripper. Still less successful is "'Lizzie Borden Took an Axe...'" (1946), in which a woman is possessed by the spirit of Lizzie Borden and commits crimes very much like hers. A much better tale is the vastly clever "I Like Blondes" (1956), in which we seem merely to be concerned with an old rake who likes blondes either for sex or for murder, but who is actually an alien from another planet who seizes blondes in order to eat them. The tale is told with Bloch's trademark humor, a mixture of the graveyard comedy of Bierce and a stand-up comic's one-liners. It was first published, interestingly, in *Playboy*.

The collection *Such Stuff as Screams Are Made Of* (1979) is devoted almost wholly to what Bloch in an afterword terms "psychological suspense" (SS 284), although a few purely supernatural tales ("The Weird Tailor," "A Case of the Stubborns") and even some science fiction stories intrude anomalously. Many are what Bloch (SS 285) frankly terms *contes cruels*, but there is one story that presents one of the most original ideas in recent weird fiction. In "I Do Not Love Thee, Dr. Fell" (1955) Clyde Bromely, feeling that his life is going nowhere and having doubts as to his own identity, begins to see a psychiatrist. It transpires that Clyde has actually *invented* his psychiatrist: he has in fact been going into his own office and lying down on the couch, imagining that he is having a session with a Dr. Fell. This tale seems authentically weird both because of the extreme bizarrerie of Clyde's psychological aberration and because Bloch relates the entire idea to witchcraft and sorcery ("Three hundred years ago ... a man who couldn't integrate his personality created a new one—he became a wizard" [SS 103]). Less successful is the long story "The Screaming People" (1959), in which a psychologist in an insane asylum manipulates his patients for his own ends, even inducing them to commit murder. This foreshadows (again in a secular manner) Blatty's use of a similiar idea in *Legion* (1983) and, in its treatment of the protagonist's amnesia, may even foreshadow some of L. P. Davies's work. But the tale is rushed in its execution and fails to develop the many interesting ramifications of the story line (a problem that dogs much of Bloch's fiction, early and late). It is obvious that Bloch has some kind of hostility against psychiatrists, but at any rate stories like these plumb unknown depths of human consciousness in ways that methodologically approach Lovecraft's and other cosmic horror writers' probing of the depths of the universe.

A number of Bloch's novels center around very disturbed individuals, but some seem clearly to be mystery-suspense works while others may well cross over into the weird. A case, however, could be made for the weirdness of two of his nonsupernatural novels, *The Scarf* (1947; revised 1966) and *Psycho* (1959). I am almost inclined to rank the former above the latter as Bloch's finest novel, and perhaps only a highly contrived and implausible ending will force us to give the palm to its more celebrated companion. *The Scarf* is the first-person account of Dan Morley, who tells of a traumatic experience he had as a youth. A handsome boy, he has attracted the attention of one of his teachers, a lonely woman in her late thirties named Miss Frazer. One day she invites him to her home and proceeds to tie him up with a maroon scarf, seal up the house, and turn on the gas so that the two of them can die together as lovers. He manages to escape, but Miss Frazer dies in the process. As a result, he confesses that "For years I hated women, books, everything" (S 9).

It is at this point that the paradoxes begin. Although he hates women, he attracts them and is attracted to them; although he hates books, he becomes a writer of them. He undergoes a pattern of latching on to a woman, writing stories about her, then killing her with the scarf. Words and reality have become inextricably confused in his mind. It is as if he kills his women only so as to provide a fitting climax to a story: "I killed Rena because she was just a story character to me. She wasn't real. She didn't exist at all" (S 17). In a fascinating and highly prophetic disquisition, Morley ponders on words and their ubiquity: "A jumble of words on a slip and a mumble of words on a lip and you're married. Or divorced. Or buried, for that matter. You can't buy, sell, or contract without a magic formula. It's all words now" (S 77). Is there a reality beyond the facade of words? Yes, but only one: "Murder isn't a word. Murder is a deed" (S 79). Morley kills not only to vent his hatred of women but, in a twisted way, to affirm his own existence.

The quasi-weirdness of this novel comes from several directions. Morley begins writing a "Black Notebook," a notebook filled with his innermost thoughts, in which he records not only his murders but the terrifying nightmares he suffers; they are among the more effective dream-sequences in modern weird literature. Moreover, it is precisely because there is no doubt of Morley's guilt, and accordingly no mystery or suspense element aside from the matter of whether he will ever be caught, that we are not distracted from the perception of his increasingly aberrant mental state. The latter part of the novel does indeed take on a suspense element as certain characters finally begin to suspect Morley of the murders and set about entrappping him; and the conclusion—rewritten in the 1966 version[3]—is more than a little contrived. Here we find that Miss Frazer did not in fact die, and she maintains that it was Morley who was in love with *her* and sought to tie her up and commit joint suicide. I believe we are to interpret this, however, as a lie fabricated by Miss Frazer in order finally to gain Morley for herself—and Morley now seems resigned to such a fate ("Miss Frazer and I are going to be married..." [S 160]). I am not especially happy with this conclusion, but perhaps Bloch felt that this ending allowed him to give Morley a more satisfactory comeuppance than merely death or incarceration. Nevertheless, *The Scarf* is a powerful work of psychological horror; because of its singleminded focus upon a disturbed mentality, it can take a place with the best weird fiction of its kind.

It is difficult to treat of *Psycho*, just as it is now difficult to read it, without reference to Alfred Hitchcock's film, but we must try to do so, for the novel reveals subtleties and moments of chilling terror that even the film has not captured. As the story is so well known, I need not recapitulate it here. I wish, however, to preface my discussion of it by examining a much earlier story, "Enoch" (1946). This story bears striking thematic resemblances to *Psycho* but is supernatural, and it perfectly exemplifies how a nonsupernatural work can be not only more frightening than a supernatural one but more psychologically compelling. "Enoch" is the tale of a man who is deemed insane for thinking that some strange entity "that lives on the top of my head" (B 22) has ordered him to commit repeated murder. At one point the man confesses that "Most people ... thought I was crazy—because of my mother" (B 26). This is not wholly explained, but it appears that the man's mother had the reputation of being a witch. In any event, the man convinces the district attorney to take Enoch over for a while; the latter, wanting to humor the man, agrees, and he inevitably finds that Enoch is a real entity. "Enoch" is in fact (if I may be excused a Blochian pun) rather innocuous: the supernaturalism of the tale undercuts any interesting psychological analysis because the man's murderous propensities are now attributed to Enoch rather than to himself. It therefore scarcely matters what the man's relationship to his mother is, or why he commits the murders, since he is not truly responsible for them. Bloch wisely did not make this mistake in *Psycho*.

One of the many details the film version of *Psycho* fails to capture is the degree to which, at the outset, Norman Bates's symbiotic, love-hate relationship with his (dead) mother is elaborated. By a transparent projection, Bates imagines that it is his mother who is mentally ill and ought to be locked away in an asylum. In a brilliant updating of the Jekyll and Hyde syndrome, Bates on occasion wholly adopts the personality of his mother and then, regaining his own personality, professes horror at what his "mother" has committed. But Bates is by no means wholly unaware of his condition, and at one point comes dangerously close to realizing it: "It was like being two people, really—the child and the adult. Whenever he thought about Mother, he became a child again, with a child's vocabulary, frames of reference, and emotional reactions. But when he was by himself—not actually by himself, but off in a book—he was a mature individual. Mature enough to understand that he might even be the victim of a mild form of schizophrenia, most likely some form of borderline neurosis" (P 83–84).

What makes *Psycho* a genuine weird tale is not primarily—or, rather, not *initially*—our awareness of Bates's profound mother fixation, which has led him to deny the fact of his mother's death, extract her body from her grave, place it in his home, and imagine her alive once more. All this we learn only toward the end of the novel, and we can now only imagine what an impact these revelations would have had on the book's first readers. What has laid the groundwork for the weirdness of this conclusion is, firstly, the *apparent* lack of mystery as to the deaths that occur at the Bates motel (they are, we believe, clearly the work of Bates's mother) and, secondly, some exceptionally fine touches of what I call the *pseudosupernatural*—the suggestion of the supernatural in details of landscape, atmosphere, or character description. The revelation that Bates's mother is actually dead comes about two-thirds through the novel. Shortly thereafter we learn that the private detective Arbogast had told Lila Crane, sister of the murdered Mary Crane, that he saw Bates's mother (actually Bates dressed as his mother) as he drove into the motel. At this point the sheriff, who knows Bates's mother is dead, remarks: "'Maybe he saw her ghost sitting in the window'" (P 120). And indeed, it is momentarily conceivable to a reader that Bates's mother is in fact a ghost and has killed Mary and Arbogast, although most ghosts in standard weird fiction do not wield knives. Another pseudosupernatural touch occurs when Bates sees Lila come to the motel and thinks it is Mary who has come out of the swamp where he dumped her (P 125).

The episode in which Lila boldly enters Bates's home in order to find out the truth of the matter is the most horrific scene in the novel. The pseudosupernatural here functions on several levels. This entire episode is an adaptation and subtilization of the conventional haunted-house story in which a protagonist explores some centuried and cobwebbed dwelling where a sheeted figure may emerge at any moment; and Bloch's use of language simultaneously enhances and subverts this convention. Lila, examining the musty and archaic surroundings, uses such terms as "ghastly" and "horrors" to describe her aesthetic response to the furnishings ("There was a bureau over in the corner ... one of those antique horrors" [P 142]), but we as readers are led to connote them very differently. Lila then enters Bates's mother's room (Bates has taken his mother's corpse down to the fruit cellar), and although she notes that all the items in it are some 50 years old, the room is *still alive* (P 144): again a double meaning is intended here, suggesting both that the mother's spirit lives because of the meticulous way in which the room has been kept and that Bates is attempting to keep his mother alive in a bodily manner. Finally, Lila, becoming increasingly affected by the eerie atmosphere of the house, repeats to herself harriedly, *"There are no ghosts"* (P 144, 145). Here again this brings to mind the conventional haunted-house character's attempts to reassure himself in the presence of the supernatural, but in fact Lila is right—there are no ghosts here; only Bates's twisted mind. The enormous skill with which this chapter, and the entire novel, is written must place it at the pinnacle of Bloch's output.

Both *The Scarf* and *Psycho* suffer somewhat from a clumsy explanatory ending that creates a sort of schoolroom atmosphere. But both are textbooks for the depiction of crazed mentalities from within; it is remarkable that *Psycho* allows for this sort of depiction in a third-person narrative. Bloch has regrettably attempted to play upon the success of *Psycho* by writing two novel-length sequels to it, both entirely unreadable. But they, along with much of the rest of his uneven output, must be forgotten and forgiven. If the film has become an imperishable cultural landmark, then the novel has itself spawned many imitations and adaptations. It is to two of those that we now turn.

THOMAS HARRIS: THE MIND OF HORROR

Thomas Harris (b. ca. 1940) is not your usual best-selling author. In the first place, in contrast to the mechanical regularity of Judith Krantz, Sidney Sheldon, and especially Stephen King, Harris has written only three novels in about 15 years. In the second place, his spare, tight, but rather colorless style is leagues away from the floridity, tawdriness, and plain bad writing of the Danielle Steels of the world. In his two best and most representative novels, Harris straddles (or, at least, is thought by some to straddle) the thin boundary between suspense and horror, but to my mind he ultimately lands in the former domain.

Black Sunday (1975) is a mere potboiler, with a preposterous premise—terrorists wish to blow up the Super Bowl from a blimp—and stereotypical characters (Dahlia Iyad, the fanatical Palestinian terrorist; Michael Lander, the embittered Vietnam War vet who seeks nothing but death and destruction; David Kabakov, the ruthless Israeli secret service agent who foils the plot). It has only one point of interest: early on a portion of a chapter is devoted to a psychological history of Lander from infancy onward, supplying the inner motives for his actions and desires. It is written in a clinical, almost emotionless manner, but it nevertheless provides the necessary psychological motivation for the entire novel.

Harris developed this idea in an ingenious way in *Red Dragon* (1981). The premise of this novel is the attempt by Will Graham, a semiretired FBI agent, to hunt down a serial killer by adopting the mindset of the criminal. Graham has an unusual sensitivity to other people's minds. (It must be emphasized that this idea is not presented as in any way supernatural or occult, and Graham is far removed from the "psychic detectives" who lumber implausibly through some of the work of Algernon Blackwood, William Hope Hodgson, and others.) The FBI, stumped in the matter, feel that this may be the only way to capture the killer.

This premise is, as I say, ingenious, but I wonder whether in fact it is actually carried out. That is to say, does Graham really solve the case, or any part of it, by entering the criminal's mind? It seems that what he really does is simply interpret the physical evidence more thoroughly, sensitively, and keenly than others have. He states his purported principles to his wife.

"Molly, an intelligent psychopath—particularly a sadist—is hard to catch for several reasons. First, there's no traceable motive. So you can't go that way. And most of the time you won't have any help from informants. See, there's a lot more stooling than sleuthing behind most arrests, but in a case like this there won't *be* any informants. He may not even know that he's doing it. So you have to take whatever evidence you have and extrapolate. You try to reconstruct his thinking. You try to find patterns" [RD 18].

This is all well and good, but let us now examine a particularly vivid example of Graham's psychological insight, as he examines a murder scene and notes that the murdered children of a family have been brought down to the bedroom where the parents have been killed.

> *Why did you move them again? Why didn't you leave them that way?* Graham asked. *There's something you don't want me to know about you. Why, there's something you're ashamed of. Or is it something you can't afford for me to know?*
>
> *Did you open their eyes?*
>
> *Mrs. Leeds was lovely, wasn't she? You turned on the light after you cut his throat so Mrs. Leeds could watch him flop, didn't you? It was maddening to have to wear gloves when you touched her, wasn't it?*
>
> There was talcum on her leg.
>
> There was no talcum in the bathroom.
>
> Someone else seemed to speak those two facts in a flat voice.
>
> *You took off your gloves, didn't you? The powder came out of a rubber glove as you pulled it off to touch her, DIDN'T IT, YOU SON OF A BITCH? You touched her with your bare hands and then you put the gloves back on and you wiped her down. But while the gloves were off, DID YOU OPEN THEIR EYES?* [RD 29–30].

The murderer perversely wanted the dead children to watch the killing of the parents. All this is rather effective, but there does not seem to be any conclusion here that has not been arrived at by anything other than very acute deduction from the evidence. If Harris or his supporters think that he has invented some "new" form of detection, then he and they had better think again.

But this is not what I wish to study here. What, if anything, makes this a weird tale? Chet Williamson, both a sharp commentator and a gifted weird fictionist, has written of this novel that it is "quite simply, the most frightening book I have ever read."[4] I suppose I cannot quarrel with Williamson on what he finds frightening, and it is, I trust, not because I am exceptionally hardened that I did not find anything particularly frightening in this book.[5] The work is highly compelling, but it is a work of detection and suspense and not horror. Much of the novel is given over to a very careful forensic analysis of evidence, until finally sufficient clues are found to identify the murderer. Harris, with unusual restraint for a popular writer, has not even peppered this novel with much overt violence: the murders have already occurred at the start of the book, and we can only infer their loathsomeness from the gradual accumulation of evidence.

It is, presumably, this whole notion of trying to enter the twisted mind of a serial killer that is supposed to generate horror in the work, and there are occasions when Harris attempts to invest this action with portentous shudders. Graham's great triumph is the capture of Dr. Hannibal Lecter, a highly learned but fiercely cynical and misanthropic psychiatrist who sports the charming soubriquet of "Hannibal the Cannibal." Graham actually seeks Lecter's advice on the serial killings, and Lecter delivers a parting shot: "The reason you caught me is that we're *just alike*" (RD 73).

This sets the stage for a psychological history of the killer very much like that in *Black Sunday*, and it is here that the parallels to *Psycho* become striking. The killer, Francis Dolarhyde, was an orphan who was raised by a hideous and tyrannical grandmother who made fun of his speech impediment and who once threatened to cut off his penis with scissors when she found him as a young boy exposing himself to a little girl. Although Dolarhyde certainly does not resurrect his grandmother's body like Norman Bates, he seems to have preserved her false teeth (one suddenly thinks of Poe's "Berenice"). And he pretends to have self-tormenting conversations with his grandmother very similar to Bates's; he fancies that it is the grandmother who is urging him to kill a young blind woman, Reba McClane, who has taken a romantic interest in him. "'YOU MAY PUT AWAY MY TEETH. YOU PITIFUL LITTLE HARELIP, YOU'D KEEP YOUR LITTLE BUDDY FROM ME, WOULD YOU? I'LL TEAR HER APART AND RUB THE PIECES IN YOUR UGLY FACE. I'LL HANG YOU WITH HER LARGE INTESTINE IF YOU OPPOSE ME. YOU KNOW I CAN" (RD 275). The parallels with Norman Bates's unacknowledged attraction to Mary Crane, and his "mother's" murder of her in order that the bond between him and his mother can be preserved, is striking. But Dolarhyde is tracked down, Reba is saved, and Lecter's plot to have Graham's wife killed is foiled.

The Silence of the Lambs (1988) has now exceeded the acclaim of *Red Dragon*, largely as a result of the success of the 1990 film version, one of the most faithful adaptations of a literary work in years. If *Silence* lacks the gripping and monomaniacal intensity of its predecessor, it is overall a finer work: in fullness of characterization, in intricacy of plot, and in cumulative suspense. But it, too, is not a weird tale. Once again much of the action revolves around the mechanics of tracking down the serial killer, and here the evidence ranges from death's-head moths (found in the victims' throats) to anomalous triangular markings discovered on the back of one victim. As in *Red Dragon*, several of the murders have already occurred, and much attention is given to rescuing the killer's latest victim, who has been abducted but is not murdered immediately.

Dr. Hannibal Lecter, who was merely a sort of sardonic commentator in *Red Dragon*, plays a much larger role in *The Silence of the Lambs*, virtually orchestrating the events even though he spends much of the novel behind bars. (It is interesting that Harris has never given a full account of Will Graham's capture of Lecter, or even of Lecter's own crimes. Perhaps a future novel will deal with these rich issues.) Lecter really is one of the more delightfully evil figures in recent literature, and his knowledge of psychiatry allows him to play the most exquisite games of mental torture upon his various targets. While there is something of the Gothic villain in Lecter, he could just as well be considered a Moriarty figure. In this case, however, the Sherlock Holmes figure is not Will Graham but Clarice M. Starling, a trainee in the FBI Academy. She has been chosen to interrogate Lecter so as to produce a psychological profile of serial killers But, because she finds that Lecter appears to know much about the serial killer known as Buffalo Bill, she becomes enmeshed in that case and ultimately helps to solve it. The sensitive portrayal of Starling is one of the quiet triumphs of this novel.

The gripping mental battle between Lecter and Starling actually ends up relegating the actual murderer to the background, and we learn relatively little about the motivations of Buffalo Bill, who is ultimately identified as one Jame Gumb. This is unfortunate, for had such a psychological history been supplied, a much better case could have been made for the weirdness of *The Silence of the Lambs*. It turns out that Gumb is profoundly confused sexually: he is not homosexual, nor does he truly fit the psychological model of the transsexual; for that reason he has been turned down for a sex change operation, and so he resorts to killing women. Why? He wishes to make an entire suit *out of women's skin*, since this will be the closest he will ever come to being a woman. So he takes various pieces of skin from each of his victims: the back from one, the thighs from another, and so on. This, certainly, is exceptionally perverse, but Harris's presentation of it is so indirect (this, in fact, is the clue to the killings, and so it cannot be fully revealed until the end) as to rob it of potential horror. This is not a criticism: it only confirms that Harris's *prime* goal in the novel is detection, not horror.

What is interesting is that the film version of *The Silence of the Lambs* is actually much more horrifying (and, accordingly, much less of a detective story) than the novel. An early scene, in which Starling must confront Lecter in his heavily guarded cell in a madhouse, is presented in the film as something out of *Melmoth the Wanderer*: we seem suddenly transported out of the present and into the horrors of the Inquisition. There is nothing like this in the novel. Jame Gumb's home in the film is a Gothic castle with a stone-encircled well in which he keeps his hapless victim. One wonders whether the director of the film was thinking of the climactic scene in Lovecraft's *The Case of Charles Dexter Ward*—Harris certainly wasn't. I am not saying that the film is unfaithful to the novel in these and other particulars; perhaps it is merely drawing out hints that were only implicit in Harris's work. Nevertheless, it is not paradoxical to say that the film *The Silence of the Lambs* is weird whereas the novel is not.

Even if *Red Dragon* and *The Silence of the Lambs* cannot be considered genuinely weird, they are certainly among the more successful works of popular fiction in recent years. I am trying not to say this condescendingly, although it is a fact that Harris tends to succumb to various conventions of popular fiction—abundance of dialogue, stereotypical conflict of good and evil, occasionally contrived plot twists, a plethora of technical knowledge of certain matters (especially forensics) that is meant to impress the reader. On the other hand, he at least avoids certain other conventions such as sentimentality, slipshod or colloquial style, and a complete resolution of all plot threads at the end (Lecter escaped toward the end of *The Silence of the Lambs* and is still on the loose). I am not sure how aware of the weird tradition Harris is, but if he is working in the field that Robert Bloch termed "psychological suspense," then he gives equal emphasis to both halves of that compound, and perhaps even a little more to the latter.

BRET EASTON ELLIS: THE BANALITY OF HORROR

And now we come to *American Psycho* (1991). It is likely that the controversy surrounding this book and its author will be forgotten in a very short time, so it is worth outlining it here. Ellis had gained a certain amount of celebrity as the author of two previous mainstream novels, *Less Than Zero* (1985) and *The Rules of Attraction* (1987), which sought to lay bare the emptiness of the twentysomething generation of the 1980s. *American Psycho* was scheduled to be released by Simon & Schuster (the publisher of his two previous books) in late 1990: it was accepted for publication, an advance was offered to Ellis, and copies were actually printed. They were about to be distributed when the head of Paramount Pictures, Simon & Schuster's parent company, saw some excerpts of the novel in a magazine and, apparently revolted by the contents (or by the furor it was already causing), decided to withdraw the book and destroy the printed copies. At this point a still greater furor arose. On the one hand, charges of censorship were leveled. On the other hand, the book was condemned—before it was released, and probably before it was even read—by some conservative critics and some feminists as being misogynist, gratuitously violent, and morally decadent. Finally the book was picked up by Vintage and released in early 1991. Ellis, although somewhat disturbed at the controversy,[6] went laughing all the way to the bank: he was allowed to keep the Simon & Schuster advance, and the novel remained on the paperback bestseller list for several weeks.

Many individuals on both sides of the issue have seriously misunderstood the work and its odd publishing history. The Author's Guild rightly protested Simon & Schuster's actions not as censorship but as a breach of contract. And hostile critics (like Roger Rosenblatt, who wrote a highly obnoxious and self-righteous prepublication review[7] that was clearly meant to prejudice readers against the book before they had had a chance to read it for themselves) have by some incredible means failed to grasp the obvious fact that this book is a satire—a satire that continues to focus, like Ellis's two previous books, on the shallowness, rootlessness, and irresponsibility of the yuppie lifestyle of the 1980s. On this level the book is a brilliant work of fiction, if a little too long; some passages toward the beginning contain some of the best social satire since Evelyn Waugh.

It is, unfortunately, not my purpose to study this novel in any detail, although it would be very rewarding to do so. I am solely concerned with whether *American Psycho* is a weird tale in any sense. It emphatically is not, despite one commentator's highly uninformed linkage of it, as well as of the work of Thomas Harris, to the splatterpunk movement.[8] The very title of the work, of course, suggests some sort of relationship to *Psycho*, whether it be the novel or the film; there is in fact an allusion to the Hitchcock film at one point (AP 108), as well as to the case of Ed Gein (AP 92), the Wisconsin murderer upon whom Bloch's *Psycho* was in part based. But beyond this there is little to suggest any direct influence of *Psycho* or any other work of weird fiction upon Ellis's novel.

I want to approach both *Psycho* and *American Psycho* in a somewhat roundabout way, and that is by briefly studying a celebrated predecessor to both works, William Faulkner's magnificent tale of necrophilia, "A Rose for Emily" (1930). The story was included in Dashiell Hammett's *Creeps by Night* (1931), one of the most heterogeneous weird-suspense anthologies ever compiled, containing everything from the cosmic horror of Donald

Wandrei's "The Red Brain" to John Collier's *conte cruel*, "Green Thoughts." The volume's appearance led to an illuminating debate between August Derleth and H. P. Lovecraft as to whether Faulkner's tale was weird, Derleth apparently averring that it was (we have lost his side of the correspondence), Lovecraft emphatically affirming the contrary. One of Lovecraft's comments is significant:

> ...I'm far from denying the Faulkner yarn a high place as a realistic story. It is a fine piece of work—but is *not weird*. This sort of gruesomeness does *not* suggest anything beyond ordinary physical life & commonplace nature. Necrophily is horrible enough—but only *physically* so, like other repellent abnormalities. It excites loathing—but does not call up anything beyond Nature. We are horrified at Emily as at a cannibal—or as at some practitioner of nameless Sabbat-rites—but we do not feel the stark glimpse or monstrous doubt hinting at subversions of basic natural law.[9]

Lovecraft's argument—fundamental to his view of weird fiction—is persuasive, but I believe it contains a few fallacies that may at least force us to qualify it. It is true enough that the horrible and the gruesome do not by themselves constitute weirdness; it is also true that necrophilia is horrible, but it is not merely "physically" so. The power of Faulkner's tale rests on our perception of the astonishing aberration of Emily's psyche that led her to kill her lover, keep the corpse in her bedroom, and lie next to it for decades, until her own death. Lovecraft's bias toward external, cosmic horror and his general lack of interest in human beings appears to have caused him to underrate the degree to which the mysteries of the mind could be nearly as powerful and bizarre as the mysteries of the universe. I will grant that there is no actual "subversion of basic natural laws" in Faulkner's tale—to say that it somehow subverts our norms of "human nature" is to say nothing in particular—and if in the end "A Rose for Emily" remains on the borderland of the weird, then it is closer to that realm than Lovecraft was willing to concede.

I am not certain of the influence of "A Rose for Emily" upon Bloch's *Psycho*, but the scenarios are in fact surprisingly close. The latter can almost be seen as a mirror image of the former: the sexes are changed, but otherwise very much the same things happen. Emily's opportunities for associating with young men were severely restricted by her father, just as Norman Bates's were by his mother; and Norman's preservation of his mother's corpse is a still more twisted version of Emily's preservation of her lover. But we have seen that what makes *Psycho* authentically weird is its playing upon the conventions of the weird tale, something generally absent in

Faulkner's story. For this reason "A Rose for Emily" must remain outside—if only just outside—the domain of the weird.

And it is for this same reason that *American Psycho* must be banished from the weird. This novel is the prototypical instance of the rule that a horror story is not necessarily a story in which horrible things happen. *American Psycho* certainly has enough of horror—vicious, mindless, cold-blooded murder, twisted sex, cannibalism—but these acts are related in exactly the same tone and spirit as the endless catalogues of high-fashion clothes and expensive furnishings, and the boring, pointless dinners and parties that the narrator Patrick Bateman and his yuppie friends attend night after night. In fact, I now believe that these latter objects and events are meant to be *just as horrifying* as the loathsome murders Bateman blandly commits. They horrify in exactly the same way as his murders: by excess.

If there were some penetrating examination of Bateman's psyche, then the novel might more closely approach the weird, but it is precisely Ellis's design not to engage in such a thing. Bateman and all his cronies are psychologically empty: there simply *are* no depths of character to fathom. He himself says at the end, "Surface, surface, surface was all that anyone found meaning in" (AP 375). A number of other factors contribute to this end: the narration of the entire novel in the present tense (the present moment is all that matters to these people); the fact that characters continually mistake one person for another (all these AmEx–carrying, mousse-wearing Wall Streeters are alike and interchangeable, and it is only an accident that Bateman commits murders and the others do not); and the flat, toneless style that reflects the utter vapidity and banality of every single character in the novel.

Toward the end *American Psycho* devolves into a sort of dream fantasy, and one long stream-of-consciousness passage (AP 347–52) approaches the weird as it records Bateman's near-capture by the police after a chase scene in which he murders victim after victim. The conclusion of the novel is as chilling (and not in a physical sense) as anything that has happened before. Bateman, who by now has killed dozens if not hundreds of people (it should be pointed out that he kills not only women but men, children, and animals), finds himself in a bar for one more round of meaningless drinking and socializing, and he reflects:

> "Well, though I know I should have done *that* instead of not doing it, I'm twenty-seven for Christ sakes and this is, uh, how life presents itself in a bar or in a club in New York, maybe *anywhere*, at the end of the century and how people, you know, *me*, behave, and this is what being *Patrick* means to me, I guess, so, well, yup, uh..." and this is followed

by a sigh, then a slight shrug and another sigh, and above one of the doors covered by red velvet drapes in Harry's is a sign and on the sign in letters that match the drapes' color are the words THIS IS NOT AN EXIT [AP 399].

This is an obvious but still powerful metaphor. Bateman's life has no exit: he will keep on making $200,000 a year and go out drinking every night and have meaningless affairs with women he doesn't care for and who don't really care for him, and he will probably continue murdering, but it will all amount to nothing. *This* is the true horror of the novel. I have remarked earlier that some works of satire are written with such ferocity and misanthropy as to border upon the weird, and it is in this sense—and this sense only—that *American Psycho* might come close to horror. As for the bloodletting, it is all incidental; or, rather, it is strictly subordinate to the satirical function. The novel is a cold, ugly work—part social commentary, part farce, part suspense story, part pseudopornography—but masterful in its cold, ugly way.

I am not certain that anyone aside from critics of the weird tale cares—or should care—whether the works of Robert Bloch, Thomas Harris, and Bret Easton Ellis, and others of their kind, are or are not weird. The distinctions, even if valid, seem purely academic and do not affect the merit of the works in question. Still, I think they are necessary in order that the weird tale, which has already become so heterogeneous and so unlike the standard classics of the field, not become so all-inclusive that anything a little out of the ordinary becomes subsumed within it. An important recent trend in weird fiction is the mingling of genres once thought distinct—mystery, suspense, science fiction, mainstream fiction. And the future appears to promise further contortions on the part of critics as we encounter new works that, consciously or not, continually pummel the already weakened boundaries of genre. But if fine writing is the result of this intermingling, then critics will be the only ones to complain.

THOMAS TRYON: RURAL HORROR

In 1971 Thomas Tryon (1926–91), a minor Hollywood actor, published *The Other*. To everyone's surprise, it became a bestseller. Two years later he published *Harvest Home*, followed by *Lady* (1974) and *Crowned Heads* (1976). After a long hiatus he then issued *All That Glitters* (1986), *The Night of the Moonbow* (1989), and *The Wings of the Morning* (1990), the last being the first of a projected four-volume saga of a Connecticut family in the nineteenth century on which Tryon was working prior to his death. The second novel in this series, *By the Waters of Babylon*, as well as a children's book, *The Adventures of Opal and Cupid*, have been announced as forthcoming, but they have not as yet appeared.

I have no idea whether Tryon chose to write horror novels because he witnessed the success of Ira Levin's *Rosemary's Baby* (1967). I tend to doubt it, for his novels have nothing of Levin's tediously conventional supernaturalism. Certainly he could not have been directly inspired by the example of William Peter Blatty's *The Exorcist* (1971), which emerged simultaneously with *The Other*. While it could be said that the fortuitous appearance of *The Exorcist* and *The Other* initiated the literary "boom" in weird fiction whose decline we are at the moment witnessing, Tryon's works are worth considering for more than sociological reasons: they are, in fact, rather good.

What *The Exorcist* did for the tale of supernatural horror, *The Other* and *Harvest Home* did for the nonsupernatural tale of psychological horror: they legitimized it and showed that in the hands of a master it formed a genuine subclass of the weird tale. We have already seen that some previous works of this type—notably the novels of Robert Bloch—so closely tread the nebulous boundary between horror and suspense that classification becomes difficult. Tryon changed all that. *The Other* and *Harvest Home* are emphatically nonsupernatural and psychological—the horror is largely or wholly internal, a product of a disturbed mind, and not external—but they are also emphatically horrific. Indeed, I know of few authors who have *simulated* what I call ontological horror (horror at the perception of some violation of natural law in the external world) better than Thomas Tryon. It is unfortunate that his purely horrific novels are limited to *The Other* and *Harvest Home*. *Lady* and *The Night of the Moonbow* are so tangentially horrific that they can hardly be classed in the field at all (although they are fine novels for all that), while *Crowned Heads* and *All That Glitters*, being purely novels of Hollywood life, will not be considered here at all.

The Other is based on a trick. To say this is not at all to say that it is somehow meretricious, for the "trick" is the whole focus of the novel and the source of Tryon's investigation of the psychology of his protagonist. In this tale of Niles and Holland Perry, twin boys growing up in rural Connecticut in the 1930s, we do not learn until about two-thirds through the novel that Holland is actually dead and that Niles, shattered by the loss of his twin brother, is desperately pretending that Holland is still alive. Neither the third-person narrator of the novel proper, nor the first-person narrator who introduces each of the three segments of the book (and who turns out to be Niles, speaking from a lunatic asylum), reveals the truth until Niles's grandmother Ada, who initially allowed him to continue pretending that Holland was alive but finally tires of it because of the tragedy it has caused, forces Niles to confront the spectacle of Holland's grave. This is one of the most powerful and shocking moments in all modern weird literature. The first-person narrator (the grown-up Niles) seems finally to concede the matter of Holland's being dead:

> Witness this astonishing reverence, this passion for a corpse; the boy is in thrall to a cadaver, obsessed by a ghoulish inamorato; not a ghost, not a vision, but a living breathing thing of flesh and blood; Holland, *he himself*. Such are the properties of the game. Be a tree, be a flower, be a bird—be *Holland*. With this—creature—he acts out his little pageants of blissful agony, the happy, subtle tyrannies, loving his twin, yet supplanting him, idolizing him, yet tearing him from his place; it is not enough to be Holland's twin, he must become Holland himself [O 209].

But the boy Niles cannot accept it, and he continues the pathetic charade that leads to still more horror and death, until he is finally put away.

The degree to which Niles rejects the truth of his brother's death is exactly reflected in the degree to which both the third-person and the first-person narrators conceal this fact from us. And the degree to which Holland seems to Niles a living being, even though he is dead, is reflected in the degree to which we unsuspectingly assume Holland's existence until little cracks in the narrative cause us to doubt it, making the shattering revelation simultaneously shocking and inevitable.

The Other is, in effect, really a detective story, but it remains a work of horror because it pretends *not* to be a detective story. We have no reason to doubt Holland's guilt in the various gruesome crimes that are committed until it is revealed that Holland is dead. At this point, our increasingly horrified awareness of Holland's psychological aberrations is suddenly and cataclysmically transferred to Niles. Throughout the novel, random utterances that seem to have the most innocent implications—or, indeed, to have no implications at all—become, once the secret is known, full of loathsome suggestion.

It is vital to Tryon's purpose to establish the psychological similarity—indeed, near-unity—of Holland and Niles. The closeness of the brothers is emphasized at every turn: "As twins should, they had been inseparable to begin with. Why, they had shared the same cradle, head to foot—that old wicker cradle, still in the storeroom—until they outgrew it, and then they slept in the same crib. You would have thought they were Siamese twins, so close they were; one being housed in two forms. What had happened? Whose fault? She could not tell. Always the same question, over and over..." (O 66). The ominousness of those last few sentences, coming well before the revelation, escapes us here: we do not know what "happened" or whose "fault" it was. But this closeness of the twins leads to the notion that "Holland could more often than not tell what he [Niles] was thinking, and vice versa" (O 34). This, along with the already quoted passage stating that Niles could mentally *be* Holland at times (the "game" referred to in that passage is a process taught to Niles and Holland by Ada whereby their minds become psychologically united with some other being or object), is important in clarifying some ambiguous matters later on. And note this remark: "Niles considered his profile against the dark sky: Holland, he thought; Holland. He needed him—they needed each other. That was the thing. He was—what?—dependent upon him. Without Holland, he felt some unidentifiable part of him had been lost" (O 103). Consider the enormous subtlety of this statement (something we again fail to realize at this point): the final sentence is in the *pluperfect* tense. If Holland were alive, surely the sentence would have been in the imperfect or subjunctive.

It is not merely that Niles, heartbroken at the loss of his twin, seeks to keep him alive in his mind; there is the suggestion that psychologically Niles is transferring his "evil" side to Holland. Niles cannot admit to himself that he, not Holland, has committed all the atrocities in the tale (and there are many of them). After "Holland" has killed his cousin Russell's pet rat, Niles even chides him in his mind: "*Oh Holland, you bastard. What a heartless thing to do*" (O 39). This sort of scenario is repeated over and over again. Even Ada states, "Niles, don't you think sometimes you blame Holland for things that perhaps are not his fault?" (O 86). Fascinatingly, at one point the first-person narrator (who of course is Niles) actually remarks: "Believe me, Niles is not entirely the paragon he appears, nor Holland quite the knave" (O 98). Of course, Holland when alive really was the "bad boy" of the two, and he ultimately caused his own death when he tried to hang Ada's cat in the well but fell down it himself. This incident itself—the most deeply repressed event in Niles's psyche—is fragmentarily related several times throughout the novel until all the details finally come out. Holland was playing with the cat on his thirteenth birthday in March. Initially the first-person narrator reports the incident in a highly oblique manner.

> A frightful scene, as you can imagine, the cat clawing, spitting, Holland chuckling–fiendishly, as it were, and now, amidst the horrible caterwauling, crying out as his body tumbled over the brink of the well, the animal with him—*miaow! miao-o-ow*—and there was one who thought, for a quick moment, that Holland was—but no, he told himself, he's only hurt. "Help! Somebody help! He's hurt! Holland is hurt! Help!" And surely there was time yet; the well was dry; the cat, poor creature, was dead as a doornail, and there was the end of that. But Holland—a patch here and there and he'd be fine, though sore for a week, which is what comes of hanging cats in wells. ("Are you sore, Holland? Does it hurt?" "Sure it hurts, what didja think?") [O 15].

There are a number of interesting things here. Even now Niles cannot admit the true state of affairs to himself (recall that he is the grown-up narrator telling the tale at this point). "Holland was—but no, he told himself, he's only hurt." But Holland is dead. The tone of mild recrimination—Holland, you really oughtn't to have hung that cat, such a mean thing to do—belies the fact that Holland brought about his own destruction. And that parenthetical remark is critical, for it is the focus of the deception here; but again, as elsewhere, it is also the point at which Niles refuses to acknowledge reality: Niles is (as we learn much later) pretending to have this conversation with Holland as he looks at him in his coffin. A little later Ada reflects on the incident:

> Ada shook her head again, thinking about her own cat—Pilakea. Pilakea was a word Holland had collected from somewhere; "trouble," it meant, in Hawaiian. Trouble indeed. But of course there wasn't any more Pilakea; that one had come to a bad end, back in March, right after St. Patrick's Day. On Holland's birthday. Died horribly, poor *koshecka*; Holland had hanged it in the well. Holland ... what senseless, what tragic destruction [O 65].

Again Tryon's subtlety of diction must be marveled at here: the "tragedy" of course is not merely the death of the cat but the death of Holland.

Ada is, of course, a critical figure in this whole chain of events. She has both, in psychological terms, encouraged Niles in his fantasy (hence the double meaning behind the seemingly innocuous phrase that she "indulg[ed] his whim" [O 50]) and, in narrative terms, assisted in the deception of the reader by pretending to acknowledge Holland's existence. One supposes that at least one such figure is necessary to this sort of narrative, since otherwise it would be nearly impossible to pull off the deception for any length of time.

Once we know the true state of affairs, all sorts of remarks and incidents, either passed over without question or else the source of undefined
puzzlement, become starkly clear. Why is Niles afraid to go to the cemetery? (O 57). What trauma did Niles's mother suffer in March? (O 142–43).
Why is Aunt Fanny anomalously horrified at the sight of what appears to
be Holland in a costume, when in fact it is Niles? (O 144). And when Ada,
seemingly talking of Niles's mother, says to him, "And sometimes it takes
longer for some people to get over things than others, do you see" (O 90),
is she really thinking only of Niles's mother or also of Niles himself?

There are only three points in the novel that become difficult to
explain on purely naturalistic grounds. First, an elderly neighbor, Mrs.
Rowe, appears to entertain Holland (actually Niles dressed up in a costume
Holland was known to wear) for tea. But it was stated earlier that "her
mind was sometimes cloudy" (O 155), so perhaps we are to assume that she
is senile, or else that she is humoring Niles. Niles's elder sister Torrie, lying
in bed with her husband Rider, refers to Niles and Holland in the present
tense ("I swear they're gypsies" [O 134]). But perhaps this remark is meant
as a sort of generic description, or, because she knows that Niles is over-
hearing them, as a way of humoring Niles in his obsession. The most troubling detail is when the imaginary Holland reveals to Niles that he saw
Torrie and Rider in bed the previous Thanksgiving, at a time when they
must have conceived the child that Torrie is about to deliver. The real Holland was still living then, but how is he able *now* to pass on this information, which comes as a shock to Niles ("'*Saw them?*' Niles was thunderstruck.
'You *watched?*'" [O 136])? Here I think we must have recourse to the anomalous, and nearly supernatural, mental synchronicity of the twins, or rather
to Niles's power to *be* Holland on occasion. This particular incident is the
only one that is not ultimately elucidated naturalistically, and it is perhaps
Tryon's way of leaving the matter fractionally open to doubt, as he does
later when Ada thinks to herself: "It was no good, she could tell. He would
never give it up, this incredible, this monstrous delusion, these *remains* he
was obsessed with. It would be with him for as long as he lived. She could
see that now. And this outburst she had just witnessed, so unlike *him*, but
so like ... the Other ... it was almost as though..." (O 270). Almost as though,
we are to understand, Niles is actually possessed by Holland.

The Other is a masterwork in every sense: in a tightness of writing that
does not preclude passages of poignant lyricism as well as clutching horror; in a succession of ghastly incidents—the death of Russell as he leaps
from a hayloft onto a pitchfork; Niles (as Holland) pushing his mother
down the stairs and crippling her; Niles abducting his sister's baby and
killing it in a particularly loathsome manner; the suspicion that the real

Holland killed his father months before his own death that almost numbs us; in an atmosphere of rural placidity that is subtly disturbed by an ever-growing undercurrent of terror and punctuated by startling incidents of sudden death. But Tryon saves the greatest horror for last, introducing it so quietly that it perhaps escapes many readers. We register the fact that the first- and third-person narrators of the novel are very different: the latter, usually seeing things through Niles's eyes, presents the world as a 13-year-old boy would perceive it; but the former, right from the beginning, makes clear his adult sophistication. The surprise, therefore, is not merely that this is Niles, and not merely that he is in an asylum for the criminally insane; it is the clear suggestion that he has been there for a long time ("But Miss DeGroot says I'm 'family,' meaning, I suppose, that I have been here that long" [O 288]) and will surely be there for a very long time to come. It is this that helps to raise this novel far above that of a mere display of sordid crime, and even above that of a penetrating study of a diseased mind, though it is that. The novel, ending with Niles finally identifying himself completely with his dead brother ("Call me his name—Niles; *Niles*, for God's sake, isn't that crazy? When I have told them, for years have told them, my name is Holland" [O 288]), becomes authentic tragedy.

Harvest Home is in some ways a still greater work, presenting a many-stranded tapestry of horror in which the diverse elements are all miraculously united in one of the most shuddersome denouements in the history of weird fiction. Like *The Other*, it is set in rural Connecticut, but in the present day; and yet, as we are introduced to the small, tightly knit village of Cornwall Coombe, we can imagine that we have entered some ageless agricultural community where the continual cycle of the planting, nurturing, and harvesting of the corn is the eternal and perhaps the only reality. It is something one of the villagers tells Ned and Beth Constantine just as they are moving into the town from New York:

> Tradition, he continued, was the important thing here; tradition and custom, customs that had been preserved through the villagers' lineage since olden times. They were a tightly knit, insular group, these corn farmers, apparently determined to cut themselves off from the rest of society in an effort to preserve their own folkways, much as had the Amish in Pennsylvania, the Mennonites in Ohio. What had been good for a man's father and grandfather was good enough for him; what they had worn, he wore; the tools they used, he used—a scythe to mow the hay, a sickle to cut the corn [HH 32–33].

The parallel with the Amish and the Mennonites seems suggestive, for the people of Cornwall Coombe appear as archaically devout as those other isolated folk: "did people still observe Whitsunday?" (HH 26), Ned wonders as he first enters the town. But what is the true religion of Cornwall Coombe? The Widow Fortune, who is the matron of the entire town, clarifies the matter. "She pointed upward. 'See that blue sky now, that's God's sky. And up there in that vasty blue is God. But see how far away He is. See how far the sky. And look here, at the earth, see how close, how abiding and faithful it is. See this little valley of ours, see the bountiful harvest we're to have. God's fine, but it's old Mother Earth that's the friend to man'" (HH 60). The god they worship seems older than the Christian god. Another resident, Mrs. Buxley, almost gives the show away at one point when she remarks: "You're bound to think us positively heathenish hereabouts" (HH 86).

It is important for Tryon at the outset to establish the apparent serenity and placidity of this forgotten and undisturbed corner of the world. Cornwall Coombe is only a short drive from New York, and yet it is "hardly on the map at all" (HH 18): the simultaneous isolation and reality of the village is critical. Will Ned and Beth fit into the community and its somewhat peculiar ways? They certainly mean to try: Ned remarks, after some months, "I felt I was becoming a fixture in the village" (HH 104). It is a fond wish. What he does not realize is that, as one villager says to his wife, "The social unit here is not the family, it's the community. And the community is founded on corn" (HH 125). This simple statement will take on ominous overtones much later.

And yet, things seem tranquil enough as Ned, an artist, wins favor by drawing portraits of the villagers and Beth participates in a sewing circle and other village activities. Although unbelievers, they gradually realize that church attendance is expected of them as a matter of social etiquette. Indeed, it becomes increasingly clear that a number of activities are either prescribed or proscribed, and that the tolerance for any deviations from the unwritten social laws of the community is very small.

Harvest Home, even more decidedly than *The Other*, proclaims the non-supernatural basis of the horrors that come to dominate its latter segments. There are frequent mentions of a ghost that is said to haunt the nearby woods, and some villagers seem to regard the phenomenon quite seriously. One tells Ned that it is the ghost of a revenuer who met a bad end (HH 123); another can still hear his bansheelike howls. Ned scoffs at this, as do some of the other, more enlightened townspeople. But then he has this experience:

> As I kicked the branch into the gully, lightning flashed again, a
> sharp electric current of blue that turned the sky a sickly green color.

Then suddenly, above me, at the top of the embankment, materializing out of the darkness, there appeared what I immediately thought must be the Ghost of Soakes's Lonesome. Ghastly, eerie, the figure was a gray ashen hue, the white garments flapping like cerements, a specter returned from the grave. I have never seen a ghost, nor do I believe that ghosts exist, but at that moment I was absolutely certain I was looking at one. It seemed to glow against the lurid sky, hovering some twelve feet above me, the body cut off by the edge of the embankment, head upraised, arms outstretched. I tried to tell myself I was imagining all this, but there it stood, a haggard, silvery shape, like some ghoul risen from the dead.

It turned on me the most terrible countenance I had ever seen. An appalling face, the flesh was as white as the clothes, except for the dark recesses of the eyes and the red, grinning mouth. It was this grin that made it seem more horrible, scarcely a smile at all, but the parody of one. A poor, painted smile, witless, demented, grim, the inane smile of a rag doll. Dark gouts of liquid erupted from the corners of the mouth while one hand—feeble, supplicating—lifted in a pitiful gesture and tore at the grin, as though to strip it away [HH 148–49].

But almost immediately Ned doubts the supernatural cause of the apparition: "I felt sure this was no ghost, no supernatural creature, but something as real as the moon itself, real enough to have been human and alive" (HH 149).

In the daytime Ned explores the woods and finds a rotting skeleton embedded in a tree root; the wind whistling through the skeleton's skull is the cause of the bansheelike sounds (HH 157). This may be a sufficient explanation for the old tradition of the ghost—perhaps it is in fact the revenuer who was killed many years ago—but it does nothing to explain Ned's recent experience with an evidently living creature. The (natural) explanation for that comes only later, when Ned stumbles into the shack of Jack Stump, formerly a genial general handyman of the village. He has been horribly mutilated: his tongue has been cut out and his mouth crudely sewn up. As Ned ponders the spectacle, he begins to connect this event with his ghastly encounter. "Then it dawned on me. The phantom in the windstorm. Not the Ghost of Soakes's Lonsome, but the mutilated Jack Stump, his mouth stitched up into the grim red smile, the face ash-smeared" (HH 248–49). A more emphatic repudiation of the supernatural could hardly be asked for.

Ned's fortunes take a critical turn when he befriends a young man, Worthy Pettinger. Worthy has been selected as the next Harvest Lord, a high honor in the eyes of the villagers; but he spurns the office and attempts to flee the community. The Widow Fortune warns him: "'Worthy, don't shirk your duty to your Lord'" (HH 236). This seemingly clumsy expression, with the pointed repetition of "your," is another of Tryon's masterstrokes of subtlety: perhaps Worthy's (and the community's) "Lord" is not everyone else's. But Worthy pays no heed. Not only that, he makes a dramatic gesture by bursting into a church meeting.

> Worthy lifted his right hand from the door panel and made a fist of it, and the fist trembled as he raised it and spoke in a loud, angry voice: "May God damn the corn!"
> Immediately a babble of sounds arose, women covering their faces with their hands, some of the men turning to one another with angry mutters.
> "May God damn the corn!"
> He remained frozen in the open doorway, his clenched fist held aloft. *"And may God damn the Mother!"* [HH 256].

That Mother, of course, is Mother Earth (cf. HH 309), and the cursing of her is the most heinous blasphemy the villagers can imagine. But Ned abets Worthy's attempts to escape and is ultimately detected. Worse, Worthy is dragged back as a virtual prisoner of the town.

Ned, increasingly disturbed by a series of odd occurrences, is already reflecting on his false sense of belonging to the community. Matters become worse when his wife Beth, who is already alienated from him because of his suspected dallying with Tamar Penrose, now reproves Ned for helping Worthy. It becomes clear that Beth has chosen the social unit of the community, not the family. This evolution is inevitable, for Beth, like all women, has a deep connection with Mother Earth, as the Widow Fortune tells Ned: "'She [earth] is all of woman, and more. She bears as a woman bears. She gives and sustains as a woman does, but a woman dies, being mortal. But she is not. She is ever fruitful. She is the Mother'" (HH 323).

Interweaved in this complicated network of strange events is the old mystery of Grace Everdeen, a young girl who was chosen as the Corn Maiden 14 years ago but who died under cloudy circumstances. Ned becomes increasingly obsessed with this mystery, questioning anyone who might have had anything to do with the matter. He has come to feel that it has a central bearing on recent events. And so it does. Ned finally discovers that Grace had contracted a rare disease, acromegaly, that made her physically grotesque. The townspeople refused to let such a disfigured person play the role of the Corn Maiden, and they killed her. It was her body, not that of a revenuer, in the woods. It was Jack Stump's discovery of the body that led to his own mutilation. And now Ned faces the prospect of being killed or harmed himself.

The climax of the novel has almost unbearable potency. It is here that Tryon *simulates* supernatural horror through skillful manipulation of atmosphere and diction. The secret ceremony of Harvest Home, in which only the women of the village, along with the Harvest Lord, participate, is explicitly compared to the Eleusinian Mysteries (HH 392); Ned recklessly bursts in on the ceremony, horror-struck that his own wife is participating. That ceremony, involving ritualistic language that becomes increasingly archaic (very reminiscent of the conclusion of Lovecraft's "The Rats in the Walls," whence Tryon probably derived the technique), involves nothing less than the death of the Harvest Lord after he has impregnated the Corn Maiden. It is this suggestion of the hoary antiquity of the ceremony, in addition to its barbaric violence, that lends a quasi-supernatural aura to the event. There are few scenes in all weird literature more powerful than the spectacle of Beth and the Harvest Lord coupling.

> She was not his lover, nor he hers, but both were instruments of the women, his arms bound, hers held outstretched on the earth as he probed her, and my cries broke from my lips again, mingling with the ecstatic chant that moment by moment mounted in tempo and pitch, "Ldhu, ldhu," thrusting their shoulders as he thrust, grunting as he grunted, "Ldhu," and "Ldhu," some moving behind him, their fingers tracing the curve of his back as it arched and bent again, rose and sank, their passion spurring his passion, she beneath him crying out in lust and pain. In the madness and the moonlight, his face contorted in spasm as he pushed his way farther. And then, in the moment of complete knowledge, they worked each other, met shudderingly, and capitulated. The corn was made [HH 407].

But again, as with *The Other*, a quieter but even more loathsome horror concludes the novel. A villager who early befriended Ned and Beth, Robert Dodd, is blind. He seems harmless enough, listening to recorded novels throughout the story. But Ned then discovers that he not merely is blind but actually has no eyes. What is the significance of the Widow Fortune's remark: "'Take Robert, for instance; he had trouble many years ago; he learned'" (HH 322)? What was that trouble? What has he learned? Could he himself have violated the Harvest Home ceremony as Ned did? It certainly seems so, for Ned suffers a like fate: he is blinded and his tongue is cut out. Only then do we realize that the entire novel has been a monumental flashback; only then do we perceive the ominousness of the opening paragraph:

> I awakened that morning to birdsong. It was only the little yellow bird who lives in the locust tree outside our bedroom window, but I

could have wrung his neck, for it was not yet six and I had a hangover. That was in late summer, before Harvest Home, before the bird left its nest for the winter. Now it is spring again, alas, and as predicted the yellow bird has returned. The Eternal Return, as they call it here. Thinking back from this day to that one nine months ago, I now imagine the bird to have been sounding a warning. But that is nonsense, of course, for who could have thought it was a bird of ill omen, that little creature? [HH 13].

Harvest Home, with its rich characterization, deft construction, fluid prose, and cumulative force, is one of the great weird novels of our time, and a virtual textbook on how to update the form while simultaneously drawing upon history to lend texture and substance. Both *The Other* and *Harvest Home* are *horror novels* in the strictest sense: though nonsupernatural, they powerfully delineate horrific scenarios, and their themes are such as to require the novel form for their execution. Richness of character portrayal, rather than being an awkward encumbrance, is a necessary component of both works; but whereas *The Other* is essentially concerned with the abnormality of a single individual, *Harvest Home* shows the increasingly aberrant nature of an entire community. It is accordingly a longer and richer work, and each character is painted with slow and careful strokes that gradually uncover the twisted mentalities lying beneath outward normality. In this regard *Harvest Home*, although seemingly padded with dialogue and descriptive passages that bear no strict relationship to the central plot, is as carefully and tightly written as *The Other*. In both novels Thomas Tryon has triumphantly demonstrated that the novel and the horror tale can be fused so that their best features work smoothly together to produce an amalgam that is greater than both. It is unfortunate that so few others have learned by his example.

Tryon may not have a well-rounded world view (it does not, at any rate, fully emerge in his novels) but he wields a narrative device that approaches a world view and links all his novels, whether weird or not. This device might be referred to as the successive peeling off of layers, whether of characters or of events. To understand how this device functions in Tryon, let us briefly consider two of his other novels.

Lady is a winsome and delightful story of a charming but enigmatic and melancholy woman, Adelaide Harleigh, who fascinates the young boy who narrates the novel. There is nothing at all weird about this work; if anything, it may approach the detective story in that there appears to be some nameless secret in Adelaide's past, and it is something we do not learn until almost the final page: she killed her husband many years ago because she had fallen in love with her black servant. All this is presented with the utmost delicacy and sympathy, and we leave the novel realizing that Adelaide could have done nothing else in order to preserve her happiness.

The worst thing about *The Night of the Moonbow* is how Tryon's publisher shamelessly attempted to capitalize upon the fame of *The Other* and *Harvest Home* by presenting this novel as weird, when it is nothing of the sort. Instead, it is the sensitively written story of a strange boy, Leo Joaquim—who, like Lady, has a mysterious past—at a summer camp. A poignant and evocative work, it has no legitimate weird elements save a "haunted house" (which, of course, is not actually haunted) at the edge of the camp, and which does not even figure centrally in the novel in any event.

What unites all four of these novels is the careful etching of character that gradually reveals more and more about the protagonists, until finally the surface layers are peeled off to display the core of their personalities: the psychotic horror of Niles Perry, the loathsome primitivism of the inhabitants of Cornwall Coombe, the crime of passion that has cast a shadow over Adelaide Harleigh, or the human tragedy that disfigures the youth of Leo Joaquim. This device functions in regard to events as well: the constant reiteration of the tale of Holland Perry and the cat, or of the murder of Grace Everdeen, each time lends more and more detail to the account until finally the truth is known. Is Tryon saying that each of us, if the external layers of our character were peeled away, would find something nameless in the depths of our past or the depths of our psyche? Although he never explicitly articulates this philosophy of human life, it structures all his work, weird and nonweird alike.

I am unsure of Tryon's actual influence upon subsequent weird fiction, specifically upon nonsupernatural horror. His work continues to be read and admired by the weird community, but the recent trend toward psychological suspense does not seem to owe a great deal, in any specific sense, to Tryon's brand of pseudosupernaturalism. Nevertheless, I believe that such works as Bloch's *Psycho* and Tryon's *The Other* provided models for the intense exploration of aberrant psychological states that one finds in Campbell's *The Face That Must Die* and other works of this kind, even if there is no effort at simulating the supernatural. As for *Harvest Home*, it seems—like Klein's *The Ceremonies*—a strange and wonderful throwback to the heyday of Machen and Lovecraft in its densely textured prose and evocation of the awe and mystery of nature.

If Thomas Tryon had continued in the vein of *The Other* and *Harvest Home*, he might well have rivaled Shirley Jackson and Ramsey Campbell for preeminence in modern weird fiction. But he chose a different path, and that was his prerogative: perhaps he did not wish to be pigeonholed as a "horror writer"; perhaps, in his first two novels, he had said all he had to say in the horrific mode. Whatever the case, the whole of Tryon's work (save perhaps his Hollywood novels, which seem to have a very restricted appeal) is worth reading, if for no other reason than for his exquisite prose, skillful character drawing, flawless plot construction, and a richly evocative atmosphere that remains long after the work is finished. There are few more accomplished works in weird fiction than *The Other* and *Harvest Home*: they will survive long after their noisier successors have been forgotten.

PETER STRAUB: FROM GHOST STORY TO THRILLER

The career of Peter Straub (b. 1943) may be very instructive. After writing a horrendous mainstream novel, *Marriages* (1973), which shamelessly aped two of his idols, D. H. Lawrence and Henry James, and after being unable to sell his second novel, *Under Venus*, an equally dreary and meandering mainstream love story, Straub was encouraged by his agent to write something more marketable—a "gothic."[10] Although he had read some horror and science fiction as a youth, he did not really know what a "gothic" was, but he managed to produce a competent supernatural tale, *Julia* (1975), even though it too labors somewhat under a heavy Henry James influence. Finding the weird tale to his liking, he wrote what may in fact be his best supernatural tale, *If You Could See Me Now* (1977). *Ghost Story* (1979) lifted Straub to bestsellerdom, but this turn of events, although good for his pocketbook, was not entirely beneficial to his literary career. Over the next decade and a half he produced the odd fantasy, *Shadowland* (1981); the confused and verbose *Floating Dragon* (1983), half supernatural and half science fiction; a disastrous collaboration with Stephen King, *The Talisman* (1984); and, after a several-year hiatus, three entirely nonsupernatural novels, *Koko* (1988), a mind-numbingly windy novel about Vietnam and its aftermath, *Mystery* (1990), which is a detective story and nothing more, and *The Throat* (1993), far and away his best book but also a murder mystery.

As early as 1984, Straub asked himself whether he would keep on writing horror novels. He responded: "No, I say, only until I think I've done everything I can do with that kind of book" (WA 9). It may be that he *has* done all he can do in the weird tale, although his recent collection of shorter tales, *Houses Without Doors* (1990), makes a partial and very adept return to supernaturalism. And his abandonment of the weird tale for the "psychological thriller" (as *Koko* was billed) may or may not be representative of the flight from supernatural horror that has characterized so much writing in this field over the last two decades.

It is, however, unwise to think of Straub as in any way a generic horror writer: he has, with a certain arch arrogance, always considered himself a mainstream writer. Much of his work is rather tiresomely and self-consciously literary, and many of his pronouncements on his own work are irksomely smug and self-congratulatory. The introduction to *Wild Animals* (1984) trumpets the influence of Saul Bellow, John Updike, John O'Hara, Alison Lurie, and Iris Murdoch upon *Under Venus*, and refers to *Julia* as "a dark book, driven and gloomy and cynical in the raw, startled manner of adolescence" (WA 8–10). And elsewhere: "*Shadowland* is close to horror, but it's really a territory I created."[11] Straub may be happy to act as his own critic and back-patter, but a more balanced view might reveal that his earlier novels are reasonably skillful, his later ones wordy and rambling beyond belief and tolerance, and his work as a whole pretty generally void of any broad philosophical meaning or resonance. Certain themes—in particular, a fascination with the mysterious power of women—crop up repeatedly in his work, but with a sameness that robs them of interest or insight. As can be said for a number of authors in this volume, Straub is not as good a writer as he thinks he is.

The bulk of Straub's weird work (I do not consider *Koko*, *Mystery*, or *The Throat* to be weird, and *Marriages* and *Under Venus* certainly are not) is structured around a single concept: the notion that a force or personality occupies the bodies of various human beings (usually women) over successive generations, sometimes over the course of centuries. This premise is utilized in *Julia*, *Ghost Story*, and *Floating Dragon*, while a slight variant is used in *If You Could See Me Now*; only *Shadowland*, in many ways an anomaly in Straub's work, does not conform to this pattern. It is not clear to me that Straub has varied this single theme such that it is worth using in four different novels, two of them very long.

Julia concerns a weak-willed and somewhat neurotic woman, Julia Lofting, whose daughter Kate died at the age of nine. Julia is shattered by the loss and eventually leaves her domineering husband Magnus. She in fact believes that Magnus killed Kate by attempting to perform an emergency tracheotomy on her when she was choking on a piece of meat; she bled to death. Strange things begin to happen in the house Julia has moved into: is Kate haunting her? Gradually this notion gives way to another and more disturbing one. Julia stumbles upon a book that tells the story of Heather

Rudge, a society queen who murdered her young daughter Olivia 25 years ago. Heather, still alive and in an asylum, bluntly tells Julia: "'Olivia was evil. She was an evil person. Evil isn't like ordinary people. It can't be got rid of. It gets revenge'" (J 131). It must be Olivia who is haunting the house Julia occupies—the very house she died in—and it may well be Olivia's spirit that is occupying the body of a wicked little girl Julia sees occasionally in the park. But why is Julia the one being haunted? What has she done to deserve the haunting? Living in the same house does not seem to be a sufficient motive. Why is the word "MURDERESS" scribbled on her bathroom mirror? Finally the truth comes out: Magnus was actually Olivia's father. And Julia, not Magnus, was the one who killed her daughter, Kate—she had been repressing the incident all along.

Julia is a compact and effective work, skillful in its execution and subtle in its portrayal of a neurotic personality. I am, however, troubled by the failure to account adequately for the origin of the supernatural element in the tale. Why is Olivia "evil"? How did she get that way? The mere remark that "murder is ... an eternal crime" (J 145) merely confuses the issue: did the murder of Olivia somehow compel her spirit to persist over the years (if so, why don't all murder victims react that way?), or was Olivia evil before she was murdered? The latter seems to be the only plausible alternative, but no account is made of the prior existence of the spirit that possesses Olivia.

Nevertheless, there are some fine touches in the novel. Straub, like his mentor Henry James, who hangs oppressively over this novel, is determined to suspend the question of the actual supernaturalism of the various weird manifestations as long as he can. We are offered three possible explanations for the weird events: they are a product of Julia's disturbed mind; they are the result of (natural) actions by various characters (Magnus, desperately seeking to win Julia back, breaks into her home at one point, which Julia interprets as the actions of Olivia or a poltergeist); and they are the result of supernaturalism. The third hypothesis finally prevails. Julia, looking up old friends of Olivia's, learns that they are being systematically killed. This clinches the matter in her mind, and we are left with the same conclusion in the novel's disturbing ending.

The premise of If You Could See Me Now is not new. Alison Greening, a fetching young girl who entrances the young Miles Teagarden, tells him just prior to her death at the age of 14 that they should make a vow to meet in their hometown in Wisconsin in 20 years. "'And if you forget, I'll come after you. If you forget, God help you'" (I 9). By golly, she does just that. Nearly 60 years prior to Straub's writing, Lovecraft jotted down the core idea in his commonplace book (and it was not new to him): "Man makes appt. with old enemy. Dies—body keeps appt."[12] This is not exactly a case of a spirit possessing successive bodies, but a spirit returning after the body is dead.

Despite the hoariness of the theme, the treatment is deft. Miles was himself blamed for the death of Alison as they were swimming in a quarry, and when he returns to the town 20 years later (ostensibly to write his Ph.D. dissertation, but in reality because he feels a strange need to adhere to Alison's portentous adjuration), he is not slow to feel the town's lingering resentment. This whole aspect is handled quite crudely. Miles, an academic from the sophisticated East, is clearly Straub's object of sympathy against the spiteful small-town hostility of the uncouth and ignorant villagers. A further awkwardness is added by frequent interjections of "statements" by the various townsfolk (taken down by the police after the events) as they reflect upon the events in hindsight. The intent is clearly to create suspense, as we are given dim foreshadowings of what is to come, but the treatment is too clumsy and obvious to be effective. And yet, as a *conte cruel* in which Miles suffers repeated humiliation by the townspeople, the novel attains cumulative power and an atmosphere of ineluctable doom. The bulk of the narrative, told from Miles's point of view, does not fail to suggest that Miles brought down much of this abuse upon himself by his own bizarre and self-centered actions, but we are clearly meant to side with him against the hypocritical minister, the small-minded and oily sheriff, his misogynist cousin, and other unsavory characters.

Like *Julia, If You Could See Me Now* plays upon the question of whether the supernatural is actually involved. As Miles enters the town, a horrible murder has just been committed, and more murders—all of teenage girls—occur during his stay. Miles quickly becomes the object of suspicion, but he himself comes to believe that the spirit of Alison has returned: "I had awakened Alison's spirit, that terrible force I had felt in the woods, and I knew now that spirit was rancid with jealousy of life. On the twenty-first she would appear ... but as the date drew nearer, she was growing in strength. She could take life. That, she had been able to do from the day I had begun to draw near the valley" (I 269).

It is at this point that Straub commits what I believe is an error of judgment. As the story is building up powerfully to the return of Alison, perhaps in the flesh, Straub stages a deliberate anticlimax. "It was two minutes past twelve. She had not come. The twenty-first of July had slipped into the past and she was not coming. She would never come. She was dead. I was stranded alone in only the human world. My guilt, moving under some impetus of its own, shifted hugely within me and came to a new relationship with my body" (I 308). But shortly thereafter the matter is reversed, as Alison's actual murderers—the sheriff and Miles's cousin—are found killed in a particularly revolting manner: only Alison could be the cause. The idea, no doubt, is that readers will have let down their defenses so that this supernatural revelation can have that much greater an impact; but to me the sensation is one of deceit and trickery—a rabbit pulled out of a hat. Straub has deliberately destroyed the atmosphere he has been building up throughout the entire novel, and he cannot resurrect it in a few pages. This is also the first of several novels in which Straub is faced with a certain awkwardness in writing a plausible conclusion. Once the spirit of Alison is raised, how is it to be quelled? It seems to have more than human strength, and yet Miles and his cousin's daughter manage somehow to destroy it by fire, allowing them to drive off happily ever after. If I say, therefore, that *If You Could See Me Now* is probably Straub's best and most satisfying weird novel, it is only because his other novels are burdened with still greater problems of conception and execution.

The core of *Ghost Story* is already evident in *If You Could See Me Now*. In the latter, the sheriff, "Polar Bears" Hovre, tells Miles: "'...we're all men alone—single men. The four of us that used to know each other. Duane, Paul Kant, you and me'" (I 182). Three of these four at least (all save Paul Kant, a loner suspected of being gay) were fascinated with Alison Greening as boys. The four old men of *Ghost Story*—Ricky Hawthorne, Sears James, John Jaffrey, and Lewis Benedikt—were similarly fascinated as youths with the actress Eva Galli, whom another member of their circle, Edward Wanderley, brought into their small New York town. By now it becomes clear that this fascination with mysterious and alluring women rests with Straub himself; and yet, I cannot help suspecting a hint of misogyny behind it. We eventually learn that these five men actually killed the actress and then concealed her body so as not to endanger their careers and reputations. Incredibly, Straub seems to lay the blame on the actress herself: she was behaving wildly, taking her clothes off and mocking the others; one of the men lashed out at her in fear, and she struck her head on the mantel and died.

The last third or so of the novel is merely an adventure story in which the men, who are being systematically killed off by the spirit of the actress, pursue and attempt to kill her. All the sympathy is on their side, and Straub manages to justify both the earlier killing and the present one by casually referring to the woman's "false humanity" (GS 540): she wasn't human anyway, so it's all right to kill her. The spirit of this creature, which has inhabited various bodies over the course of decades and has entered the lives of each of the male protagonists in various disastrous ways, is finally referred to as follows:

> ...what you saw when you looked at Eva Galli on screen was a young
> woman who was not likable. Even Alma had not been likable; even
> Anna Mostyn, when truly seen—as at the Barnes's party—seemed
> coldly perverse, driven by willpower. They could for a time evoke
> human love, but nothing in them could return it. What you finally saw
> was their hollowness. They could disguise it for a time, but never
> finally, and that was their greatest mistake; a mistake in being [GS 547].

I pity the lot of women if they can be killed with insouciance merely for
being unlikable and hollow.

But I am not concerned about the misogyny underlying the entire
conception of this novel: it suffers from greater problems than this. It is
obvious that *Ghost Story* is not merely a sort of combination of *Julia* and *If
You Could See Me Now* (the idea of a spirit inhabiting various bodies over
generations, taken from the former; the idea of a group of men all fascinated with the same woman, taken from the latter), but is transparently
derived from Machen's "The Great God Pan," in which several individuals compare notes and find that the strange woman who, under different
guises, haunted their lives is the same person. This connection would be
clear even if Straub had not confessed to it in an interview.[13] He has not
done anything in particular with the root conception save to elaborate it
with a mass of background detail and character description. Much of this
is admittedly adept, but once the secret is out, the novel devolves into a
very extended chase sequence, as each of the principals strives to kill off
the evil spirit before it kills him.

Straub's penchant for happy endings (every one of his novels except
Julia and perhaps *Koko* ends with the complete elimination of the horror,
whether it be natural or supernatural) betrays him more painfully in *Ghost
Story* than in any of his other works. We are to understand that the spirit
animating Eva Galli and all her other incarnations is a manitou. The problem is that according to legend a manitou is immortal or nearly immortal;
how, then, does one dispose of such a wearily persistent entity? The present incarnation of the manitou remarks that "'I have lived since the times
when your continent was lighted only by small fires in the forest, since
Americans dressed in hides and feathers'" (GS 469). Straub attempts to set
the stage by noting that, since the young men who ganged up on Eva Galli
managed to kill her (although at the last moment the spirit escaped the
body and entered that of a lynx, thereby continuing its existence), it is in
some way vulnerable. The men manage first to kill off two repulsive sidekicks she has brought along for the ride, then finally her current incarnation. But of course this would be too easy, and so we are treated to the
ludicrous spectacle of one of the men pursuing the spirit as it changes

forms over and over again, until finally it enters the body of a wasp. The man captures the wasp and chops it up with a knife, causing a certain amount of unfortunate injury to his hand in the process. But the thing is evidently gone for good, and we humans can all breathe easier for it. Straub sums things up by remarking: "Creatures like Anna Mostyn or Eva Galli are behind every ghost story and supernatural tale ever written" (GS 422)—every tale, that is, written by those who like Straub seem to find the focus of horror and fascination in females. It would be interesting to see how Straub would incorporate the entities in Lovecraft's "The Colour out of Space" or *At the Mountains of Madness* into his scheme.

I do not wish to be unduly harsh on *Ghost Story*. The landscape of Milburn, an idyllic suburban town in New York state, is depicted with admirable affection and lyricism; the male characters are all rendered distinctly and lovingly. The structure of the novel is highly complex and could be described as a sort of spiral: we are first led down from the recent past (the death of Edward Wanderley a year before the novel opens, the first victim of the manitou's revenge) to the story of Don Wanderley and his brother David, who years before both fell in love with the same woman (another incarnation of the manitou), to the fateful death of Eva Galli 50 years in the past, then back to the present and the quest to eliminate the manitou. Some of the most powerful scenes in the novel are those in which the manitou induces hallucinations in its enemies. These hallucinations, heart-rending or horrific in turn, touch upon exactly those sources of love and fear that make the human characters human, and the lightning quickness with which Straub introduces these sequences seriously disrupts our own hold on truth and reality.

The first appearance of the manitou's sidekicks—the evil Gregory Bate and his brother Fenny, who live in appalling ignorance and squalor in rural New York—is one of the most arresting tableaux in the entire novel. It is tiresome, however, to read the stereotypical moral condemnation of the villains of the piece: "...the man ... was not merely a wolf, but a supernatural being in wolf form whose only purpose was to kill, to create terror and chaos and to take life as savagely as possible ... pain and death were the only poles of its being" (GS 378). Well, we certainly can't sympathize with such a creature, can we? Lovecraft amusingly speculates on according sympathy to a protagonist whose sole desire is the extirpation of the human race,[14] but Straub will have none of this: his villains are *bad*, and all you can do is kill 'em. And for a near-immortal entity, our manitou seems to have curiously limited horizons: "'I am going to shatter Milburn, Donald. My friends and I will tear the soul from this pathetic town and crush its bare bones between our teeth'" (GS 469). Surely this creature has bigger fish to fry.

I want to bypass *Shadowland* temporarily and turn to *Floating Dragon*, since it continues the theme of an evil spirit possessing a succession of bodies. The entity in question occupies male bodies this time; but otherwise the novel is startlingly, almost embarrassingly, similar in conception to *Ghost Story*. As in that novel, we are treated to a complex interweaving of different narrative voices, as the various protagonists gradually come together in the small and wealthy suburban town of Hampstead, Connecticut, to confront the horror. This horror is not mobile, as was the manitou in *Ghost Story*, but generally keeps pretty close to home. It has been causing periodic disasters in the town since colonial times, and for some entirely unaccountable reason it seems stronger once every hundred years (FD 430). Alas, we are in one of those periods now, and people die like flies before our stalwart heroes unite to dispel the creature—apparently by singing happy songs.

The biggest problem with *Floating Dragon* is that it goes on too long. Straub has fallen in love with his own narrative voice and cannot prevent himself from elaborating every incident in entirely needless detail—even such an utterly inconsequential thing as the weird suicide of a dog, which throws itself under the wheels of a car. (Even here is emphasis is not on the dog—the true focus of the scene—but on two unimportant human characters who argue over who is responsible for the animal's death.) We are not meant to forget that Straub is a *novelist*, and novelists (all the writing manuals say so) have to have plenty of character description, realistic dialogue (even if the dialogue serves no purpose), and background description. There is, as a result, a grotesque lack of *proportion* in this novel: Straub does not know what incidents to elaborate and what incidents to compress.

Another serious, indeed crippling, flaw is a fundamental confusion in the very premise of the work. The novel opens with the release of a poison gas from a chemical plant secretly operated by the government. This chemical, DRG-16, has miraculous properties: "'Skin lesions, hallucinations, outright madness, flu, changes in pigmentation, even narcotization— some percentage of a treated population will simply be mildly tranquilized. There may even have been evidence of fugue state and telepathic ability...'" (FD 42). That's quite a lot to ask of a drug, even one produced by the Defense Department, but let it pass. What nearly disfigures this novel is Straub's apparent confusion over how this quasi-science-fiction premise and the supernatural premise of the body- and century-hopping spirit are supposed to interact. Through large parts of the novel the chemical issue is not even addressed, and the spirit is the focus of all the attention; finally, toward the end, Straub makes some half-hearted attempts at integration, and his final statement on the matter is as follows:

> "Graham," Richard said, "I still don't know what really happened."
>
> "No," the old man said.
>
> "I thought I would somehow understand it better as time went on. I thought I'd come around to thinking that the Telpro business was more important than we thought at the time."
>
> "That Telpro installation was just out there in the world," Graham said. "I think Gideon Winter could grab it and use it because of the name—DRG. Or the other position is that the name was a coincidence, and the accident was a real accident, and Winter simply capitalized on it" [FD 511].

It can hardly be clearer from this that Straub has not thought out the matter in his own mind. It was an enormous mistake to mingle a quasi-science-fiction and a supernatural conception in this novel; one or the other would have sufficed. It is also irresponsible of him to have undertaken a sizeable novel of this sort without having worked out the issue in advance. As it is, the two disparate elements continually jostle each other awkwardly, and he does not have the ability to harmonize them.

And then there is *Shadowland*.[15] It is clear that Straub is trying to do something very different from his other works here. It is as if the very success of *Ghost Story* impelled him to write a novel as unlike it as possible. In a way this is admirable—we have grown all too tired of writers who adhere mechanically to a once-successful formula—but I am not sure what we are to make of the result here. At about the time he was writing *Shadowland*, I heard Straub speak at a convention[16] about his desire to inject more of a "fantasy" element into his work. Puzzled by the multifarious use of this term, I asked him what, specifically, he meant by it. He replied (I quote from memory): "You know—gnomes, elves, that sort of thing." I confess that I quailed at the prospect of a very promising proponent of supernatural horror writing about gnomes and elves, but I assume that Straub was referring more generally to the creation of an alternate reality or realm of magic and wonder. This is in fact what he has done both in *Shadowland* and in his collaboration with Stephen King, *The Talisman*.

The result in each case is not, to my mind, successful. *Shadowland* has its supporters, but I find the novel simply fatiguing. The mechanism or metaphor by which the bounds of reality are broken or expanded is sleight of hand—progressing from card tricks to more and more elaborate feats of prestidigitation until finally we are evidently to perceive the utter instability and superficiality of a world that purports to be governed by science and rationality. At the outset it is made clear what a magician's function is:

"A magician uses all of himself. Uncle Cole says a magician is in synthesis. *Synthesis.* He says you're part music and part blood, part thinker and part killer. And if you can find all that in you and control it, then you deserve to be set apart."

"So it's about control. About power."

"Sure it is. It's about being God" [S 54–55].

Later, as more and more inexplicable things occur, one character ponders earnestly: "magic existed in the teeth of all the hypocrites and bores, in the teeth of all the proprieties too" (S 190).

But the novel ends up numbing and stupefying the reader with its plethora of bizarre events; toward the end they simply lose force through sheer surfeit. Add to this a highly pretentious writing style and highly unpleasant and unsympathetic characters, and the result is a noble failure.

The critical juncture in Straub's career to date is *The Talisman*, his heroically awful collaboration with Stephen King. At the time it seemed a good gimmick to have the two leading horror writers of the day team up on a novel, but the result is such utter confusion that one is better off forgetting that this work ever existed. Straub, however, seemed in a quandary what to do next. While King continued to grind out bestseller after bestseller every year, or sometimes twice a year, four years passed before another book bearing Peter Straub's name appeared. It seemed as if he had tried everything the field had to offer: the ambiguous horror tale (*Julia, If You Could See Me Now*), pure supernatural horror (*Ghost Story*), an awkward combination of supernatural horror and quasi-science fiction (*Floating Dragon*), and two forays into imaginary-world fantasy (*Shadowland, The Talisman*). What was there left to do? In an interview conducted shortly after the publication of *The Talisman*, Straub confessed: "I'm tired of using the typical materials of the genre. I don't want to write anymore about animated corpses, about devils, about inexplicable fires, about loathsome diseases. I want to work with material closer to the human vein" (FF 232). It is interesting that in this same interview Straub already announced that he was working on *Koko*, and that he stated bluntly: "*Koko* won't be a horror novel."

Koko is the ploddingly tedious and long-winded story of some Vietnam veterans who seek to find a fellow soldier, Tim Underhill, whom they suspect of committing some particularly grisly murders in Singapore and Bangkok. Straub owlishly attempts to inject the novel with sociological significance: the vets have bad dreams about being back in Nam; one character opines: "'The goddamned war still isn't over, I guess'" (K 40); and so on and so forth. This may all be closer to the human vein, but Straub just doesn't have the talent to enliven this realistic material beyond the level of superficiality and unintended caricature. He has chosen a subject he does not have the capability of handling. All the characters are flat and boring— and there is not a little misogyny in the vicious portrayal of Michael Poole's estranged wife Judy, who comes off (and is meant to come off) as a small-minded and conventional bitch who doesn't understand her husband's need to come to terms with what happened in Vietnam. As in *Floating Dragon*, every incident is elaborated in endless detail, as Straub evidently believes that mere bulk may create the illusion of weight and significance.

If *Koko* is nothing more than an extremely drawn-out detective story, in which the identity of the killer is ultimately revealed to be not Underhill but another soldier in the company, then the very title of *Mystery* proclaims that it too is a detective story. Although scarcely shorter than *Koko*, it is rather more effective because the core of the mystery is more intrinsically complex. And, for once, Straub has shed his literary pretensions to write a fairly straightforward work that does not make windy claims to be anything other than the entertaining narrative it is. Let us ignore the fact that we are initially introduced to a very hackneyed know-it-all detective, Lamont von Heilitz ("'I am an amateur of crime'" [M 81]): most of the novel—and the mystery—is focused on young Tom Pasmore, who acts as von Heilitz's eyes, ears, and legs as he explores a decades-old murder in a Wisconsin resort. *Mystery* is, to be sure, longer than the average detective story. Only two writers have managed to write mysteries of such length with any real success: Dorothy L. Sayers (I think not so much of *Gaudy Night* as of *Have His Carcase* and *Busman's Honeymoon*) and P. D. James (*A Taste for Death*, *Devices and Desires*). *Mystery* is, of course, entirely devoid of philosophical significance, but it is a good story.

The Throat seeks to unite both the themes and the characters of its two predecessors; indeed, *Koko*, *Mystery*, and *The Throat* comprise a sort of trilogy concerning the Blue Rose murders that occurred in the mythical Illinois town of Millhaven. At the outset one becomes a little concerned that Straub has become excessively fond of his own characters and as a result has made his work too coyly self-referential. The novel is narrated in the first person by the now middle-aged Tim Underhill, who turns out to be a friend of Tom Pasmore, now an older man living in Millhaven. More curiously, the strange out-of-body experience related at the outset of *Mystery* as occurring to Pasmore actually happened to Underhill as a boy when he saw his sister murdered. I am not sure what purpose is served by Straub's revision of his own work; but I am heartened to announce that once *The Throat* gets underway, it proves to be a thoroughly satisfying sequel to *Koko* and *Mystery*, and somehow manages to lend them a substance and richness that they did not possess on their own.

The Throat, at 700 pages, is Straub's longest book, and yet it is his most compellingly readable: all the arch pretentiousness that marred his earlier work has fallen away, and he tells his detective story with verve, vigor, and panache. I wish I could study this novel in detail, with its extraordinarily complex and very skillfully told plot, its vivid and crisply realized characters, and its sheer narrative drive. But since it is nothing more than a murder mystery I cannot justify any lengthy discussion of it here. Suffice it to say that Straub has successfully and seamlessly united the Vietnam theme of *Koko* and the murder mystery theme of *Mystery* ("Millhaven and Vietnam were oddly interchangeable, fragments of some greater whole, some larger story" [T 79]). The opening scenes in Vietnam are told with a compactness and bland irony that puts the verbosity of *Koko* to shame, while the elucidation and resolution of both the original Blue Rose murders of the 1950s and the apparent recrudescence of them in the present surpass *Mystery* in deftness of execution. I am not wholly convinced of one critic's assessment that these three Blue Rose books "confront many of the same themes and problems as Straub's supernatural books";[17] indeed, the only "message" I can derive from these novels is the platitude that child abuse and war trauma can lead to hideous violence. This message is elaborated in a windy and superficial way in *Koko*, but is not even given much attention in *The Throat*: if it had been, then a case might have been made that these works are of the "psychological horror" type. But, like Harris's *Silence of the Lambs*, the overwhelming bulk of *The Throat* is simply given over (quite enthrallingly) to Underhill's and Pasmore's discovery and analysis of critical evidence in the case, so that in the end we get very little in the way of a psychological portrait of the killer. The attempt to trace deep themes in *The Throat* may not even be worth making, for there do not seem to be any; the novel is simply a thoroughly entertaining read. I trust I may be permitted some hyperbole in saying that *The Throat* is not merely Straub's best book but perhaps the best single detective story ever written, surpassing anything by Agatha Christie, John Dickson Carr, Dorothy L. Sayers, Margery Allingham, Margaret Millar, Ruth Rendell, P. D. James, or anyone else. But it is not a weird tale.

Houses Without Doors has both its reassuring and its disturbing sides: it is reassuring that Straub has not entirely abandoned the domain of the supernatural, but it is troubling to see him returning to a pompous, pretentious, and self-consciously literary approach that he seemed on the brink of shedding with *Mystery*. In the first place, this collection of stories of widely varying length (from five pages to 125) were clearly written at different times, and yet Straub attempts to link them by adding meaningless "interludes" that reveal little save his own literary posturing. Moreover, two stories explicitly derive from (or, as Straub self-importantly announces in an author's note, have "deep connections to" [HD 357]) *Koko*. "Blue Rose" and "The Juniper Tree" are both mentioned in *Koko* as stories written by Tim Underhill, but does Straub really expect us to care what "deep connections" exist between these stories and his tiresome novel? Both tales are quite effective, but they are not weird. "Blue Rose" may be marginally so, as it involves a young boy who hypnotizes his little brother and does all sorts of nasty things to him while he is under hypnosis; but I believe that the phenomena related here are too clearly associated with what is actually known of the powers of hypnosis to be classified as *weird*. If Lovecraft is correct in saying that the weird tale describes events *"which could not possibly happen"*[18] (i.e., those not encompassed by science *as presently known*), then "Blue Rose" is not weird because hypnosis of the sort described in the story "could possibly happen." As for "The Juniper Tree," it is certainly a moving tale about a boy who is sexually abused in a movie theatre, but there is nothing at all weird about it.

The real drawing cards in *Houses Without Doors* are two long stories, "The Buffalo Hunter" and "Mrs. God." Both are powerfully atmospheric and lyrical tales and show that Straub has finally mastered the art of characterization and the ability to introduce the weird in the most subtle and insidious manner.

The disturbed protagonist of "The Buffalo Hunter" could rival any of Ramsey Campbell's psychotics in his gradual deterioration from seeming normalcy to lunacy and death. Bob Bunting, lonely, inhibited, and working at a dead-end job as an accountant for a pornographer, invents a fantasy life as a ladies' man so that his parents will think him a normal guy with a healthy interest in women. In fact, he is terrified of women, has an unhealthy relationship with his father, and clearly yearns for the closeness to his mother that he had as an infant. A blind date tells Bunting the brutal truth: "'I know guys like you,' she said, her eyes blazing at him.... 'I know a few inadequate children who can't handle relationships, one in particular, but I thought I was all done hanging around a guy who spent half the night making phone calls and the other half in the bathroom...'" (HD 181). She doesn't know the worst of it: Bunting becomes fascinated with baby bottles and begins to affix them to the walls of his room. This is an obvious symbol for Bunting's longing for the responsibility-free life of infancy, but Straub handles it well.

The weird element in the story is introduced with great deftness. Bunting, reading a western by Luke Short called *The Buffalo Hunter*, seems actually to enter the world of the book, spending time riding a horse on the prairie. The same thing happens with a Raymond Chandler novel. We are clearly intended at the outset to interpret this phenomenon psychologically, as merely another aspect of Bunting's yearning to escape from life. But then he picks up *Anna Karenina* and reads the line: "And all at once she thought of the man crushed by the train the day she had met Vronsky..." (HD 199). Later the superintendent of his building finds him dead in his room: "'It looked like he got hit by a train. It's crazy, but that's what I thought when I saw him. He was smashed up against the wall, and the bed was all smashed...'" (HD 206). This idea, to be sure, is not new, but sufficient praise cannot be extended to the subtlety and elegance of Straub's handling of it. "The Buffalo Hunter" comes close to redeeming all Straub's missteps of the previous decade.

"Mrs. God" is ultimately rather less successful, although it has a pervasive atmosphere of weirdness found nowhere else in his work. Straub states in his author's note that the story is a pastiche of Robert Aickman, but he need not have made such a declaration: the setting in an English country house, the inexplicable events, and the polished, erudite atmosphere all proclaim allegiance to the elusive and occasionally confusing Aickman. As with Aickman's work, we are not entirely sure what exactly has transpired here, and it would be futile to trace the plot of this long and somewhat rambling story: everything is subordinate to mood. Although Straub stated that one of the things he "learned" from Stephen King was that a weird tale could be "bad-mannered, noisy, and operatic,"[19] "Mrs. God" indicates that Straub has wisely abandoned an approach that does not suit him at all and returned to well-mannered weird writing.

I do not, in the end, know what significance Straub's possibly temporary abandonment of the supernatural in *Koko*, *Mystery*, and *The Throat* really has. It is true that Stephen King himself has made a few excursions into nonsupernaturalism (disastrously in *Cujo*, more successfully in *Different Seasons*, *Misery*, and others), and many other writers have recently written very powerful tales that involve nothing supernatural; but the course of Straub's career displays an exhaustion of conventional supernatural elements, often with a single work, so that there was no alternative but to enter the adjacent but fundamentally different mode of the detective story. But this may have more to do with Straub's unoriginality than with any supposed lack of intrinsic variety in supernatural themes. He has, after all, essentially written one work four times: *Julia*, *If You Could See Me Now*, *Ghost Story*, and *Floating Dragon* all concern the endurance of a human or quasi-human spirit over the course of years. Even his detective trilogy, excellent as its final two components are, furrows the same ground over and over again.

It is also true that Straub's work savors rather too much of the study and the library. Peter Penzoldt's remark about Lovecraft—"He was too well read"[20]—is far more applicable to Straub. The influence of Henry James, Arthur Machen, Stephen King, and Robert Aickman hangs heavily over Straub's work, to such a degree that there is a real question over what is genuinely Straub and what is some conscious or unconscious recollection of a prior literary text. If he is to continue in the weird vein (and there is no guarantee that he will do so), then he will have to find some ideas that are actually his, learn a little more concision, and harness a prose style that at its best is one of the most precise, well-modulated, and evocative in the entire realm of modern literature. If he can do this, he may one day accomplish what he has yet to accomplish in nearly 30 years of writing: produce a wholly satisfying and significant work of supernatural horror.

V. PSEUDO-, QUASI-, AND ANTI-WEIRD FICTION

ROBERT AICKMAN: "SO LITTLE IS DEFINITE"

Robert Aickman (1914–81) is an exceptionally odd writer. He earned his living as founder and chairman of the Inland Waterways Association, an early environmentalist concern devoted to preserving England's inland rivers from destruction and pollution. He seems to have taken to writing weird fiction relatively late in life, publishing his first collection—*We Are for the Dark* (1951), containing three stories by him and three by Elizabeth Jane Howard—when he was well into his thirties. More than ten years would pass before the issuance of Aickman's next collection, *Dark Entries* (1964). In all, eleven collections of Aickman's tales have been published (three are posthumous), a seemingly significant sum for a life's work, but the figure is deceptive. There are, in fact, only a total of 48 short stories by Robert Aickman, and these are distributed in such a peculiar fashion in his various collections that a given story may appear in two or even three different volumes. Aickman also wrote two novels—*The Late Breakfasters* (1964), which, aside from a few ghostly effects, turns out rather surprisingly to be a sensitive and poignant story of lesbianism, and *The Model* (posthumously published in 1987), a charming but ultimately insubstantial quasi-fairy tale set in Tsarist Russia. One of his most delightful works is his autobiography, *The Attempted Rescue* (1966), as Aickman follows the curious tradition of piquant autobiographies by weird writers established by Arthur Machen (*Far Off Things*, 1922), Algernon Blackwood (*Episodes Before Thirty*, 1923), Lord Dunsany (*Patches of Sunlight*, 1938), and a number of others.

217

I certainly mean no criticism of Aickman's relatively modest literary output, for his literary gifts were of an extremely high order. His prose style—supple, urbane, sophisticated, restrained, yet capable of surprisingly powerful emotive effects—never falters from the beginning to the end of his work. There are few writers who are as purely pleasurable to read, regardless of their subject matter or the success or failure of their actual work, as Robert Aickman. His major literary influences (it might be better to say analogues) appear to be M. R. James and Walter de la Mare, yet he excels the former in richness and variety of texture and the latter in the sustained intensity of all his literary work.

But Aickman based his work upon a very odd theory of weird fiction, a theory he evolved seemingly early in life and maintained to the end. His most succinct enunciation of it appears in *The Second Fontana Book of Great Ghost Stories* (1965), which he edited:

> In my Introduction to the first Fontana Book of Great Ghost Stories, I tried to define what seem to me the basic facts about the genre. I pointed out that the ghost story must be distinguished both from the mere horror story and from the scientific extravaganza. I suggested that the ghost story draws upon the unconscious mind, in the manner of poetry; that it need offer neither logic nor moral; that it is an art form of altogether exceptional delicacy and subtlety; and that, not surprisingly, there are only about thirty or forty first-class specimens in the whole of western literature [F2, 7].

The supposed support for these claims is to be found in Aickman's introduction to *The Fontana Book of Great Ghost Stories* (1964), but in many ways his reasoning seems either flawed or insufficient. I do not wish to concern myself overmuch with his apparent denigration of either science fiction or what he calls the "horror story": he refers to the latter as "purely sadistic; it depends entirely upon power to shock" (F1, 7). But since he never tells us what specific tales he considers horror stories as opposed to ghost stories, this is not of much help. His remark would be very apt if applied to the recent splatterpunk movement, but I suspect his condemnation extends much more widely than this. In any event, the crux of the matter, as regards Aickman's own work, is the assertion that the ghost story appeals to the unconscious mind and that it "need offer neither logic nor moral." These are, it is no surprise, the distinguishing features of his tales.

The curious thing about Aickman's notion of the unconscious is that he assumes as self-evidently true Freud's assertion that "only a small part, perhaps one-tenth, of the human mental and emotional organisation is conscious" (F1, 7). When faced with manifest evidence that Freud is no longer uniformly accepted on this point, Aickman merely launches into one of his frequent denunciations of the excessive rationalism of the modern world: "Our main response to this discovery has been to reject the nine-tenths unconscious more completely and more systematically than ever before.... The most advanced psychologists have begun even to claim that the unconscious mind has no existence, and that unhappiness can be cured physically, like, say, cancer" (F1, 7). Aickman will not win a place among leading philosophers or psychologists with things like this.

Still more curious is the idea of the ghost story requiring neither moral nor logic. The first part of this assertion is not especially problematical, and Aickman's targets are such obviously didactic weird tales as *Dr. Jekyll and Mr. Hyde.* But in the same breath he speaks of the ultimate message of weird fiction: "...what the ghost story hints to us is that there is a world elsewhere, as Coriolanus put it (meaning something rather different, but that is just like a ghost); that as flies to wanton boys are we to the gods; that luck's a chance, but trouble's sure; that achievement and comfort are (like the poor ghosts themselves) immaterial" (F1, 8). But, mind you, the ghost story does not teach or preach. Perhaps there is no direct contradiction in all this, and what Aickman is saying here may be what I have maintained all along: that the weird tale offers a unique opportunity for a writer to express his world view because it allows for a reordering of the universe in accordance with the author's vision. Aickman implies here that that world view is likely to be either avowedly cosmic (although I find his own work not at all cosmic, certainly not in the manner of Lovecraft or Blackwood) or generally pessimistic, as his own view of life certainly was.

But what of the claim that the weird tale need offer no "logic"? What does this exactly mean, and how does Aickman justify it? Well, to my mind he doesn't. I can find no passage in that first introduction to the Fontana series in which he presents his case for the alogicality of weird fiction; in fact, the closest he comes is in the introduction to *The Third Fontana Book of Great Ghost Stories:* "The successful ghost story does not close a door and leave inside it still another definition, a still further solution. On the contrary, it must open a door, preferably where no one had previously noticed a door to exist; and, at the end, leave it open, or, possibly, ajar" (F3, 7). This is unexceptionable: a tale in which every feature is explained would be science fiction or, at any rate, not a weird tale. But this is in no sense a justification for the weird tale's lack of logic even on the level of plot. I think Aickman's position on this matter has to be inferred from his notion of the unconscious: if a weird tale can reach those depths of the unconscious toward which it ought to be striving, then the surface plot need not "make sense" because that is an appeal to that conscious one-tenth in which

Aickman has no interest. It is a widespread complaint against Aickman that his stories are oftentimes highly confusing, ambiguous, and obscure, hence the subtitle to this article, "so little is definite" (AR 11), which I have quoted somewhat out of context from *The Attempted Rescue*. It is, indeed, a tribute to the consistency of his philosophy of the weird tale (and to his lack of interest in commercial success) that, even to the end of his life, he disdained the mere dovetailing of a plot. He never made it easy for his readers.

The problem with the scorn of "logic" on this level is that it can lead to great abuses, especially in writers far less gifted and far more intellectually lazy than Aickman. There is a real danger that the events in a tale will seem random and unmotivated if they are not somehow brought together into a coherent scenario. If nothing else, there seems to be a violation—or, at the very least, a stretching to the uttermost limits—of Poe's notion of the unity of effect. The symbolism in Aickman's stories is at times so obscure and, I believe, so related to personal symbols that conveyed meaning for him but which he was perhaps not entirely successful in conveying to others, that the reader cannot help feeling dissatisfied and, accordingly, failing to absorb those "hints" ("that there is a world elsewhere ... that as flies to wanton boys are we to the gods") that Aickman saw as the function of the weird tale. He seems to have felt that the mere creation of a sense of the inexplicable was a sufficient purpose for weird writing. He would certainly not have agreed with L. P. Hartley, a master of weird fiction in his own right who presented an argument exactly contrary to Aickman's: "The ghost-story writer's task is the more difficult [i.e., than the detective story writer's], for not only must he create a world in which reason doesn't hold sway, but he must invent laws for it. Chaos is not enough. Even ghosts must have rules and obey them."[1] What is more, those tales that Aickman himself singles out for praise—Blackwood's "The Wendigo," Hichens' "How Love Came to Professor Guildea," Onions' "The Beckoning Fair One"—all "make sense" on the level of surface plot as well as on the level of philosophical import. The only philosophy I can detect in the mass of Aickman's fiction is the idea that the world is a little odder than it seems to be.

I wonder whether Aickman's belief in the occult has anything to do with all this. His tales themselves are singularly, and thankfully, devoid of occultist trappings, but in one of the Fontana introductions he finally makes this confession:

> While it is true that serious psychic research (as distinct from psychological) and the ghost stories of fiction are far apart, yet the latter would lose much, and become mere playthings, if the former had nothing

to investigate. It is my belief and my experience that "paranormal phenomena" do occur; and my opinion that the future well-being of man
might be forwarded by more attention being paid to them. There is evidence that a mystical, clairvoyant faculty of a most practical kind is
commonly taken for granted in many "primitive" societies, from pre-
communist Tibet to the Hebrides; and is merely bred out and killed off
by industrialism, compulsory education, and the belief that every question has an answer [F5, 8].

I hardly know how to respond to this farrago of nonsense. Weird tales were
hardly "mere playthings" to Lovecraft, Dunsany, and other unbelievers, but
rather their means for conveying their deepest and sincerest visions of the
universe. Indeed, Lovecraft frequently states that it is exactly *because* he
could not believe in conventional religion or in spiritualism that he required
the imaginative outlet of weird fiction. And it never seems to occur to Aickman, foe to all modernism that he is, that clairvoyance has been beaten
out of modern man because it is very likely to be false. In any event, it is
conceivable that Aickman, like Machen and Blackwood, is so intent on
shaking us from our ingrained rationalism that he wishes to present the
inexplicable simply as such. In this sense he may be doing exactly the sort
of preaching that he chides others for.

It may be of some interest to note that, whether in spite or because
of his interest in the paranormal, Aickman appears to disavow conventional religious belief. In *The Attempted Rescue* he speaks of the influence
of Norman Douglas, whose "combination of anti–Christianity with political and social traditionalism" (AR 119) greatly affected him. He also notes
the influence of two other great foes of religion, H. L. Mencken and Bernard
Shaw (AR 119). Later, when speaking of his fondness for the music of Delius,
he notes: "Delius offers deep, mystical feeling without implications of conventional religion" (AR 168). There is, however, little explicit anticlerical-
ism in Aickman's stories: "Larger Than Oneself" appears to open with
considerable cynicism directed toward spiritualism and perhaps toward religion in general, but the story nevertheless seems an instantiation of the
rather curious idea, stated by one of the characters, that "Sin is a sense of
something larger than oneself" (PD 189). Similarly, the quasi-spiritualist ceremony in "A Roman Question" is initially treated as something of a joke,
but it does in fact appear to cause the ghostly manifestation in the tale.

The curious thing is that Aickman could write stories that "make
sense" in terms of plot when he chose, and I cannot help but feel that they
are among the strongest of his tales. As for the stories that don't "make
sense," it seems that their effectiveness will depend, firstly, upon a given

reader's tolerance for the lack of explanation and, secondly, a sensitivity to the particular images and symbols utilized by Aickman in the story in question. I myself find such tales as "Meeting Mr Millar" and "Letters to the Postman" extremely unnerving, but can imagine that they may not so affect other readers or that other tales will. Since Aickman placed so much importance on the unconscious as a motivating force for the composition of weird fiction, it seems evident that he attempted, insofar as is possible, to tap his own unconscious for some of the more disturbing particulars in his tales or, at the very least, that he depicted or transmogrified phenomena that were personally disturbing to himself. Hence the importance or validity of an autobiographical interpretation of his work.

There is no question that Aickman belongs somewhere within the realm of weird fiction; but where exactly his place is in that realm is a singularly vexing question. His general similarity in *tone* to writers like M. R. James, Walter de la Mare, Oliver Onions, and L. P. Hartley does not to my mind make him in any sense a "traditional" writer of ghost stories. Aickman used the term "ghost story" only because "no other suggested name ... has come my way"; and he realizes that "often there is no actual ghost" (F2, 9). There are, in fact, very few ghosts in Aickman, and in many cases perhaps not even anything supernatural—certainly not conventionally so. In many tales the weird is engendered by the increasingly odd behavior of various characters; but for all that he cannot be called a writer of psychological horror, for he is not interested in the psychology of his protagonists except insofar as he wishes to delineate (and does delineate with exquisite delicacy and sensitivity) their psychological reactions to the weird phenomena. Aickman himself subtitled nearly all his collections "Strange Stories" or "Strange Tales"; and in the end perhaps no more precise a designation is possible.

Aickman did not write short stories so much as novelettes—they tend rather uniformly to be about 10,000 words in length. He requires this length to create and sustain the mood of strangeness that makes his work so uniquely compelling; indeed, it is exactly on those few occasions when he tries to compress that he lapses into triteness and conventionality. "The Waiting Room" is an undistinguished story about ghosts appearing in the waiting room of a remote train station; they are the former inmates of a prison previously existing on the site. Even an additional twist at the very end cannot make this tale anything but routine. On the other hand, some stories drag on interminably, not because Aickman's writing is anything less than polished and elegant, but because of a curious lack of focus on the central weird phenomenon. "Residents Only" has some magnificent descriptions of a decrepit cemetery, but Aickman seems to feel that the weird component of this story requires so much "subtlety" and indirection that he devotes the majority of the tale to a tiresome account of the inconclusive actions of a governmental committee overseeing the cemetery. For long periods the true heart of the story—the fate of Rogerson, the cemetery's caretaker—is virtually forgotten.

"My Poor Friend" is another example of how Aickman's excessive reticence in regard to the actual supernatural manifestation and its origin mars an otherwise potent tale. The narrator becomes associated with a peculiar and rather harried M.P., Walter Enright, who makes the startling admission that his wife has left him, taking their two children, who are "not human at all. They ought not to live" (PD 221). This certainly sounds promising. Is the wife some sort of alien entity? It is difficult to tell, since the narrator only gets fleeting glimpses of a "woman in the black dress" (PD 236) whom he thinks is the woman in question. As for the children, their harrowing appearance in a very gripping conclusion is introduced by the simple words: "It seemed as if a bird had got in" (PD 237). Evocative as this is, it really causes the tale to break down logically: if the children are birdlike creatures, how can they be the offspring of a woman who appears to be more or less human? Aickman has simply failed to provide a sufficient rationale for the birth of these anomalous creatures. Contrast Lovecraft's "The Shadow over Innsmouth": the idea of fish creatures mating with humans to produce loathsome hybrids is probably equally ridiculous scientifically, but it contains that aesthetic logic which the supernatural tale requires if it is not to lapse into absurdity and unbelievability. Because Aickman has not laid the foundations properly, the result seems arbitrary: why bird creatures as opposed to anything else?

But it would be unfair to Aickman to keep harping upon his possible failures when he has so many undoubted successes to his credit. I believe that the most efficient way to examine these successes is to start with his stimulating autobiography.

The Attempted Rescue (1966) is one of the most poignant books I have ever read. Without the least inelegance of diction, Aickman manages to be startlingly revelatory about his profoundest sentiments (e.g., "For years I suffered unspeakable agonies from sex frustration" [AR 156]). It is unfortunate that the autobiography proceeds only up to the outbreak of World War II; Aickman's continuation of it, *The River Runs Uphill*, has recently been published, but I have not had access to it. And yet, it becomes rapidly clear that Aickman's early years were so central to the development of his entire world view that perhaps much or all that we need to know about him can be found in *The Attempted Rescue*, even though he says virtually nothing about his writing there. To be sure, his upbringing was extremely odd. He lived in terror of his demonic father, had a love-hate relationship with his mother, was appalled by the constant wrangling of his parents, and, as an only child, led a generally solitary and inward-looking existence. The degree to which he bravely articulates his conflicting and clearly painful early memories makes his autobiography an act of great courage.

I do not believe that an autobiographical approach is necessarily the ideal or even a universally useful method of exegesis; but it is very clear that Aickman's fiction has pronounced autobiographical overtones, although they are never presented bluntly and are always skillfully and seamlessly enmeshed in the narrative. Some of the autobiographical touches may be either obvious or thematically insignificant—the meticulous chronicling of parliamentary activity in "My Poor Friend" is surely a product of Aickman's own experience with his Inland Waterways Association, as is the endless sequence of inconclusive meetings of an Open Spaces and Cemeteries Committee in "Residents Only." Elsewhere, however, autobiography so infuses a tale that it becomes extremely tempting to examine it with care, especially when some central tenet of Aickman's general philosophy is involved.

There are, I think, four autobiographical points that may be worth studying in detail: Aickman's nostalgia for the past; his relations with women; his sense of class; and his fondness for travel.

I actually wish to study the last point first, even though it may appear to be the least significant. Travel was, certainly, important to Aickman, as he makes clear: "Travel, the *art* of travel, is the great impersonal passion of my life, though personal also, because I need a perfect companion, and cannot make art without" (AR 89). But what becomes quickly obvious when reading his weird fiction is that in virtually every story the intrusion of the weird depends upon the protagonist's traveling to some unfamiliar locale—not necessarily remote or intrinsically anomalous, but simply some realm other than his or her own. "No Stronger Than a Flower" appears to be one of the few stories set in a locale familiar to the protagonists (the apartment of a married couple), and yet it too involves a journey to the unknown, and it is exactly such a journey that triggers the strange. A wife, tired of her husband's complaints that she takes no particular interest or care in her appearance, decides to go to a peculiar beauty shop advertised in a magazine, and finds that "the address was in a street, and indeed a part of the town, which were outside her restricted topography" (UD 98). Her slow degeneration begins at this point.

One of Aickman's earliest stories, "The Trains," establishes a pattern that would hold true for most of his career. Here two young women are hiking on foot in the north of England. The region they have entered is already sufficiently remote and forbidding, but Aickman casts further doubt on rationality when one of the women finds that the map she is consulting does not appear to be correct in certain very small particulars. By a fairly obvious but still effective sequence of symbols, it later turns out that the map, which "hasn't proved too accurate" (WDS 56), is destroyed in the rain. With the shackles of known reality sloughed off, the weird adventure can begin.

This notion of entering an unfamiliar realm is the key to one of the most distinctive features of Aickman's horrific technique. Although he appears on the surface to be a "supernatural realist," describing the real world meticulously and slyly inserting the weird through the accumulation of background details, the true secret of his weird artistry is his ability to portray seemingly normal regions that are somehow *wrong*. A statement by a character in "Hand in Glove" gets to the heart of the matter: "There's something very wrong with almost everything" (I 17). The realms he describes do not, in the end, correspond to anything we know, even though the characters attempt to move within them as if there were nothing intrinsically odd about them; they are, in the end, as fantastic as Dunsany's Pegana or any of Thomas Ligotti's dream-worlds. This notion of wrongness could, indeed, be extended to virtually everything that happens in Aickman's fiction—landscape, psychological reactions of characters, and even the smallest details of what appear to be mundane transactions.

One of Aickman's favorite devices is simply *imprecision* in topographical detail. At least three of his stories take place on islands. This would in itself be a sufficiently isolating technique, but he compounds it by failing to specify the name of the island or where exactly it is located. In "The View" we appear to be on an island just off the coast of England; in "The Wine-Dark Sea" it is off the coast of Greece; in "The Houses of the Russians" it is evidently off the coast of Finland. But no more precise delineation is to be found, and once we are there we are in a sort of hazy topography where anything can happen. Every one of Aickman's stories, whether set in an intrinsically remote area or not, is of this type.

"The Hospice" is an enormously powerful story with an extremely simple premise. A man named Maybury is traveling on business and finds that he is short of gas late one evening, and he is compelled to stop at a roadside inn simply called "The Hospice." At first, everything seems normal as he sits down to dinner in the inn's dining room; but, with the most exquisite pacing and subtlety, weird details begin to accumulate. Maybury is first given an enormous bowl of soup, followed by an equally enormous serving of a main course. Then he notices that the other diners, all but one of whom are seated at a long central table, are elderly people eating "as if their lives depended on it" (CHM 132). Later he "had the horrid idea about them that eating was all they did do" (CHM 134). Finally he notices that one of the old men has his leg attached to a rail beneath the table (CHM 136)—what can this possibly mean? There follows what seems to be a hackneyed scenario whereby Maybury is pressured to stay the night, with all sorts of obstacles being put up against his leaving. But he finally does leave, albeit by an unusual avenue: one of the inn's guests has evidently died, and Maybury is allowed to ride away in the hearse. Throughout the tale there has been the most delicate balance between farce and horror, and this conclusion—in which Maybury eventually alights from the hearse at a bus stop—should not be seen as an anticlimax: firstly, the inn's proprietor has already had his sadistic pleasure by witnessing Maybury's discomfiture throughout his stay and by compelling him to depart in this ignominious and hideous manner; secondly, it is the simple realization that such a place can exist just off the beaten track that is the true source of horror.

There is something very strange about Aickman's nostalgia for the past. It is not his loathing of the machine (AR 7), which he thinks will overtake human beings and become our master (Lovecraft and Dunsany said as much); it is rather his nostalgia for a past that he never experienced, namely the period prior to 1914, the very year of his birth. Aickman certainly perceives this difficulty. When he remarks that "It may be doubted whether there has ever been so much happiness in England at any other time as there was between 1880 and 1914" (AR 26), he is quick to add: "I discovered long ago that it and not this was my world too, though I never knew it" (AR 26). Aickman evidently believes that he gained so thorough a knowledge of this vanished world from his father and other older relatives that he inevitably felt a part of it. It is peculiar how tenaciously he clings to this view of a pre–1914 Eden; even when discoursing upon restaurants, he veers off into an aside: "The great age of restaurants, as indeed of all civilized pleasures, ended in 1914, and I saw only the epilogue, but even the epilogue was incomparably brighter, more varied, and, not least, cheaper than now seems imaginable" (AR 87).

This belief that he is living in a time in which he manifestly has no business, and which is trampling so many of the beliefs he cherishes, very largely accounts for Aickman's profound pessimism. *The Attempted Rescue* leaves no doubt of the fact of his pessimism, although there is no real account of its origin: at the very outset he remarks that we live in "a world where happiness is impossible" (AR 8); later, when recounting one of his few successful relationships with women, he remarks: "...when, at last, you are really happy, die at once" (AR 58). Perhaps it is incorrect to attribute Aickman's pessimism wholly or even largely to his nostalgia. No doubt that was an important contributory factor, but his relations with women, as well as his class consciousness, were also of significance.

Given this tendency to look backward, it is a little odd that only a few of Aickman's stories are actually set in the past. Those that are—for example, "Pages from a Young Girl's Journal," set in the time of Byron—do not strike me as among his most successful. But perhaps it is not odd at all; for it is by locating his work either in the contemporary world or in the interwar years, as the bulk of his tales tend to be located, that Aickman can allow himself his lugubrious references to the lost world of the Edwardians and the barren hopelessness of the present. He is not at all to be condemned for his nostalgia (surely no thinking person can be content with the current state of civilization) and in fact this longing for a vanished era lends a distinctively somber or melancholy cast to his work and actually facilitates the subtle incursion of the weird.

"Growing Boys" is an ingenious story that can be studied in this context. Initially it seems to be the comic tale of a mother's difficulty in controlling her two large, rowdy, voracious 15-year-old sons, who storm into the house only for meals and then storm out again. But this is only the beginning. The boys have been expelled from their school, either for poor work or perhaps for more serious derelictions. Then a policemen comes to the house and reports that the boys have gone on some sort of rampage. The charges "'include a long list of assaults, fifteen at least so far, and we are expecting more.... There are a couple of attempted rapes expected to be reported soon'" (TLD 28). When we read the policeman's remark that "'violence ... [is] growing fast pretty well everywhere in the world'" (TLD 28)—a remark that echoes the boys' father's comment that "'some boys grow faster than some other boys'" (TLD 28)—we begin to perceive the drift of the tale: the boys are symbols for the increasing violence in modern society. It is even said at a later point that "'Those two are like children of the future'" (TLD 37–38); and still later: "they were passing unnoticed amidst the freaks and zanies that people urban and suburban areas in the later part of the twentieth century" (TLD 45). The symbolism is completed by the boys' Uncle Stephen, a relic of the past, who says, "'I know all about times changing, none better... The fact remains that I have not changed. I am older, unfortunately, but otherwise exactly the same'" (TLD 37). He becomes the boys' opponent and in the end destroys them—no doubt to Aickman's great relish.

Just as nearly all of Aickman's stories involve a journey into the unfamiliar, so do they almost all involve a sexual tension between the protagonist (usually male, but on a surprising number of occasions female) and an alluring figure of the opposite sex. The title of a later Aickman collection,

Tales of Love and Death (1977), could serve for almost any of his volumes, as could the epigraph from Yeats cited in *Powers of Darkness* (1966): "I am still of the opinion that only two topics can be of the least interest to a serious and studious mind—sex and the dead."

All this, understandably, has its origins in Aickman's own life, as narrated in *The Attempted Rescue*. It is remarkable how forthright he is about his relations with women: if it was courageous of him to admit to a "sex frustration" for much of his early life, then it was equally courageous of him to have stated: "Possibly the most formative thing of all about my childhood was that love was never mentioned about the house, or seldom at all and never seriously; let alone sensuality, which was taken hardly to exist, and where it did exist, to be criminal" (AR 97). In this aspect Aickman's household did not differ greatly from that of his post–Edwardian peers, and it would be a very facile and inexpert psychoanalysis that lays all the peculiarities of his relations with women at the door of his repressed upbringing. Aickman did marry briefly (although it must have occurred subsequent to World War II, as it is not recounted in *The Attempted Rescue*) and had a number of affairs with women, but in the end he confesses that in his youth "there were only the infrequent, fleeting girls and women I have mentioned, all untouchable; supplemented by an occasional distant actress, totally inaccessible. I have been pursuing them ever since" (AR 98). That penultimate phrase, of course, makes us immediately think of "The Visiting Star," about the arrival of a world-famous actress to participate in a local theatre production.

Aickman confesses that "Always (or, rather, when I have had anyone at all) there has been one woman for whom I have felt affection, and occasionally passion, but mainly dependence, often almost total; and sometimes another woman who has been a beauty, an inspiration, and in dream, an unreality far more powerful in the directing of my life than any person or things of substance" (AR 44). I cannot actually find any clear parallel to this scenario in his fiction; perhaps the closest we get is the very delicate story, "Marriage."

Here a man, Laming Gatestead, meets and feels attracted to a woman, Helen Black, but later finds himself still more attracted to her roommate, Ellen Brown. The coincidence of their names does not pass unnoticed, and Helen remarks that Ellen "'happens to be the exact opposite to me in almost every way'" (TLD 72). This is so not only physically—one has fair hair, the other dark; one's hand, when Laming shakes it, is dry, the other's is moist—but temperamentally: Helen proves to be quite unanimated, whereas Ellen, although seemingly reticent, turns out to be a seductress who engages in sex with Laming at every opportunity after their first meeting, once lying with him in a park.

Autobiographically, Helen seems to be the woman for whom Aickman feels mere "affection," whereas Ellen is the "unreality" who directs his life. The critical remark in this context is made by Helen: "'I sometimes feel quite a shadow when I'm with her'" (TLD 72). The word "shadow" was used frequently by Aickman in *The Attempted Rescue* (generally of his father) to refer to a sort of imp of the perverse that led a person to do things detrimental to his or her own best interest. If this meaning is applied to the story, then Ellen is in fact Helen's shadow, and is nothing more than another side of her personality. And yet, Aickman refrains from stating definitively which one of the women is the real one and which the shadow. Laming's mother concludes with the remark: "'There's always the one you take, and the one you might have taken'" (TLD 84).

"Letters to the Postman" is one of the oddest stories I have ever read. A young man, Robin Breeze, takes over the postal route in a remote region of England. He hears strange things about a woman, Rosetta Fearon, living apparently alone in a house along his route: she never gets any mail, and indeed is hardly seen by any of the villagers. Then one day he finds a note in her mailbox addressed to him: "Something strange has happened to me. I find that I am married to someone I do not know. A man, I mean. His name is Paul. He is kind to me, and in a way I am happy, but I feel I should keep in touch. Just occasional little messages. Do you mind? Nothing more, for God's sake. That you must promise me. Write to me that you promise" (I 188–89). Only Aickman could have come up with such a scenario. This brings up, however, an interesting point that applies nearly uniformly to his entire work: we are evidently to accept this statement at face value. Unlike Shirley Jackson, Aickman does not appear interested in the psychological issues raised by the possibility that characters may be deliberately lying, possibly for sadistic or cynical reasons; and as this tale progresses it seems that Rosetta is indeed telling the truth. Robin and Rosetta continue exchanging anomalous little notes, and Robin finds that he has fallen in love with her, even though he has seen her—or, rather, even though he thinks he has seen heronly at random moments in the village. "The woman wore long gloves, stretching up casually over her wrists, or over the sleeves of her slim dress, different every day. Always she seemed about to smile" (I 193).

Rosetta's relations with her husband appear to deteriorate over time, and gradually she comes to feel that she must escape. Naturally, she calls upon Robin to aid her. He now becomes convinced that she is as much in love with him as he is with her: he rents a small apartment for her to use when she leaves her husband, and he imagines the bliss of living with her or even marrying her at some point. Rosetta does indeed flee her house and husband, coming to stay in Robin's apartment; but she has very different ideas about their relationship. She is grateful for his help, of course, but that was all she asked of him, and she lectures him sternly before departing out of his life. I have no idea whether this story is some twisted version of an episode in Aickman's own life; but it shows once again the difficulty of categorizing Aickman within the realm of weird fiction. There is nothing supernatural in this tale, but for all that one can hardly call it a mainstream story—it is simply "strange."

A little more conventionally supernatural, but only a little, is "The Swords." This is one of the few stories in which Aickman adopts a slightly more colloquial style than is his custom, as he narrates the tale of a boy attracted by a curious exhibit at a fair. A woman lies on a chair while the master of ceremonies invites members of the audience—only eight of them, and all male—to take one of a pile of evidently sharp swords next to her and plunge it into her body. They do so, first with reluctance, then more eagerly, as they see that the swords have no appreciable effect aside from making a loathsome hiss when they enter her flesh. Afterwards they are allowed to kiss her. The symbolism of this action does not, I imagine, need to be belabored. And yet, the tale effects as harrowing a union of sex and weirdness as anything in Ramsey Campbell. The master of ceremonies lets the woman come to the boy's apartment for a "private show" (CHM 20). He attempts to have sex with her, but is dissatisfied with her lack of enthu-siasm. He pulls her arm and finds that it has come off in his hand. The woman hastily arises, dresses, and leaves, snatching the body part away from him at the last minute. Comical as this may sound when baldly told, Aickman's narration of the entire episode—a boy's worst nightmare of his "first experience" (CHM 1)—is chilling.

"I believe that magnificence, elegance, and charm are the things that matter most in daily life" (AR 15). With this pronouncement, and many others, Aickman unhesitatingly claims allegiance to the idea of life as a fine art, and it is inevitable that this notion melds into his sense of aristocracy. His family was only on the fringe of the British aristocracy, but he sam-pled enough of it in youth—particularly through visits to relations who were actual aristocrats—that he came to find comfort in "a patrician household, such as I was determined to soar to later" (AR 70). Aristocracy mingles with nostalgia for the past when Aickman speaks of the pre–1914 world: "Of course it was a world for the few, but almost all good things are for the few, and almost everything is depreciated when too many people have it" (AR 26). Such an opinion would scarcely win favor in the democratic tyranny of today; but I have no inclination to pass judgment upon Aickman for beliefs such as this: not only did he defend them ably and live by them throughout his life, but they can be found just as commonly in the thought of Lovecraft, Machen, and Dunsany, and can even be said to strengthen their work by lending it an austerity and dignity lacking in the work of their more egalitarian contemporaries. And perhaps we ought all to consider whether the following does not have more than a modicum of truth: "Not to be able to phrase things finely, is, in general, not to be able to feel them finely" (AR 133). On this criterion Aickman could feel things very finely.

What is interesting about Aickman's attitude toward class is that some of the weird events in his stories are triggered by, or perhaps simply *are*, violations of social etiquette. "Ravissante" is a prototypical example. This tale is nothing more than the encounter between a man and the eccentric widow of a painter whom he admires. The widow commands the man more and more imperiously to examine, feel, and even fondle the clothes of her adopted daughter. That is, in effect, the entire story. I am not convinced, however, that the conclusions the narrator draws from this encounter are entirely sound or plausibly derived: "Human relationships can be so fantastically oblique that one can never be sure" (PD 3) and "The sheer oddity of life seems to me of more and more importance" (PD 7). Here again the symbolism of the tale is either too obscure or too obvious: fondling a woman's clothes is a clear metaphor for the man's desire to fondle the woman herself—but what of it?

"The Unsettled Dust" is a little more interesting along the same lines, but it too is ultimately unsatisfying. Here a member of the Psychic and Occult Research Committee of the Historic Structures Fund comes to visit a manor house, inhabited by two sisters, which is reputed to be haunted. Aickman's attacks on modern life (which "seems every day to grow more uniform, regulated, and unambitious" [UD 9]) and democracy ("...as patrician standards merge with plebeian ones, and there is less opportunity for the graces of entertainment as distinct from the utilities" [UD 24]) are blunter than usual; but the atmosphere of weirdness is in large part created by the man's uneasiness in trying to deal amicably with the two sisters, who obviously don't like each other or at the very least are "utterly bored with one another" (UD 23). This social tension gradually metamorphoses into a quasi-supernatural one: the dust that the narrator notes with embarrassment all around the house (doesn't the maid clean properly?) finally becomes a huge cloud rolling along the back lawn like the exhaust from some enormous automobile. But again the symbolism of the dust eludes me: are we to understand it as suggesting the decrepitude of the "patrician" way of life?

Other of Aickman's stories suggest that he shares the class consciousness attributed to his characters. In "No Stronger Than a Flower" the husband of the woman who has sought the beauty treatment is "sincerely shocked" (UD 103) when his wife refuses to change into proper attire to receive their friends. Indeed, the entire story urges us to find actual horror in the wife's increasing disregard for social convention.

Two of Aickman's stories, "Ringing the Changes" and "Meeting Mr Millar," unite many or all of his important themes in an exceptionally powerful way. In "Ringing the Changes" we have the idea of travel (a pair of newlyweds, Gerald and Phrynne Pascoe, visit an obscure coastal town in England for their honeymoon), frustrated sex (Gerald feels increasingly disturbed at the odd milieu into which he has fallen), and nostalgia (the town seems untouched by modernity). The place has a reputation for its church bells, but the volume of the bells on this particular night seems highly anomalous. How can all the churches be practicing their bell ringing at the same time? The sound continues without cessation, growing louder and louder. The hotel's proprietors are getting drunker and drunker, as if seeking oblivion for the night. Why? What is the meaning of the bells? An old commander who lives in the hotel finally tells the couple: "'They're ringing to wake the dead'" (PD 102). Blunt as this sounds, it carries great potency after the enormously subtle and gradual build-up. Gerald and the commander discuss this outrageous proposition:

> "I don't believe in the resurrection of the body," said Gerald. As the hour grew later, the bells grew louder. "Not of the body."
> "What other kind of resurrection is possible? Everything else is only theory. You can't even imagine it. No one can" [PD 102].

The idea of ringing all the bells in a town on a special night in order to raise the dead is no doubt illogical, but it has that aesthetic logic I mentioned earlier—it taps our unconscious in the sense that it is a very short step from ringing bells to commemorate the dead to ringing them to raise the dead. Accordingly, this tale satisfies where others of Aickman's do not. It would require a long commentary to trace the seamless way in which Aickman builds up the cumulative suspense in this story, and the spectacular climax—where the dead (if that is who they are) are only *heard*, never seen—is a masterstroke of suggestiveness.

"Meeting Mr Millar" also plays upon many of Aickman's central themes. A starving writer moves into a cheap flat, and is forced to take a job as editor for a pornography publisher. The large apartment below him seems occupied by a company ("Stallabrass, Hoskins and Cramp. Chartered Accountants"), but it does not seem to engage in much actual business. The writer hears "endless giggling, shouting, and banging of doors" (CHM 196); the employees' conversation, which he occasionally overhears, "was always of unbelievable commonplaceness or banality" (CHM 198). Peculiar details accumulate, including a strange encounter with Mr. Millar, evidently the head of the company: rarely has such an entirely colorless individual inspired so much vague terror. Finally, after a series of strangely disturbing but curiously inconclusive incidents, another tenant makes an odd suggestion: "'It just struck me for one moment that you might have seen into the future. All these people slavishly doing nothing. It'll be exactly like that one day, you know, if we go on as we are. For a moment it all sounded to me like a vision of 40 years on—if as much'" (CHM 225). It is not clear how seriously we are to take this explanation; I do not imagine that Aickman simply wishes to reduce his story to a sociological dystopia. Nevertheless, the tale's odd twists and turns all seem to work, achieving a cumulative power in no way marred by the lack of an explanation. "Meeting Mr Millar" is also one of Aickman's most autobiographical stories, and much could be written on its connections with passages and sentiments in *The Attempted Rescue*. It may well be his greatest success.

I feel almost impertinent criticizing Robert Aickman, for his purely literary gifts—a prose style of impeccable fluidity, urbanity, and elegance; a high sensitivity to those nuances and details productive of a weird scenario; a keen insight into all aspects of human psychology, not merely those touching upon the strange; and some very powerful weird conceptions that do not require copious, or any, bloodletting for their effectiveness—make his work a triumph, even if one violently disagrees with his theory of weird fiction, as I do. That theory of weird fiction—especially in its absence of "logic"—results not so much in *stories* as in vignettes or impressions, which we are evidently to value regardless of their coherence or ultimate significance. But Aickman is certainly an assured master of the type of weird fiction he chose to write, and his work is a wondrously refreshing contrast to the slovenliness, crudity, and gratuitous violence that increasingly passes for weird fiction nowadays. His younger contemporaries could learn much from him about the philosophy and methodology of the weird tale; but I do not think many of them are listening.

ANNE RICE:
THE PHILOSOPHY OF VAMPIRISM

In 1976, Anne Rice (b. 1941) published *Interview with the Vampire*. Surprisingly, it became a bestseller. After writing two mainstream novels, *The Feast of All Saints* (1980) and *Cry to Heaven* (1982), she wrote three sequels to her first novel, *The Vampire Lestat* (1985), *The Queen of the Damned* (1988), and *The Tale of the Body Thief* (1992). She also published three other horror novels, *The Mummy; or, Ramses the Damned* (1989), *The Witching Hour* (1990), and *Lasher* (1993), two other mainstream novels under the pseudonym Anne Rampling, and three volumes of soft-core pornography (tactfully labeled "erotica") under the name A. N. Roquelaure.

Rice is worth considering in the context of modern weird fiction if for no other reason than that her first novel is strikingly original and evocative. She resembles Shirley Jackson in the sense (and only in the sense) that she is approaching the field from the realm of mainstream literature and does not appear to be especially familiar with the long history of weird fiction, even specifically of the fiction of vampirism which she has explored so voluminously in her own work. As a result, her writing exhibits a number of traits characteristic of the mainstream experimenter in the weird: a concern not so much with the weird phenomenon itself as with its function and ramifications in a network of human relationships; an originality of conception and treatment born, curiously, of a lack of awareness of the many similar works in the field; and a lush, richly textured, almost florid style, but a style in no way derived from Lovecraft, Machen, Dunsany, Shiel, or other masters of weird prose.

Interview with the Vampire is a remarkable piece of writing. The premise—a vampire in modern-day San Francisco agrees to be interviewed on tape and tells the story of his two centuries of existence does not sound especially prepossessing, and indeed the novel is not so much a narrative as a series of often striking set pieces and tableaux. Louis (we are never told his last name here), a Frenchman, became a vampire at the age of 25 in 1791 (I 4) after he had moved to Louisiana. The process by which he becomes a vampire, at the hands of the vampire Lestat, is arresting: he is nearly drained of blood, then is forced to drink Lestat's blood, now mixed with his own, from the vampire's wrist. This entire process seems to be a transparent metaphor for homosexual love, and in some senses it is exactly that: "'Never had I felt this, never had I experienced it, this yielding of a conscious mortal.... He was pressing the length of his body against me now, and I felt the hard strength of his sex beneath his clothes pressing against my leg'" (I 231). But there is always more to the procedure than mere sex, as Louis learns in the end: "'For vampires, physical love culminates and is satisfied in one thing, the kill'" (I 256).

What Rice must first establish is the nature and functions of her vampires. Perhaps because she is not thoroughly versed in the literature of vampirism, she dispenses with some of the standard vampiric traits with insouciance. It is true that her vampires must go about only at night, but it is symptomatic of her writing that Louis responds to this not with horror but with pathos when he sees the sun rise for the last time: "'I said good-bye to the sunrise and went out to become a vampire'" (I 14). Analogously, Lestat informs him scornfully that other traditions of the vampire—fear of the cross, ability to turn to smoke, death by the driving of a stake through the heart—are all "'bull-shit'" (I 23). What is more, vampires need not sustain themselves merely on human beings: animals can serve the purpose just as well. In *The Vampire Lestat* several other conventional traits of the vampire are done away with: vampires can now see themselves in mirrors (V 104); they need not spend the days in coffins filled with the earth of their native land—any resting place will suffice, even the ground (V 336).

But what makes *Interview with the Vampire* so unclassifiable—what makes it fit very uneasily into either the realm of weird fiction or that of mainstream fiction—is, firstly, its emphasis on the vibrant and sensual physical sensations of being a vampire (sensations that cannot be seen as mere metaphors for normal human states) and, secondly, its moral disquisitions on the nature of vampirism and the inevitable bloodletting caused by such a state. I am not sure that any portion of the novel is *horrifying* or *frightening* in any real sense, even though we read nearly the whole of it with a certain awed fascination.

Consider Louis's first sight of the vampire: "'...the moment I saw him, saw his extraordinary aura and knew him to be no creature I'd ever known, I was reduced to nothing. That ego which could not accept the presence of an extraordinary human being in its midst was crushed. All my conceptions, even my guilt and wish to die, seemed utterly unimportant. I completely forgot *myself!*'" (I 13). This is rather uncannily similar to that perception of the supernatural which shatters the psyches of so many of Lovecraft's characters, but it is here bereft of any sensation of fear. Similarly, a later scene, in which a little girl, Claudia, is turned into a vampire, must rank as one of the most stunning tableaux in modern weird fiction, and yet it too contains more of pathos and eroticism than of horror:

> "'Where is Mamma?' asked the child softly. She had a voice equal to her physical beauty, clear like a little silver bell. It was sensual. She

was sensual.... I found her on my lap, my arms around her, feeling again how soft she was, how plump her skin was, like the skin of warm fruit, plums warmed by sunlight; her huge luminescent eyes were fixed on me with trusting curiosity. 'This is Louis, and I am Lestat,' he said to her, dropping down beside her. She looked about and said that it was a pretty room, very pretty, but she wanted her mamma" [I 93–94].

Being a vampire is an anomalous condition: one was once human but is no longer so; one must subsist by killing. Louis, who can never forget his former humanness, reflects plangently on his condition: "'... I ... had presided over the death of my own body, seeing all I called human wither and die only to form an unbreakable chain which held me fast to this world yet made me forever its exile, a specter with a beating heart'" (I 168). Louis had earlier maintained that he had experienced a "'divorce from human emotions'" (I 24), but it is obvious that this is more a wish than a reality. It is Lestat, perhaps because of his longer tenure in the vampiric state, who asserts the amorality of vampirism: "'We are immortal. And what we have before us are the rich feasts that conscience cannot appreciate and mortal men cannot know without regret. God kills, and so shall we; indiscriminately He takes the richest and the poorest, and so shall we; for no creatures under God are as we are, none so like Him as ourselves, dark angels not confined to the stinking limits of hell but wandering His earth and all its kingdoms'" (I 89).

But let us not be deceived at the transparently religious symbolism in this speech of Lestat's: not only is he doubtful of God's existence (hence Satan's), he is openly atheistic. Louis claims to be so ("'God did not live in this church; these statues gave an image to nothingness. *I* was the supernatural in this cathedral. I was the only supernatural thing that stood conscious under this roof!'" [I 145]), but he cannot bring himself to accept this belief wholeheartedly. He is shattered by a later conversation with an old vampire in Europe:

> "'Then God does not exist ... you have no knowledge of His existence?'
> "'None,' he said.
> "'No knowledge!' I said it again, unafraid of my simplicity, my miserable human pain.
> "'None.'
> "'And no vampire here has discourse with God or with the devil!'
> "'No vampire that I've ever known,' he said, musing, the fire dancing in his eyes. 'And as far as I know today, after four hundred years, I am the oldest living vampire in the world'" [I 239–40].

An amusing passage in *The Vampire Lestat* seems to clinch the matter: "'What if they're right,' she said. 'And we don't belong in the House of God.' 'Gibberish and nonsense. God isn't in the House of God'" (V 190). This leads Louis to a quasi-humanist position: "'Because if God doesn't exist we are the creatures of highest consciousness in the universe. We alone understand the passage of time and the value of every minute of human life. And what constitutes evil, real evil, is the taking of a single human life. Whether a man would have died tomorrow or the day after or eventually ... it doesn't matter. Because if God does not exist, this life ... every second of it ... is all we have'" (I 238). I shall refrain from harping upon the obvious fallacy of that first sentence.

The substance of *Interview with the Vampire* derives from its richly sensual and evocative prose and its probing of complex metaphysical and emotional issues dealing with the vampiric state. The tortured Louis, by turns coldly cynical and pitiably human, is a fine creation, although the child vampire Claudia, who as she continues her unnatural existence maintains the pristine innocence of her little girl's body but becomes morally more ruthless and savage than either Louis or even Lestat, is perhaps a still greater triumph of conception and characterization. The sheer vitality of this novel ought to make it survive in spite of its somewhat rambling structure and slight repetitiveness.

Where *Interview with the Vampire* fails is in its portrayal of the historic backdrop against which the action is presumably set. Louis has been on the earth for more than 200 years—and 200 of the most eventful years of human history—but he seems to have gained remarkably little insight from his long existence on two continents. After spending the first 70 or so years of his vampiric life in Louisiana, he and Claudia make their way to the France of Napoleon III (I 205): it appears that the American Civil War came and went without his noticing it. Louis remarks at one point that "'I had now lived in two centuries, seen the illusions of the one utterly shattered by the other, been eternally young and eternally ancient, possessing no illusions'" (I 142), but nothing in his account justifies such a cocksure opinion. It is in this absence of historical perspective that Rice's novels in general suffer by comparison with those of Les Daniels. It would be facile to say that this somehow points to a difference between the male perspective, focusing upon the realities of political and social history, and the female perspective, emphasizing emotional values; it is more likely that Rice simply doesn't know as much about history as Daniels, who always researches the historical settings of his novels with scrupulous care. Kathy Mackay, in an interview with Rice, notes in reference to *The Feast of All Saints* (a novel begun prior to *Interview* but completed and published later),

"She found that as soon as she tried to write about these people [the Creoles of New Orleans], she didn't know enough about the 19th Century and her writing didn't work."[2] It does not appear as if she had remedied the fault with *Interview*.

And yet, as if conscious of this failing, Rice makes *The Vampire Lestat* more explicitly embedded in the very wide-ranging historical epochs in which it is set. Some rank this novel still higher than *Interview*, but I am not one of them. It is true that it not so much follows up on as subsumes and envelops its predecessor, but to my mind it already reveals that long-windedness and excessive fondness for her own voice and her own creations which mar most of Rice's later works. This novel is narrated entirely by Lestat, whom we find in San Francisco in 1984 in the rather charming role of a rock star. Right from the beginning he reflects at great length upon the differences between the eighteenth and the twentieth centuries, in the course of which he makes a number of statements (e.g., "In fact the poverty and filth that had been common in the big cities of the earth since time immemorial were almost completely washed away" [V 8]) that make us highly skeptical of his, and Rice's, grasp of historical reality. (And what are we to make of the fact that a review of a play in the time of Mozart is cited from the *Spectator* [V 69], a paper that came and went half a century earlier?) Unfortunately, Rice does not allow Lestat to elaborate upon his rock stardom, a potentially interesting subject,[3] but instead compels him to tell at appalling length the not very compelling story of his life from childhood to vampiredom. I fail to understand the significance or value of much of this narrative, especially as there seem to be no new conceptions developed here. There is some interest provided when Lestat transforms his own mother, Gabrielle, into a vampire, after which time they become pseudolovers, but otherwise we have heard it all before in *Interview*. Indeed, the portrayal of Lestat here is not even consistent with that in *Interview*, as he gains the same tormented moralism that typified Louis in *Interview* but which Lestat entirely repudiated: "'I can live without God. I can even come to live with the idea there is no life after. But I do not think I could go on if I did not believe in the possibility of goodness'" (V 72). Perhaps we are to understand that all vampires, in the infancy of their vampiredom, are afflicted with human morality until the decades and centuries finally bludgeon it out of them.

Interest in the novel finally appears toward the conclusion, in which Rice attempts something no less grandiose than a sort of origin of species for vampires. Marius, a Roman vampire who has lived for nearly two millennia, stumbles upon the mother and father of all vampires in Egypt, Akasha and Enkil, who are the real figures behind the myth of Isis and

Osiris. It transpires that the lives of all the vampires in the world depend upon the continued existence of this pair—or, more specifically, of Akasha, who seems to have vastly greater power than her consort. The convoluted but riveting tale Rice spins here, after 400 pages, is indeed worth the wait and comes close to redeeming this otherwise bloated novel. Her writing finally attains the vibrancy and dynamism we found in *Interview*, and even Lestat—who through worldweariness buries himself in the ground for much of the nineteenth century—finds himself at last capable of an interesting historical reflection when he awakens early in the twentieth: "I do not remember when it became the twentieth century, only that everything was uglier and darker, and the beauty I'd known in the old eighteenth-century days seemed more than ever some kind of fanciful idea. The bourgeois ran the world now upon dreary principles and with a distrust of the sensuality and the excess that the ancient regime had so loved" (V 509). And the final scene, in which Akasha awakens and apocalyptically disrupts Lestat's rock concert, brings the novel to a fittingly cataclysmic conclusion.

Unfortunately, Rice found herself so enraptured by the figure of Akasha that she brought her back for the interminable *Queen of the Damned*, a nearly unreadable novel full of angst-ridden maunderings by various vampires, ponderously prophetic dreams, and an extraordinarily clumsy structure of shifting narrative voices. Rice's writing has now become flabby, verbose, and self-indulgent, and this book's lack of focus, pacing, and ultimate purpose make us blanch when we finally reach the end and see the ominous words on the last page: "The Vampire Chronicles Will Continue."

That continuation took another four years to materialize, and one would be justified, after reading Rice's next two published novels—*The Mummy* (1989), a silly but entertaining potboiler, and *The Witching Hour* (1990), a staggeringly prolix and pointless nonvampiric novel—to be wary of *The Tale of the Body Thief* (1992). Had Rice completely lost the art of telling a good story? Had bestsellerism laid its heavy hand on her as it has on so many others? It is with some relief that one can announce that *The Tale of the Body Thief*, while by no means the best of Rice's novels, ably picks up the thread of *Interview with the Vampire* and *The Vampire Lestat* and, remarkably enough, actually introduces a new idea in the Vampire Chronicles.

That new idea is personality exchange. It is, of course, not in fact new in the history of weird fiction, and Rice herself is aware of it. In the early parts of the novel her human protagonist Raglan James slyly presents Lestat, who narrates the entire novel in the first person, with various horror tales (Lovecraft's "The Thing on the Doorstep," Robert Bloch's "Eyes of the Mummy") and films (*Vice Versa*, *All of Me*) dealing—as Lestat finally deduces—with the swapping of personalities. James, it appears, has the ability to effect this exchange if he has a willing partner, and much of the early part of the novel is spent in his attempts to seduce (the word is not too strong) Lestat into agreeing to this exchange.

Lestat, now a vampire for several centuries, yearns for the human form and the human condition. Would it not be a delight to see the sun again, to eat fine food and drink the best wines, to have sex with men or women— to be, in other words, once again a part of the human race instead of a loathed outsider? Lestat agrees to switch bodies with James for a mere two days, with the possibility of a longer exchange if he likes the human state; and, in spite of vehement objections from his human friend David Talbot, he effects the exchange. And the inevitable happens: James "steals" his body, vanishing and leaving Lestat in a strong, handsome, but unfamiliar and uncomfortable human form.

If being a vampire is anomalous, Lestat has forgotten how many inconveniences the human condition has: the finest food tastes like sand or dirt, wine is a poor substitute for blood, and the tedious human necessities of eating, sleeping, and defecating prove unutterably wearying. Meanwhile Raglan James, in his vampiric state, goes on a murderous rampage while Lestat and Talbot spend the bulk of the novel tracking him down. Ultimately, they corner him on the *Queen Elizabeth 2* and force him to switch back to his own form. Some further twists occur hereafter, but they do not add appreciably to the novel's significance.

The Tale of the Body Thief is in part an adventure story, in part a rumination on God, and in part a sort of modern *Gulliver's Travels*. If Gulliver, after becoming accustomed to the high civilization of the Houyhnhnms, finds the human form repellent and disgusting, Lestat can see only the brutish side of being mortal. Even sex proves unsatisfying, since he ends up clumsily raping a waitress and failing to persuade his dear friend Talbot to have a homosexual encounter, although Talbot has leanings in that direction. As with Louis in *Interview with the Vampire*, it is only the awesome sight of the sun that reconciles him, momentarily, to being human. But in the end he learns his true nature: "I was Lestat, drifting between hell and heaven, and content to be so—*perhaps for the first time*" (T 343).

One would think that such a novel would allow Rice to make interesting reflections on the nature of identity, but in fact the philosophical substance of the novel lies in the various discussions of God conducted by Lestat, Talbot, and Gretchen, a nun whom Lestat encounters in his human state. Talbot is convinced he has seen God and the Devil talking in a cafe; Gretchen presents a vigorous defense of altruism: "'God may or may not exist. But misery is real. It is absolutely real, and utterly undeniable. And in that reality lies my commitment—the core of my faith. I have to do something about it!'" (T 246). Lestat provisionally accepts Talbot's vision, and is also momentarily shaken out of his cynicism by Gretchen's devotion; but in the end he reverts to his old atheistic self, discounting Talbot's account and even making Gretchen confess that there is no God (T 253). It is not clear what relevance these theological discussions have to the core of the novel, but they are admirably presented.

As with all her novels, *The Tale of the Body Thief* works best as a succession of striking images: the exchange of personalities between James and Lestat, involving their respective souls floating up out of their own bodies and plunging like divers into each other's torpid form; the spectacular dreams or hallucinations Lestat experiences when he falls ill in his human state, as he conducts bizarre dialogues with the spirit of Claudia; the account of Talbot's experiences among primitive magicians in Brazil; and, toward the last, Lestat's search (in his own body) for Gretchen in the jungles of South America, and her rejection of him as a monster and abomination. This novel has a somewhat better sense of narrative pacing than some of Rice's previous works, but it too goes on a little too long.

In *The Vampire Lestat* there is a mention of the "vampire Ramses" (V 302), but much later Marius corrects this impression, declaring that Ramses is not a vampire at all because he has "'never drunk blood'" and "'can walk in the daylight as well as in the dark'" (V 474). In fact, Ramses is a mummy. I do not know what led Rice to write *The Mummy*, nor do I know whether it is some early, much-rejected novel or one that was written hastily to capitalize upon the success of the Vampire Chronicles. The fact that it was published only in a trade paperback suggests that even her publisher did not feel it worth the dignity of hard covers. And yet, I find it more enjoyable than such overblown and pretentious things as *The Queen of the Damned* or *The Witching Hour*. It is nothing more than a cheap pulp thriller, but an entertaining one for all that. All the characters are stereotypes— Lawrence Stratford, an explorer singlemindedly devoted to the cause of science; Henry Stratford, his wastrel nephew; Julie Stratford, his feminist daughter determined to carry on her father's mission; Samir Ibrahaim, the wise native assistant. Ramses himself is, as it were, the only character who comes alive as a vibrant and complex personality, as perhaps does Elliot, Lord Rutherford, Stratford's friend (and one-time lover) who finds the figure of Ramses powerfully fascinating and plunges himself into the mystery of his existence as one final intellectual thrill at the end of a long and hard life.

Ramses is no dusty and bandage-wrapped relic stalking about blindly and mindlessly. After being revived by the sun, he becomes a compellingly suave and enigmatic figure who easily wins the doting love of Julie. But

Ramses' own love for his long-lost Queen Cleopatra is the driving force of his resurrected life. Conveniently enough, he discovers the body of Cleopatra in an Egyptian museum, where it is ignorantly labeled as an anonymous woman of the Graeco-Roman period, and he revives her after a fashion with the elixir by which he himself gained immortality. Unfortunately, Cleopatra's body is not wholly intact, and the resurrected queen, although physically alluring, proves to be a lustful and murderous maniac who goes on a rampage until finally perishing in a railway accident (although in Rice's works one never quite seems to perish). All this is great fun, even though much of the novel makes us wince at Rice's ponderous attempts to inspire fear ("*What if there* were *an immortal being under those wrappings?*" [M 22]) or romance (Julie on yielding her virginity to Ramses: "'Batter down the door... The virgin door. Open it, I am yours forever'" [M 230]). And Ramses' pontifications on the contrast between ancient and modern times are no more interesting than Louis's or Lestat's. I cannot decide whether this novel is meant seriously or as a parody. If it is meant seriously, then it is simply bad; if it is a parody, then Rice has concealed her intentions rather too well. I am half inclined to think that she *began* the work as a parody (the writing is much poorer, by ordinary standards, at the beginning than at the end), but, as she warmed to the task and got into the flow of the narrative, changed her mind and tried to write a serious pulp romantic adventure. But there is no such thing as a *serious* pulp romantic adventure. *The Mummy* also concludes with the note that the adventures of Ramses the Damned will continue, but to date no sequel has emerged.

And now we come—reluctantly—to *The Witching Hour*. It is the nadir of Rice's works. By now a best-selling author with the assurance that any new work will sell many copies and bring her lots of money, she has spawned a 965-page novel that goes nowhere and should have been cut by a full two-thirds. By no means should an author so utterly lacking in narrative drive be allowed to write a novel of this length. One might imagine that Rice thinks of herself as an old-time pulpster, getting paid by the word.

The plot of this novel is deceptively simple. A mysterious force or entity named Lasher seems to hang around all the members of the Mayfair family. This is Rice's excuse for undertaking the stupefyingly tedious account of the lives of the "Mayfair witches" from the late seventeenth century to the present—an account whose utter lack of vital connection with the main narrative, set in the present, is rendered painfully obtrusive by the use of a different typeface. That main narrative is the sentimentalized story of Rowan Mayfair, the latest of the Mayfair clan, and Michael Curry, a young man whom Rowan saved from drowning. At long last, after 850 pages, one finally gets some vague idea of who or what Lasher is: he is a force from some other plane of existence who desperately wishes to become human. He infuses himself into the body of the baby being carried by Rowan, and when he is born—a man of full stature but with the delicate physique of a baby—he and Rowan dash off to Europe, leaving Michael disconsolate, full of flatulent philosophical maunderings ("'I believe in Free Will, the Force Almighty by which we conduct ourselves as if we were the sons and daughters of a just and wise God, even if there is no such Supreme Being'" [W 963]) and waiting for Rowan to return. Although there is no note that the Witching Hour chronicles will continue, Rice has now produced a windy and pointless sequel in *Lasher*. One can only hope that she does not follow through on her threat to alternate the Vampire and Witching Hour cycles.

When *The Witching Hour* was published, coming hard on the heels of *The Mummy*, there began to develop the ominous idea that Anne Rice was already finished as a writer; that the curse of bestsellerdom, and the arrogant self-indulgence it very often brings, had descended upon her as it has descended upon Stephen King, Peter Straub, and Clive Barker, and would prevent her from ever producing a work as vital and powerful as *Interview with the Vampire*. But *The Tale of the Body Thief* should have restored at least some of our faith that Rice still has the power, skill, and self-restraint to write vibrantly in the weird mode. She is not, and probably never will be, one of the great masters of weird fiction—she will never deserve to be ranked with Poe, Machen, Blackwood, Lovecraft, Shirley Jackson, and Ramsey Campbell—but she has contributed some highly creditable novels to a field whose masterworks are still very few in number.

THOMAS LIGOTTI:
THE ESCAPE FROM LIFE

"There is no field other than the weird in which I have any aptitude or inclination for fictional composition. Life has never interested me so much as the escape from life."[4] Ironically, this utterance by H. P. Lovecraft was made when he was well into what he himself called his "quasi-realistic"[5] phase, in which the weird is introduced subtly and gradually through the painstaking accumulation of realistic details in every aspect of the tale *except* that pertaining to the weird manifestation. And that Lovecraft was far from truly wishing for an "escape from life" is evident in his earnest concern for economic justice and political reform as the depression of the 1930s grinded on. *At the Mountains of Madness* could only have been written by one for whom the real world manifestly existed.

The whole notion of escaping from life—escaping, that is, from the mundane, the actual, the real—can apply much more pertinently to a recent writer, Thomas Ligotti (b. 1953). Ligotti's interest is focused more intensely and exclusively on the weird, than any author's in the history of weird fiction. I do not think it would be possible to study, for example, the sociopolitical aspects of Ligotti's fiction—there do not seem to be any. His portrayal of human relationships, when it occurs at all, is either perfunctory or sardonic. Human characters, indeed, are virtually insignificant in themselves in his work, serving only as embodiments of or conduits to the unreal.

Ligotti is himself one of the strangest phenomena in weird fiction, not only for the utter bizarrerie of his own work but for the curious way in which he has emerged as a leading writer in the field. Having published a certain number of stories in fan magazines (*Nyctalops*) or what might at best be called "semi-pro" magazines (*Fantasy Tales, Eldritch Tales*) in the early 1980s, he issued a collection of short stories, *Songs of a Dead Dreamer*, through the specialty firm of Silver Scarab Press, operated by Harry O. Morris, Jr. When this volume emerged in 1986, Ligotti was still almost entirely unknown: I myself received a review copy of it and rather hastily and ignorantly dismissed it as mere "fan fiction." But Morris had, as it were, backed the right horse, for very shortly thereafter Ligotti was embraced by many of the leading writers and critics of the field (Ramsey Campbell had written an introduction to *Songs of a Dead Dreamer*) and his reputation began to grow, although still in a sort of subterranean fashion. A British trade paperback of his collection, augmented with new stories (and, it must be admitted, with some of the more embarrassingly poor ones removed), emerged in 1989. This was reprinted in hardcover in this country in 1990 and in paperback the next year. A second and still more substantial collection, *Grimscribe*, appeared in late 1991, and a third collection, *Noctuary*, was published in 1994. Liggoti is, however, still content to publish the majority of his work in the small press, although he has made occasional forays into full-fledged professional journals (*Magazine of Fantasy and Science Fiction*) and anthologies (Douglas E. Winter's *Prime Evil*, 1988). Perhaps this is just as well, for his work is certainly not bestseller material in the manner of Stephen King's or Clive Barker's.

If Ligotti's refreshing lack of self-promotion is virtually unique in what has become the big-business world of weird fiction, then his actual work is also entirely original and unclassifiable. His is the most distinctive voice in the field. This is not to say that he is necessarily the best weird fictionist now writing—Ramsey Campbell and T. E. D. Klein, at least, are still his superiors—but his work is perhaps the most easily recognizable of any current writer's because of its sheer difference from that of his contemporaries. Ligotti is one of the few modern weird writers to draw extensively from the older masters of the weird tale—Poe, Lovecraft, Blackwood, Machen—but his work is so far from being pastiche that it is difficult in all but a few cases to pinpoint actual literary influences.

The focus of all Ligotti's work is a systematic assault on the real world and the replacement of it with the unreal, the dreamlike, and the hallucinatory. Reality is, for him, a "grossly overrated affair" ("Alice's Last Adventure" [SDD 38–39]). It is simply too prosy and dull, lacking in intrinsic value or dramatic interest: "It would be difficult to conceive of a creature for whom *this* world—its bare form seen with open eyes—represented a coveted paradise" ("Vastarien" [SDD 263]). Accordingly, Ligotti's literary goal is to suggest that other realm which we glimpse either through dreams or, worse, stumble upon by accident in obscure corners of this world. Ligotti has neatly summed up his aesthetic of the weird in "The Consolations of Horror," a magnificent essay that ranks among his finest works:

> The horror story does the work of a certain kind of dream we all know. Sometimes it does this so well that even the most irrational and unlikely subject matter can infect the reader with a sense of realism beyond the realistic, a trick usually not seen outside the vaudeville of sleep. When is the last time you failed to be fooled by a nightmare, didn't suspend disbelief because its incidents weren't sufficiently true-to-life? The horror story is only true to dreams, especially those which involve us in mysterious ordeals, the passing of secrets, the passages of forbidden knowledge, and, in more ways than one, the spilling of guts.[6]

This tells us many things: the importance and prevalence of dream imagery in Ligotti's work; the scorn of the "true-to-life"; and the notion of the quest—the quest for "secrets" and "knowledge" of the realm of the unreal. I shall examine all these points more detailedly later, but what I wish to consider now is the difficulty of classifying Ligotti's work within the standard distinctions existing within the weird tale. Many of his tales do not conform to the conventions of supernatural horror, which Maurice Lévy has compactly defined as work in which "the irrational makes an irruption into the real world":[7] the "real world" exists so fragmentarily for Ligotti that the contrast between the "natural" and the "supernatural" is never sufficiently established. This is not (or not yet) meant as a criticism, but simply as a defining characteristic of Ligotti's writing. Nor can his tales be classified as "fantasy" (by which I mean the otherworldly fantasy of a Dunsany or Tolkien) because they are set in what is more or less recognizable as the "real world," but a real world depicted so sketchily—and, perhaps, with such a lack of enthusiasm—that its sole function seems to be as a springboard for the beyond. "Victor Keirion belonged to that wretched sect of souls who believe that the only value of this world lies in its power—at certain times—to suggest another world" ("Vastarien" [SDD 263]). Ligotti in fact rejects such divisions in weird fiction as ontological or psychological horror:

> What seems important to me is not whether the spectre is within or outside of a character ... but the power of the language and images of a story and the ultimate vision that they help to convey. For all that, everything that happens in every story ever written is merely an event in someone's imagination—exactly as are dreams, which take place on their own little plane of unreality, a realm of nowhere in which outside and inside are of equivalent ontological status, where within *is* without and both are phantasmal in essence [F 33].

And yet, does Ligotti flee from the real world simply because it is boring or "overrated"? In "Professor Nobody's Little Lectures on Supernatural Horror" he speaks of the "logic of supernatural horror" as "a logic that is founded on fear; it is a logic whose sole principle states: 'Existence equals Nightmare.' Unless life is a dream, nothing makes sense. For as a reality, it is a rank failure" (SDD 206). Compare this with the character in "The Mystics of Muelenberg" who has found "a greater truth: that all is unreal" (G 112–13), or the statement of the narrator of "Allan and Adelaide: An Arabesque": "I have seen the soul of the universe ... and it is insane,"[8] or that of the narrator of "The Sect of the Idiot": "Life is the nightmare that leaves its mark upon you in order to prove that it is, in fact, real" (SDD 234), or a random remark in "In the Shadow of Another World" that speaks of the "marriage of insanity and metaphysics" (G 130). What statements like these suggest is that what we all take to be the real world is actually unreal and also mad. Consider "The Journal of J. P. Drapeau":

> From the earliest days of man there has endured the conviction that there is an order of existence which is entirely strange to him. It does indeed seem that the strict order of the visible world is only a semblance, one providing certain gross materials which become the basis for subtle *improvisations* of invisible powers. Hence, it may appear to some that a leafless tree is not a tree but a signpost to another realm; that an old house is not a house but a thing possessing a will of its own; that the dead may throw off that heavy blanket of earth to walk in their sleep, and in ours. And these are merely a few of the

infinite variations on the themes of the natural order as it is usually conceived.

But is there *really* a strange world? Of course. Are there, then, two worlds? Not at all. There is only our own world and it alone is alien to us, intrinsically so by virtue of its lack of mysteries [SDD 257].

This utterance conveys, perhaps as succinctly as any, Ligotti's own quest: it is not, in the end, a replacement of the real world by the unreal, but a sort of turning the real world inside out to show that it has been unreal all along.

The vehicle for this transformation is language. Ligotti has evolved a highly distinctive and idiosyncratic style that, with seeming effortlessness, metamorphoses existence into nightmare. Its closest analogue, on purely stylistic grounds, is the eccentric idiom of M. P. Shiel, although he is not a writer whom Ligotti acknowledges as an influence or model. And yet, the analogy is apt in more than one way. Lovecraft referred to Shiel's "Xélucha" as a "noxiously hideous fragment,"[9] and much of Ligotti's work could be so labeled: it stylistically echoes Shiel's tortuous, metaphor-laden prose poetry while at the same time seeking to capture that atmosphere of nightmarish or hallucinatory strangeness that typifies Shiel's best short work. Plot is almost everywhere negligible, and everything is subordinate to mood. There is also in Ligotti a considerable dose of Blackwood's searching exploration of the precise psychological effect of the weird upon human consciousness.

Ligotti, indeed, in essays, interviews, and stories, talks much of style and language, and every one of his stories, successful or otherwise, is written with impeccable meticulousness. In speaking of the need for subtlety in relating a weird tale, he has remarked that "extraordinary subjects require a certain deviousness in the telling, that a twisted or obscure technique is needed to realize the maximum power of the strange" (R 21). This is reminiscent of T. S. Eliot's celebrated justification for the obscurity of Modernist poetry: "We can only say that it appears likely that poets in our civilization, as it exists at present, must be *difficult*. Our civilization comprehends great variety and complexity, and this variety and complexity, playing upon a refined sensibility, must produce various and complex results. The poet must become more and more comprehensive, more allusive, more indirect, in order to force, to dislocate if necessary, language into his meaning."[10] The resemblance may in fact not be entirely adventitious: the absence of any vivid or realistic description of the contemporary world gives Ligotti's tales a curiously archaic cast, but in their allusiveness and disregard for the mechanics of plot they are strikingly modern. However much Ligotti draws upon the weird masters of the early part of the century, his work could only have been written by one sensitive to the ambiguities of his *fin de siècle*. If he errs rather more frequently than I would like on the side of excessive obscurity and excessive plotlessness, and if his style remains just on this side (and sometimes on the other side) of bombast and fustian, then it is perhaps an occupational hazard in the sort of highly intellectualized and self-conscious weird fiction Ligotti has chosen to write.

One of Ligotti's many distinctive attributes is the frequency with which he can metafictionally enunciate his own literary agenda in his tales. Many of his stories are just as much about the writing of horror tales as they are horror tales. In "The Frolic," a psychiatrist's report of a madman's visions are uncannily like Ligotti's own aesthetic quest for the unreal: "'There's actually quite a poetic geography to his interior dreamland as he describes it. He talked about a place that sounded like the back alleys of some cosmic slum, an inner-dimensional dead end.... Less fathomable are his memories of a moonlit corridor where mirrors scream and laugh, dark peaks of some kind that won't remain still, a stairway that's "broken" in a very strange way...'" (SDD 13). The book Victor Keirion finds in "Vastarien" is similar:

> It seemed to be a chronicle of strange dreams. Yet somehow the passages he examined were less a recollection of unruled visions than a tangible incarnation of them, not mere rhetoric but the thing itself. The use of language in the book was arrantly unnatural and the book's author unknown. Indeed, the text conveyed the impression of speaking for itself and speaking only to itself, the words flowing together like shadows that were cast by no forms outside the book. But although this volume appeared to be composed in a vernacular of mysteries, its words did inspire a sure understanding and created in their reader a visceral apprehension of the world they described, existing inseparable from it [SDD 269].

It is not surprising, therefore, that Ligotti has written, in addition to the actual essay "The Consolations of Horror," several pseudoessays on the writing of weird fiction. The most interesting of these is "Notes on the Writing of Horror: A Story." This work proposes to narrate a tale in three distinct styles—the realistic, the traditional Gothic, and the experimental. In the course of this disquisition it becomes clear where Ligotti's own sympathies lie. He dispenses with the realistic technique, viciously parodying the Stephen King style of mundane realism: "Nathan is a normal and real character, sure.... And to make him a bit more real, one could supply his coat, his car, and grandfather's wristwatch with specific brand names, perhaps autobiographically borrowed from one's own closet, garage, and wrist" (SDD 105). The traditional Gothic style is a little more to Ligotti's liking, but only because "isolated supernatural incidents don't look as silly in a Gothic tale as they do in a realistic one" (SDD 108). One would imagine that the experimental technique is in fact Ligotti's own, but his lukewarm account of it makes this doubtful. Then we find a fourth technique, and it gains Ligotti's resounding vote of approval: "...the proper style of horror is really that of the *personal confession*" (SDD 113). This connects with a sentiment in "The Consolations of Horror": "Nothing is worse than that which happens personally to a person."[11] This may be nothing more than the old adage that you can't frighten anyone else unless you yourself are frightened, but in some fashion or other it leads to the curious notion that "the tale teller, ideally, should himself be a writer of horror fiction by trade" (SDD 114). The number of writers in Ligotti's fiction is unusually high.

There are, of course, certain drawbacks to this extreme self-consciousness and awareness of the heritage of horror on Ligotti's part. I have already cited, in connection with Peter Straub, Peter Penzoldt's comment that Lovecraft "was too well read,"[12] and I fear that criticism may apply even more aptly to Ligotti. The original edition of *Songs of a Dead Dreamer* contained some disastrous attempts at comic rewritings of classic horror tales—*The Island of Dr. Moreau, Dr. Jekyll and Mr. Hyde, Frankenstein*—which Ligotti wisely removed in the later edition. Elsewhere he has perpetrated still more arid and jejune rewritings of Poe ("Selections of Poe") and Lovecraft ("Selections of Lovecraft"). I am utterly at a loss to understand the purpose of these writings. Even a work such as "Studies in Horror"—a series of prose poems or vignettes each narrated in a different style ("Transcendent Horror," "Gothic Horror," "Spectral Horror," so on)—is certainly a tour de force of sorts and reveals Ligotti's mastery of these varied idioms, but the whole seems dry and academic. And a story like "The Mystics of Muelenberg" suffers from an attention to the niceties of language so excessive as to rob the words of their imagistic power. They don't add up to anything beyond themselves.

At this point I wish to make a brief digression to consider Ligotti's attitude to Lovecraft, since I believe it will enlighten us on his precise place in weird fiction. Ligotti has remarked: "I hope my stories are in the Lovecraftian tradition in that they may evoke a sense of terror whose source is something nightmarishly unreal, the implications of which are disturbingly weird and, in the magical sense, charming" (R 21). But in explaining why he does not use the framework and nomenclature of Lovecraft's myth cycle, Ligotti adds that "Lovecraft's universe ... is a very specific model of reality, one whose portrayal demands a more realistic approach to fiction writing than mine is" (R 21). The relatively tactful reference to realism is to be noted, since it contrasts violently with the snide attack on supernatural realism in "Notes on the Writing of Horror." And yet, Lovecraft *was* a supernatural realist, and the difference between him and the brand-name realism of Stephen King is a difference of methodology and not, fundamentally, one of approach. Ligotti has flatly declared that he is most attracted to Lovecraft's early tales (F 34; DM 117), in which the dream element is more prevalent and the supernatural elements not always satisfactorily accounted for; he has remarked of the later work that "I find Lovecraft's fastidious attempts at creating a documentary style 'reality' an obstacle to appreciating his work" (F 33). Two stories by Ligotti are markedly Lovecraftian. "The Sect of the Idiot" appears to be influenced most by "The Music of Erich Zann" and "The Festival." "The Last Feast of Harlequin," dedicated "To the memory of H. P. Lovecraft" (G 45), does indeed draw upon Lovecraft's late tale "The Shadow over Innsmouth" (although more perhaps upon "The Festival," his earlier working out of the same idea), but shall see that this story is an extreme anomaly in Ligotti's fiction. In any event, a very crude distinction between Lovecraft and Ligotti might be enunciated as follows: whereas Lovecraft tries to make the unreal (i.e., the supernatural) real, Ligotti tries to make the real unreal (i.e., everything is "supernatural," or at any rate unnatural and monstrous).

Ligotti's emphasis on language has led him, like Lovecraft, to be very prodigal in the inventing of mythical books. *Vastarien, Cynothoglys, The Noctuary of Tine*—these are only a few of the cryptic volumes in the Ligottian library. The author has remarked: "I have some notes about the 'forbidden book,' in the Lovecraftian sense, that is, a kind of metaphysical obscenity, an offense against all conception of order. I think my conclusion was that the forbidden book would require the forbidden author to write it, though it might be a work of imagination and not, like the *Necronomicon*, a book of genuine revelation" (DM 116). Imagination as opposed to revelation: here again is a critical distinction between the Ligottian and the Lovecraftian universe. Lovecraft's tomes reveal loathsome truths about the real world; Ligotti's transport one to the unreal.

"Vastarien" is Ligotti's most searching exploration of the forbidden book theme. The plot of this richly atmospheric tale—which stands with "The Last Feast of Harlequin" at the pinnacle of his achievement—is deceptively simple: a man finds a book and it drives him mad. But what a wealth of dense imagery is created by means of this seemingly hackneyed device! Victor Keirion searches for a book to transport him out of this world, but most of the "forbidden" books he finds are insufficient for the task: they are all "sodden with an obscene reality, falsely hermetic ventures which consisted of circling the same absurd landscape. The other worlds portrayed in these books inevitably served as annexes of this one; they were impostors of the authentic unreality which was the only realm of redemption, how-ever gruesome it might appear" (SDD 264–65). But *Vastarien* is different: it is "'not *about* something, but actually is that something'" (SDD 267). This is a piquant conception, and a very neat resolution of the inveterate prob-lem of the relation between the signifier and the signified—here they are one! But what sort of book is *Vastarien*? "To all appearances it seemed he had discovered the summit or abyss of the unreal, that paradise of exhaus-tion, confusion, and debris where reality ends and where one may dwell among its ruins" (SDD 271). I shall return to this conception later.

Another extraordinarily powerful tale, "Nethescurial," strikes me as a very subtle—and perhaps unconscious—adaptation of Lovecraft's seminal story "The Call of Cthulhu." This is not to deny the essential originality of Ligotti's work, or to suggest that the tale in any way incorporates the now hackneyed "Cthulhu Mythos" in the manner of an August Derleth or a Brian Lumley, but I believe that the basic framework of the two tales is strikingly similar. Lovecraft's tale is divided into three sections. In the first, a man discovers papers left by his grand uncle attesting to the existence of a cult worshipping a hideous god, Cthulhu, and the possible existence of that entity itself; the second section narrates a policeman's discovery of this cult and its beliefs; the third finally reveals—although again through a doc-ument—the actual existence of Cthulhu as he attacks the hapless crew of a derelict ship.

It can be seen that the basic pattern in Lovecraft's story is the grad-ual transformation of words into reality: whereas at the outset we only read of Cthulhu from the narrator's paraphrase of documents, at the end we vicariously experience the proximity of the nameless creature. Ligotti adapts this pattern and in a sense even surpasses it. "Nethescurial" is presented as a letter written by one friend to another; it begins: "I have uncovered a rather wonderful manuscript" (G 69). This manuscript tells of a man who comes to a mysterious island named Nethescurial and, in the course of dis-cussions with a Dr. N——, learns of an "omnipresent evil in the living world" (G 71), "an absolute evil whose reality is mitigated only by our blind-ness to it" (G 75). Suggestive as this is, the horrors remain curiously abstract. The letter writer even remarks that the "words of this peculiar manuscript seem rather weak in this regard"—i.e., in the matter of actually conveying the bizarrerie of the situation. Thus ends the first section of the tale.

In the second section the letter writer has experienced a disturbing dream in which he is in a room poring over maps, all of which feature some island named Nethescurial. In the room is an altar with an idol on it. When a weird band of worshipers comes to pray before it, one of the wor-shipers loathsomely melds with the idol.

The third section of the tale opens with the remark: "Well, it seems this letter has mutated into a chronicle of my adventures Nethescurialian" (G 81). The writer speaks more truly than he knows, for as this section proceeds we learn that the writer's own words are insidiously being mutated by Nethescurial (whatever it may be), as he unwittingly begins to duplicate the expressions of the manuscript he had so desultorily examined at the outset. The relations to Lovecraft's story are obscure but significant—Nethescurial as a parallel for the sunken island of R'lyeh; worshipers praying before an entity whose true nature they themselves may not understand; Cthulhu's influence of dreams mirrored by the narrator's loss of control over his own language. And Ligotti brings home the *reality* of the weird phenomenon in a way that perhaps even exceeds Lovecraft: the letter writer can only conclude with a pitiable denial of the true state of affairs—"I am not dying in a nightmare" (G 84).

It is already evident that one vehicle by which the unreal is reached is dream. I have no doubt that many of Ligotti's tales incorporate fragments of his own dreams, but there is certainly more to it than that. Consider another comment on Lovecraft: "Lovecraft dreamed the great dream of supernatural literature—to convey with the greatest possible intensity a vision of the universe as a kind of enchanting nightmare" (F 32). This, too, is clearly Ligotti's dream. It is suggestive that, in answering a query as to why he took to writing horror fiction, he noted: "I've never been tempted to write anything that was not essentially nightmarish" (F 30)—as if horror and nightmare are fundamentally synonymous.

Ligotti's treatment of the dream theme is complex and multifarious. On occasion it can be very simple, as in "Oneiric Horror," an exquisite prose poem that does nothing but paint a dream. I wonder whether Ligotti wrote this vignette as a sort of elaboration or commentary on the illustration by Harry O. Morris, Jr., that accompanies it, as Dunsany did in his *Book of Wonder*. In any event, the details and objects of this dream are described with all the meticulous realism that other writers would bestow upon the real world. A very suggestive phrase in "The Dream of a Mannikin"—"the divinity of the dream" (SDD 56)—is capable of two meanings: in the surface plot of the story it refers to the sense of irrefutable reality a dream conveys to its dreamer for the duration of its existence; but it also suggests—again metafictionally—the dominance of dream over reality.

This dream world or other realm (although recall that it is not an "other" realm but merely an aspect—perhaps the "true" aspect—of this realm) takes a peculiar form in Ligotti. We have already cited some characteristics of it: the "back alleys of some cosmic slum" in "The Frolic," the "paradise of exhaustion, confusion, and debris" in "Vastarien." Or consider the sinister movie theatre in "The Glamour": "...the round-backed seats were at the same time rows of headstones in a graveyard; the aisles were endless filthy alleys, long desolate corridors in an old asylum, or the dripping passages of a sewer narrowing into the distance; the pale movie screen was a dust-blinded window in a dark unvisited cellar, a mirror gone rheumy with age in an abandoned house; the chandelier and smaller fixtures were the facets of murky crystals embedded in the sticky walls of an unknown cavern" (G 166). This notion of the world-as-junkheap is obsessively pervasive in Ligotti, and, although he himself merely states that this sort of imagery has "haunted me since childhood" (DM 117), I wonder whether it has to do with his general world view. "Being something of a pessimist, I tend to think, in those rare moments when I really think, that existence is by nature evil. And nothing is good" (DM 116).

"Mad Night of Atonement," a rather tiresome and long-winded story, enunciates this idea. Dr. Francis Haxhausen, a sort of itinerant showman very much like Lovecraft's Nyarlathotep, has discovered the "law and the truth of the Creator": "what delight His heart" are "ruins and the ghosts of puppets." "'All the lonesome pathetic things, all the desolate dusty things, all the misbegotten things, ruined things, failed things, all the imperfect semblances and deteriorating remnants of what we arrogantly deign to call the Real, to call ... Life. In brief, the entire realm of the unreal—wherein He abides—is what He loves like nothing in this world'" (N 113). This is, I take it, what Robert M. Price has termed Ligotti's Gnostic vision–the notion of the "imbecilic demiurge, a distant relation of the true divinity and the ill-advised creator of the dreadful material world."[13] Ligotti himself confirms this conception in "Nethescurial": "Imagine the universe as the dream, the feverish nightmare of a demonic demiurge" (G 76). I wonder, too, whether the mannikin or puppet theme, which also recurs with great frequency in Ligotti's work, can be related to this idea. On the most elementary level the mannikin theme simply suggests a mockery of the human: Dr. Haxhausen can momentarily turn human beings into puppets, and perhaps vice versa, and at the end of the tale it appears that his audience—and perhaps the entire world—has been so transformed (or perhaps was so all along). On another level the notion relates to Ligotti's conception of characterization in weird fiction, as enunciated in "The Consolations of Horror." In discussing "The Fall of the House of Usher" Ligotti notes that we do not genuinely care about the fates of the human characters in the tale—our perspective as readers is more godlike: "This is a world created with built-in obsolescence, and to appreciate fully this downrunning cosmos one must take the perspective of its creator, which is all perspectives without getting sidetracked into a single one.... And the consolation in this is that we are supremely removed from the maddeningly tragic viewpoint of the human."[14]

I cannot help feeling that there is a strain of misanthropy running through Ligotti's work (I hardly need add that this is not meant pejoratively): the protagonist of "Alice's Last Adventure" remarks acidly, "Thank goodness there's only one of everybody" (SDD 40). The clinical detachment of Ligotti's narrative voice, the sardonic (or, in his poorer work, cheaply sarcastic) tone he adopts in reference to his human puppets, and the number of characters who reveal themselves by their own words to be grotesque buffoons certainly underscore a refreshing scorn for human life.

Some of Ligotti's tales allow a little more of the observably real world than others, and a few of these are among his great successes. "The Frolic," an early and relatively conventional story, is still powerful for the visions of a lunatic that so hideously defy the inept rationalizations of a psychiatrist to account for them naturalistically. "Alice's Last Adventure" recounts a rather old idea—fictional characters coming to life—but does so with great adeptness and cumulative power. I could have done without the trite ending—the author, overtaken by her creations, scribbles away to the bitter end—and I also think that this tale is remarkably similar in conception to Jonathan Carroll's *The Land of Laughs* (1980), although perhaps the idea was probably not derived directly from that work.

"Les Fleurs" is emblematic of the "twisted or obscure technique" that Ligotti employs in his work. Here again the plot seems simple—a man evidently lures and kills a series of women—but a profound unease is engendered in the reader because of the many features of the story that are left tantalizingly unexplained. The protagonist has apparently already killed one woman, Clare (it is never revealed how), and is now pursuing another one, Daisy. At his apartment he shows her an odd object that looks something like a cactus or perhaps a furry animal (the function of this object is never clarified). He attends meetings of some sort (their nature and purpose are never elucidated). Finally he shows her a painting, but her reaction is not what he was expecting: she is nonplussed and perhaps a little disturbed. And when we read that Daisy now "truly possesse[s] a sure knowledge of my secrets" (SDD 26) and that her fate is accordingly sealed, we realize the truth (or, at least, a fragment of the truth): the man is not a mere homicidal maniac but one who wishes to indoctrinate a woman of the proper sensitivity into his mysterious sect, but who must kill any who are not suitable.

Incredibly, "The Last Feast of Harlequin" is a relatively early tale of Ligotti's (F 34), and yet it is leagues away from the nightmarish unreality of the rest of his work. I trust it is not simply my bias toward supernatural realism that makes me rank this tale as his best. If nothing else, it may perhaps be the very best homage to Lovecraft ever written. To call it a mere pastiche would be to do it an injustice.

The story follows traditional Lovecraftian lines: an anthropologist interested in exploring the "significance of the clown figure in diverse cultural contexts" (G 3) reads an article by a former professor of his, Dr. Raymond Thoss (who, I take it, is not the same as the Dr. Thoss of "The Troubles of Dr. Thoss" [SDD 155–67]), about a festival that takes place every year in December in the Midwestern town of Mirocaw. He visits the town in the summer and thinks he sees Dr. Thoss there, although he appears transformed into an inarticulate derelict. This compels him actually to go to the town during the festival. He insinuates himself into the goings-on, dresses up as one of the many derelicts who seem to serve some cryptic ritual function, and is led by them into an underground chamber where horrors of various sorts transpire. This superficial and incomplete synopsis cannot even begin to suggest the tale's richness of texture, density of atmosphere, psychological and topographical realism, and—the most Lovecraftian feature of all—the notion of ancient and loathsome rituals surviving into the present day, related to and perhaps the origin of the most ancient human myth cycles. If there is any complaint to be made of this story, it is that it appears to lack the cosmicism of Lovecraft's most representative work. The bulk of the story is very likely derived from Lovecraft's "The Festival" (1923), with a brief nod to "The Shadow over Innsmouth" at the end. The horror of the story seems to affect only random individuals rather than, as in the later Lovecraft, the entire race or the entire cosmos. Nevertheless, "The Last Feast of Harlequin" clearly demonstrates that Ligotti can write the sort of documentary realism he appears to scorn without losing the individuality of his own voice.

Ligotti's third collection, *Noctuary* (1994), reveals some disturbing features. In the first place, most of the stories are reprints, and Ligotti has seriously erred both in opening the volume with "The Medusa," which displays him at his worst in a long-winded tale full of self-indulgent, smart-alecky, high-sounding sentences that in the end mean nothing, and in closing it with an augmented version of the "Studies in Horror" (now collectively titled "Notebook of the Night"). It might be thought, given Ligotti's general scorn for the mechanics of plot and his emphasis on mood, that the prose poem would be an ideal form for him, but it is exactly here that his single-minded emphasis on pure verbal witchery presents its greatest drawbacks. He has failed to note that even the most delicate prose poems—whether by Baudelaire or Clark Ashton Smith or Dunsany (*Fifty-one Tales*)—must present some unified or coherent narrative if they are to have any effect. Most of the items in *Noctuary* are simply too insubstantial, fragmentary, and directionless to amount to much. A passage from "The Spectral Estate" typifies their essence. "Long exasperated by questions without answers, by answers without consequences, by truths which change nothing, we learn to become intoxicated by the mood of mystery itself, by the odor of the unknown. We are entranced by the subtle scents and wavering reflections of the unimaginable" (N 175–76). This is an ideal that Ligotti does not always fulfill, and most of these items, written with undeniable panache as they are, simply leave no impression upon the reader and are forgotten the moment they are finished.

The other disturbing thing about *Noctuary* is that there is only one original work in the volume. And yet, this tale, "The Tsalal," is almost worth all the other stories combined. It concerns an individual, Andrew Maness, who is the incarnation of the Tsalal (a term taken consciously from Poe's *Narrative of Arthur Gordon Pym*), or "a *perfect blackness*" (N 86). Maness's father, a reverend, has written a book called *Tsalal*, and Andrew ponders its significance.

> "'There is no nature to things,' you wrote in the book. 'There are no faces except masks held tight against the pitching chaos behind them.' You wrote that there is not true growth or evolution in the life of this world but only transformations of appearance, an incessant melting and molding of surfaces without underlying essence. Above all you pronounced that there is no salvation of any being because no beings exist as such, nothing exists to be saved—everything, everyone exists only to be drawn into the slow and endless swirling of mutations that we may see every second of our lives if we simply gaze through the eyes of the Tsalal" [N 80].

I do not know if this accurately represents Ligotti's philosophy, but it is an ideal instance of that *intellectualized horror* of which he is such a master. Somehow Andrew Maness is the embodiment of this nihilistic existentialism, and only Ligotti could have written so compellingly hypnotic a tale around such a dryly philosophical conception.

The fact that Ligotti has written (or published) so few new tales in the last few years is indeed a cause for worry, and one hopes that he is not prematurely "written out." My feeling (perhaps it is only a hope) is that he is undergoing a fallow period while searching for something new to say, or a new way to say it. He has surely done all that one can possibly do in his current idiom. My respect for Ligotti is considerable: he has literary gifts beyond what most other writers in this field could even dream of; he has a uniqueness of vision that sets his work radically apart from all others; he is a highly articulate spokesman for his brand of weird fiction; and he has read exhaustively in the best work in the field and has profited enormously thereby. But I am troubled by a number of things: his writing is so self-conscious and self-referential that it utterly lacks spontaneity and emotional vigor; its appeal seems directed almost wholly to the intellect; he seems, apparently by design, not to care about the complete reconciliation of the various supernatural features in a given tale; and a number of his stories—like "The Shadow at the Bottom of the World" (G 203–14), one of the most exquisitely modulated pieces of prose I have ever read—are flawlessly written by the sentence but do not in the end convey a very powerful impression. I fervently hope (especially in light of the recent championing of his work by leading critics in the field) that Ligotti is not in danger of becoming self-indulgent, overly obscure, and, worst of all, content to remain at the level he has attained. He will, I believe, have to start writing more *stories*—as opposed to the vignettes, prose poems, sketches, and fragments that so far constitute the bulk of his output—if he is to gain preeminence in the field. Ligotti's own tastes notwithstanding, few will doubt that Lovecraft initiated the most representative phase of his career when he adopted the documentary realism of "The Call of Cthulhu" in 1926; if he had stopped writing before that point, we would have little reason to remember him. This is not to say that Ligotti's current work is somehow qualitatively equal to Lovecraft's pre–1926 work (it is, in some ways, rather better). Nor, of course, is it possible to say that "The Last Feast of Harlequin" is a harbinger of a realistic phase on Ligotti's part, since it is an early work. But I think that Ligotti will have to write more tales like "The Last Feast of Harlequin," "Vastarien," or "Nethescurial" if he is to join the ranks of Lovecraft, Blackwood, Dunsany, Jackson, Campbell, and Klein, as he is on the verge of doing.

EPILOGUE

It should be obvious to any reader that one of my objectives in this book is to lay down a canon of modern weird writing. No one need be reminded of the problematical nature of such an enterprise, although one hopes there may be less scepticism of it in light of Harold Bloom's *The Western Canon* (1994), which argues more cogently for the necessity of canon formation than I can do. In essence, Bloom's argument is as follows:

There must be canons (and, indeed, there will always be canons whether anyone wants them or not) because there is only a limited time for reading amidst the myriad other activities of life. Such canons need not be exclusive, although by their very nature canons establish certain criteria that some works will meet and others will not; and any single critic's or reader's canon need be nothing more than suggestive, not prescriptive. What is criticism, after all, but an individual's exercise of critical judgment? The degree to which that judgment is coherent, informed, and sensitive will determine its validity.

Turning to our humble field of weird fiction, it should be clear that no one has sufficient leisure to read all the works in this realm that have been written in the past 200 years, even if anyone were so foolish as to undertake such a task. Some principle of selectivity must be had, and I can state unequivocally that my principle—hence my canon—is based upon the actual literary merits, as best I can assess them, of the works and authors I have read. I am aware that utilizing something so elitist and antidemocratic as literary quality as a yardstick must seem very anomalous, but my whole training as a critic leads me to it. There might conceivably be other criteria by which a canon is formed, but I am not interested in them. I am not, for example, interested in what weird fiction can tell us about our society because I am not interested in society. This may or may not be a deficiency on my part.

The overriding question, addressed sporadically in this book, is

258

whether literary merit coincides with popular appeal. The question is relevant to the weird tale because of the widespread conception that weird fiction is, pure and simple, a "popular" literary mode and that there are no other criteria of value in this realm other than popularity. I do not know how such a conception could have gained currency except through a very myopic view of the history of the field. Certainly, after the initial popularity of the Gothic novels of the late eighteenth century, it could never be said that serious weird fiction—including the work of Poe, LeFanu, Machen, Dunsany, Blackwood, Lovecraft, Aickman, and so many others— was "popular" in any meaningful sense. I have attempted to address the disjunction of popularity and literary merit throughout this book, but the matter really boils down to certain basic if uncomfortable truths about society: in particular, the truth that, for a variety of complex reasons, the "mass reading public" is incapable of assessing a literary work on its purely literary merits.

The brute fact of the matter is that public education in the English-speaking world—especially in America—does not inculcate literary values into its charges or permit them to distinguish literature from hackwork. Many untutored readers cannot make a distinction between what happens to tickle their fancy and what actually makes for a substantial work of literature. Since such readers are by far in the majority, and since democratic capitalism has given them purchasing power undreamed of in prior ages, it is natural that many writers would seek to cater to their tastes in order to make a living. This tendency became evident as early as the advent of the dime novels at the turn of the century—whose readership was almost exclusively among the ill-educated—and advanced through the pulp magazines to the paperbacks of today. Lovecraft was keenly aware of the situation and of its sociological causes.

> Bourgeois capitalism gave artistic excellence and sincerity a death-blow by enthroning cheap *amusement-value* at the expense of that *intrinsic excellence* which only cultivated, non-acquisitive persons of assumed position can enjoy. The determinant market for written ... and other heretofore aesthetic material ceased to be a small circle of truly educated persons, but became a substantially larger ... circle of mixed origin numerically dominated by crude, half-educated clods whose systematically perverted ideals ... prevented them from ever achieving the tastes and perspectives of the gentlefolk whose dress and speech and external manners they so assiduously mimicked. This herd of acquisitive boors brought up from the shop and the counting-house a complete set of artificial attitudes, oversimplifications, and mawkish sentimentalities which no sincere art or literature could gratify—and

they so outnumbered the remaining educated gentlefolk that most of
the purveying agencies became at once reoriented to them. Literature
and art lost most of their market; and writing, painting, drama, etc.
became engulfed more and more in the domain of *amusement enter-
prises*.[1]

If anyone has doubts about Lovecraft's assessment, one glance at any week's
bestseller lists should relieve them. Critics who equate popular appeal with
literary merit had best occupy their time writing studies of Danielle Steel
and Sidney Sheldon.

Turning to realities, my vaunting of Shirley Jackson, Ramsey Campbell, T. E. D. Klein, and Thomas Ligotti—and my devaluation of Stephen
King, Clive Barker, Peter Straub, and Anne Rice—should come as no surprise. I repeat that there are ways in which the writers I have demoted
could be raised in one's estimation, but I do not think it could be done
on the basis of pure literary merit. And I repeat that that is the only basis
which interests me.

NOTES

Introduction

1. Winfield Townley Scott, "A Parenthesis on Lovecraft as Poet" (1945), in S. T. Joshi, ed., *H. P. Lovecraft: Four Decades of Criticism* (Athens: Ohio University Press, 1980), p. 215.

2. See Harlan Ellison, "Harlan Ellison's Watching," *Magazine of Fantasy and Science Fiction* 80, No. 1 (January 1991): 104–10.

3. On this point see Douglas E. Winter's introduction to *Prime Evil* (New York: New American Library, 1988), p. 2. See also, more generally, Ramsey Campbell in *Necrofile* No. 2 (Fall 1991): 12–13, and Steve Rasnic Tem, "The Subject Matter of Horror," *Necrofile* No. 3 (Winter 1991): 18–19.

4. Lovecraft to Jonquil Leiber (20 December 1936), *Selected Letters 1934–1937*, ed. August Derleth and James Turner (Sauk City, WI: Arkham, 1976), p. 380.

5. See Lovecraft to August Derleth (23 May 1931), ms., August Derleth Papers, State Historical Society of Wisconsin: "The Simon & Schuster request I spoke of was made first a year ago, when their book editor Clifton P. Fadiman wrote me ... to ask if I had any book MSS. to submit—& saying he would give careful attention to anything I did submit. I replied that I had nothing of novel length, but would like very much to get a short story collection published—to which, however, he responded that they do not consider short story collections."

6. Both volumes appeared on the *New York Times* bestseller list for June 20, 1971. By July 25 *The Exorcist* had risen to No. 1, remaining there for 11 weeks, until October 10. It was on the bestseller list for a total of 55 weeks, until July 9, 1972. *The Other* ranked No. 2 on the bestseller list on August 15, 1971, remaining in that position off and on for the next several weeks. It was on the bestseller list for a total of 24 weeks, until November 28, 1971.

7. See Stefan Dziemianowicz, "Lovecraft and the Modern Horror Writer," in *The H. P. Lovecraft Centennial Conference: Proceedings*, ed. S. T. Joshi (West Warwick, RI: Necronomicon Press, 1991), p. 45, where the term "familiarization of horror" is used. In private discussions Dziemianowicz has used the term "banalization" to refer to a particularly flat or superficial use of familiar elements of ordinary life.

8. "The Defence Remains Open!" (1921), *Miscellaneous Writings*, ed. S. T. Joshi (Sauk City, WI: Arkham House, 1995), p. 155.

9. Thomas Ligotti, "Notes on the Writing of Horror: An Interview with Thomas Ligotti [by Carl Ford]," *Dagon* Nos. 22/23 (September–December 1988): 5.

I. Shirley Jackson: Domestic Horror

1. Jackson's year of birth is usually given as 1919, a date she herself gave in later years. But her biographer, Judy Oppenheimer, has determined that Jackson was actually born on December 14, 1916, and that 1919 was given as the year of her birth so that she could seem to be younger than her husband, Stanley Edgar Hyman. (See O 11, 88.)

2. Some of these stories have now been gathered in *Just an Ordinary Day*, ed. Laurence Jackson Hyman and Sarah Hyman Stewart (New York: Bantam, 1997).

3. "Sanctuary: Shirley Jackson's Domestic and Fantastic Parables," *Studies in Weird Fiction* No. 6 (Fall 1989): 15.

4. "One Last Chance," *McCall's* 83, No. 7 (April 1956): 112. The reprint in RD is considerably more elaborated.

5. "On Being a Faculty Wife," *Mademoiselle* 44, No. 2 (December 1956): 136.

6. Plautus, *Amphitryo*, in *The Rope and Other Plays*, tr. E. F. Watling (Harmondsworth: Penguin, 1964), p. 230.

7. "The House," *Woman's Day* 15, No. 8 (May 1952): 116.

8. Ibid., p. 118.

9. "Bulletin" (1954), rpt. in *The Best from Fantasy and Science Fiction: Fourth Series*, ed. Anthony Boucher (Garden City, NY: Doubleday, 1955), pp. 182–85.

10. H. P. Lovecraft, "The Outsider" (1921), in *The Dunwich Horror and Others*, ed. S. T. Joshi (Sauk City, WI: Arkham House, 1984), p. 52.

11. "The Possibility of Evil," *Saturday Evening Post* 238, No. 25 (December 18, 1965): 68–69.

12. The number of paired women in Jackson's fiction is certainly large. Jackson claimed to be horrified at one reviewer's suspicion of a lesbian undercurrent to *Hangsaman* (O 232–33), but this novel, as well as *The Haunting of Hill House* and *We Have Always Lived in the Castle*, certainly dwells at great length on a potentially intimate relationship between two women. Perhaps not much is to be made of this: recall the frequency of paired male characters in Lovecraft.

13. "Strangers in Town," *Saturday Evening Post* 231, No. 48 (May 30, 1959): 77, 79.

14. *Lovecraft: A Study in the Fantastic*, tr. S. T. Joshi (Detroit: Wayne State University Press, 1988), p. 14.

15. See Dale J. Nelson, "Arthur Jermyn Was a Yahoo: Swift and Modern Horror Fiction," *Studies in Weird Fiction* No. 7 (Spring 1990): 3–7.

16. A chapter from this novel, "Du côté de chez Todd," has frequently been

included in horror anthologies under the title "The Man Who Liked Dickens." It is one of the nastiest *contes cruels* ever written.

17. "One Ordinary Day, with Peanuts" (1955), in *Best American Short Stories 1956*, ed. Martha Foley (Boston: Houghton Mifflin, 1956), p. 204.

II. The Persistence of Supernaturalism

1. "'So Much Mystery...': The Work of William Peter Blatty," *Studies in Weird Fiction* No. 9 (Spring 1991): 13–17.

2. This same problem haunts the windy novelette "The Sun Dog" (FPM), about a supernatural camera.

3. If King wished a word for this phenomenon based upon the analogy with "telekinesis" (movement from a distance), the term would not be "pyrokinesis" but "telepyrosis" (fire from a distance).

4. *Rage* may have had its origin in a very early short story, "Cain Rose Up" (1968; SC), involving a college student who suddenly begins shooting people with a rifle. Here, however, there is insufficient psychological analysis of the murderer to produce a compelling scenario.

5. One detail will suffice. At one point King writes a dramatic one-sentence segment—"Nothing much happened for the next two weeks" (I 878)—which no informed reader can fail to recognize as a plagiarism of a one-sentence chapter in Bradbury's *Something Wicked This Way Comes* (1962; rpt. New York: Bantam, 1963, p. 112): "Nothing much else happened, all the rest of that night." Many other similarities could be pointed out.

6. Mary Pharr, "Of Women and Wolves," *Necrofile* No. 8 (Spring 1993): 2.

7. See Magistrale's *Landscape of Fear: Stephen King's American Gothic* (1988).

8. "T. E. D. Klein: Master of Ceremonies" (interview by Carl T. Ford), *Dagon* Nos. 18/19 (July–October 1987): 46.

9. This is exactly what Les Daniels has condemned as "melodrama"; see "Lovecraft and Modern Horror," *The H. P. Lovecraft Centennial Conference: Proceedings*, p. 43.

10. "T. E. D. Klein: Master of Ceremonies," pp. 47–48.

11. It may be well to note here that Klein's second novel, *Nighttown*, is to be, in his words, a "paranoid horror novel set entirely in New York City" (FF 135). This may suggest that the novel will be nonsupernatural, but Klein has told me that it will in fact be supernatural.

12. See Steven J. Mariconda, "The Hints and Portents of T. E. D. Klein," *Studies in Weird Fiction* No. 1 (Summer 1986): 19–28.

13. The influence of Lovecraft's "The Dunwich Horror" becomes evident at this point.

14. Arthur Machen, *The House of Souls* (New York: Knopf, 1922), p. 149. Hereafter abbreviated as M in the text.

15. S. T. Joshi, "'The Events at Poroth Farm' and the Literature of Horror," *Dagon* Nos. 18/19 (July–October 1987): 10–12.

16. *Collected Ghost Stories of M. R. James* (London: Edward Arnold, 1931), p. 148.

17. See note 9.

18. Stephen Haff, "Clive Barker: Spokesman for the Strange," *Other Dimensions* No. 1 (Summer 1993): 3.

III. Ramsey Campbell: The Fiction of Paranoia

1. "Introduction" to *Demons by Daylight* (New York: Tor, 1990), n.p. Further citations will not be specifically footnoted.

2. A numerical breakdown of his short-story writing by year from 1962 onward is as follows: 1962 (5); 1963 (8); 1964 (3); 1965 (7); 1966 (2); 1966–67 (1); 1967 (6); 1968 (13); 1969 (12); 1970 (4); 1971 (5); 1972 (2); 1973 (17); 1974 (27); 1975 (10); 1976 (11); 1977 (10); 1978 (11); 1979 (5); 1980 (4); 1981 (0); 1982 (0); 1983 (6); 1984 (1); 1985 (3); 1986 (3); 1987 (3); 1988 (4); 1989 (0); 1990 (8).

3. In *Demons by Daylight* "The Franklyn Paragraphs" and "The Interloper" appear in a section entitled "Errol Undercliffe: A Tribute," the latter story bearing Undercliffe's byline as author. Campbell seems to have been successful in passing off Undercliffe as a real author: I have noted cross-references to Undercliffe in the catalogues of several libraries I have visited.

4. H. P. Lovecraft to Maurice W. Moe (15 May 1918), *Selected Letters 1911–1925*, ed. August Derleth and Donald Wandrei (Sauk City, WI: Arkham House, 1965), p. 63.

5. H. P. Lovecraft, *Commonplace Book*, ed. David E. Schultz (West Warwick, RI: Necronomicon Press, 1987), Vol. 1, p. 4 (entry 56).

6. "The Gap," in *The Year's Best Horror Stories* X, ed. Karl Edward Wagner (New York: DAW, 1981), p. 65.

7. M. R. James, "The Treasure of Abbot Thomas," in *Collected Ghost Stories*, p. 175.

8. Joel Lane, Review of *Waking Nightmares* and *The Count of Eleven*, *Studies in Weird Fiction* No. 11 (Spring 1992): 33.

9. H. P. Lovecraft to Woodburn Harris (25 February–1 March 1929), *Selected Letters 1925–1929*, ed. August Derleth and Donald Wandrei (Sauk City, WI: Arkham House, 1968), pp. 308–9.

10. Steven J. Mariconda, Review of *Needing Ghosts* and *Midnight Sun*, *Studies in Weird Fiction* No. 9 (Spring 1991): 33.

11. In his author's note to the story in *Masters of Darkness*, ed. Dennis Etchison (New York: Tor, 1986), pp. 128–29.

12. T. E. D. Klein, "Ramsey Campbell: An Appreciation," in *Discovering Modern Horror Fiction II*, ed. Darrell Schweitzer (Mercer Island, WA: Starmont House, 1988), p. 99.

IV. The Alternatives to Supernaturalism

1. A serviceable bibliography can be found in Randall D. Larson's *Robert Bloch* (Mercer Island, WA: Starmont House, 1986).

2. Bloch's Lovecraftian stories have now been collected in *Mysteries of the Worm* (1981).

3. See Larson, pp. 63–64.

4. *Horror: 100 Best Books*, ed. Stephen Jones and Kim Newman (New York: Carroll & Graf, 1988), p. 184.

5. I am not being entirely flippant in saying that the most horrifying moment in *Red Dragon* for me was not the murders or the psychological probing of the murderer, but the scene in which Dolarhyde goes to the Brooklyn Museum and *eats* the original Blake watercolor of the "Great Red Dragon," a picture that has haunted him since youth. People come and go, but one cannot destroy great art like that!

6. See the enlightening interview of him by Roger Cohen, "Bret Easton Ellis Answers Critics of 'American Psycho,'" *New York Times*, March 6, 1991, pp. C13, 18.

7. *New York Times Book Review*, December 16, 1990, pp. 3, 16.

8. Ken Tucker, "The Splatterpunk Trend, and Welcome to It," *New York Times Book Review*, March 24, 1991, pp. 13–14.

9. Lovecraft to August Derleth (6 November 1931), ms., August Derleth Papers, State Historical Society of Wisconsin.

10. Jay Gregory, "Peter Straub" [interview], *Twilight Zone* 1, No. 2 (May 1981): 14.

11. Jack Sullivan, "Breaking In," *Twilight Zone* 6, No. 1 (April 1986): 27.

12. Lovecraft, *Commonplace Book*, 1:1 (entry 8).

13. Gregory, p. 13.

14. "Take a werewolf story, for instance—who ever wrote a story from the point of view of the wolf, and sympathising strongly with the devil to whom he has sold himself? Who ever wrote a story from the point of view that man is a blemish on the cosmos, who ought to be eradicated?" Lovecraft to Edwin Baird (c. August 1923), *Weird Tales*, March 1924; rpt. in *Miscellaneous Writings*, p. 509.

15. I confess to be somewhat uncertain as to the correct title for this work. The title page and spine of the book clearly read *Shadow Land*, but the running heads and the text itself read *Shadowland*. I assume that the latter is correct, and that the variant is the product of incompetence by copy editors or designers at Coward, McCann & Geogheghan.

16. The Northeastern Regional Fantasy Convention (NECON) at Bristol, RI. I cannot recall the year, but it was 1981 or 1982.

17. Bernadette Lynn Bosky, Review of *The Throat*, *Necrofile* No. 9 (Summer 1993): 4.

18. Lovecraft to August Derleth (20 November 1931), *Selected Letters 1929–1931*, ed. Augut Derleth and Donald Wandrei (Sauk City, WI: Arkham House, 1971), p. 434.

19. Gregory, p. 15.

20. Penzoldt, *The Supernatural in Fiction* (1952); portions rpt. in S. T. Joshi, ed., *H. P. Lovecraft: Four Decades of Criticism*, p. 64.

V. Pseudo-, Quasi-, and Anti-Weird Fiction

1. L. P. Hartley, "Introduction" to *The Third Ghost Book*, ed. Cynthia Asquith (1955; rpt. New York: Beagle Books, 1970), p. viii.

2. Kathy Mackay, "Anne Rice: Risks Fuel Success in Her World of Imagination," *Los Angeles Times Book Review*, February 3, 1980, p. 3.

3. This is also the subject of S. P. Somtow's novel *Vampire Junction* (1984), but this obscure if brilliant work is not likely to have been read by Rice.

4. H. P. Lovecraft, Letter to J. Vernon Shea (7 August 1931), *Selected Letters 1929–1931*, p. 395.

5. H. P. Lovecraft, Letter to Robert E. Howard (25–29 March 1933), *Selected Letters 1932–1934*, ed. August Derleth and James Turner (Sauk City, WI; Arkham House, 1976), p. 170. Lovecraft dates this phase to "The Colour out of Space" (1927).

6. "The Consolations of Horror," *Crypt of Cthulhu* No. 68 (Hallowmass 1989): 48.

7. Maurice Lévy, *Lovecraft: A Study in the Fantastic*, p. 107.

8. "Allan and Adelaide: An Arabesque," *Crypt of Cthulhu* No. 68 (Hallowmass 1989): 13.

9. "Supernatural Horror in Literature," in *Dagon and Other Macabre Tales*, ed. S. T. Joshi (Sauk City, WI: Arkham House, 1986), p. 413.

10. "The Metaphysical Poets" (1921), in *Selected Essays* (New York: Harcourt, Brace, 1950), p. 248.

11. "The Consolations of Horror," p. 43.

12. See Section IV, note 20.

13. Robert M. Price, "Thomas Ligotti's Gnostic Quest," *Studies in Weird Fiction* No. 9 (Spring 1991): 29.

14. "The Consolations of Horror," p. 47.

Epilogue

1. H. P. Lovecraft, Letter to C. L. Moore [7 February 1937], *Selected Letters 1934–1937*, pp. 397–98.

BIBLIOGRAPHY

General

Barron, Neil, ed. *Horror Literature: A Reader's Guide*. New York: Garland, 1990. Rev. as *Fantasy and Horror*. Lanham, MD: Scarecrow Press, 1999.

Bleiler, E. F., ed. *Supernatural Fiction Writers*. New York: Scribner's, 1985. 2 vols.

Carroll, Noël. *The Philosophy of Horror; or, Paradoxes of the Heart*. New York: Routledge, 1990.

Daniels, Les. *Living in Fear: A History of Horror in the Mass Media*. New York: Scribner's, 1975.

Joshi, S. T. *The Weird Tale*. Austin: University of Texas Press, 1990.

Reginald, Robert, ed. *Science Fiction and Fantasy Literature: A Checklist 1975-1991*. Detroit: Gale Research Co., 1992.

Schweitzer, Darrell, ed. *Discovering Modern Horror Fiction I*. Mercer Island, WA: Starmont House, 1985.

_____, ed. *Discovering Modern Horror Fiction II*. Mercer Island, WA: Starmont House, 1988.

Sullivan, Jack, ed. *The Penguin Encyclopedia of Horror and the Supernatural*. New York: Viking Penguin, 1986.

Tymn, Marshall, ed. *Horror Literature: A Core Collection and Reference Guide*. New York: Bowker, 1981.

Wiater, Stanley. *Dark Dreamers: Conversations with the Masters of Horror*. New York: Avon, 1990.

Winter, Douglas E. *Faces of Fear: Encounters with the Creators of Modern Horror*. New York: Berkley, 1985.

Robert Aickman

A. PRIMARY

The Attempted Rescue. London: Gollancz, 1966. [AR]

267

Cold Hand in Mind. London: Gollancz, 1975. New York: Scribner's, 1977. *New York: Berkley, 1979. [CHM]

Dark Entries. London: Collins, 1964. [DE]

The Fontana Book of Great Ghost Stories (editor). London: Fontana, 1966–72. 8 vols. [F1, F2, etc.]

Intrusions. London: Gollancz, 1980. [I]

The Late Breakfasters. London: Gollancz, 1964.

The Model. New York: Arbor House (William Morrow), 1987.

Night Voices. London: Gollancz, 1985. [NV]

Painted Devils. New York: Scribner's, 1979. [PD]

Powers of Darkness. London: Collins, 1966. [PoD]

The River Runs Uphill: A Story of Success and Failure. Burton-on-Trent: Pearson, 1986.

Sub Rosa. London: Gollancz, 1968. [SR]

Tales of Love and Death. London: Gollancz, 1977. [TLD]

The Unsettled Dust. London: Mandarin, 1990. [UD]

We Are for the Dark (with Elizabeth Jane Howard). London: Jonathan Cape, 1951. [WFD]

The Wine-Dark Sea. *New York: Arbor House (William Morrow), 1988. London: Mandarin, 1990 (abridged). [WDS]

B. Secondary

Briggs, Scott D. "Robert Aickman: Sojourns into the Unknown." *Studies in Weird Fiction* No. 12 (Spring 1993): 7–12.

Crawford, Gary William. "The Poetics of the Unconscious: The 'Strange Stories' of Robert Aickman." In *Discovering Modern Horror Fiction II,* ed. Darrell Schweitzer. Mercer Island, WA: Starmont House, 1988, pp. 43–50.

Morris, Christine Pasanen. "The Female 'Outsider' in the Short Fiction of Robert Aickman." *Nyctalops* No. 18 (April 1983): 55–58.

Clive Barker

A. Primary

Books of Blood, Volume 1. London: Sphere, 1984. *New York: Berkley, 1986. [BB1]

Books of Blood, Volume 2. London: Sphere, 1984. *New York: Berkley, 1986. [BB2]

Books of Blood, Volume 3. London: Sphere, 1984. *New York: Berkley, 1986. [BB3]

Books of Blood, Volume 4. *London: Sphere, 1985. New York: Poseidon Press, 1986 (as *The Inhuman Condition*). [BB4]

Books of Blood, Volume 5. *London: Sphere, 1985. New York: Poseidon Press, 1987 (as *In the Flesh*). [BB5]

Books of Blood, Volume 6. *London: Sphere, 1985. [BB6]

Cabal. London: Collins, 1988. *New York: Poseidon Press, 1988 (with *Books of Blood, Volume 6*). [C]

The Damnation Game. London: Weidenfeld & Nicolson, 1985. *New York: Ace/Putnam, 1987. [DG]

The Great and Secret Show. *London: Collins, 1989. New York: Harper & Row, 1990. [GS]

"The Hellbound Heart." In *Night Visions 3* (with Lisa Tuttle and Ramsey Campbell). Arlington Heights, IL: Dark Harvest, 1986. *New York: Berkley, 1988 (as *Night Visions: The Hellbound Heart*). [NV] Separate publication New York: HarperPaperbacks, 1991.

Imajica. New York: HarperCollins, 1991. [I]

The Thief of Always. New York: HarperCollins, 1992.

Weaveworld. London: Collins, 1987. *New York: Poseidon Press, 1987. [W]

B. SECONDARY

Brown, Michael, ed. *Pandemonium: Further Explorations into the Worlds of Clive Barker.* Forestville, CA: Eclipse, 1991.

Haff, Stephen. "Clive Barker: Spokesman for the Strange" [interview]. *Other Dimensions* No. 1 (Summer 1993): 2–8.

Jones, Stephen, ed. *Clive Barker's Shadows in Eden.* Lancaster, PA: Underwood-Miller, 1991. [SE]

Winter, Douglas E. "Clive Barker." In *Faces of Fear.* New York: Berkley, 1985, pp. 207–20.

William Peter Blatty

A. PRIMARY

The Exorcist. New York: Harper & Row, 1971. [E]

I, Billy Shakespeare! Garden City, NY: Doubleday, 1966.

I'll Tell Them I Remember You. New York: Norton, 1973.

John Goldfarb, Please Come Home! Garden City, NY: Doubleday, 1963.

Legion. New York: Simon & Schuster, 1983. [L]

The Ninth Configuration. New York: Harper & Row, 1978. [N]

Twinkle, Twinkle, "Killer" Kane! Garden City, NY: Doubleday, 1966. [T]

Which Way to Mecca, Jack? New York: Bernard Geis Associates, 1960.

B. SECONDARY

Briggs, Scott D. "'So Much Mystery ...': The Fiction of William Peter Blatty." *Studies in Weird Fiction* No. 9 (Spring 1991): 13–17.

Winter, Douglas E. "William Peter Blatty." In *Faces of Fear.* New York: Berkley, 1985, pp. 36–49. [FF]

Robert Bloch

A. PRIMARY (NOT COMPLETE)

The Best of Robert Bloch. Edited by Lester Del Rey. New York: Ballantine, 1977. [B]

Firebug. New York: Regency, 1961. New York: Tor, 1988.

The Kidnaper. New York: Lion Pocketbooks, 1954. New York: Tor, 1988 (as *The Kidnapper*).

The Opener of the Way. Sauk City, WI: Arkham House, 1945. *St Albans: Panther, 1976 (abridged). [OW]

Psycho. New York: Simon & Schuster, 1959. *Greenwich, CT: Fawcett Crest, 1960. [P]

The Scarf. New York: Dial, 1947. Rev. ed. *Greenwich, CT: Fawcett Gold Medal, 1966. [S]

Screams [includes *The Will to Kill, Firebug,* and *The Star Stalker*]. San Rafael, CA: Underwood-Miller, 1989.

The Skull of the Marquis de Sade and Other Stories. London: Robert Hale, 1975. *London: Corgi, 1976.

Such Stuff as Screams Are Made Of. New York: Ballantine, 1979. [SS]

B. SECONDARY

Larson, Randall. *Robert Bloch.* Mercer Island, WA: Starmont House, 1986.

Ramsey Campbell

A. PRIMARY

Alone with the Horrors: The Great Short Fiction of Ramsey Campbell 1961-1991. Sauk City, WI: Arkham House, 1993.

Ancient Images. London: Legend/Century, 1989. *New York: Scribner's, 1989. [AI]

Black Wine (with Charles L. Grant). Niles, IL: Dark Harvest, 1986. [BW]

The Claw. *London: Futura, 1983 (as *Claw*; as by Jay Ramsey). New York: St Martin's Press, 1983 (as *Night of the Claw*; as by Jay Ramsey). [C]

Cold Print. Santa Cruz, CA: Scream/Press, 1985. *New York: Tor, 1987. [CP]

The Count of Eleven. London: Macdonald, 1991. *New York: Tor, 1992. [CE]

Dark Companions. New York: Macmillan, 1982. [DC]

Dark Feasts: The World of Ramsey Campbell. London: Robinson, 1987. [DF]

Demons by Daylight. *Sauk City, WI: Arkham House, 1973. New York: Carroll & Graf, 1990. [DD]

The Doll Who Ate His Mother. Indianapolis: Bobbs-Merrill, 1976. *New York: Jove/HBJ, 1978. Rev. ed. New York: Tor, 1985. [DM]

The Face That Must Die. London: Star, 1979. Rev. ed. *Santa Cruz, CA: Scream/Press, 1983. [FD]

"The Gap." In *The Year's Best Horror Stories X*, ed. Karl Edward Wagner. New York: DAW, 1981, pp. 55–66.

Ghostly Tales. Special issue of *Crypt of Cthulhu* No. 50 (Michaelmas 1987). [GT]

The Height of the Scream. Sauk City, WI: Arkham House, 1976. [HS]

The Hungry Moon. New York: Macmillan, 1986. [HM]

Incarnate. New York: Macmillan, 1983. *New York: Tor, 1984. [I]

The Influence. New York: Macmillan, 1988. [In]

The Inhabitant of the Lake and Less Welcome Tenants. Sauk City, WI: Arkham House, 1964.

The Long Lost. London: Headline, 1993. [LL]

Medusa. Round Top, NY: Footsteps Press, 1987.

Midnight Sun. London: Macdonald, 1990. *New York: Tor, 1991. [MS]

The Nameless. Glasgow: Fontana, 1981. New York: Macmillan, 1981. Rev. ed. *New York: Tor, 1985.

Needing Ghosts. London: Legend/Century, 1990. [NG]

New Tales of the Cthulhu Mythos (editor). Sauk City, WI: Arkham House, 1980. [NT]

Night Visions 3 (with Lisa Tuttle and Clive Barker). Niles, IL: Dark Harvest, 1986. *New York: Berkley, 1988 (as *Night Visions: The Hellbound Heart*). [NV]

Obsession. New York: Macmillan, 1985. [O]

The Parasite. London: Millington, 1980 (as *To Wake the Dead*). Rev. ed. *New York: Macmillan, 1980. [P]

Scared Stiff: Tales of Sex and Death. Los Angeles: Scream/Press, 1986; *rev. ed. 1987. [SS]

Slow. Round Top, NY: Footsteps Press, 1986.

Strange Things and Stranger Places. New York: Tor, 1993. [ST]

The Tomb-Herd and Others. Special issue of *Crypt of Cthulhu* No. 43 (Hallowmass 1986). [TH]

Two Obscure Tales. West Warwick, RI: Necronomicon Press, 1993.

Waking Nightmares. New York: Tor, 1991. [WN]

B. SECONDARY

Campbell, Ramsey. *The Core of Ramsey Campbell: A Bibliography and Reader's Guide*. Edited by S. T. Joshi and Stefan Dziemianowicz. West Warwick, RI: Necronomicon Press, 1995.

Crawford, Gary William. *Ramsey Campbell*. Mercer Island, WA: Starmont House, 1988.

Joshi, S. T., ed. *The Count of Thirty: A Tribute to Ramsey Campbell*. West Warwick, RI: Necronomicon Press, 1993.

Klein, T. E. D. "Ramsey Campbell: An Appreciation." *Nyctalops* No. 13 (May 1977). Rpt. in *Discovering Modern Horror Fiction II*, ed. Darrell Schweitzer. Mercer Island, WA: Starmont House, 1988, pp. 88–102.

Lane, Joel. "Negatives in Print: The Novels of Ramsey Campbell." *Foundation* No. 36 (Summer 1986): 35–45.

Morrison, Michael A. "The Forms of Things Unknown: Metaphysical and Domestic

Horror in Ramsey Campbell's *Incarnate* and *Night of the Claw*." *Studies in Weird Fiction* No. 6 (Fall 1989): 3–9.

Vine, Phillip. "Ramsey Campbell" [interview]. *Interzone*, March–April 1989, pp. 11–16.

Winter, Douglas E. "Ramsey Campbell." In *Faces of Fear*. New York: Berkley, 1985, pp. 65–78. [FF]

Bret Easton Ellis

American Psycho. New York: Vintage, 1991. [AP]
Less Than Zero. New York: Simon & Schuster, 1985.
The Rules of Attraction. New York: Simon & Schuster, 1987.

Thomas Harris

Black Sunday. New York: Putnam's, 1975.
Red Dragon. New York: Putnam's, 1981. [RD]
The Silence of the Lambs. New York: St. Martin's Press, 1988. *New York: St. Martin's Press, 1989. [SL]

Shirley Jackson

A. PRIMARY

I. BOOKS

The Bird's Nest. New York: Farrar, Straus, 1954. Rpt. in *The Magic of Shirley Jackson*. New York: Farrar, Straus & Giroux, 1966, pp. 147–380. [B]

Come Along with Me. Ed. Stanley Edgar Hyman. New York: Viking, 1968. Rpt. *New York: Popular Library, n.d. [C]

Hangsaman. New York: Farrar, Straus, 1951. Rpt. *New York: Popular Library, 1976. [H]

The Haunting of Hill House. New York: Viking, 1959. Rpt. *New York: Popular Library, 1977. [HH]

Life among the Savages. New York: Farrar, Straus, 1953. Rpt. in *The Magic of Shirley Jackson*. New York: Farrar, Straus & Giroux, 1966, pp. 383–530. [LS]

The Lottery. New York: Farrar, Straus, 1949. Rpt. *New York: Popular Library, n.d. [L]

Raising Demons. New York: Farrar, Straus, 1957. Rpt. in *The Magic of Shirley Jackson*. New York: Farrar, Straus & Giroux, 1966, pp. 531–753. [RD]

The Road through the Wall. New York: Farrar, Straus, 1948.
The Sundial. New York: Farrar, Straus, 1958. Rpt. *New York: Ace, n.d. [S]

We Have Always Lived in the Castle. New York: Viking, 1962. Rpt. *New York: Popular Library, n.d. [W]

II. SHORT STORIES

"'All She Said Was "Yes."'" *Vogue* 140, No. 8 (November 1, 1962): 142–43, 169, 171, 174–75.
"The Box." *Woman's Home Companion*, November 1952, pp. 25, 82–83. In LS.
"Bulletin." *Magazine of Fantasy and Science Fiction* 6, No. 3 (March 1954): 46–48. Rpt. *The Best from* Fantasy and Science Fiction: *Fourth Series*, ed. Anthony Boucher. Garden City, NY: Doubleday, 1955, pp. 182–85.
"Family Magician." *Woman's Home Companion*, September 1949, pp. 23, 92–93, 98, 100.
"The House." *Woman's Day* 15, No. 8 (May 1952): 62–63, 115–16, 118–19. In LS (in part).
"Karen's Complaint." *Good Housekeeping* 149, No. 5 (November 1959): 38, 40, 42, 46.
"The Life Romantic." *Good Housekeeping* 129, No. 6 (December 1949): 165–67. In LS.
"Look, Ma, We're Moving." *Good Housekeeping* 134, No. 2 (February 1952): 49, 173–75.
"Lucky to Get Away." *Woman's Day* 16, No. 11 (August 1953): 26, 117–19. In RD.
"Monday Morning." *Woman's Home Companion*, November 1951, pp. 21, 57, 60. In LS.
"On Being a Faculty Wife." *Mademoiselle* 44, No. 2 (December 1956): 116–17, 135–36. In RD (in part).
"One Last Chance." *McCall's* 83, No. 7 (April 1956): 52, 112, 114, 116. In RD.
"One Ordinary Day, with Peanuts." *Magazine of Fantasy and Science Fiction* 8, No. 1 (January 1955): 53–61. Rpt. *The Best American Short Stories 1956*, ed. Martha Foley. Boston: Houghton Mifflin, 1956, pp. 195–204.
"The Possibility of Evil." *Saturday Evening Post* 238, No. 25 (December 18, 1965): 61–64, 68–69.
"Queen of the May." *McCall's* 82, No. 7 (April 1955): 47, 73, 75, 78. In RD.
"Shopping Trip." *Woman's Home Companion*, June 1953, pp. 40, 85–87. In LS.
"Strangers in Town." *Saturday Evening Post* 231, No. 48 (May 30, 1959): 18, 76–77, 79.
"Worldly Goods." *Woman's Day* 16, No. 8 (May 1953): 10–11, 178–79. In RD.

B. SECONDARY

Egan, James. "Sanctuary: Shirley Jackson's Domestic and Fantastic Parables." *Studies in Weird Fiction* No. 6 (Fall 1989): 15–24.
Friedman, Lenemaja. *Shirley Jackson.* Boston: Twayne, 1980.
Hall, Joan Wylie. *Shirley Jackson: A Study of the Short Fiction.* New York: Twayne, 1993.
Oppenheimer, Judy. *Private Demons: The Life of Shirley Jackson.* New York: Putnam's, 1988. [O]

Parks, John G. "Chambers of Yearning: Shirley Jackson's Use of the Gothic." *Twentieth Century Literature* 30 (1984): 15–29.

Stephen King

A. PRIMARY

The Bachman Books. New York: New American Library, 1985. [BB]
Carrie. Garden City, NY: Doubleday, 1974. *New York: Signet, 1975. [C]
Christine. New York: Viking, 1983. *New York: Signet, 1983. [Ch]
Cujo. New York: Viking, 1981. *New York: Signet, 1982. [Cu]
Danse Macabre. New York: Everest House, 1979. *New York: Berkley, 1982. [DM]
The Dark Half. New York: Viking, 1989. [DH]
The Dark Tower I: The Gunslinger. West Kingston, RI: Donald M. Grant, 1982. [G]
The Dark Tower II: The Drawing of the Three. West Kingston, RI: Donald M. Grant, 1987.
The Dark Tower III: The Waste Lands. West Kingston, RI: Donald M. Grant, 1991.
The Dead Zone. New York: Viking, 1979. [DZ]
Different Seasons. New York: Viking, 1982. [DS]
Dolores Claiborne. New York: Viking, 1993. [DC]
The Eyes of the Dragon. New York: Viking Penguin, 1987. *New York: Signet, 1988. [ED]
Firestarter. New York: Viking, 1980. *New York: Signet, 1981. [F]
Four Past Midnight. New York: Viking, 1990. [FPM]
Gerald's Game. New York: Viking, 1992. [GG]
It. New York: Viking, 1986. [I]
The Long Walk (as by Richard Bachman). New York: New American Library, 1979. *New York: New American Library, 1985 (in *The Bachman Books*). [BB]
Misery. New York: Viking, 1987. [M]
Needful Things. New York: Viking, 1991. [NT]
Night Shift. Garden City, NY: Doubleday, 1978. [NS]
Nightmares & Dreamscapes. New York: Viking, 1993.
Pet Sematary. Garden City, NY: Doubleday, 1983. [PS]
Rage (as by Richard Bachman). New York: New American Library, 1977. *New York: New American Library, 1985 (in *The Bachman Books*). [BB]
Roadwork (as by Richard Bachman). New York: New American Library, 1981. *New York: New American Library, 1985 (in *The Bachman Books*). [BB]
The Running Man (as by Richard Bachman). New York: New American Library, 1982. *New York: New American Library, 1985 (in *The Bachman Books*). [BB]
'Salem's Lot. Garden City, NY: Doubleday, 1975. *New York: Signet, 1976. [SL]
The Shining. Garden City, NY: Doubleday, 1977. *New York: Signet, 1978. [S]
Skeleton Crew. New York: Putnam's, 1985. [SC]
The Stand. Garden City, NY: Doubleday, 1978. Complete ed. *New York: Doubleday, 1990. [St]

The Talisman (with Peter Straub). New York: Viking/Putnam's, 1984. [T]

Thinner (as by Richard Bachman). New York: New American Library, 1984. *New York: Signet, 1985. [Th]

The Tommyknockers. New York: Putnam's, 1987. [To]

B. SECONDARY

Magistrale, Tony. *Landscape of Fear: Stephen King's American Gothic.* Bowling Green, OH: Bowling Green State University Popular Press, 1988.

_____. *Stephen King: The Second Decade.* New York: Twayne, 1992.

_____, ed. *The Dark Descent: Essays Defining Stephen King's Horrorscape.* Westport, CT: Greenwood Press, 1992.

Reino, Joseph. *Stephen King: The First Decade.* Boston: Twayne, 1988.

Underwood, Tim, and Chuck Miller, ed. *Bare Bones: Conversations on Terror with Stephen King.* New York: McGraw-Hill, 1988. New York: Warner, 1989. [UM]

_____, ed. *Fear Itself: The Horror Fiction of Stephen King.* Lancaster, PA: Underwood-Miller, 1982.

_____, ed. *Kingdom of Fear: The World of Stephen King.* Lancaster, PA: Underwood-Miller, 1986.

Winter, Douglas. *Stephen King: The Art of Darkness.* New York: New American Library, 1984 (rev. ed. 1986).

T. E. D. Klein

A. PRIMARY

"Camera Shy." *Crypt of Cthulhu* No. 56 (Roodmas 1988): 21–27.

The Ceremonies. New York: Viking, 1984. [C]

Dark Gods. New York: Viking, 1985. [DG]

"Dr. Van Helsing's Handy Guide to Ghost Stories." *Twilight Zone* 1, No. 5 (August 1981): 69–75; 1, No. 6 (September 1981): 74–77; 1, No. 7 (October 1981): 56–60; 1, No. 8 (November 1981): 62–66 (as by "Kurt Van Helsing").

"The Events at Poroth Farm." *From Beyond the Dark Gateway* 1, No. 2 (December 1972). Rev. ed. *West Warwick, RI: Necronomicon Press, 1990 (with introduction by the author). [EP]

"Hagendorn's House." *Country Inns,* Spring 1987, pp. 82–88. *Dagon* Nos. 18/19 (July–September 1987): 52–61 (as "Well-Connected").

"Ladder." In *Borderlands,* ed. Thomas F. Monteleone. New York: Avon, 1990, pp. 188–200. [L]

"Magic Carpet." *Myrddin* No. 3 (1976): 18–22.

Raising Goosebumps for Fun and Profit. Round Top, NY: Footsteps Press, 1988. [RG]

"Renaissance Man." *Space* 2 (1974). Rpt. in *Microcosmic Tales,* ed. Isaac Asimov, Martin Harry Greenberg, and Joseph D. Olander. New York: Taplinger, 1980, pp. 59–64.

"S.F." In *The Year's Best Horror Stories: Series III*, ed. Richard Davis. New York: DAW, 1975, pp. 39–55.

B. SECONDARY

Dagon Nos. 18/19 (July–October 1987). Special T. E. D. Klein issue. Articles by S. T. Joshi, Robert M. Price, Steven J. Mariconda, Mark Valentine, Mark Morrison, Carl T. Ford (interview), Peter F. Jeffery, and Peter Cannon.
Mariconda, Steven J. "The Hints and Portents of T. E. D. Klein." *Studies in Weird Fiction* No. 1 (Summer 1986): 19–28.
Price, Robert M. "T. E. D. Klein." In *Discovering Modern Horror Fiction I*, ed. Darrell Schweitzer. Mercer Island, WA: Starmont House, 1985, pp. 68–85.
Winter, Douglas E. "T. E. D. Klein." In *Faces of Fear*. New York: Berkley, 1985, pp. 122–35. [FF]

Thomas Ligotti

A. PRIMARY

"Allan and Adelaide: An Arabesque." *Crypt of Cthulhu* No. 68 (Hallowmass 1989): 10–16.
"Charnelhouse of the Moon." *Crypt of Cthulhu* No. 68 (Hallowmass 1989): 35–36.
"The Consolations of Horror." *Crypt of Cthulhu* No. 68 (Hallowmass 1989): 42–48.
"Ghost Stories for the Dead." *Crypt of Cthulhu* No. 68 (Hallowmass 1989): 18–20.
Grimscribe: His Lives and Works. London: Robinson, 1991. *New York: Carroll & Graf, 1991. [G]
Noctuary. London: Robinson, 1994. *New York: Carroll & Graf, 1994. [N]
"Oneiric Horror." *Dagon* Nos. 22/23 (September–December 1988): 55–56.
"The Real Wolf." *Nocturne* No. 1 (1988): 6–9.
"A Selection of Poe." *Fantasy and Terror* No. 6 (1985): 20–24.
"Selections of Lovecraft." *Crypt of Cthulhu* No. 68 (Hallowmass 1989): 38–41.
Songs of a Dead Dreamer. Albuquerque, NM: Silver Scarab Press, 1986. Rev. ed. *London: Robinson, 1989. [SDD]
"Ten Steps to Thin Mountain." *Crypt of Cthulhu* No. 68 (Hallowmass 1989): 37, 36.

B. SECONDARY

Dagon Nos. 22/23 (September–December 1988). Special Thomas Ligotti issue. Articles by Mike Ashley, Christine Morris, Robert M. Price, Stefan R. Dziemianowicz, and Simon MacCulloch.
Dziemianowicz, Stefan, and Michael A. Morrison. "The Language of Dread: An Interview with Thomas Ligotti." In *Science Fiction & Fantasy Book Review Annual 1990*, ed. Robert A. Collins and Robert Latham. Westport, CT: Greenwood Press, 1991, pp. 109–18. [DM]

Ford, Carl T. "Notes on the Writing of Horror: An Interview with Thomas Ligotti." *Dagon* Nos. 22/23 (September–December 1988): 30–35. [F]

Price, Robert M. "Thomas Ligotti's Gnostic Quest." *Studies in Weird Fiction* No. 9 (Spring 1991): 27–31.

Ramsey, Shawn. "A Graveside Chat: Interview with Thomas Ligotti." *Deathrealm* No. 8 (Spring 1989): 21–23. [R]

Schweitzer, Darrell. "*Weird Tales* Talks with Thomas Ligotti." *Weird Tales* No. 302 (Winter 1991–92): 51–55.

Anne Rice

A. PRIMARY

Interview with the Vampire. New York: Knopf, 1976. *New York: Ballantine, 1977. [I]

Lasher. New York: Knopf, 1993.

"The Master of Rampling Gate." *Redbook*, February 1984. Rpt. in *The Ultimate Dracula*, ed. Byron Preiss. New York: Dell, 1991, pp. 11–33.

The Mummy; or, Ramses the Damned. New York: Ballantine, 1989. [M]

The Queen of the Damned. New York: Knopf, 1988. [Q]

The Tale of the Body Thief. New York: Knopf, 1992. [TBT]

The Vampire Lestat. New York: Knopf, 1985. *New York: Ballantine, 1986. [V]

The Witching Hour. New York: Knopf, 1990. [W]

B. SECONDARY

Mackay, Kathy. "Anne Rice: Risks Fuel Success in Her World of Imagination." *Los Angeles Times Book Review*, February 3, 1980, p. 3.

Ramsland, Katherine. *Prism of the Night: A Biography of Anne Rice.* New York: Dutton, 1991.

Wiater, Stanley. "Anne Rice." In *Dark Dreamers*. New York: Avon, 1990, pp. 163–71.

Peter Straub

A. PRIMARY

Floating Dragon. New York: Putnam's, 1983. [FD]

"The General's Wife." *Twilight Zone* 2, No. 2 (May 1982): 25–38. West Kingston, RI: Donald M. Grant, 1982.

Ghost Story. New York: Coward, McCann & Geogheghan, 1979. *New York: Pocket, 1980. [GS]

Houses without Doors. New York: Dutton, 1990. [HD]

If You Could See Me Now. New York: Coward, McCann & Geogheghan, 1977. *New York: Pocket, 1979. [I]

Julia. New York: Coward, McCann & Geogheghan, 1975. *New York: Pocket, 1976. [J]

Koko. New York: Dutton, 1988. [K]

Marriages. New York: Coward, McCann, 1973. New York: Pocket, 1977.

Mrs. God. West Kingston, RI: Donald M. Grant, 1991.

Mystery. New York: Dutton, 1990. [M]

The Talisman (with Stephen King). New York: Viking/Putnam's, 1984.

The Throat. New York: Dutton, 1993. [T]

Wild Animals: Julia, If You Could See Me Now, Under Venus. New York: Putnam's, 1984. [WA]

B. SECONDARY

Gregory, Jay. "Peter Straub" [interview]. *Twilight Zone* 1, No. 2 (May 1981): 13–16.

Winter, Douglas E. "Peter Straub." In *Faces of Fear.* New York: Berkley, 1985, pp. 221–34. [FF]

Thomas Tryon

All That Glitters. New York: Knopf, 1986.

By the Rivers of Babylon. New York: Knopf, 1992.

Crowned Heads. New York: Knopf, 1976.

Harvest Home. New York: Knopf, 1973. *Greenwich, CT: Fawcett Crest, 1974. [H]

Lady. New York: Knopf, 1974. [L]

The Night of the Moonbow. New York: Knopf, 1989.

The Other. New York: Knopf, 1971. *Greenwich, CT: Fawcett Crest, 1972. [O]

The Wings of the Morning. New York: Knopf, 1990.